INDIA AND THE WEST

SOUTH ASIA INSTITUTE
UNIVERSITY OF HEIDELBERG
NEW DELHI BRANCH

South Asian Studies No. XV

INDIA AND THE WEST

Proceedings of a Seminar Dedicated to the Memory of Hermann Goetz

Edited by

JOACHIM DEPPERT

MANOHAR
2024

First published 1983
Reprinted 2023, 2024

ISBN 978-93-94262-39-3

Published by
Ajay Kumar Jain *for*
Manohar Publishers & Distributors
4753/23 Ansari Road, Daryaganj
New Delhi 110 002

Printed at
Replika Press Pvt. Ltd.

PREFACE

This book presents a selection from the papers read on occasion of a seminar which was organized by the South Asia Institute, the Max Müller Bhavan, and the Embassy of the Federal Republic of Germany, New Delhi, and held February 25 – 28, 1982, in the frame of the celebrations of the 25th anniversary of the Max Müller Bhavan, New Delhi.

The seminar was dedicated to the memory of the well-known Indian Art historian Hermann Goetz. It endeavoured to consider two main tenets of Hermann Goetz's life work: that significant research into Indian Art history is only possible in collaboration with indology, comparative religion and philosophy, archeology, history, ethnology, sociology, and general history of civilization; and that India in all her manifoldness is not at all to be isolated from, but put into the context with the West—with the Iranian, Muslim, and Christian Cultures west of India—inasmuch as the many-layered prehistorical and historical mutual influences help to establish the autonomy as well as to corroborate the complementarity and the root-relationship of the Indian and Western cultural fields.

The printing of the book would not have come off without the generous donations of the Siemens Foundation, Bombay, the Max Müller Bhavan, New Delhi, its central office, Munich, and the South Asia Institute, Heidelberg. I want to express my warmest thanks to Mr D. Briese and Mr S.K. Thakersey (Siemens), to Dr W. Breuer (MMB), and to Professor D. Rothermund and Dr D. Halcour (SAI) for their advocacy of the financial support required. Moreover I thank Dr Ch. Niemöller and Mrs M. Duckwitz of the German Embassy, New Delhi, for kind advice, Mr Aman Nath, New Delhi, for grammatical assistance, and Mrs Susan Gole, New Delhi, for copy-editing.

Joachim Deppert
New Delhi
14 June, 1983

CONTENTS

Inaugural Address

MIR NASRULLAH
Additional Secretary
Ministry of Education, Govt. of India, New Delhi

Excellency, Dr Joachim Deppert, Dr Breuer, Ladies and Gentlemen.

I consider this a privilege to inaugurate the seminar India and the West, dedicated to the memory of Hermann Goetz.

The occasion is one of retrospect of the history of Indology, a field in which the extent of my ignorance is mercifully limited only by the time allotted to me.

The learned scholars listed to speak in this seminar would, I am sure, do ample justice to the comprehensive theme. The fact, however, that it is organized by the University of Heidelberg in memory of Goetz, obliges me to speak chiefly on German contributions to Indology.

The German connection in this respect has been so vital to us Indians that a mere enumeration of the names of the great German Indologists, and an assessment of their contributions, would themselves constitute a valid curriculum.

We are all fortunate to participate in the present tribute to Hermann Goetz who lived a little beyond the Biblical gift of three score and ten years, out of which a full quarter of a century was spent in this country. His work in India chiefly related to the organization of museums, at Chamba and Baroda, also at New Delhi where he built up our National Gallery of Modern Art.

Delivering the Jawaharlal Nehru Memorial Lecture in 1971 under the title "World Perspective of Indian Art", Goetz furnished some interesting illustrations of his favourite thesis, namely, intercommunication of cultures. Two of the illustrations are of the Vaishnava iconography of the *varāha* form, which he perhaps noticed initially on the metal image of Vaikuṇṭha Chatur-mūrti worshipped in the Hari Raj temple at Chamba where he had a tenure with archaeology. (This image was recovered by the authorities from the Bombay airport in 1974 as it was being smuggled out, and was on display at the A.S.I. HQ before its return to Chamba. This image was developed from a motif of the Gupta age.) In the same lecture, he refers to the Padmanābha form and cites a similar form, "Tree of Jesse", representing Jesus as emanating from a lotus. From my limited knowledge I may say that Goetz seems to have been the first to cite a Christian parallel to the Padmanābha motif.

One of the books published by Goetz is titled "5000 years of Indian Art", which I have not seen, but which reminds me of the assumptions of the commencement of Indological studies by our former English rulers. The wording of this title speaks of a generosity of outlook which was wanting in the early English traders, rulers and scholars. For instance, while speaking before the University of Oxford in 1840, H.H. Wilson, the celebrated translator of Viṣṇu Purāṇa, spelt out the objects of Indian studies to be "to contribute to the religious enlightenment of a benighted, but intelligent and interesting and amiable people", and "to confute the falsities of Hinduism, and affirm to the conviction of a *reasonable* Hindu the truths of Christianity". He went on to describe the Vedas as "invocations of the deities ... in return for ...temporal blessings upon the worshipper ... the short-sighted vanities of human desire, which constituted the sum of *heathen* prayer in all heathen countries". It is a reasonable surmise that such prejudices of this important Indologist echoed the magisterial opinion handed down five years earlier (in 1835) by the colonialist administrator, Macaulay, who went on record to say:

> A single shelf of a good European library was worth the whole native literature of India and Arabia. Neither as languages of law, nor as the languages of religion, have Sanskrit or Arabic any particular claim to our encouragement.

More light has recently been thrown on this early English scepticism towards Indian literature. I refer to a paper presented by Garland Cannon of Texas to the Fourth World Sanskrit Conference held in Weimar in 1979, detailing the reaction of British periodicals to Sir William Jones's introduction of Sanskrit culture to the West. Cannon points out that "the English judged Sanskrit culture (with) a Christian bias to depict the Indians as ignorant, remote from civilization" and that the reaction to Jones's moving Hymn to Narayana was "reserved". Cannon adds a footnote to say that it was "the German romanticists' and philologists' study of Sanskrit (which) finally verified Herder's view that the nobility of Hindu culture would ultimately shame European colonists".

While noticing such prejudices, we have to allow for the historic reality that the English came to India to trade and to rule, and it is far from my mind to under-rate the valuable contribution of the English Indologists to the editing and translating of Indian texts.

What was wanting in Wilson and others of his tribe was "empathy", which could be the literary equivalent of Goethe's key word "Anschauung", defined as "the mental process by which we spontaneously grasp through observation aided by intuition, a thing in its *wholeness*". This deficiency was somewhat corrected later by men like Monier Williams, a disciple of Wilson, whose remarks on India are worth quoting:

> It will not be supposed that in our Eastern Empire we have to deal with ordinary races of men ... [or] savage tribes who melt away before the superior force and intelligence of Europeans. Rather, we are placed in the midst of great and ancient people who ... attained a high degree of civilization when our forefathers were barbarians, ... centuries before English existed even in name.

On the other hand the Bavarian author, Johannes Aubanus in the 16th century said :

> As they [the Indians] trust one another in business transactions, they have no need of laws, seals and testimonies. The only law recognised by the Brahmanic nation is never to violate the Natural Law.

Albiruni, an orthodox Muslim had, I think, a much better insight in at least trying to understand the aspects of Hindu way of life which were not in conformity with his faith. While writing on the subject of image-worship in India, though not exactly defending it, he takes considerable pains to explain the circumstances of this religious development.

We in India believe that the German soil has been a second home of Sanskrit. August W. Schlegel, who established the basis for philological penetration of Sanskrit, Franz Bopp who spread Sanskrit in Europe with his clearly structured grammarbooks and dictionaries, and Weber who edited the Shukla Yajurveda, and not the least, Max Mueller who presided over the truly monumental publication of the Sacred Books of The East — these are among the brightest stars of the Indological firmament. Thanks to these German scholars' discovery of India, the subject of Indology is no longer a curious study of a few names like Kālidāsa, nor the sentimental identification of Sanskrit as the "original language" of the Indo-European peoples. The monumental work on the first edition and translation of the Rig Veda by the great Trinity of Grassman, Ludwig and Max Mueller was an acknowledgement of it as the oldest surviving record of human literature, its voluminous text having been "preserved with a faithfulness that is unparalleled in the literature of all peoples in the world".

It is interesting that not a few of the Indologists, (the Germans especially) were mathematicians, which explains their resort to the tool of philology in establishing the authentic text. When it came to writing on philosophical systems, the etymology method was extensively used. It happened often that these two important tools made for excessive certitude of opinion and interpretation, mechanically explaining every esoterism as an allegory.

A mere allegory, however, does not sustain a living culture. This kind of approach, again, failed to take into account the Indian exegetic tradition of *samanvaya* or "systematization", which employed *arthī nirukti* or semantic etymology, in preference to *śabdī nirukti* or phonetic etymology. The esoterism seems to have vexed many a "scientific" Indologist who chose the easier task of explaining it etymologically. The English writer, Thomas Carlyle, provoked by such investigation of the identity of the Scandinavian deity Odin, exclaimed, "We cannot annihilate a man for etymologies like that." A reaction to the obsession with etymology is noticeable in the great Max Mueller himself who thought that the history of religion was more important than the history of language. I am given to understand that, in recent years, the work of Otto Schrader who pioneered the edition of the Pañcarātra Agama, displays the integrated approach as compared to the time-honoured exclusive addiction to philology and etymology.

Indology remains an exciting and fertile field for research and interpretation. More tools like archaeology, epigraphy, and the literary and religious traditions of the South Indian languages, have become available. Goetz's enunciation of "intercommunication of cultures" is particularly appropriate in this context.

One of the references I have consulted is the highly researched and invaluable directory, German Indologists, compiled by the late Mrs Valentina Stache-Rosen, and published by the Max Mueller Bhavan. Her work deserves to be held in great esteem, and I have great pleasure in releasing the book.

Life and Work of Hermann Goetz

HERMANN KULKE
Heidelberg

It is a great privilege and honour to talk on behalf of my colleagues of the South Asia Institute of Heidelberg University on our great scholar, guru and genuine grand old friend, the late Professor Hermann Goetz. The members of the South Asia Institute at Heidelberg feel grateful to all those institutions who have organized this seminar dedicated to the memory of Hermann Goetz, particularly to the Max Mueller Bhavan and its Director Dr Breuer, the German Embassy and to our Representative Dr Deppert. But I have been asked by colleagues and friends in Heidelberg to thank especially all participants of this seminar whose scholarly contributions are keeping alive the memory of the life and work of Hermann Goetz.

The organizers of this seminar were well advised and have to be congratulated on having convened this seminar under the subject "India and the West". For all who had the chance to meet Hermann Goetz during his last years were impressed by his sincere persistence in emphasizing again and again the drawing together of nations and continents. Well equipped with the sensitivity of an art historian and the analytical capacity of a historian he observed, studied and participated actively for nearly half a century in the cultural and political development of Europe and Asia. He therefore was able to see "unity in diversity" not only in India *or* in the West but envisaged cultural convergence and unity as a major aim of future mankind as a whole. In the 1940s, at a time when the world was experiencing the holocaust of Auschwitz, Dresden and Hiroshima, Hermann Goetz wrote about his grand vision in a book with the title "The Commonwealth of Tomorrow". In this "commonwealth of tomorrow", which meanwhile has become the world of today, Hermann Goetz assigned an important role to art historians in rediscovering cultural movements which had once united the Eurasian continent to an extent that we sometimes tend to understand as a benefit of modern means of communication.

It was in this broader perspective that Hermann Goetz placed his various studies on the interrelation between India and the West. His intention was to discover and expose cultural and intellectual movements which linked continents and peoples rather than discovering, for instance, yet another hitherto unknown architectural detail of early Gupta temples borrowed from provincial Roman architecture of Western Asia. I remember very well the vivid discussions with Professor Hermann Goetz when I had the pleasure to re-edit in 1974 his key article on "Imperial Rome and the Genesis of Gupta Art" in his second volume of collected articles "Studies in the History, Religion and Art of Classical and Medieval India". This article certainly does contain a large number of tiny details of possible Roman prototypes of Gupta architecture which Hermann Goetz was able to bring out in his characteristic thoroughness. The framework in which he did these detailed studies becomes quite clear from Goetz' own words: "However, now we have to put the question very differently: Not what did the Indians learn, as a novel art, technique, subjects, etc. from the Greeks (and Romans). Rather, did any already existing and already highly developed cultural aspects in India get their final shape or final function in contact with or as counterforms to late Hellenistic-Roman civilization? Respectively, were late Hellenistic-Roman forms borrowed and consciously transformed almost beyond recognition, for the purposes of any new aspects of Indian development?"[1]

It is highly revealing that the last two articles ever published by Hermann Goetz were both devoted to India's contacts with the wider world. Both of them reflect clearly his balanced approach towards India's contacts with the West as a continuous process of give and take. His last but one article dealt with an unfinished early Indian temple which Goetz had been able to detect in far-off Petra in Transjordania. And in his last article published during his lifetime, which he had contributed to the Professor Sherwani Felicitation Volume, he traced Ottoman-Turkish Art in the Gol Gumbaz at Bijapur in Central India.[2] Another earlier major contribution of Hermann Goetz to the study of Europe's relations with the East and India in particular is his extensive article on the Orient of the crusades and on North India in Wolfram von Eschenbach's Parzival.[3] It is through Hermann Goetz' studies that we know now that the famous medieval German poet Wolfram von Eschenbach, on whose Parzival Richard Wagner's great opera was based, had an exceptional knowledge of India in the early 13th century. Wolfram enlarged the original Celtic-French version by introducing information about India which he must have collected from ex-crusaders and their respective Muslim informants. So we learn from Goetz that Feirefitz, Parzival's "uncle", stands for Sultan Iltutmish of Delhi and Secundille, queen of Tribalibot (i.e. Hindu India), was no other than the widow of Prithvi Raj of Delhi. Furthermore the description of the "Tomb of Camille" in all probability is a description of Kanishka's famous stupa of Buddha the "Perfect One" (al-Kamil) at Peshawar. And the grail in India probably stands for the begging bowl of Buddha preserved near Jalalabad. Thus we learn from Goetz about the existence of a highly developed pre-modern system of communication between India and the West from source material which hitherto seems to have been the "monopoly" of historians of Germanic literature.

Hermann Goetz' extensive work on India's art and its relation with the world was crowned by the invitation of the Government of India to deliver the Jawaharlal Nehru Memorial Lecture of 1971.[4] As title for his lecture he chose "The World Perspectives of Indian Art", a subject which gave him an opportunity to bring to harvest his enormous studies of nearly half a century on Indian Art and to put the results into the broader context which forms also the subject of the present seminar in his memory. It seems to be more than a mere coincidence that his stay in India, when he delivered this Jawaharlal Nehru Memorial Lecture on World Perspectives of Indian Art, was to be his last visit to the country which had already become his destiny more than fifty years ago soon after he had begun his studies.

Hermann Goetz was born at Karlsruhe on July 17th, 1898. His father Hermann (1848 1901) was an artist and the Director of the College of Arts and Crafts at Karlsruhe. Already during his schooltime at the Gymnasium (secondary school) young Hermann showed a deep interest in the history and culture of the Orient. He began his studies at Munich in 1917, immediately after passing his Abitur, though they were interrupted for one term in 1918 by military service. It is highly interesting and revealing to have a thorough look at his study programme and I am therefore most grateful to Mrs Annemarie Goetz for having provided me with these detailed records of her late husband. Already in his first term Hermann Goetz attended classes on the History of Ancient Egypt (Prof. Bissing), participated in an introduction into cuneiform writing (Hommel) and attended classes on the History of Greek Art (Wolters), and Religion and Art of Buddhism in India (by Professor Scherman, his doctor father). And what is most interesting in regard to the topic of our present seminar, already in his first term Hermann Goetz attended a class by Professor Lindl on cultural relationship between the Orient and Occident. After having been drafted in early 1918 he continued his studies in

Munich for one more term. During this time he concentrated on economic history (Brentano), law and even political science (Dyroff). In May 1919 he matriculated at the University of Berlin. During the following term Hermann Goetz seems to have been on the verge of taking up a full-fledged study of Near Eastern languages and cultures (or "Orientalistics"). He began the study of Arabistics under the renowned Professor Bergsträsser, took up classes in middle Iranian language and an introduction into modern Persian language (Marquart). At the same time he attended an introductory course held by Professor Bergsträsser in Turkish studies and two other classes in Turkish language (Bolland) and Turkish literature (Frank). During the same term Hermann Goez had the opportunity to study archaeology under two famous Professors of the Berlin University. Under Professor Herzfeld, the renowned scholar of Near Eastern archäeology, he attended a class on Samarra in Iraq where Herzfeld had been excavating in the years 1912-13. Under Professor Lüders, the famous Indologist and editor of the Bharhut inscriptions, he attended a class on the excavations in Eastern Turkestan. Here we are, for the first time, confronted with Hermann Goetz' insatiable thirst for knowledge. The burden of varied subjects and three languages he took up during his third term already foreshadows his future pleasure in, and his eagerness for work which characterized his whole life.

But fortunately for the Indological studies, Hermann Goetz' occupation with Near Eastern subjects turned out to be only an intermediate though important stage on his way to and in his discovery of India. But he never lost his deep interest in the cultures of the Near East. On the contrary, his respective studies in Berlin and Munich enabled him throughout his lifetime to view "India *and* the West" and to keep in his mind "the world perspective of Indian art" and culture. He began his Indological studies during a short intermediary term in 1919. Hermann Goetz' first teacher of Indology during this and the following terms was Professor Schubring who later on became famous for his studies on Jainism. But at the same time Goetz continued his Iranistic studies in Avesta (Marquart). During the summer term in 1920 he changed over to Jena University where he studied Indology under Professor Cappeller who is known to German students of Indology for his short but excellent Sanskrit-German dictionary already published in 1886. In October 1920 Goetz returned to Munich where he remained till 1923 when he received his Ph.D.

During his final years at the University he studied regularly Indology (Sanskrit and Pali) under Professor Geiger, the renowned scholar of Ceylonese studies and editor of the Pali chronicles of Sri Lanka. Throughout these years he attended the classes of Professor Scherman who had specialized on ethnology of India and Buddhist art. But we should mention that even during these last terms, when he was already working for his Ph.D thesis, Goetz still attended classes in Arabic, Turkish and Greek languages and even participated in two courses on ancient Meso-America, particularly on the culture of the Mayas. In 1923, at the age of 25, he obtained his doctorate under Professor Scherman for a thesis on "The Court Dresses of the Moghul Empire", an abridged version of which was published the following year in the first volume of the Jahrbuch der Asiatischen Kunst (Yearbook of Asian Art).[5]

With this Ph.D. thesis Hermann Goetz began a series of illuminating and essential studies on Indian miniature painting, a hitherto rather neglected field of Indological research. This work was of course inspired by the renowned A. Coomaraswamy, the guru of the whole generation to which Hermann Goetz belonged. These studies remained throughout his life one of Goetz' major interests of research. A splendid starting point for his further studies was the famous Jahāngīr album which, owing to its unusual format, had long lain concealed in the midst of the map collection of the Staatsbibliothek of Berlin.[6]. These studies on "Indian Book Painting from Jahāngīr's Album in the State Library at Berlin" were jointly published with Ernst Kühnel in 1924 and were translated into English and re-edited by Kegan Paul in London two years later in 1926.[7] At this young age of less than thirty years Hermann Goetz was thus looked upon as being a scholar of international repute. In 1923 the journal "Rupam" had devoted several editorial articles to his studies on Rajput painting.[8] His studies on Indian miniature painting culminated in further monumental works, e.g. his "Pictorial Atlas of the Cultural History of India during the Time of the Great Moghuls", published in 1930[9] and in a series of articles published in 1931/32 in the Ostasiatische Zeitschrift (Eastern Journal) on the "History of Indian Miniature Painting". These articles were re-published as a monograph in 1934 by de Gruyter in Leipzig.[10] His earlier studies in Near Eastern and Central Asian languages and cultures and his ethnographic knowledge enabled him to trace on a scientific basis Near Eastern and Central Asian influences on the culture of Mughal India, an empire which had been founded by a princely adventurer belonging to one of the last migratory movements to reach India from the north-west.

During the early years when Hermann Goetz was fully occupied with his studies on Indian miniature painting he was still able to contribute several important works in other fields. One year after his doctorate he published for instance a substantial article on the importance of the Indian Chronicles in the context of Indian Historiography.[11] It is quite likely that he was stimulated and encouraged to do this work by his Indological guru at Munich, Professor W. Geiger, who edited the Pali chronicles of Sri Lanka. In a way, Goetz tried to prove that Hindu India, too, had its own historiographical tradition. Though his hope that new important royal and dynastic chronicles might be discovered in the near future did not come true, this article proved to be an essential contribution to the neglected field of Indian historiography. In 1929, when Hermann Goetz had just become thirty years old, he brought out another monograph under the title "Epochs of Indian Culture".[12] This voluminous book of more than 600 pages contains mainly selections from original literary source material, a conception which reminds one of the "Sources of Indian Tradition", edited by Th. de Bary thirty years later. Another major contribution to Indological studies and the establishment of a separate discipline of Indian Art in Germany was the German translation of A. Coomaraswamy's "History of Indian and Indonesian Art" which Hermann Goetz published in 1927.[13]

Hermann Goetz was able to perform all this immense work despite his administrative work at the Indian Department of the Museum of Ethnology at Berlin where he was employed as an Assistant during the years 1926-31. And one should not forget to mention the difficult economic conditions during these years of the world depression which hit his family severely, particularly since his father, as mentioned above, had died in 1901. I think it is no exaggeration to state that a new era in Hermann Goetz' life began in 1927 when he married Annemarie, née Bartels, whom we have the pleasure and honour to have with us during this conference dedicated to the memory of her late husband. As daughter of a Professor of Medicine and granddaughter of the renowned scholar L. Fuchs, Professor of Mathematics at Heidelberg and Berlin, she remained his true life companion throughout the various stages of his life. Only those who happen to know the Goetzes over a longer period were able to detect to what an extent Mrs Annemarie Goetz participated in and contributed to the work of Hermann Goetz. As members of the world-wide community of Indologists who learned and gained from the work of Hermann Goetz, we should make use of this opportunity to thank Mrs Annemarie Goetz for the continuous help she rendered to Hermann Goetz and his work. Without her help he would have been unable to continue his work during his later years of vanishing health.

In 1931 Hermann Goetz accepted an invitation of Prof. J. Ph. Vogel, former Director-General of the Archaeological Survey of India, who had become the Director of the newly established Kern-Institute and edited the famous "Annual Bibliography of Indian Art and Archaeology" which under his scrutinizing editorship became a "*hiraṇyakośa*" for all students of art and history of India and "Greater India", too. Time forbids mention in detail of the outcome of his research work during these years. Among his scholarly contributions were several articles on Indian miniatures in Dutch collections which became known to the scholarly world only through Hermann Goetz' studies at Leyden.[14]

In 1936, when a storm was already gathering over Europe and refugees from Germany were crowding Holland, Hermann Goetz accepted a travel grant from the Kern-Institute to India. He continued to stay in India with his wife even after the fellowship expired, earning his money as a visiting fellow of several Indian Universities and as a correspondent for European newspapers. It was under these difficult conditions that Hermann Goetz began his studies on Indian art in India itself. During the following years he laid the foundation of his immense and "first hand" knowledge of Indian art and cultural history by an uninterrupted series of study tours in various parts of India which were often quite strenuous for him and his wife. As a matter of course he continued his studies on Indian miniature painting. But staying now in India, he extended his range of interest considerably and became more and more interested in more general "Studies in the History, Religion and Art of Classical and Medieval India" as the second volume of his selected articles has been named. The various stages of Hermann Goetz' life and activities in India are too well known to this audience, so a few remarks may suffice.

Initially he was pursuing the work of his mentor Professor Vogel and concentrated particularly on the history and art of the Punjab Hill States and the Indian Himalaya,[15] a work which culminated in his assignment to undertake an extensive archaeological survey of the state of Chamba. The outcome of the study was his well-known book on "The Early Wooden Temples of Chamba."[16] During the following years he undertook a similar comprehensive survey on the "Art and Architecture of Bikaner State".[17] As a consequence of these studies and his earlier work on Rajput painting, the history and art of the Rajput states became one of the major fields of his research in India. He contributed more than a hundred articles to various fields of Rajput studies, a selection of which was republished recently by the South Asia Institute as Volume Three of his selected works.[18] During his stay in India Hermann Goetz became increasingly interested in Indian architecture. Initially his studies focused mainly on the hitherto rather neglected history of Muslim monuments in India, an interest which certainly had been influenced by his previous studies in Near Eastern Cultures in Munich and Berlin.[19] But soon he extended the scope of his studies and contributed several important articles on the history of several "key monuments" of medieval Hindu architecture, e.g. the Kailasa of Ellora and the Teli-ka-Mandir at Gwalior.[20] But since Hermann Goetz never treated these monuments as isolated manifestations of Indian culture, he carried out also extensive studies on their religious social and historical context. A well-known piece of this line of research is his article on "The Historical Background of the Great Temples of Khajuraho". And looking at the bibliography of his work it is impressive to note the large number of articles which he contributed on purely historical topics too. They include, for instance, his early Calcutta University Readership Lecture on the "Crisis of the Indian Civilization in the 18th and early 19th Centuries"[21] and such topics as "The Policy of the Grand Mughals vis-à-vis the Rajput States", a paper which he read at the Indian History Congress at Bombay in 1947.[22] His historical studies culminated in his History of India, the first comprehensive monograph ever written on Indian history in German language.[23]

Though determined adversaries of the Nazi regime in Germany, the Goetzes were interned twice during war times for altogether three years. But in his characteristic way of overcoming difficulties through work Goetz was able to make use even of these severe restrictions. During the internment in Purandhar he began to survey the surroundings of this fortress and collected material for several articles which he published during the following years on the history and art of Purandhar.[24] In 1940, at the request of the Maharaja of Baroda, he became the Director of the new Baroda Museum and Picture Gallery, where he founded and edited the Museum's renowned Bulletin. In 1951 he also joined the newly established University of Baroda as Honorary Professor of History of Indian Art. In 1953, at the time of his retirement at Baroda, he was appointed Director of the newly established National Gallery of Modern Art in New Delhi. In this capacity he proved that his research was not restricted to history and art forms of the past.[25]

In 1955, after residing continuously in India for nearly twenty years, Hermann Goetz and his wife returned to Germany mainly for medical reasons. This two and a half years' stay in Germany was not an easy one for either of them. During the decades of their absence, Germany had changed fundamentally and many of their old friends and former colleagues were no more. His hope of becoming associated with a German University did not materialize because the establishment of new Indological chairs and institutes which led to a tremendous expansion of Indological studies in Germany in the early sixties was not yet taking place when Goetz returned to Germany in 1955. So the Goetzes returned to India in 1958 at the invitation of the Maharaja of Baroda to build up the new Maharaja Fatehsingh Museum. In 1959, they stayed again for a few months in Germany where Hermann Goetz participated actively in the organization of the famous exhibition "5000 Years of Indian Art" at Essen and Zürich. The extensive introduction to the catalogue was written by him. During these years of personal hardship and first signs of weakening health, Hermann Goetz again overcame these troubles in his characteristic way and wrote his magnum opus "India — Five Thousand Years of Indian Art" which was published simultaneously in English and German in 1959.[26] Re-edited several times and translated into nearly ten languages it became within a few years the standard book for the history of Indian Art, perhaps with the widest circulation in the world.

In 1961, at an age already far beyond the bureaucratic age-limit for becoming a so-called "full professor", he joined the newly established South Asia Institute of the Heidelberg University as Honorary Professor. Till 1971, he was Director of the Department of History of Indian Art which he built up as one of the most flourishing departments of the whole institute. As already mentioned, Goetz became deeply interested in the interrelations between different cultures after returning from the East to the West. Fascinated by the new possibilities of communication and cultural interaction offered by means of our modern civilization, he began again, as in his early years in India, his own intensive travel programme. But this time it led him, in his old age and together with Mrs Goetz, to Morocco and Cyprus, and twice to Southeast Asia as far as Cambodia and Indonesia. After having spent nearly a quarter of a century in India itself, it was as if he were now searching for the peripheral areas of the ancient world which had once been influenced by India's culture and from where India herself had drawn ideas and inspirations.

Though having returned only recently from the seemingly far-off India to post-war Germany, the Goetzes soon became a centre of the academic social life in Heidelberg. Their radiant spell made them and their modest flat, lovingly decorated with Indian textiles, a continuous attraction to many visitors from different countries and of different ages. The last two years of Hermann Goetz, however, were literally overshadowed by illness and failing eye-sight. Initially his illness could only hinder, but finally it prevented him from pursuing actively his own research. But he remained a source of ideas and inspiration for all his friends and students till he died suddenly on July 8th, 1976. Looking back at his life and work six years after his death, one is still fascinated by the impressive number and the wide scope of his 383 publications mentioned in his bibliography.[27] Yet one feels that it is not this mere number, but the synthesis of his gigantic work with his modest style of life and his personal deep humanity which made his life and work so unique.

NOTES

1. Imperial Rome and the Genesis of Classical Indian Art, in: H. Goetz, Studies in History, Religion, and Art of Classical and Medieval India, ed. by H. Kulke, Wiesbaden, 1974. p.44.
2. An Unfinished Early Indian Temple at Petra, Transjordania, in: East and West, XXIV 1974, pp. 245-48; Ottoman-Turkish Art in India. The Architecture of the Gol Gumbaz at Bijapur, in Prof. H.K. Sherwani, Felicitation Volume, Hyderabad, 1975, pp. 522-26.

3. Der Orient der Kreuzzüge in Wolframs Parzival, in Archiv für Kulturgeschicte, 49, 1967, pp. 1-42.
4. The World Perspective of Indian Art, Jawaharlal Nehru Memorial Lecture, 1971, pp. 39.
5. Kostüm and Mode an den indischen Fürstenhöfen der Grossmoghul-Zeit (16 — 19. Jh.). Ein Beitrag zur Chronologie und Kulturgeschichte der indischen Miniaturma lerei, in Jahrbuch der Asiatischen Kunst, I, 1924, pp. 67-102.
6. See K. Jettmar's obituary on Hermann Goetz in: East and West, XXVI, 1976, pp. 539f.
7. Indian Book Painting from Jahangir's Album in the State Library in Berlin, London, 1926.
8. The Indian Art Exhibition in Berlin: Dr Goetz in the "Kunstchronik" in Rupam, Nos. 15-16, 1923, pp. 82ff; Dr Goetz on Rajput Painting, in Rupam, Nos 15-16, 1923, pp. 66-72, 104-06.
9. Bilderatlas zur Kulturgeschichte Indiens in der Grossmoghul-Zeit. Die materielle Kultur des Alltags, ihre Wurzeln, Wandlungen und Beziehungen zu anderen Völkern, aufgrund der indischen Miniaturmalereien und anderen Quellen dargestellt, Berlin, 1930.
10. Geschichte der Indischen Miniatur-Malerei, Leipzig, de Gruyter, 1934.
11. Die Stellung der indischen Chroniken im Rahmen der indischen Geschichte, in: Zeitschrift für Buddhismus, VI, 1924, pp. 139-59.
12. Epoche der Indischen Kultur, Leipzig, 1929.
13. (Translation) A. Coomaraswamy, Geschichte der indischen und indonesischen Kunst, Leipzig, 1927.
14. e.g.: Some Court Portraits of the Pahari School in Dutch Collections, in J. of the Indian Society of Oriental Art, I, 1933, pp. 120-23; Een belangrijk Indisch miniaturen-album in het Rijksprentenkabinet te Amsterdam, Maandblad voor beeldenden Kunsten, XI, 1934, pp. 310-14.
15. Studies in the History and Art of Kashmir and the Indian Himalaya, Schriftenreihe des Südasien-Instituts der Universität Heidelberg, Vol. 4, Wiesbaden, 1969.
16. The Early Wooden Temples of Chamba. Leiden, 1955.
17. The Art and Architecture of the Bikaner State. Published for the Government of the Bikaner State and the Royal India and Pakistan Society, Oxford, Cassirer, 1950.
18. Rajput Art and Architecture, ed. by Jyotindra Jain and Jutta Jain-Neubauer, Schriftenreihe des Südasien-Instituts, Vol. 26, Wiesbaden, 1978.
19. The Central Asian Mausoleum in India, in: Islamic Culture, XII, 1938, pp. 419-23; Persian Architecture in India, in: Bulletin, Iranian Institute of America, V, 1938, pp. 262-69; The Pathan Tombs of Sarhind, in: Islamic Culture, XIII, 1939, pp. 313–18.
20. The Kailasa of Ellora and the Chronology of Rashtrakuta Art, in Artibus Asiae, XV, 1952, pp. 84-107; The Last Masterpiece of Gupta Art. The Great Temple of Yaśovarman of Kanauj ('Teli-ka-Mandir') at Gwalior, in: Art and Letters, XXIX, 1955, pp. 47-59.
21. The Crisis of Indian Civilization in the 18th and Early 19th Centuries. — The Genesis of Indo-Muslim Civilization, Calcutta University, 1938.
22. The Policy of the Grand Mughals vis-à-vis the Rajput States, in: Proc. of the 10th Session of the Indian History Congress, Allahabad, 1949, Vol.X, pp. 340-349.
23. Geschichte Indiens, Stuttgart, Kohlhammer, 1962.
24. Notes on the Siege of Purandhar by Maharaja Jai Singh, in: Poona Orientalist, VII, 1942/43, pp. 181-86; Purandhar: Its Monuments and their History, Annals of the Bhandarkar Oriental Research Institute, XXX, 1949, pp. 215-40; Unidentified Caves at Purandhar, in: J. of the Royal Asiatic Society, 1950 pp. 158–62.
25. Between 1923 and 1929 Goetz had already published three small articles on modern

Indian painting, e.g. Ausstellung moderner indischer Aquarelle im Kronprinzenpalais zu Berlin, in: Kunstchronik (Nuremberg), LVIII, 1923, pp. 433-35.

26. India: Five Thousand Years of Indian Art, London, Methuen, 1959.
27. Published in The History, Religion and Art of Classical and Medieval India, pp. 124-58 (see above note 1).

ANANDA K. COOMARASWAMY

HERMANN GOETZ

The Relevance of Coomaraswamy and Goetz to the History of Ideas— Some Aesthetic Considerations

A. RANGANATHAN
Madras

"An artist" observed Dr Ananda Coomaraswamy, "is not a special kind of man but every man is, or should be a special kind of artist". An exponent of the tradition in art, religion and philosophy, he was also a modern scientist associated with the discoveries of serendibite and thorianite. The frame of his thought is traditional but the picture within the frame can be said to come close sometimes to the aesthetic experiences of poets, philosophers, scientists and mathematicians as different as Śaṃkara and Marie Curie, Aśvagoṣa and G.H. Hardy. Behind these seeming paradoxes is a modern Renaissance figure whose creative achievements in the fields of modern science and perennial metaphysics can be attributed to that tension of the mind which ultimately inheres in the human situation. For genius, ripeness is all; and he drew the main tension of his creativity from the clash between Mediaeval thought and the Renaissance mind. It is not an eclectic combination but that maturity of mind which is derived from the varieties of aesthetic experience. Just as the quantum theory which postulates the relationship between different aspects of one and the same physical process led Niels Bohr to arrive at an epistemological truth of the principle of complementarity, so did Coomaraswamy forge the traditional symbols and figures of thought into the reaffirmation of the Imagination and the dimension of the Sacred in all significant art.

Hermann Goetz's interpretations of Coomaraswamy's specific contributions such as the Coomaraswamy assessment of E.B. Havell as an art critic and the Coomaraswamy exposition of the Tree of Jesse and its Oriental Parallels, we shall analyse here. This analysis is necessary for three reasons. First of all, Dr Goetz had not only translated Coomaraswamy's classic work History of Indian and Indonesian Art but also clarified our understanding of the Coomaraswamy contribution to comparative aesthetics—an achievement which is reminiscent of similar parallels in other related disciplines like the contributions of Max Mueller and J.E. Carpenter in Comparative Religion and Mircea Eliade in Comparative Mythology. Second, Dr Goetz could be at once sympathetic and critical; in this process he revealed the aesthetic values that contributed to the uniqueness of Coomaraswamy—historical empathy, aesthetic sensibility and tonal complexity. And finally Dr Goetz, who began his career as an art critic in the wake of the publication of his doctoral thesis on The Court Attire of the Great Mughal Empire, made distinguished contributions to the very fields in which Coomaraswamy had pioneering achievements to his credit—Rajput Art in its wider perspective, the world perspective of Indian Art and the East–West cultural dialogue.

Like Ananda Coomaraswamy, E.B. Havell paid one of the most charming tributes ever offered to the spirit of India. Just as Coomaraswamy perceived the aesthetic significance of Indian Nationalism in his earlier writings, so was Havell very much a product of that phase of nationalism. Havell is best represented by his works on Indian Sculpture and Painting, The Ideals of Indian Art, A Handbook of Indian Art, Benares, the Sacred City and the Himalayas in Indian Art. However, Havell's approach to the study of Indian art history was more impassioned than accurate, depending rather upon imagination than upon scholarship. For instance, his book on the Ideals of Indian Art is based on the argument that modern India "needs more art in its archaeology and less archaeology in its art". Not surprisingly, in a review of Havell's The Ancient and Mediaeval Architecture of India in The Times (London, March 2, 1915), Coomaraswamy noted: "While the present beautifully illustrated volume is full of suggestive interpretation, it is also bewildering, because so many difficult and complex problems are solved with such facility, and yet the working out of the problem is rarely supplied; and nothing is gained by assuming that every archaeologist must be wrong merely because he is an archaeologist". And several decades later Dr Goetz correctly argued[1] that Havell "had restored the self-esteem of Indian art, often in a one-sided and crudely chauvinistic manner, but too often misunderstood the themes and the objects of art for art itself".

"Since A.K. Coomaraswamy discovered Rajput Painting as a perfect expression of some of the ideals which India had to offer to humanity" wrote Dr Goetz[2] in 1937, "the progress of our knowledge of this art has been rather one-sided. Much has been done to elucidate its individuality and its characteristic themes, but its historical position and development are on the whole still a matter of conjecture and guesswork. Most of these paintings were first brought to the notice of collectors by art dealers whose statements about their place of origin had to be vague and unreliable for commercial reasons or due to indifference. The application of historical and aesthetic criticism has on the other hand proved very unsatisfactory; whereas in the case of Mughal art we have to do with the creations of one dynasty and one civilization of essentially the same standard everywhere, Rajput art is split up in many local schools the standards and fates of which differ as much as the kaleidoscopic history of the Rajput clans. Coomaraswamy as well as the author of these lines had made some attempts to come at least to some chronological sequence by tracing contemporary features in the dresses and buildings depicted in Mughal and Rajput paintings; but for the just mentioned reasons these can at best be regarded as a terminus post quem, the more as our knowledge of the history of Rajput architecture is still in the beginning. And the same might be said of our classification of local schools". Indeed Coomaraswamy and Goetz were the only two scholars who understood the meaning of Rajput Art in terms of what Panofsky would have described as iconological roots. And the three Coomaraswamy–Goetz landmark publications—Rajput Painting by Coomaraswamy, Oxford, 1916, Rajput Painting by Coomaraswamy, Harvard, 1926 and Rajput Art and Architecture by Goetz, Heidelberg, 1978 — are brilliant studies to illustrate how the history of ideas flows through the different intellectual and artistic currents that compartmentalize as well as constitute a mediaeval civilization and way of life. It is this methodology which enabled Coomaraswamy and Goetz to focus their almost ecumenical scholarship on the totality of Rajput Art ranging from literature and paintings to sociology and architecture. Furthermore, this Coomaraswamy–Goetz methodology has raised the level of scholarship to view the Rajput aesthetic sensibility not only as a fundamental contribution to the mediaeval history of art but to the larger domain of South Asian Studies.

Commenting on the apparently paradoxical nature of the Coomaraswamy contribution to art history, Dr Goetz wrote that "in his Western orientation he was a late follower of the Romantic School, of those who opposed the traditional classicism in the name of a return to the intensive religiosity and the Mysticism of the Middle Ages. He became, indeed, himself an expert in the philosophy of Mediaeval Christianity. And this knowledge, a knowledge not only of the brain, but also of the heart, permitted him to interpret to our living understanding not only the classic philosophy of the East, but the symbolic language of all virginal stages of world experience . . . But this great discovery was also Coomaraswamy's one great failure. It made him an archaist who extolled the East against

West, the Middle Ages against the Modern World . . . Thus he evoked an idealized Mediaeval world and an East such as had never existed except as the vision of few extraordinary personalities and contrasted one type of civilization to another, extolling the young and condemning the later ones, and treating each of them as something permanent". Undoubtedly it would be accurate to describe Coomaraswamy as the nearest twentieth-century approximation to the ideal of the Renaissance Man. A distinguished scientist–writer, he was also a master of several languages, an artist who excelled in that difficult art form relating to the drawings of the nude woman figure, an interpreter of the arts of India and Indonesia, Mughal and Rajput Paintings, iconography and sculpture, a philosopher who made excursions into metaphysics particularly in relation to aesthetics, Hindus, Buddhist, Greek and Chinese and an authority on Sacred Art.

In order to interpret the traditions of Sacred Art, more than mere scholarship is necessary. "For the meaning of symbols" stressed Coomaraswamy, "we must rely on the explicit statements of authoritative texts, on comparative usage, and on that of those who still employ the traditional symbols as the customary form of their thought and daily conversation". Actually what is required for a significantly authentic interpretation is the power of creative thinking in the specious perspective of the tradition. Furthermore, Titus Burckhardt has explained in his Sacred Art in East and West that "a symbol is not merely a conventional sign. It manifests its archetype by virtue of a definite ontological law; as Coomaraswamy has observed, a symbol is in a certain sense that to which it gives expression. For this very reason traditional symbolism is never without beauty". And concerning the interpretation of Sacred Art, an American critic Howard Nemerov makes the following comment in his speculations: On Poetry and Painting with a thought of Music: "It will be worthwhile to remember here Coomaraswamy's demonstration that in traditions of sacred art, the Mediaeval Christian as much as the Hindu, painting was treated as Linguistic; the characters of iconography were dictated at least as much by the codified formulas of priesthoods as by any free observation of the visible world; which offers an answer, and a good one, to the question of how, in a world without photography, the features of gods and saviours become so quickly fixed and invariant".

Coomaraswamy's ability to switch from science to art history, and again from art history through religion on to metaphysics revealed an impressive many-sidedness that was possible only to one whose mind was cast in the mould of the Renaissance and Post-Renaissance artists like Leonardo da Vinci, Galileo and Goethe. However, viewed in historical perspective, it is clear that Coomaraswamy is, in a sense, the Renaissance Man in reverse; whereas the Renaissance was in many respects a process of secularization, the great importance of Coomaraswamy is that he was seeking to reaffirm the sacred nature of art and human crafts and activities within traditional cultures both of East and West. And just as S.H. Butcher described Aristotle's Poetics as the criticism of "a Greek summing up Greek experience", so could Coomaraswamy's work be regarded as the contribution of a post-Renaissance figure summing up pre-Renaissance experience.

Leonardo da Vinci emphasized in one of his notebooks, "that figure is most laudable which by its action best expresses the passion which animates it". Furthermore he noted that a sophisticated painter ought to know anatomy. In fact, the memorable quality of the fresco of the Last Supper at Milan relies no less upon Leonardo's religious passion, than upon his use of the anatomical form, subtle chiaroscuro and aerial perspective. But the canons and conventions of Indian art are different. And Coomaraswamy argued in his essay on The Technique and Theory of Indian Painting that "the Indian artist sees indeed ideally, but he does not idealize, he imitates. He does not draw according to his taste but from the intellectual image; not 'knowing what he likes' but liking what he knows ... The Indian artist painted in the express likeness of what he saw 'as if in a mirror', and yet not such a 'looking-glass image' as we see in the mirror ... That art is thus essentially an intellectual experience, which view is also presupposed in the unsatisfactory word 'aesthetic', for which there is no Sanskrit equivalent; but it cannot be distinguished from the view of art that prevailed in Europe throughout the Middle Ages and of which full account must be taken by every student of Byzantine or Romanesque". In this way, he laid the foundations of what may be termed as the new discipline of comparative aesthetics.

The breadth and polymathic nature of Coomaraswamy's writings have spanned geology, art history, aesthetics, religions, civilizations, even time and eternity. He distilled his impeccable scholarship into volumes such as Mediaeval Sinhalese Art, Rajput Painting, Hinduism and Buddhism, Buddha and the Gospel of Buddhism and Elements of Buddhist Iconography. However, his polyvalent genius can be perceived in such major works as The Transformation of Nature in Art, Figures of Speech or Figures of Thought, A New Approach to the Vedas, Time and Eternity as well as in the shorter ones like Recollection, Indian and Platonic, On the One and Only Transmigrant and Two Passages in Dante's Paradiso.

The Coomaraswamy corpus is truly impressive. Interestingly, the nature of Coomaraswamy's achievement in the field of art criticism recalls the shaping of the Auden sensibility in the field of modern English poetry. For the relationship between the earlier revolutionary poetry of Auden and his later theological poetry is reminiscent of Coomaraswamy's migration from the state of Indian Nationalism into the shores of the

Perennial Philosophy. And just as Auden's poetics flashed through Beowulf and Troilus and Criseyde to the contemporary English poets, so was Coomaraswamy's aesthetic imagination shaped by works ranging from Sir Gawain and the Green Knight, Shakespeare's Plays and Paradise Lost to Aśvaghoṣa's Buddha Carita, Laṅkāvatāra Sūtra and Ānandavardhana's Dhvanyāloka. Again Coomaraswamy's contributions to the traditional theory of literature, derived from the perennial streams of literary symbolism, aesthetic sensibility and aphoristic insight, entitle him to be ranked among the major figures in the history of literary criticism. To cite an example, Prof. L.C. Knights' suggestive essay King Lear as Metaphor links Coomaraswamy's gloss on Hsieh Ho's concept of Yun in The Transformation of Nature in Art to the central thesis of Prof. Martin Foss's seminal work Symbol and Metaphor in Human Experience. As Prof. Knights has shown, Coomaraswamy's comparison of the Indian *dhvani* with the Chinese *yun* not only suggests the concept of reverberation but also highlights the metaphoric process defined by Martin Foss as "a process of tension and energy". For Coomaraswamy's profoundly original interpretation of *dhvani* as the verbal noun "sounding" rather than the noun "sound" is present both in *dhvanyāloka* and in Chinese aesthetics. And the appositeness of this concept resulting from the energy to hold in tension the apprehension of meanings in King Lear to Coomaraswamy's explication of "an echoing in the heart of the heart of the hearer" is a key to Prof. Knights' understanding of King Lear as "a moving image of life . . . that sets in motion those powers of apprehension through which we simultaneously become aware of, and make our world".

"There is hardly a branch of Indian art to which Ananda Coomaraswamy has not contributed pioneer research work. But there is one aspect of which he can claim to be the sole discoverer: Rajput Art. Not that he had been the first to study and publish works of this style . . . but he has been the first to discover Rajput Art as a distinct branch of the Indian tradition, with a strong individuality of its own and with no less distinct ideals and conventions" wrote Dr Goetz in a celebrated essay, Rajput Art: Its Problems[3] in 1947 where he not only highlighted the historic significance but also assessed the pioneering nature of Coomaraswamy's memorable work on Rajput Painting.[4] Indeed sixty-six years ago, Coomaraswamy awoke one morning in London to find that his publication Rajput Painting . . . "an account of the Hindu paintings of Rajasthan and the Punjab Himalayas from the sixteenth to the nineteenth century described in their relation to contemporary thought" was an immediate success. In fact, it became and has remained an authentic classic of Indian art history.

Although Coomaraswamy was a versatile and prolific writer, his interpretative work on Rajput Painting is his most significant contribution to Indian art history. True, long before Coomaraswamy published his original essays on Rajput Painting in the Burlington Magazine in 1912, certain art critics had already written on some aspects of Rajput art—a contribution to architecture by J. Fergusson, an occasional piece on painting by Hendley and essays on the decorative arts by Sir George Birdwood and Percy Brown. However, these art critics mistook surface qualities and expressions for fundamentals and universals. Naturally their inability to comprehend the attitude and level of vision attained by the Rajput artists accounted for shallow understanding. And in the process of identifying Rajput Painting with a tradition different from that of the Mughals, Coomaraswamy discovered the actual headwaters of the stream of Rajput art.

The two Coomaraswamy publications—the 1916 classic on Rajput Painting and the fifth volume of the Catalogue of Indian Collections pertaining to Rajput Paintings which came out in 1926, the three Goetz essays—the 1937 Notes, the 1947 assessment and the 1952 critique—as well as the Coomaraswamy–Goetz correspondence are so interrelated as to shed light, from a number of vantage points, on several aspects of Rajput art history. Here a few representative examples of the Coomaraswamy–Goetz aesthetic assessments and responses will be cited to suggest the integration and total perspective that these two scholars brought to bear on the subject of Rajput art over the decades.

Coomaraswamy's letter to Dr Goetz dated May 15, 1923[5] which raised several important issues must be quoted at some length: " . . . I am delighted to know that my books have been the means of assisting you in the study of a culture which you say is not merely of aesthetic interest but of profound spiritual significance. I continue to work on the subject, and have been glad to receive your article in "Über Land and Meer" and also to see your article in the current No: 7 *Ostasiatische Zeitschrift.* I shall study them with care. I have not seen any reason to change my view that the early Rajasthani Raga paintings are of 16th century, or at least very early 17th century date and feel rather more sure of this than before. The Kangra School on the other hand is in the main development of the second half of the eighteenth century, mainly under the patronage of Raja Samsara Cand. I still think that the early Rajasthan paintings in particular do represent a continuation of the old national school and are related exactly as the Tertiary Prakrits are related to the older forms of the language. But as you say, however that may be, I am so glad that the art itself has a meaning for you apart from these questions of history, I am glad to find another scholar who will work in this field in which one student alone cannot hope to find the way without error. You will recognize that mine has been entirely a *pioneer work* and I hope that the work will secure your pardon for what you may in it regard as serious errors". And in a characteristic passage, Dr Coomaraswamy highlights his difference of opinion with Dr Geotz in the 1926 volume of Rajput Painting:[6] "Dr Hermann Goetz in *Studien zur Rajputen Malerei,* Ostasiatische Zeitschrift, X, 1922-23, pages 54 and 56 has argued from the costume and facial angles that this series must be assigned to the beginning of the eighteenth century. In subsequent correspondence (1923) and O.Z., N.F., 1, p. 121, Dr Goetz assigns this series to about 1616–20 on account of the correspondence of the costume with that of the Mughal paintings of the school of Jahangir. The costume and armpit shadow show that they cannot in any case be later than this. I am still inclined to place them somewhat earlier; there is nothing in the costume or architecture that cannot as well or better be assigned to the later part of the reign of Akbar as to that of Jahangir.

To mention only two points: (1) the abundant use of large black pompoms is paralled in the illustrations of the Rasikapriya MS which must certainly be dated about 1600, and in some Mughal paintings of the Akbar period, while the wearing of many large pompoms went out of fashion very early in the seventeenth century and (2) while it is true that in S.2 the skirt of the jama lacks the pointed extensions which are characteristic of the Akbar fashion (Rasikapriya MS: portrait of Man Singh, C.P.I.A. P1, XC and Hamza Nama illustrations, in Gulck, C. Die indische Miniaturen des Haemzae Romanes, 1925) it should be observed that the pointed and the plain-skirted jama, were simulataneoulsy worn (both forms are represented in the Rasikapriya MS and in the Bankipore Tarikh-i- Khandan-i-Timuriyah). The plain jama indeed already occurs in Jaina MS illustrations of the fifteenth and sixteenth centuries (C.C.I.C., Part IV, No. vi, P1 XXII). I have therefore assigned S.2 'to about 1600' and have described S.I. represented by No. 1 of this catalogue, which has a rather more 'primitive' aspect as late sixteenth century". Dr Goetz's 1947 essay on Rajput art not only underscrores the state of knowledge in respect of Rajput painting during this period, but is also a tribute to the pioneering genius of Coomaraswamy. As he rightly put it, "under the circumstances under which *Rajput Painting* was written, it could not be more than a first approach to a new field of research. As such it is the work of a genius, and its fundamental results stand still unchallenged until the present day".

Coomaraswamy's letter[7] to Dr Goetz dated January 22, 1947 which is not only a gracious acknowledgement of the 1947 Goetz essay (this essay was sent by Dr Goetz to Coomaraswamy before it was published) but also an explication of the Coomaraswamy shift of interest from descriptive iconography to the seminal nature of iconographic development, deserves to be quoted at length in this context: "You connect my change of interest from art history to metaphysics with age and no doubt that is in a measure true, though I would perhaps rather say 'maturity' than 'age'. However, I would also like to explain that this was also a natural and necessary development arising from my former work in which the iconographic interest prevails. I was no longer satisfied with a merely *descriptive* iconography and had to be able to explain the *reasons* of the forms; and for this it was necessary to go back to the Vedas and to metaphysics in general, for there lies the seminal reasons of iconographic development. I could not, of course, be satisfied with mere 'sociological' explanations since the forms of traditional societies themselves can only be explained metaphysically".

Coomaraswamy had that rarest of scholarly gifts, a mind which was at once sensitive and interdisciplinary. His contributions to the study of Rajput painting over the years—the original work on Rajput Painting, Part V of the Catalogue of the Indian Collections in the Museum of Fine Arts, Boston which is devoted to Rajput painting and the section dealing with Rajput painting in the History of Indian and Indonesian Art—reflect a wide spectrum of moods and insights. Here is an evocation of Cowdust which translates Krishna from the merely mortal realm of time and place into an immutable product of the Vaishnava imagination. "In the Museum of Fine Arts Collections", Coomaraswamy observed "there is no more lovely painting of the Kangra School than the well-known Cowdust where Krishna is seen returning with the herds and herdsmen to Brindavan at sunset . . . he is an Orphic power whose music charms and beguiles all nature, animate and inanimate alike, and the very rivers stay their courses to hear it . . . In innumerable paintings we find varied combinations of the theme". Again Coomaraswamy's exposition of the Hindi Rāgmāla Texts reveals a new insight into the nature of Rajput aesthetics. He defined the Rāgmāla as "profoundly imagined pictures of human passion". In these Rāgmāla, with their interweaving of mood and suggestion as colours and designs in a piece of embroidery, we have an aesthetic fragment of fine art. For example, the aim and method of the Bundi Painting Madhu Mādhavī Rāgiṇī are expressed in Coomaraswamy's translation of a Rāgmāla text. To cite another example, the Bundi painting depicting the lover's dalliance can be visualized in the Rāga Malkaus.

At least three aesthetic reasons exist for calling Coomaraswamy's book on Rajput Painting a classic. First, there is a vernal freshness here which forecasts its more sensitive use in Coomaraswamy's next book History of Indian and Indonesian Art as the following aesthetic response suggests: "What Chinese art achieved for landscape, is here accomplished for human love. Here, if never and nowhere else in the world, the Western Gates are opened wide. The arms of lovers are about each other's necks, eye meets eye, the whispering *sakhis* speak of nothing else but the course of Krishna's courtship, the very animals are spell-bound by the sound of Krishna's flute and the elements stand still to hear ragas and raginis. The art is only concerned with the realities of life, above all, with passionate love service, conceived as the means and symbol of all Union. If Rajput art at first appears to lack the material charm of Persian Pastorals, or the significance of Mughal portraiture, it more than compensates in tenderness and depth of feeling, in gravity and reverence".

Second Coomaraswamy traced with a revealing sensitivity as of a painter, the shimmeringly exquisite colour scheme in sky and valley, shrub and dew drop and to his seeing eye the aesthetic inspiration of the Rajput paintings had its radiating point in Vaishnava mysticism. Here it is well to recall that Wordsworth wrote of that "inward eye which is the bliss of solitude" while relecting upon the Ullswater daffodils. To see into the life of things is to enable the seeing eye to perceive an entire spectrum of beauty. Again just as Shelley perceived a ray of what he termed as "a light of laughing flowers", so is Coomaraswamy's book full of a passionate conviction that "the sound of Krishna's flute is the voice of Eternity heard by the dwellers in Time". Furthermore, it would be a mistake to disassociate Coomaraswamy's interpretation from his historical method in general, for it is the way in which he translated the limitations of man's existence in an attempt to understand the aesthetic significance of Vaishnava mysticism, that his greatness as an interpreter of Rajput Painting lay. Above all, Coomaraswamy was aware of the haunting presence of Krishna that moved behind the thought and feeling of the Rajput painters, and communicated this aesthetic awareness in sensitive prose: "In Rajput art it is not through landscape or through animal painting that the highest universality is reached. There is no such philosophic interpretation of Nature, as we recognize in Chinese interpretations of mist and mountain, dragon and tiger. The universalism of Vaishnava art is attained in another way, its philosophic language is that of human love; its pair of opposites—Mist and Mountain, Yin and Yang, Being and Becoming, Rest and Energy, Spirit and Matter—are typified by Man and Woman ... In this convention of its own so different from and complementary to that of Chinese Art, the Vaishnava art of Hindusthan is none the less the Indian equivalent of Ch'an or Zen Buddhistic culture of the Far East. Each in its own way achieves the union of Nirvāṇa or Saṃsāra, renunciation and pleasure, religion with the world, Man with Nature".

This leads to the last point. It speaks of the universality of Coomaraswamy's genius that he, the historian of Rajput Painting, should have looked beyond the frontiers of Indian culture. His enchanting descriptions of Rajput Paintings which are expressed in meticulously chosen flicks of words, remind one of Watteau and possibly Blake. Again his translations bring out the similarities between the Rajput lyric poets and the Troubadours. Similarly the Rajput mystics have as their comrades St. John of the Cross, Francis Thomson, Rainer Maria Rilke and others who constitute the Christian hierarchy of immortal song. Thus in the pages of Coomaraswamy's Rajput Painting one looks beyond India and across Europe to that timeless Holy Land of aesthetic experience which is memorably recreated in the following paragraph: "The typical examples of Rajput painting, like every other expression of mystical intuition, have for us this lesson, that what we cannot discover at home and in familiar events, we cannot discover anywhere. The Holy land is the land of our own experience. All is in all and if beauty is not apparent to us in the well-known, we shall not find it in things that are strange and far away".

Coomaraswamy expresses his agreement with Dr Goetz in a noteworthy passage[8] on the origin of Basholi Painting in the 1926 Rajput Painting volume: "It has been stated that the so-called 'Tibeti' pictures (the Amritsar dealer's name for the pictures here classified as Jamwal, on which inscriptions in Takri characters are commonly found) should be described as Balauria (Basholi) rather than Jamuali (Jamu). In any case these represent the oldest and most peculiar type of Pahari art, and the continuation of some older tradition. I am inclined to agree with a suggestion made to me by Dr Goetz in correspondence that Pahari painting perhaps together with Taranatha's Kashmir School was separated at a relatively early date fron the school of the Ancient West, and evolved on the basis of material originating somewhere between the Pala and Jaina miniature styles, and perhaps near to that of the Vasantha-Villasa MS. On the other hand, after this, apparently influences proceding from the Mughal court tended to the elimination of old forms and the formation of a unified style in works and later on dispensed with every trace of the past."

Dr Goetz' 1952[9] essay on Coomaraswamy is at once an essay in general understanding of the methodology of art criticism that may be applied effectively to Coomaraswamy's individual situation and a censure of the smallness to which the present century is subjected. In fact, according to Dr Goetz, the Coomaraswamy sensitiveness was derived from an aesthetically satisfying combination of erudition and general culture. "This sensitiveness" argued Dr Goetz "made his judgement of Indian art history, often based on quite insufficient evidence so sure that it proves correct even in the light of the much more specified information available to us today . . . His work on Rajput painting has opened a new chapter of Indian art history, i.e. that of living Hindu art subsequent to the Muslim conquest. His judgement of quality was infallible".

In retrospect, Coomaraswamy's Rajput Painting is the work of a pioneer which reveals a new world of romance and mysticism, heroism and chivalry. Not surprisingly, it inspired several informative publications by O.C. Gangoly, N.C. Mehta, J.C. French, L. Binyon, H. Goetz, W.G. Archer, Eric Dickinson, Karl Khandalavala, M.S. Randhawa, B.N. Goswamy and several others. For instance, the importance of Archer's work is derived from his accent on the styles and centres of Pahari Painting. Equally important is the jointly authored publication of Eric Dickinson and Karl which highlights the romantic lyricism of the Khandalavala school. Similarly Randhawa's focus[10] is on the brilliance of colours which constitutes the peculiar appeal of Basholi painting.

It is easy to be unfair[11] to a pioneer like Coomaraswamy. It is easier to stir up old controversies about "styles" and "bias". Yet, significantly, Coomaraswamy's Rajput Painting has not become outdated amid the flood of "new material" pertaining to the Rajasthani, Basholi, Kangra and related styles that appeared over the decades. In fact, Karl Khandalavala has correctly remarked[12] that Coomaraswamy's "interpretation of Rajput painting, despite certain debatable and even misconceived viewpoints, has yet to be bettered. He possessed the remarkable gift of saying more effectively in a few simple lines what many others sought to express in involved dissertations lacking that clarity and precision of language and that economy of words which are so characteristic of his writing on Indian painting and sculpture". For instance, Karl Khandalavala has stated[13] that "the development of Pahari painting which is the name by which the painting of the Rajput Hill states of the Punjab is known appears to be a later manifestation. It first makes its appearance in what Coomaraswamy called the Jammu school but that nomenclature is obsolete and it is now more correctly referred to as Basholi painting ." This discovery does not alter the fundamental quality of Coomaraswamy's judgement of the nature of Rajput painting. Again the fact that Mughal influences have played on important part in the evolution of the Rajasthani style is hardly relevant in an assessment of Coomaraswamy's contribution to the study of Rajput painting as a part of the mediaeval background of the history of ideas.

Like Coomaraswamy, Dr Goetz did not confine himself to mere academic specialization. In fact, his 1971 Nehru Memorial lecture entitled The World Perspective of Indian Art[14] was a brilliant essay in tracing the works of Indian art to the sociological factors and the cultural roots from which they had arisen. Underlining the Hellenic factor in Indian art history, Dr Goetz wrote that "during the centuries between the birth of Christ and the Guptas, Hellenistic influence seems to have been considerable, just because it was not imposed ... The body canon of Hellenistic art has been studied but replaced by an Indian canon, its type of canon replaced by a Buddhist, later by a Hindu one. Perhaps an attitude quite natural with people who, convinced of their superior culture, had to deal with princes, courtiers and officers whom, though their political and military masters, they regarded as semi-barbarians. This circumstances explains why Indian sculpture attained its classic stage at Mathura in the North as well as at Amaravathi in the South in the second century A.D. and why Kanishka's attempt at Iranizing the Kushana empire after the collapse of Roman 'Hellenism' failed and the Indian party retained the upper hand in both semi-nomadic states. This probably facilitated their conquest by the Guptas."

The foregoing analysis reveals an insight which reminds us of the Coomaraswamy approach to Buddhist Art. Actually, in order to arrive at a balanced perspective of the aesthetics of Buddhism, the art historian must step back out of the details of the Buddhist art history; he must also get beyond the pages of mere scholarship to grasp the full significance of the aesthetics of Buddhism. This is the process through which Coomaraswamy's genius has expressed itself. His interpretation is, in the best sense, modern, for it sees with the evolutionary eye the origin of the Buddha image along the surface of life; and it also sees with the inner eye the accumulation of legends that lifts the mind towards an intuitive understanding of the deeper messages of Hindu-Buddhist aesthetics.

"It becomes impossible" wrote Coomaraswamy in his essay on The Origin of the Buddha Image, "to treat the phrase 'Greek Origin of the Buddha Image' as representing anything more than a rhetorical misuse of language; if art of the Gandharan School, as its students admit, is half Indian, art of the Kushana and Gupta periods in Ganges Valley is altogether Indian, for it deals with the same ideas, and uses a plastic language that is in direct continuity with that of the preceding centuries". However the problem of determining the origin of the Buddha Image must be understood at different levels of aesthetic perception. For a Buddha image, whether Gandharan-Greek, Mathura-early Indian or Gupta-Classical Indian, reflects the same tranquillity of the spirit awakened to itself. Again the creations of Buddhist art comprise two poles, the first being the Gandharan images while the second constitute the Japanese paintings. Actually the Gandharan image is important in the history of art on two counts. For the artistic process of using the secular idiom of the Roman West in an attempt to express the spirit of Buddhism began in the holy land of Gandhara. Furthermore the Gandharan perspective derived from the head of Apollo, had contributed to a dimension of Greek beauty of Buddhist art. Similarly the tenth century Japanese paintings of Amida (Amitabha) which were partly inspired by the techniques of Taoist art, had introduced an element of Japanese daintiness into Buddhist art.

Just as the Coomaraswamy sensitiveness — the term coined by Dr Goetz — enabled Coomaraswamy to discover the historic signature of Rajput painting in the Mediaeval Indian Landscape, so was the

Coomaraswamy discovery of the artistic signature of the Buddha image equally historic. Indeed the monumental 1978 UNESCO publication on The Image of the Buddha[15] reinforces the Coomaraswamy theory of the origin of the Buddha which was formulated in Coomaraswamy's 1927 publication of the History of Indian and Indonesian Art. "For present purposes a satisfactory conclusion" writes an art historian in a chapter contributed to this UNESCO publication "is that of Ananda Coomaraswamy, namely[16] 'that the Buddha image must have been produced simultaneously, probably in the middle or near the beginning of the first century A.D., in Gandhara and in Mathura, in response to a demand created by the internal development of the Buddhism which was common ground in both areas, in each case, by local craftsmen, working in the local tradition'."

The fundamental significance of Coomaraswamy's interpretation lies in its appeal to men to go beyond the textual, critical analyses to deeper meaning. Beyond the icons of Buddhist art is the Buddhist concept of 'Saṃvega' or the power of aesthetic shock, enabling man to understand the aesthetics of the Buddha-lotus equation as well as gain an aesthetic insight into the nature of reality. And he set forth this idea in the concluding paragraph of his perceptive essay on The Nature of Buddhist Art: "One must have learnt that an access to reality cannot be had by making a choice between matter and spirit considered as things unlike in all respects, but rather by seeing in things material and sensible a formal likeness to spiritual prototypes of which the senses can give no direct report. It is not a question of religion versus science, but of a reality on different levels of reference, or better, perhaps of different orders of reality, not mutually exclusive".

Here it is well to note different aspects of Coomaraswamy's scholarly and literary impact as an art critic. First, Coomaraswamy had co-authored with Sister Niveditha in bringing out The Myths of Hindus and Buddhists which was a significant contribution to comparative mythology. Second, his studies in Yaksha, Brahminical and Buddhist iconography exercised a considerable influence on scholars like T.A. Gopinatha Rao and J.N. Banerjea. Third, through Coomaraswamy the Naṭarājā image profoundly influenced the mind of Rodin. And Rodin's aesthetic response to the Naṭarājā image is reminiscent of Goethe's lyric on Kālidāsa's Śakuntalā, but at a different level. Fourth, Coomaraswamy's essay on The Dance of Shiva inspired the creation of the celebrated Tagore Ballet Nataraj and the Uday Shankar 'Shiva-Tandava' dance item as well as the publication of Dr G.S. Arundale's singularly interesting work The Lotus Fire which is a study in symbolic yoga. Fifth, the general outline of Coomaraswamy's theory underlying Rajput Painting still holds in an examination of the nature of Rajput art, although new definitions and assessments have been provided by art critics like Hermann Goetz, Eric Dickinson, M.S. Randhawa and B.N. Goswamy. Sixth Coomaraswamy inaugurated the study of Terracota art which was continued by the scholarly investigations of Dr V.S. Agrawala, H.D. Sankalia, Moti Chandra and others. Seventh, Coomaraswamy influenced the thinking of Paul Mus, a French scholar who is well known for his work on Barabudur. Eighth, Coomaraswamy's work on Buddhism and the Gospel of Buddhism (1916) made a deep impression on the mind of Prof. A.L. Basham, author of The Wonder that was India and Christmas Humphreys, the founder of the British Buddhist Society. Ninth, the architectonic quality of Coomaraswamy's exposition of Indian art — which can be perceived in the History of Indian and Indonesian Art — has set a compelling pattern for his successors like Vogel, Hermann Goetz, Zimmer, Stella Kramrisch and V.S. Agrawala. And finally, Coomaraswamy's interpretations of the parallels between the Chaitya Hall, Hindu Temple and Christian Cathedral were developed further by Hermann Goetz as a fascinating chapter in the history of ideas.

The quality of Coomaraswamy's later writings touches all places and times, and moves likewise above time and place; and nowhere is this quality better shown than in his interpretations of the Indian lotus and the Christian rose. Here Coomaraswamy makes a subtle distinction between the *parokṣa* and the *pratyakṣa* use of terms. He pointed out that *parokṣa* terms are "proper to angels" who are "fond of" the symbolic; *pratyakṣa* language on the other hand is "proper to man ... as individual ... who is 'fond of' the obvious ..." To cite an instance, the Sanskrit word *puṣkara* means the lotus flower on the *pratyakṣa* level; it refers to something that can be aesthetically experienced. However, in terms of *parokṣa* terminology it constitutes "the symbol and image of all spatial extension". Here it is worth noting that just as the rose is used in Christian mythology, so is the lotus adopted in the Orient in a similar sense. In fact, Coomaraswamy observed: "What presents itself directly to men (e.g., the sensible aspect of the flower) presents itself indirectly (or metaphysically) to the Angels, and what presents itself indirectly to men presents itself directly to the Angels". He also added: "There has often been brought out the common valency of the Christian rose and the Indian lotus as representations of the ground of all manifestation, the support of being when it proceeds or seems to proceed from being to becoming". Redefined in this way, the examples of symbolic imagery discussed above gain a new dimension of aesthetic perception. More importantly, Coomaraswamy realized that the lotus of Indian and Buddhist aesthetics is also the rose of Christian theology and is no less distinctively Western than Yeats' "Rose of all Roses" which exists not as a rose of the physical earth but as the transmitter of deeper meanings, or Eliot's lotus which is weighted with Eastern metaphysical associations. Interestingly enough, Elizabeth Drew discusses the connection of Eliot's lotus with the rose, the circle and the "still point" as representations of the *maṇḍala* pattern in her book T.S. Eliot: The Design of his Poetry. And in the final analysis, it is clear that the content of Coomaraswamy's later writings is not that of an art critic, but of a seer who used the things of art such as the Indian lotus and the Christian rose for the purpose of the spirit.

Coomaraswamy's mind was a perpetual chrestomathy which synthesized the different confluences of art, religion and literature into a prose of artistic significance. Here is an elegant attempt to locate omphalic points at which the totality of the Buddhist aesthetic imagination is caught in an inspired moment: "The Buddha is invariably represented iconographically as supported by a lotus, his feet never touching any physical or local earth ... The ultimate support of the lotus can also be represented as a stem identical with the axis of the universe, rooted in a universal depth, and inflorescent at all levels of reference; and if in Brahminical art this stem springs from the navel of Narayana, the central ground of the Godhead recumbent on the face of the waters, and bears in its flower the figure of Brahma (with whom the Buddha is virtually identified) the universality of this symbolism is sufficiently evident in the stem of Jesse and in the symbolic representation of the Christian Theotokos by the rose".

Of all the ideas developed by Coomaraswamy and Dr Goetz, that which is culturally significant is the principle of the application of Christian theology to illuminate ancient Indian art. Indeed the use of Christian theology as a tool for the illumination of some problems of Indian and Buddhist art has been perfected by Coomaraswamy, Dr Goetz and Dr Heimo Rau. In a perceptive essay[17] on The Meeting of Eyes Coomaraswamy argued that "Nicholas of Cusa's description of the icon of Christ has a striking parallel in the Dhammapada Attakatha, 1. 406 ... A Buddha seems to stand face to face with every individual, no matter where the individual may stand ... The effect, in other words, is not an accident, but a necessity of the iconography; if the eyes of an allseeing God are to be iconostasized truly and correctly, they must appear to be all-seeing". Here one is reminded of Dr Heimo Rau's exposition[18] in another context: "In all forms of art expression, most peoples have been faced with the challenge to achieve a formal solution of the 'reclining' female or male figure. We think here of the 'Burial of Christ', the 'Vesper pictures' in the Christian Art of the Occident, or also of the reclining female nudes from Titian and Giorgione up to Picasso and Henry Moore. The Buddhistic art was faced with this motif when portraying parinirvana and when depicting Maya's dream. With Parinirvana, the solution was naive. A standing figure was simply placed in a horizontal position without making any changes with regard to the position of the limbs or the drapery of the related garment. The viewer does not see the narrow side of the reclining figure but has a full front view. We must not presume that the figure was meant to be lying on its side. This is made clear by the treatment of the garment; the arrangement of the pleats is the same as on a standing figure. This style has been developed in Gandhara and from there it spread to North and South".

Dr Goetz has referred to the representation of the Tree of Jesse in his Nehru Memorial lecture. Actually the Tree of Jesse emerges as a full-fledged Christian iconographic formula in the twelfth century. Indeed Coomaraswamy is right[19] in arguing that the idea of a cosmic tree rising from the navel of an ultimate source of life is a well-known characteristic of Indian cosmology. However, it is difficult to be certain whether the Christian iconography of the Tree of Jesse can be traced to an Indian influence. But the similarities in the iconographic representations of Brahma seated upon a lotus whose stem rises from the navel of the recumbent Narayana and the Tree of Jesse ought to be studied in order to view these problems in their proper perspective. And here are some of Dr Goetz's aesthetic considerations[20] relating to this problem. "The Tree of Jesse, i.e., the pedigree of Christ, in the form of a lotus stem springing from the navel of his ancestor Jesse, out of each flower emerging the upper part of the body of some saintly person, until from the top flowers there emerge St. Mary and Christ. Everybody will immediately feel reminded of many frescoes in Buddhist monasteries, or of Vishnu-Narayana lying asleep, the stem of a lotus growing out of his navel, and on the open lotus flower the creator Brahma sitting. There are many more such-like motifs e.g., mandalas wherein the Buddhist deities are replaced by Christian saints, in the centre the Holy Trinity. And on closer investigation one discovers many more motifs e.g., the Biblical scenes over Gothic Cathedral doors have exactly the same framework as religious scenes in Pala miniatures; or at the Abbey of St. Denis near Paris, there are Kirtimukha friezes so Indian in the smallest particularity that everybody would—isolated—classify them so". Furthermore what makes this reasoning methodologically acceptable is a theoretical framework which, though not fully adequate, meaningfully extends the premises of comparative aesthetics. Consider as an example the following passage from Coomaraswamy's review[21] of Arthur Watson's Early Iconography of the Tree of Jesse: "... in the Gupta representation at Deogarh the stem of the lotus that supports Brahma is not directly connected with the navel of Narayana but rises behind him and this often happens in the representations of the Tree of Jesse. Still, the connection of the root with the navel is even correct formulation, and this will be evident if we reflect that the stem' after all represents the fruition of the 'seed' of Jesse, as is especially evident when the Tree becomes a veritable genealogy, and that the navel according to all ancient tradition both Western and Eastern is the progenitive centre and a centre in every sense of the word, and as such the starting point of manifestation".

Despite differing backgrounds, Dr Coomaraswamy and Dr Goetz not only contributed to but also hoped for a more fruitful era in East-West Cultural Relations. In his book[22] The Commonwealth of Tomorrow, Dr Goetz stated the case for an East-West cultural dialogue. In fact, he went to the extent of stating that "modern philosophical and religious trends are unintelligible without an understanding of the Upanishads, the Bhagavat Gita, Confucius or Laotse." Furthermore, he commented[23] in his History of India that "in our world today, in which technology brings us close to the remotest countries, an outlook or attitude centred on Europe alone, means cultural suicide. We must learn to understand distant countries—not as fairy tale lands for tourists or research travellers or objects of economic exploitation, but as cultures with their own right and value system along with ours". And Coomaraswamy wrote in a similar strain in his essay on Intellectual Fraternity[24] "Who that has breathed the clear mountain air of the Upanishads, of Gautama, Sankara and Kabir, of Rumi, of Laotse, and Jesus (I mention so far Asian prophets only) can be alien to those who have sat at the feet of Plato and Kant, Tauler, Boehme and Ruysbroeck, Whitman, Nietzsche and Blake."

In a letter to Dr Goetz dated November 1, 1944, Coomaraswamy made the following reflections[25] : "I am always insisting that the 'gulf' between East and West, while it is a present fact exists only as between the Modern West and the Surviving East. I have repeatedly emphasized that it is no question of geography, but of Zeitgeist; also that the modern Western position, temporarily provincial as it is, is accidental, rather than essential, and all that is needed is for the West to recover its sanity and for the East not to lose it; given that, the fundamental unity of humanity reappears". Small wonder that Coomaraswamy was greatly attracted by Blake, whose ethereal Illustrations in his Prophetic Books are reminiscent of mediaeval manuscript illumination. And in sum, the Coomaraswamy–Goetz range of cultural studies and aesthetic insights as well as their view of Mediaeval art history projected on to the history of ideas are not only major contributions to the discipline of comparative aesthetics but also constitute a value system of singular beauty in our time.

NOTES

1. H. Goetz, A.K. Coomaraswamy: A Critical Appreciation, J. of the M.S. University of Baroda, Vol.I, No.1, 1952.
2. H. Goetz, Notes on Some Schools of Rajput Painting, J. of the Indian Society of

Oriental Art, Calcutta, Vol.V, 1937.

3. H. Goetz, Rajput Art: Its Problems in: Art and Thought, ed. by K. Bharatha Iyer, Luzac & Co. London, 1947, pp. 87-94. This essay is included in the Hermann Goetz volume of essays on Rajput Art and Architecture, ed. by Jyotindra Jain and Jutta Jain-Neubauer, Franz Steiner Verlag, Wiesbaden, 1978.
4. Ananda Coomaraswamy, Rajput Painting, Motilal Banarsidas, Delhi, 1976, Indian Edition.
5. Letters of Ananda Coomaraswamy, ed. by S. Durai Raja Singam in: An Unpublished Private Collection, Malaysia, Vol.3, 1974.
6. Rajput Painting — Catalogue of the Indian Collections in the Museum of Fine Arts, Boston, Part V, in: Rajput Painting, Harvard University Press, Cambridge, Mass, 1926, pp. 71-72.
7. Letters of Ananda Coomaraswamy, ed. by S. Durai Raja Singam in: An Unpublished Private Collection, Malaysia, Vol.I, 1972.
8. Rajput Painting — Catalogue of the Indian Collections in the Museum of Fine Arts, Boston, Part V, in: Rajput Painting, Harvard University Press, Cambridge, Mass, 1926, pp. 7-8.
9. A critical Appreciation by Dr H. Goetz, J. of the M.S. University of Baroda, Vol.I, No.1, 1952; this essay is reproduced in Remembering and Remembering Again and Again ed. by S. Durai Raja Singam, Malaysia, 1974, pp. 71-73.
10. Basholi Painting by M.S. Randhawa, Publications Division, Government of India, New Delhi, 1959.
11. Ananda Coomaraswamy as a Historian of Rajput Painting by B.N. Goswamy in: Historians of Mediaeval India, Delhi, 1968 and reprinted in S. Durai Raja Singam's Ananda Coomaraswamy: Remembering and Remembering Again and Again, Malaysia, 1974.
12. Rajput Painting, Vol.I. Text, Foreword by Karl J. Khandalavala, Motilal Banarsidass, Delhi, 1976, p. 5, Indian Edition.
13. Ibid, p. 12.
14. The World Perspective of Indian Art, Jawaharlal Nehru Memorial Lectures, Bharatiya Vidya Bhavan, Bombay, 1973, p. 162-63.
15. The Image of the Buddha, ed. by David L. Snellgrove, Serindia Publications, UNESCO, 1978, p. 59.
16. History of Indian and Indonesian Art, Ananda K. Coomaraswamy, Dover, New York, 1965, p. 60.
17. The Meeting of Eyes, included in Roger Lipsey's Coomaraswamy: Selected Papers, Vol.I, Princeton, 1971, p. 236.
18. Reflections on Indian Art, Heimo Rau, Shakuntala Publishing House, Bombay, 1979, p. 55.
19. Tree of Jesse and Indian Parallels have influenced Christian Era, Ananda K. Coomaraswamy, Parnassus, Vol.27, II, February, 1929.
20. The World Perspective of Indian Art, H. Goetz, Jawaharlal Nehru Memorial Lectures, Bharatiya Vidya Bhavan, Bombay, 1973, pp. 160-61.
21. The Tree of Jesse and Oriental Parallels, Ananda K. Coomaraswamy, Parnassus, Vol.7, 1, January, 1935.
22. The Commonwealth of Tomorrow, H. Goetz, Indian Periodicals Limited, Allahabad, 1944.
23. History of India, Hermann Goetz, pocket edition, 1962.
24. Intellectual Fraternity included in Coomaraswamy's The Dance of Shiva, Noonday Press, New York, 1957, p. 136.
25. Letters of Ananda Coomaraswamy ed. by S. Durai Raja Singam, An Unpublished Private Collection, Malaysia, Vol.t, 1975.

East or West — The Precedent: The Aryan Schism[1]

JOACHIM DEPPERT
New Delhi/Heidelberg

For Benno and Ebba

What suits to gods and men is not at all different.
What does not suit them is the same.

A Hittite statement (KUB XIII 4 I 21f.)

I The Protagonists

There is no denying the fact that the Aryan authors of the Avesta and the Veda attracted the attention of the world less for their real properties than for the misappropriation of their name and the distortion of their image by some self-conceited would-be heirs to their legacy, in the first place by Hitler's Germans, in the second by some more harmless Indians.

Hitler and his (not only German) camp of the Third Reich coveted to recognize their self-alleged assorted abilities in the antagonistic arts of abstract thought and armed assault, and to relate their (not always) towering stature, their superwhite skin, superblond hair, and superblue eyes with the Aryans. The inferiority-complexed obsession of the Nazis with their contrived Aryan superiority over the world, and above all the Jews, conjured up the well-known calamitous consequences, from which the Aryans have to be acquitted.

To be sure, Hitler could lay claim to some Aryan models of vigorous pugnacity and ideological — even racial — discriminations. The Irano-Aryans of the Avesta drastically split the world into good and bad; and the fair-skinned *(śvitnya)*[2] and golden-haired *(harikeśa)*[3] Indo-Aryans of the Veda exceeded in warfare and abstained from deliberately condescending to the level of the dark-hued *(kṛṣṇa)*,[4] "flat-nosed" *(anās)*,[5] moreover "foul-speeched" *(mṛdhravāc)*,[6] let alone impious and idolatrous[7] Dravidian and Austro-Asian *dasyu-, dāsa-,* and *paṇi*-races they encountered in India. But in the first case the discrimination was downright religious and free from ethnic considerations; and in the second it vibrated on the wave length of the well-known archaic mentality comprehending nothing but the own tribal community as the sole island of humanity in an otherwise animal world.[8] This attitude does not necessarily have to do with the misfiring of the race hatred of the Nazis.

Not to mention that their claim was a misappropriation also with regard to the non-Aryan descent of the Germans. All the ancestors of the recent Indo-European peoples in Europe may at best be considered branches of one and the same trunk, of the Indo-European pedigree, but not scions of the Aryan branch.[9] Only the Iranians, the Afghans, the Dards-Kafirs, and some North-Indians of high caste may feel just claim upon direct provenance from it. While Islam made the former three forget their Aryan ancestry, the latter upheld the beacon of what they dubbed the Aryan spirit, and connived to thoroughly transform at the threshold from the Indo-Aryan culture to Hinduism. They rather soaked the Veda with the spirit of Hinduism, although it was still destitute, at least in its "classical" or RV manifestation, of castes, temple-cult, the protection of the cow, vegetarianism, etc.

However, the Indian image of the Aryans is suffering from a set of idler half-truths and even lies pertaining more to "spiritual" and intellectual than to racial superiority — despite the undue reputation Hitler enjoys in modern India for the Aryan myth. In her idiosyncratic propensity for eternalization, Hindu India has persisted in transfiguring the Aryans into a quasi pre-Cambrian past, so that no other people should contest their all-inclusive depth so close to god, and their inventiveness, to which the world is understood to owe the bliss of electricity, tele-communications, and whatever else is up to date on the international market. The profundity of the Aryan spirit is at least not untrue in the face of Vedic Monism, (which is any case was less Vedāntic than Śaṃkara and his followers would have us believe). But the imputation of technocratic superiority is downright wrong. The word *agni* denotes "fire" and nothing but "fire", the more so as — apart from the horse chariots and various sacrifical implements — Aryan technology appears to have come to a halt at the iron nail scissors of the Chāndogya-Upaniṣad.[10]

After all, the impact of the Aryans on the cultural history of the Indo-European and Eurasian peoples is deeper-seated and farther-reaching than the Indian or German misappropriations would implicate. The most archaic and the smallest branch of the Aryan pedigree, the *mariịannu* of

Naharin and Mitanni in Northern Mesopotamia, on whom we'll occasionally touch, are reported as having made their neighbours — the civilizations of Mesopotamia, Anatolia, Canaan, Palestine, and Egypt — familiar with the horse and chariot.[11] But this is less significant than the antagonism dividing their younger, more numerous and momentous kin, the Indo-Iranians, into the Irano-Aryans and the Indo-Aryans, or rather into the cultures of the Avesta and of the Veda. These created the precedents of the world outlook prevailing west of India, in Zarathustrian Iran, quite a lot in Judaism, Christianity and Islam, and east of Iran, in Vedic, Jaina, Buddhist and Hindu India.

The Aryan family tree had struck roots independently from its Indo-European relatives in closer or farther neighbourhood — somewhere between the lower Wolga basin (Jamna-culture) and the southern Ural Mountains — in the early 3rd millenium B.C.[12] Its growing trunk had set some hundred annual circles, before it branched off in two successive bifurcations between *c.* 2000 - 1400 B.C. and disseminated the three aforementioned scions. First the *mari̯annu* seceded from the trunk (*c.* 2000–1750/1600 B.C.),[13] then the Irano-Aryans and Indo-Aryans separated from one another (*c.* 1600 – 1400 B.C.).

The secession of the *mari̯annu* is a rather hidden secret of Aryan prehistory. It appears to have followed a common Aryan migration from the Wolga basin to the south, to Gorgan and the Araxes basin (Southwest of the Caspian Sea), and/or to the steppes of southern Middle Asia (between the Aral Sea, its two tributaries Jaxartes and Oxus, the Alai Tau and Pamir Mountains and the Afghan-Iranian highlands).[14] Three possibilities attached to three migrational routes have to be taken into account:

1. Via the eastern flank of the Caucasus to Gorgan. The area housed and obviously disunited an Aryan population in the later 3rd millennium B.C.[15] The ancestors of the *mari̯annu* stayed behind, whereas the still united Indo-Iranians are supposed to have set out on their migration to Middle Asia through Iran.

However, the conjecture of an eastbound migration raises problems. It inverts the usual east/north — west/south direction of prehistorical and historical migrations from and within Eurasia. With the exception of the Tokharians, who got stuck in Sinkiang while trying to reach China from their original homeland on the upper Wolga (?), all the other emigrators, both Indo-European (Old Europeans, Hittites, Greeks, Latins, Celts, Germanics, etc.) and non-Indo-European (Huns, Bulgars, Avars, Magyars, Mongols, Seljuk and Ottoman Turks) attained their final destinations from the east/north. Moreover, although otherwise reminiscent of mythical and astronomical traditions of the remotest Indo-European past,[16] neither the Avesta nor the Veda make mention of an eastbound

migration. Therefore two other options are likely:
2. From the Wolga basin to the northern flank of the Caucasus. From here only the ancestors of the *mariịannu* proceeded to Gorgan. The Indo-Iranians ranged the northern Caspian shore into Middle Asia.
3. From the Wolga basin to the Middle Asian steppes. Here the ancestors of the *mariịannu* broke away to settle in Gorgan and later on in Northern Mesopotamia.

Despite their utter scantness — some inscriptions, some evidence in Hurrian, Hittite and Akkado-Egyptian texts[17] — the traces of the historical *mariịannu* are of rather unequivocal datability. This is a consequence of their being so densely interwoven with the destinies, and so accessibly eternalized in the cuneiform or hieroglyphic characters of their urbanized and script-addicted Mesopotamian, Anatolian, Levantine, and African neighbours. On the other hand the disputable archeological evidence[18] and the voluminous oral literature of the Avesta and the Veda do not admit of more than an approximate temporal frame.[19] In other words, in the case of the Irano-Aryans and the Indo-Aryans the notion of history has to be divorced from its implication of exact chronology. This does not, however, mean that the two peoples have to be confined to the half-shadows of merely hypothetical prehistory. For otherwise — the Veda nearly to the extent of a chronicle — they depict the material and spiritual cultures involving and evolving from the historical events in lively, radiant colours.

The transition of the Indo-Iranians from prehistory to history came to pass after the secession of the *mariịannu* in Middle Asia, and from *c.* 1600–1500 onwards in Afghanistan, where their cultural harmony fell apart. After a short Afghan stay, not more than a few generations,[20] the Vedic tribes invaded India via the Khyber Pass and the Kurram valley *c.* 1400–1200 B.C. whereas — but only after a protracted stay and rather slowly altogether some 13–15 generations after the *mariịannu* — the supporters of the Avesta gained ground in more westerly Iran and finally in Gorgan too.

The Indian heyday of the Indo-Aryans lasted from *c.* 14/1200–600 B.C. and fell into two phases, of the RV (1400-900 B.C.) and of the Late Veda (900–600 B.C.), i.e. of the SV, YV, AV and the Brāhmaṇas, partly overlapping with, but of definitely less archaic language than the RV, and of the still younger Āraṇyakas, (early) Upaniṣads, and Sūtras.

Some faint and fading memories in the texts testify to the Middle Asian transition period of the Vedic culture. The river Rasā of the RV may not only denote a mythical river as according to the bulk of the references, but may also be identified with the Avestan Ranha, *ossìa* the Jaxartes.[21] Moreover the Balhikas, a tribe figuring in the AV,[22] may be localized in Bactrian Balkh.[23] Otherwise the scene of RV history was well established in the north-west of the Indian subcontinent, between the western (Kurram, Kabul, Gomal, Swat)[24] and the eastern or Punjabi tributaries (Jhelum, Chenab, Ravi, Beas, Sutlej)[25] of the frequently mentioned Indus (Sindhu), the still well-watered Sarasvatī[26], and the already known, however not yet very vital Yamunā and Gaṅgā.[27]

The Eurasian law of mainly westbound migrations is invalid within India. As if striving after the abodes of its most popular gods Indra (east) and Agni (south-east), later Vedic culture was shifting its centre from the Punjab to the land between Yamunā and Gaṅgā, to be called Madhyadeśa, Āryāvarta, or Brahmāvarta in the Hindu texts.[28] The west beyond the Sarasvatī fell victim to oblivion, not to say depreciation, a process already initiated in the RV. After all one of its more important historical events, the famous "battle of the ten kings" (*dāśarājña*)[29] on the banks of the Ravi (Paruṣṇī) was decided to the detriment of a confederation of five western tribes (Pūrus, Yadus, Turvaśas, Anus, Druhyus) and their northwestern allies (Alinas, Pakthas, Bhalānas, Śivas, Viṣāṇins), but in favour of the eastern Bharātas and Tṛtsus of the Madhyadeśa. Finally the Aryan colonization of the east transgressed the Gaṅgā, establishing Aryan settlements in Kosala (Oudh) and Videha (Tirhut)[30], in Kāśī (Benares), Magadha (South Bihar), Aṅga (Son-valley) and Vaṅga (Bengal).[31] By the end of the second phase of Vedic history the sphere of Aryan influence comprised the whole of India to the north and partly also to the south of the river Narmadā.[32]

While the east was won, the Vedic culture underwent considerable changes. The tribal order of the RV declined, the tribes fused into a state-like organization[33] dominated by the Kuru-Pañcālas, the people *par excellence* of the Brāhmaṇas.[34] At the same time — the question had not yet been fully settled in the RV — the function of the king became exclusively restricted to profane duties (jurisdiction, administration, warfare) without religious privileges. The Brahmins were the usufructuaries of this development. They made much money now, throwing on the intricate magical machine of a pompous *l'art pour l'art* ritualism, which was only thwarted by the Monism of the Upaniṣads. Grown from the spontaneous and fearless acquaintancy with the divine, an intrinsic property of the RV mentality (*infra*), the monist philosophy was presented now for the first time in a form to be called systematized.

The social structure of the Aryans changed too. The strict separations of the non-Aryan *dāsa-* and *dasyu*-tribes from the Aryans so upheld by the RV slackened. By the name of Sūdra — and with the obligation to serve the Aryans in class-conscious modesty — the autochthons became attached to the three classes (*varṇa*) of RV society (*brahman, kṣatra, viś*). But this concession was counteracted by a greater rigidity and hierarchization of class-distinctions. Not that the three Aryan *varṇas* lacked in the awareness of their basic superiority, they kept on emphasizing their aloofness. To salvage the Aryan purity from possible obscurations — which in the long run could not be prevented anyhow — the Brahmins had decreed a canon of contact rules concerning matrimonial (isogamy), alimentary (commensality), and religious communications (seclusion) with Sūdras.[35] It not only recommended insurmountable borders between Aryans and non-Aryans, but also ever more between the formerly open Aryan *varṇas* themselves.[36] Caste (*jāti*) was born, in which the Aryans transformed into Hindus and nevertheless lost their purity.

Contrary to the Vedic tradition merging into and overwhelmed by the vast ocean of Hinduism, the Avestan religion is still alive, upheld by the Parsis in central Iranian Yezd — let us at least hope so[37] — and on the Indian west coast (Surat, Bombay). Its faithful and comparatively undiluted preservation is a result of the solidarity cementing minorities, moreover supported in India by the traditionally detached Hindu tolerance towards other creeds. But even in Iran the destructive fundamentalist zeal can hardly make preparations for more than its fifth anniversary. Although never particularly conciliatory — the reason why some Parsis decided to permanently emigrate to India — the Muslim seizure of power after the battle of Nihāvand (642 A.D.) was not immediately disastrous for Zarathustra's followers.[38]

Notwithstanding the intact survival of the Avestan faith its literary sources have come down to us in quite fragmentary a condition. Three quarters of the canonical texts are said to be lost for whatsoever pre-Muslim reasons. Only the Yasnas, among them Zarathustra's five Gāthās,[39] the Visperad, the 18 (of originally 30) Yashts, the Vendīdād, and some minor poetical categories[40] have remained. Their present redaction is even of post-Christian date. Together with a rich exegetic literature in Middle Persian or Pehlevī on Avestan fundamentals, it was sponsored by the first kings of the Sassanid era (226 – 642 A.D.)[41], who tried to compensate the probable hostilities the literature may have been exposed to during the Parthian (250 B.C. – 226 A.D.) and the Greek (330 – 250 B.C.) eras.

Before the Parthian and Greek rules, however, it flourished as the state religion of the Achaemenian Empire (555 – 330 B.C.). But in spite of the Iranian view synchronizing the lifetimes of Zarathustra, Buddha and Orpheus,[42] the Avestan sources antedate the days of the founder of the Achaemenian dynasty, of emperor Vistaspa (555 – 522 B.C.), under no circumstances to be mistaken for Zarathustra's champion of the same name. Zarathustra's characteristic interference with the undivided Indo-Iranian bequest, his reform establishing the Moral Dualism, is already evidenced by an inscription of king Assurbanipal of Assyria (*c.* 700 B.C.), which mentions the good god Assara Mazas (Ahura Mazda) along with seven good angels (the Amesha Spentas) and seven bad spirits (Angra Mainyu and his inner circle).[43] But even then some centuries had already passed since the reform. Being most closely related with RV Sanskrit — two Aryan dialects rather than two distinct languages — the idiom of the Gāthās and consequently the age of their author Zarathustra have to be dated within the span of the RV period in India (1400 - 900 B.C.), whilst the linguistically younger Yashts, the Vendīdād, etc. counterpoint the Late Vedic phase (900 - 600 B.C.).

The pre-Achaemenian heyday of Zarathustra and the primitive Irano-Aryan culture evades a reconstruction as easy as in the Vedic case not only by dint of the fragmentation and late compilation of the Avesta — intrinsic psychological differences between the Irano-Aryans and their Indian siblings have a finger in the affair. The Middle Asian scene of early Irano-Aryan history is not to be contested irrespective of the western localization of Zarathustra's cradle and activities according to late and dubious allegations.[44] His eastern roots are corroborated by several more reliable references. The closeness of the Gāthic and Vedic languages could be invalidated with a similar root relationship between Sanskrit and Achaemenian Old Persian having originated in the central Iranian province of Pars, of which the place Ragha (Raï) is specified as Zarathustra's hometown.[45] We can, of course, think of a coexistence of Avestan and Old Persian in Pars, all the more Assurbanipal's aforementioned inscription sanctions an already early, a pre-Achaemenian transfer of the tradition to the west.

But it had come to Pars from the east, as evidenced by two further statements revealing Middle Asia. Zarathustra is understood to have received the sacred law from Ahura Mazda on a mountain by the river Daregha.[46] To be sure, this stream has been identified with the Darah, a tributary of the Gorganian Araxes.[47] But the question is rather of a branch or tributary of the Vangvi Daitya or the Ranha, of the Oxus or the Jaxartes, of the Syr Darya or the Amu Darya, in which the name survives in modern form.[48] And after all, if we acknowledge a chronological succession in the enumeration of the 16 Iranian provinces created by Ahura Mazda according to the Vendīdād,[49] the way of the Avestan culture from Middle Asia into the Achaemenian Empire and into a more nominal than genuine racial Aryanhood can be traced.

II The Indo-Iranian Schism

The antagonistic direction — the Veda to the Indian east, the Avesta to the Iranian west of Afghanistan — portend more than a *fait accompli* imposed on the cultural diffusion by random topographical features calling upon migrators in virtue of easy access. They epitomize the fundamental, the conscious and subconscious attitudes of the two Aryan cultures against each other, governed by mutual contradictions and suspensions in terms of complementary couples, of binomials yoked together by mutual inversion or negative determination of pole and generic antipole, like east/west.

a. *Pure and Useful/Impure and Noxious Animals*

Or like pure/impure, useful/noxious. The two binomials are quite suitable for embarking on the phenomenon of mutual Indian/Iranian inversions. They governed the reputation and treatment of some animals. The Avesta considered asses, pigs, dogs, crows and ravens, and cocks pure and useful, consequently honoured their existence, and handled them with care. On the other hand the Indo-Aryans degraded the very same species on account of alleged impurity. But they extolled the purity and usefulness of ants, frogs, and tortoises, three animals which the Irano-Aryans loathed. They considered them noxious animals, earmarked for pious killing.

In Iran the ass was so pure, that even in monstrous form — with three legs, six eyes, nine mouths (each as big as a cottage), and a horn — it guarded the island in holy lake Vourukasha, the abode of all fresh waters in the universe, where the sacred white *haoma*-tree, the tree "of all seeds", the tree "opposed to harm" grew.[50] The meat of asses and pigs served for the preparation of sacrificial dishes.[51] Moreover the boar figured among the theriomorphic disguises of Verethraghna, the genius of victory.[52]

But no other quadruped was heaped with more honours than the dog, or let us better say the dogs, for the hierarchy of the dogs proper culminated in the shepherd's dog,[53] and the hierarchy of the so-called or non-Darwinist dogs culminated in the "water-dog", *ossìa* the beaver.[54] Meticulous instructions regulated the right treatment of the dogs, the care to be taken for the correct covering of bitches,[55] their pregnancy,[56] and the bringing up of their whelps.[57] Neglect was punished severely. Feeding bad food — too hot, or bones too hard — to a shepherd's dog for example was to be requited with twice 200 lashes, killing it even with twice 800 lashes with the whips called *aspaheaštra* and *sraošočarana.*[58] Even if the two instruments of torture might be one and the same — the former referring to the type ("horse whip"), the latter to the function ("instrument of penalty")[59] — 200 and so much more 800 stripes are enough indeed not to wipe out, if at all to survive, the experience!

Such sacrosanctity was decided by the dog's authority over the sheep, an important factor of Avestan economy, as we shall see later, its watchfulness as guardian of the house, and last, but not least, its contribution to the solution of the problem how to protect the corpses from corruption — according to Zarathustrian orthodoxy they had to be exposed in *daxmas*. The stray dog (*vohunazga*) devoured them, before the Nasūs, the evil demons of corruption, could obstruct the soul's path to paradise.[60] For the very same reason the life of crows,[61] the "most precious of all creatures"[62], of ravens,[63] "protecting from enemies and maintaining glory"[64], and of vultures[65] was treated with indulgence. Pious speculations even furnished the vulture with a flask of musk under its wing, lest it should swoon from the stench of its chosen environment.[66] Finally cocks, the holy birds of Sraosha, the embodiment of religious obedience, were considered holy birds.[67]

However, already in RV India the cock was accused of dubious confederacies with unholy witchcraft. A short hymn against the powers of evil asked Indra "to slay every screecher (*parikrośa*), to strangle the cock (*kṛkadāśu*)."[68] A noxious spell was cast on it,[69] it symbolized the impure mouth of Nirṛti, the goddess of untruth and decay.[70] Later on the mere sight of a cock polluted the ceremony in honour of dead relatives (*śrāddha*).[71] Cock's meat was, of course, not to be eaten.[72] As for the vulture, the RV may refer to its majestic flight in neutral metaphors,[73] the AV, however, to its ill foreboding bringing diseases[74] and assaults of evil sorcerers (*yātu*).[75] Likewise crows harbingered black magic.[76] They were libelled to pollute the sacrifice,[77] to defile food,[78] and to embody untruth *par excellence* together with Śūdras, women, and dogs.[79]

Apart from some very sporadic exceptions testifying to human[80] and divine (Rudra,[81] Indra,[82] Yama[83]) dog keeping and sympathy for dogs, the Indo-Aryan tradition did not call the animal's inferiority and impurity in question. Evil sorcerers would assume the disguise of a dog.[84] Dogs polluted the site of a sacrifice,[85] and graduated Veda-students (*snātaka*) were ordered to not even look at them.[86] Pigs too spread impurity.[87] The sight of a pig suspended a *śrāddha*,[88] and its meat was on the index of forbidden food.[89] Finally asses were dubbed Śūdras by birth,[90] and had to be sacrificed for the requital of polluting perpetrations against the precepts of chastity.[91] Their braying endangered religious instructions,[92] and their meat was exempted from consumption.[93]

But to ants, frogs, and tortoises the Vedic tradition granted a seat of honour regarding their medicinal and/or hydrological usefulness, or rather their cosmographic relevance. The pungent acid of ants served as an antidote against poison,[94] particularly of serpents, scorpions, and biting insects.[95] Earth of an anthill was given to the sick,[96] since ants were reputed to dig remedies into the ground,[97] moreover to convey water from the depths of the earth, which the gods had poured for them there,[98] as a reward for their help in killing the demon Makha.[99]

Frogs betokened the transition from scorching heat to soothing cool. Compared with brahmins, frogs croaking happily and jumping playfully around announced the rainy season, the most important event of the water cycle in India.[100] In medicine they were reported as allaying fever,[101] in magic as quenching fire,[102] and a frog pond was supposed to originate from the water poured over the cremation fire at the end of the obsequies.[103] Furthermore a frog — besides a lotus flower and a bamboo shoot — was to be drawn across the completed fire altar that it might appease the wrath of Rudrāgni.[104]

Another phase of the rituals prescribed for the piling up of the fire altar provided for the deposition of a living tortoise,[105] a "lord of the waters",[106] symbolizing the creator (Prajāpati)[107] or the earth floating on the primeval ocean.[108] The tortoise was said to furnish the altar with the "life sap of these worlds."[109] The Indo-Aryans lived inside a tortoise, as it were. The earth formed its lower shell, the sky with its ends bent down an upper shell, and the atmosphere the hollow space between the shells.[110]

The Avesta had meted out a fate far less lucky to tortoises, frogs, and ants. They were reckoned among the "noxious animals" (*xrafstra*) in possession of and possessed by the evil Daeva-demons, the antagonists of the good Ahura-gods. Consequently they were reputed to pollute the waters instead of representing their bliss and to destroy life instead of preserving it.

Who was the "evil creature among the creatures of the evil spirit, roaming around from midnight till the sun is up to kill thousands of creatures of the good spirit?"[111] The "dog" of Anghra Mainyu, the archfiend, the tortoise called Zairimyangura, "injurer of the fresh water."[112] And which hateful creature "went swimming around the *haoma*-tree in lake Vourukasha, and would never cease to gnaw it down?"[113] The water frog. And who stole more corn than was necessary for its nutrition?[114] The corn-carrying ant.

In India the *ahiṃsā*-doctrine interceded for the protection of all, even of impure life. So, the impure animals of the Indo-Aryan tradition were at best punished with passive neglect. But in Iran the killing of noxious creatures yielded pious rewards. "For everyone who kills a corn-dragging ant it is as good as for anyone who recites the Hōrmazd Yasht",[115] and "killing a frog is as good a work as thousand and two–hundred *dirhams* in weight."[116] And the murderer of a beaver could not get rid of his lethal sin but by slaying "10000 tortoises, 10000 land frogs, 10000 water frogs, 10000 corn-carrying ants, and 10000 ants of these who dig holes and work mischief."[117]

b. *The Agent of the Schism and the Gods*

Similar inversions have been carved out from the perplexingly variegated and seemingly heterogeneous inventory of American Red Indian mythology by Claude Lévi-Strauss[118] in the meticulous and — to the detriment of his opponents — irrefutable *clarté française* distinguishing his structuralist method and its presentation. His four volume "Mythologiques" point out that myth cycles and their supporting cultures may radically invert each other, as evidenced by some central and south Brazilian vs. some Pacific Canadian systems. The more as some Latin American myths regarding the origin of certain constellations (Orion, Corvus) turn some Graeco-Roman antitypes upside down,[119] the amazing phenomenon may be interpreted as an automatic development brought about by the axioms of human awareness (objective consciousness)[120] in Hegel's sense.[121]

But it is not necessary to attribute the phenomenon to nothing but the blind sway of awareness according to its axioms. Stochastic, purpose- and wilful diacritic activities of awareness are also possible — and they are repeatedly shown proof of on the level of primitive tribal or early civilized societies. No victims of the modern middle class mindset deriving its self-assertion from the possession of the very same status symbols as the people next door, they make good their cultural identity by arbitrary inversions of alien models. Some tribes of Australian aborigines for example are reported as having calculated their intricate socio-parental organization by simply turning the models of their neighbours upside down.[122] Likewise the utterly receptive Hittites appear to have underpinned their religious and mythological identity with inversions of Sumero-Akkadian, Egyptian, even of Aryan sources supplied by the *mariẙannu.*[123]

A similar desire for cultural identity from mutual inversion, however of much wider range and complexity, has to be taken for granted in the case of the Irano-Aryans and the Indo-Aryans. The basic symbols, patterns, notions, concepts, the centres of gravity, as it were, consolidating the superficial polymorphism of various profane and sacred aspects of Avestan and Vedic daily life are encompassed and governed by the phenomenon: Avestan economy devolved on peaceful agriculture, enriched by means of stockfarming, first of all of sheep, and only in the second place of cows, whereas Vedic economy promoted martial cattle nomadism in grand style, minimizing the tending of sheep, not to mention the pursuit of agriculture. Vedic kinship organization hinged on patriarchy of such an exclusive purity as has never since been achieved by any other culture, whilst the Avestan conventions concealed a considerable matriarchal bias at their very base. Avestan orthodoxy recommended and welcomed "next-of-kin-marriage", while Vedic society drastically forbade incest with the consequence of well-considered, often conspicuously demonstrative exogamic matrimonial alliances. Vedic philosophy propagated Upaniṣadic Monism, prefigured in the RV version of the Indo-Iranian pantheon, the Avesta, on the other hand, decreed a rigid Moral Dualism, rooted in Zarathustra's version of the Indo-Iranian pantheon. Avestan obsequies would not acknowledge but exposure of the corpses in *daxmas,* the Veda, however, proposed cremation.

This state of affairs gives such a systematic impression that a development at random is to be excluded from a possible explanation. After all, the two Aryan cultures grew from one and the same prehistorical root. With regards to this a veritable schism has to be taken into consideration, the die of which was cast in Afghanistan *c.* 1500 – 1400 B.C. It bisected the Irano-Aryan bequest into the antagonistic shares of the Avesta and the Veda, turning, as it were, their backs upon each other and gravitating towards opposite geographical and ideological directions the moment their supporters entered the stage of history, autonomous and independent from each other.

The postulate of a veritable schism alienating the Avestan and Vedic tribes from one another has met its *pros* and *contras* among scholarly circles. Its first and most convinced assertor was the German Indo–Iranist Haug (1827–1876). He rummaged the texts, still very, very knotty then, keen on tracking down the invectives and maledictions which the two hostile camps were supposed to have hurled at each other's heads. He found much more noisy and much less silent concomitants than there actually are, but his theory was right, although, of course — *ho polemos patēr pantōn tōn chrēmatōn* — denied by others who wielded more or less convincing arguments (*infra*).

Applying the term schism with the qualification "veritable" our attention has to be directed towards two fundamental prerequisites, religion and the instigating agent. The term schism implicates religious dissent between a new and an old denomination — as, for example, in the case of Amenophis IV-Akhenaton's (1364–1347 B.C.) monotheist Aton-reform against the polytheism of the priests of Amûn and other state gods in Ancient Egypt; or between two opposed streams of the Catholic/Arian schism between the confessors of the Nicene Creed (identity of Father and Son in the Trinity) and of Arian's doctrine (mere similarity of Father and Son) enacted on occasion of the (first) Council of Nicaea (325 A.D.).

On the other hand, particularly the Avesta testifies to economic controversies between the ancestors of the Avestan and Vedic tribes, which we'll adjourn for the time being. They certainly played midwife to the Indo-Iranian schism about to be born. But a schism dealing with religious questions, and the machinations behind the scenes, are too consciously staged and too subtle to be reconducted with two swarms of siblings crushing their skulls about material problems. Peoples have never taken decisions by themselves but they were — or are — governed by trendsetting individuals — Soviet Russia is no exception, although her pundits toil at the counterevidence. Had pharaoh Akhenaton not been so keen on having his whole kingdom take part in his rapturous visions of the sole god, and on clipping the wings of the powerful Amûn-priests, or emperor Constantine not convened the bishops to Nicaea, the peoples of Egypt or of the Christian world would not have had any other choice but to live and to die in the long-lasting hostilities imposed on them by the schismatic decisions.[124]

The Indo-Iranian schism satisfies the two conditions of religion — two antipodal trends within the common heritage — and the instigating agent. The name of the manipulator was Zarathustra — even if he was called so only later on by a rearguard straining the reminiscences of preceding paragonal personalities. Doubtlessly dwelling on the disadvantages of the economic situation, Zarathustra sealed the separation of the Iranian from the Indian branch. He inaugurated the religious movement documented in his Gāthās, instituting the dualist doctrine in opposition to the still latent monist bias of the Veda. And that way he betokened the standard attitudes future generations of Avestan and Vedic proselytes would automatically embrace against each other. Even if the antipodal manifestation of their two cultures and world outlooks might not yet have been settled by Zarathustra in the "classical" dimensions of the centuries to follow him, *he* had nevertheless already shifted the points by interfering in the Indo-Iranian pantheon.

The inhabitants of the pre-schismatic Indo-Iranian, and later on of the Indian and the Iranian pantheon, fell into two groups, the Devas and Asuras of the Veda, and the Ahuras and Daevas of the Avesta.[125] The nomenclature requires some preliminary remarks. In the RV the appellative *deva,* and, at least sporadically in the oldest, quasi pre-schismatic layers of the Avesta the isoglosse *daeva* denoted a god as such in contrast with man, and could also connote a member of the Asura-Ahura-group. In the oldest Avesta the main Daeva-group itself was not yet demonized by Zarathustra's reform, whereas the still godly Asuras of the RV must neither be mistaken for the genuine Deva-gods, nor for the demons of the name populating Indian mythology from the Brāhmaṇas onwards. Although there are some overlappings between the old and godly, and the new and demoniac Asuras concerning a common symbolism now and then, the latter were no "lords" any more — such is the significance of the word *asura/ahura.*

The nucleus of the Deva-group included: a creator, Dyauṣpitā or Viśvakarman in the RV, Prajāpati in the Brāhmaṇas.[126] Indra, the most popular god of the RV tribes, the king of the universe, of gods, both Devas and Asuras, men, animals, plants, and lifeless nature. The wind- and storm-gods Vāyu, Vāta and the Maruts, a band of youthful warriors. Vivasvat, originally a mortal sacrificer turned sun god. His sons, the Aśvin- or Nāsatya-twins,[127] and Yama, the god of death. Awe-inspiring Rudra, the hunter and archer of the gods. Uṣas, the goddess Dawn. Agni, the fire god, and Soma, the god of the sacred intoxicant of the Indo-Aryan cultus. Both are turncoats from the Asuras to the Devas,[128] whence they display both Asuric and Devic features.

The oustanding personalities among the Asuras were: a creator, Asura, Father Asura, or Tvaṣṭā-Savitā-Viśvarūpa,[129] a complex deity composed of three also separable components.[130] A creatrix, Aditi, the great mother of the three, four, six, seven, or more[131] Āditya-brothers[132] — according as Dakṣa,[133] Aryaman,[134] Varuṇa[135] Mitra,[136] Aṃśa,[137] Bhaga,[138] and Savitā.[139] They embodied moral, ethical, and communal values. Dakṣa, also a creator, came to be associated with priestly skill. Aryaman controlled marriage and guided his worshippers along safe and easy paths. Apart from creative activities, Varuṇa was entrusted with the superintendence over the waters, the moral order of the cosmos (*ṛta*), and the punishment of sins. Mitra represented faith and reciprocity in mutually dependent relationships. Aṃśa apportioned booty and luck in gaining wealth. Bhaga divided the communal wealth and fertility. Savitā, a sun god often very close to Bhaga,[140] dispelled ignorance. Pūṣan[141] a pastoral god, and Apāṃ Napāt,[142] the "Son (or Grandson) of the waters," conclude the enumeration of the RV Asuras.

The RV preserved the pre-schismatic or Indo-Iranian names of both Devas and Asuras. But Zarathustra renamed and abstracted the more important members of both camps in order to emphasize the decided emancipation from the past. But his new identities and names do not downright conceal their old roots. Ahura Mazda, the "Wise Lord", the creator of what is good in the world, mixed features of (Father) Asura, of Dakṣa, and — especially regarding his superintendence over the moral order (*arta, asha*) — of Varuṇa. The Amesha Spentas, a hexad or heptad[143] of his hypostasies echoed the strong moral bias of the Ādityas. They personified eminent moral and existential qualities — like Asha Vahista (Highest Truth), Vohu Manah (Good Will), Āramaiti (Piety), Xshathra Vairya (Good Government), Haurvatāt (Health and Waters), Ameretāt (Immortality), and Sraosha (Obedience). However, two Vedic Ādityas had Iranian namesakes and were disbanded from the ensemble of the Amesha Spentas, namely Mithra, here a sun god of the *sol invictus*-type, and Airyaman, a warder-off of diseases, sorcerers, demons.

In Iran Haoma, the holy intoxicant, and the fire god, here called Ātar, kept faith to their Asuric provenance. But some Ahuras had deserted their innate devaship: Vāyu and Verethragha, a replica of Indra Vṛtrahan ("the Slayer of Vṛtra", viz. of the enemy as such), Vīvanghvant (Vivasvat) and his son Yima (Yama). The latter did not conceal his Devic descent. In spite of being the primeval sovereign, the first with whom Ahura Mazda conversed, Yima committed an apostasy and neglected the righteous religion.[144]

Otherwise there were only a few and moreover rarely mentioned namesakes of the Devas among the evil Daevas: Indara, Naonghaithya (Nāsatya), and Saurva (Śarva = Rudra).[145] Together with countless demons of diseases, pains, tortures, perversions, lies, loss, decay, corruption, etc., and an inner circle of anti-Amesha Spentas — Untruth, Bad Will, Bad Government, etc. — they made up the retinue of Angra Mainyu (Ahriman), the devil of devils of, *and* Zarathustra's creation.

Supposed to have been furnished with equal power in the Indo-Iranian pantheon, at least in terms of an ideal conjecture, the two groups lost balance with the schism. Zarathustra bowed before the Ahuras, whilst the Vedic tribes extolled the Devas. Consequently divine sovereignity changed signs, confronting the rulers with a depreciated or subjected group, according as the Daevas in the Avesta, and the Asuras in the Veda. As we shall see in detail later, the confrontation happened in concordance with the very essence of either superior group. Walled up in nothing but goodness and heavenly light, the dualist Ahuras broke up an untraversable moat between themselves and the nothing but bad, blackened and forever excluded Devas. However, due to the monist spirit of the Devas, the two groups drew much closer together in the RV, cross-fertilized each other, so to say, and occasionally exchanged their roles. As an Asura could not only be dubbed *deva,* but also display Devic faculties now and then, the Devas would casually be addressed *asura,* "lord", an honorificum in this case, or be endowed with *āsurya,* the specific power of the Asuras. But nevertheless, the more vigorous, spontaneous and decided Devas, and the principally inferior but honoured Asuras never completely shunned their basic lines of demarcation.

The bipartition of the pantheon would have made no sense without the opposition of the two groups and accordingly their association with two contrasting fields of functions, marks, symbols, etc. Their tracking is our aim now. To be sure, Zarathustra strictly separated the Daevas from the Ahuras, but nevertheless his rigid polarization knocked their antagonism only into the good/bad-shape underpinning the validity of his Moral Dualism. It aggravates inferences about the contrast within the pre-schismatic coexistence of the two groups, the reconstruction of which is indispensable for statements regarding the schism. For, so much the more in an age determining and measuring human behaviour by divine paradigms, Zarathustra is understood to have rooted and solidified his decisive steps in the lives of the gods, in other words, to have reflected his Ahura-centric values in the inverse and deterrent mirror of the Devas and their worshippers. On the other hand, the feedback from the Ahura-culture placed negative footholds at the disposal of the Vedic tribes about to establish valid conventions of their own. These however, do not leave us in the lurch as for our present ends. Despite the generosity of Monism, eclipsing the lines of hostile demarcation between the Devas and the Asuras, the Veda consents to the reconstruction of their innate antagonism, as evidenced by a considerable number of complementary oppositions on various levels of divine — and consequently of human — life.

c. *"The Farmer and the Cowman Should Be Friends"*

As already alluded to above, Zarathustra's steps may have been catalyzed to the point of no return by economic controversies, bloody skirmishes between peace-loving, sedentary husbandmen and small stockfarmers on the Iranian, and martial, nomadic cattle barons on the Vedic side. Particularly Zarathustra's Gāthās show proof of such an economic antagonism. It is confirmed by the economic systems prevailing in the Avesta and the Veda. And it was prefigured in the "occupations" of the gods presiding at either pantheon.

An extensive cattle terminology — special denominations for calves and young cattle of different age, for heifers, various types of miscarrying cows, for milchcows, for bulls and oxen, apart from the very, very frequent collective term *gauḥ*[146] — leaves no doubt about the importance of cattle in the economy of the Vedic tribes, and betrays the keen interest of seasoned experts whose hearts leapt with joy in the face of their horned darlings. The cow was "everybody's friend."[147]. It vouched for wealth, prosperity, food. It made the standard of exchange and valuation. Cows *en masse* served as the usual sacrifical fees for the bards (*kavi*) and the officiating priests (*ṛtvij*), who at times received flocks of 1,000, 1,100, even 10,000 heads at once.[148] Flocks of 30,000,[149] 100,000 and more[150] are mentioned.

Bragging exaggerations? — And yet, we can be sure, that the Vedic cattle barons swam, as it were, in cows, and lived on their milk (*gauḥ, gāvaḥ, kṣīra, payas*), its products like butter (*ājya*), ghee (*ghṛta*), or curds (*dadhi*), and on their meat.[151] The references to cow leather (*gauḥ*),[152] to the RV obsequies,[153] to sacrifices of cows,[154] to cow butchers (*goghāta, govikartana*)[155] testify that the Vedic tribes were no orthodox Hindus, and enjoyed beef as a dish. Even their saints of sorts partook freely of it. A sacrifice of 100 cows was credited to Agastya.[156] And Yajñavalkya, obviously a gourmet, would not abstain from the meat of milchcows, if it was only "tender" or "from the shoulder" (*aṃśala*).[157] The Late Vedic doctrine of *ahiṃsā* which was focused on the protection of the cow could not immediately impede the enjoyment.[158] Despite its general acknowledgement on the threshold from the Vedic to the Hindu culture, the texts kept on prescribing beef for the guest reception[159] and the wedding feast.[160]

The tending of small livestock, of sheep (*avi, meṣa, meṣī*) and goats (*aja, ajā, basta, tūpara*)[161] was neatly distinguished from the tending of cows,[162] and obviously of inferior economic relevance. Even in early RV times, when the tribes still inhabited the colder landscapes of the extreme Indian north-west, necessitating wool as the prevalent raw material for garments[163] and for the Soma-sieve,[164] and the best breeds came from Gandhāra,[165] of sheep tending in grand style there can be no question — the solitary and merely conjectural reference to the shepherd's dog[166] may corroborate this state of affairs. Later on, when the Indo-Aryans had settled down in the warmer climates of the Āryāvarta and beyond, and unlearned the old Soma-cult,[167] sheep became rather degraded. Although still figuring among the five animals fit for sacrifice (man, horse, bull, sheep, goat),[168] some branches at least of the Vedic tradition excluded the "vicious ram" (*dureḍaka*),[169] and exempted sheep's milk from consumption under any circumstances. Goat's milk, however, was not forbidden,[170] because goats were reputed to be the sacrifical animals *par excellence*. The vital energy had stayed longer in them than in the rest of the sacrificial animals — to finally penetrate into the earth and transform into rice (*vrīhi*).[171]

As evidenced by the rare and moreover comparatively young references to ploughing,[172] and the vague collectiva for grain (*dhāna, dhanya*), RV agriculture was rather overshadowed by cattle breeding. Only barley was specified (*yava*)[173] and probably grown during the winter (mid-October–February).[174] Rice was not yet known then, at least unconcernedly passed over by the RV tribes. Its rather tricky cultivation was a consequence of the gradual integration of its authors, the Indian aborigines now called Śūdra, into Aryan society during Later Vedic days, when the agriculture of various crops, ploughed in the fields with the help of many-headed teams (6, 8, 12, etc.) of oxen[175] gained ground as an important economic factor anyhow.[176]

Only during the wintry cultivation of barley the RV tribes would comply with the sedentary way of life prerequisite to agriculture. Now the cattle did not demand excessive care. During the day they had not to be sheltered from the heat and could freely graze on the pastures yielding lush grass. The nights they spent close to men in the pens around the solid, half-subterranean (?) houses (*harmya, gṛha*).[177] These were not constructed anew every year, but abandoned and reoccupied by their owners, setting out on and returning from the seasonal migrations in search of more appropriate environments for the benefit of the cows.[178]

Then oxcarts (*anas, vāhana*) were furnished to escort the wandering flocks. Such a nomadic trek and the ringshaped corral, erected in the evening from the oxcarts around the cows driven together, was called *grāma*. Later on the word came to denote the sedentary village developed from trek and corral.[179]. The changing significance of *grāma* epitomizes the gradual adoption of a completely sedentary way of life, to which the Indo-Aryans were urged during Later Vedic times by dint of the greater immobility implicated by the decline of the old tribal order in favour of a statelike political and hierarchically stratified social organisation — the *four* classes — and, last but not least, by their considerably accomplished agriculture.[180]

The oxcarts of the nomadic treks had two groaning compact wheels[181] revolving with the axle, and a shade against sun and rain.[182] But there was also a prouder, lordlier type of vehicle. It was mainly anchored to the warrior class, and used for racing — a sport quite popular in the Veda[183] — and for warfare: the chariot (*ratha*)! It was harnessed to normally two, but also to three,[184] four,[185] even to five horses,[186] animals congenial to its agility and speed. The *ratha* owed its advantages to two spoked wheels with felloe, metal tyre, and hub revolving round (and not with) the axle, which was fixed to the box by means of cow leather strings.[187] The box offered two or three[188] sheltered seats or standing places for the charioteer (*yantā, rathī, rathin, sārathi*)[189] — unless he preferred "sitting on the yoke" (*dhūrṣad*)[190] — and one-two fighters called "standing on the chariot" (*ratheṣtha, ratheṣṭhā*)[191] to the left[192] of the driver.

The chariots were often transported on the oxcarts,[193] not to use them up unnecessarily on roads too rugged or rock-strewn — in Afghanistan for example, or whenever there was no special task for them, no race, no war, and the warriors, impeded from displaying their glamour, and exonerated from their duties of defending the flocks against, or increasing their numbers by misappropriation, hung around, drank, and played at dice. But they had come to a country of vast plains inhabited by the aborigines whom they called *dasyu, dāsa, paṇi*. These lived in tribal communities of different cultural levels ranking from primitive hunting-collecting to agriculture of rice and cattle breeding, pursued in the vicinity of fortfied settlements (*pur*).[194] Then the warriors had their chariots taken down from the oxcarts and the teams of horses yoked to them, in order to set out on a cowraid (*gaviṣṭi*),[195] the most quotidian form of RV warfare, waged by means of horses and chariots,[196] and a vital factor of RV cattle nomadism. That way, while penetrating deeper and deeper into the east of the subcontinent, the Vedic tribes conquered cows, pastures, water places, conquered the Indians and their land, until they became sedentary, grew rice, proclaimed the protection of the cow, developed castes, reckoned the once honoured chariot builder (*rathakāra*) among the untouchables,[197] and transformed into Hindus.

The ruling Deva-gods were predestined for the affection of the RV cattle barons. They roamed about a lot, on foot or with horses and chariots. They were expert horse racers and warriors, and used their skills for winning and conquering cows. And they superintended the raising of big livestock.

Rudra, the "lord of roads, of wayfarers"[198] "wandered about" (*niceru, paricara*).[199] So did the Aśvin, "hiking on Rudra's path" (*rudravartanī*)[200] and among men.[201] And so did Indra, the "friend of the wayfarer."[202] Rudra set out on his travels mostly on foot. Only now and then he was accosted "lord of horses" or "lord of lords of horses."[203] Of chariots he was completely destitute. The forests, jungles, thickets of his realm[204] advised against their utilization. Rudra was the hunter and archer of the gods, furnished with "good arrows and good bow",[205] and "clad in animals's skin" (*kṛttivāsas*).[206] To him belonged the different species of beasts.[207] And the domestic animals belonged to him, above all cattle.[208] He was worshipped for cows,[209] he slaughtered cows,[210] and received sacrifices of bulls and cows.[211] Having been ruthless enough to even kill his own father (Dyauṣpitā, Prajāpati) about to commit an incest with his daughter (Uṣas), the gods had rewarded him with the title Paśupati, "lord of livestock", and the overlordship over the cows.[212]

The decoration of the pedestrian Rudra with the superintendence over cattle is Late Vedic. It might have been determined by the gradual transition of the tribes to a sedentary way of life, as the RV itself, in accordance with the "classical" heyday of the Indo-Aryan cattle nomadism, establishes a conspicuous correlation between horses, chariots and cows. So abundant are the references to the Devas having their teams of horses daily yoked to their chariots, and possessing or bestowing cows, that they appear *quasi ad aperturam libri.*

White or dappled horses, occasionally also asses, bulls, and other animals,[213] drew the three-seated and three-wheeled golden chariot of the Aśvin on its daily circumnavigation (*parijman*) of heaven and earth.[214] The Aśvin tended and made gifts of cows.[215] Every morning Uṣas, the "mother of the cows",[216] and a giver of cows,[217] took seat in her flaming chariot(s) yoked to bulls, cows, or horses of red colour.[218] Every daybreak Vāyu, an owner of cows,[219] set out on his round trip with his shining chariot(s) and his teams of bay or ruddy horses, normally called *niyut.*[220]

Day by day the Maruts navigated their dappled, bay, ruddy, or red horses[221] and their flashing or golden chariots[222] "in all directions."[223] They possessed and bestowed cows.[224] Day by day ruddy, dappled, golden-maned, peacock-coloured steeds,[225] sometimes Vāta's or Vāyu's *niyut*-horses[226] but above all a team of two bay horses (*harī*)[227] yoked themselves by mere order to the golden chariot,[228] with which Indra would inspect his realm, the universe and the Aryan territories, and visit the homes of the Soma-pressers on the way. Indra was a very rich "lord of cows" (*gopati*)[229] and, famed for his utter generosity (*maghavan*)[230] he "had many flocks to present."[231] He bestowed cows *en masse* on his favourites and worshippers, who celebrated him, the "giver of cows" (*godā, godatra*)[233].

Race meetings and warfare formed the links between the Maruts or Indra, their horses and chariots, and their bovine wealth. They championed horse-and-chariot races rewarding the winners with flocks of cows.[234] And they waged — or afforded assistance in the — wars, the cow-raids (*gaviṣṭi*) against Aryan or non-Aryan enemies rich in cows.

The hymns bristle with descriptions and praises of the martial arts of the Maruts and Indra. The Maruts, furnished with lances,[235] bows, arrows, clubs, and slingstones,[236] and famed for their pugnacity, courage, and confidence in the battles,[237] typified the troops of India.[238] Indra was the general and leader in war, invoked by the two hostile camps,[239] the warrior without equal.[240] He killed his enemies with bow and arrow,[241] sling and stone,[242] and above all with his *vajra* or different types of *vajras*[243] — not the double-crowned delicate thunderbolts wielded by Tantric deities derived from Indra (e.g. Vajrapāṇi), but wooden or brazen clubs, maces, or cudgels.[244]

He flung them from his chariot. India was the divine chariot fighter (*ratheṣṭha, ratheṣṭhā*) as such,[245] who "raised dust in dense heaps",[246] when he stormed and crushed the fortresses (*puraṃdara, purohan*)[247] of the hostile *dasyus, dāsas,* or *paṇis*[248] and "drove the(ir) cows out with his chariot."[249] Once and forever Indra had set up the divine standards of earthly cowraids by his victory over the demon Vala and his allies, the *paṇis* (M 1b):[250]

> They had kidnapped the cows of the Aṅgiras, a clan of seven semidivine bards and sacrificers, and hidden them, together with horses, Uṣas, Sūrya, and Soma, in a rock cave deep down south yonder the Rasā. Indra traced, besieged, and conquered the secret hiding place, rescued the three gods, so that day dawned and the sun and the moon (Soma) set out on their regular course, 'drove the cows out with his golden chariot', and distributed them justly among their legitimate owners.

Or he broke open the byre of Tvaṣṭā's greedy son Viśvarūpa Tvāṣṭra, released his cows, and bestowed them on his helper, a certain Trita.[251]

Agni and Soma affirm the correlation between horses, chariots, racing, warfare, and cows. Agni was a racer[252] and waged cowraids[255] with his ruddy or many-coloured steeds[256] and his golden chariot.[257] Hence one dubbed him a "producer of cows" (cf. also *infra*),[258] a knower of their secret name,[259] a "cowherd with cows",[260] and even honoured him with sacrifices of bulls and cows.[261] Soma too was the recipient of a cow sacrifice — the arrival of the Soma plants at the sacrificial site provided for the slaughter of a cow in the frame of the ceremonies for the guest reception.[262] Moreover he owned and bestowed cows,[263] which he had implicitely conquered in war — he inspired each of Indra's heroic deeds[264] — or rather won in race meetings, because he typified the speedy and victorious racing horse.[265]

Agni and Soma, the turncoats from the Asuras to the Devas, leave no doubts about the engrossment of cattle nomadism and its auxiliary means, horses and chariots, racing and warfare, by the Devas. Their desertion was, as it were, rewarded with the typically Devic paraphernalia, of which the real Asuras were rather destitute. Only Mitra and Varuṇa — in the case they are coupled together in the *dvaṃdva mitravaruṇau* — appear to establish the proverbial exception corroborating the general rule. Their twice mentioned horses[266] and their once mentioned chariot[267] might have served them as instruments for the conquest of their cows.[268]

Otherwise the attributions of horses, chariots, and cows to the Asuras are sporadic and relate to different contexts. Bhaga was called "lord of the chariot" (*rathaspati*),[269] obviously with regard to the races and competitions,[270] which he, however, did not take part in himself. As god of good luck[271] he distributed their prizes, among them chariots. Savitā orbited the earth with horses and chariots,[272] a locomotion becoming of a sun god. Tvaṣṭā (in the RV)[273] and Varuṇa (in the Late Veda)[274] had some connexions with the horse of the *aśvamedha,* or rather the primeval horse. Moreover Tvaṣṭā was reputed to "lay speed into the feet of the chariot horse,"[275] to possess a "secret cow",[276] and to sponsor the raising of livestock in general.[277] These features rather evoke his fathership of all the animals[278] and his superintendence over human, animal, and vegetal fertility,[279] but no cowraids.

On the contrary, the Asuras presided over peace, sedentary life, small lifestock, agriculture in particular, and the world of plants in general, a correlation of functions, of which the Devas were nearly or completely destitute.[280]

In the case of Varuṇa, their ace, the disinclination of the Asuras from warfare, was conspicuously contrasted with Indra's realistic political and economic superiority as the leader in war.[281] Peace and harmony in different fields of life were put under the shelter of Mitra. "Peace-loving" Mitra[282] guarded the harmony among men in general,[283] among friends,[284] and among married couples.[285]

At the same time the Asuras displayed an unequivocal inclination towards a sedentary way of life: "The Devas drove out in chariots, the Asuras stayed at home."[286] To be sure, the statement is of concern to the

Asura demons of the Brāhmaṇas, but they turn out to be the dignified heirs to the godly Asuras of the RV. Even the "path" of Mitra,[287] of Mitravaruṇau,[288] or of Aryaman[289] hardly served for wayfaring in the real sense, but for the progress of the cosmic order (*ṛta*),[290] hence for a morally responsible way of life. Moreover Aryaman's path may be identified with the zodiac or the milky way,[291]two paths studded with *fixed* stars. The remark is less arbitrary than it sounds, because according to Avestan mythology, giving expression to the basic difference between static Ahuras and dynamic Daevas, Ahura Mazda created the fixed stars, the arch-Daeva Ahriman, however, the moving planets, comets, and meteors.[292]

Consequently the Asuras inhabited firm houses. Like trees and mountains[293] the dwellings of all the Āditya's,[294] of Mitravaruṇau,[295] and of Varuṇa alone[296] were firmly fixed (*dhruvakṣema*).[297] Varuṇa lived in a palatial stone house (*harmya*).[298] A "house" (*gṛha, dama*) prominently figured in the myths of Tvaṣṭā,[299] the "sedentary (*nidhruviḥ*) among the gods."[300] And Agni was honoured in the "perennial residences" (*dhruvāsu kṣitiṣu*)[301] and inhabited a stone house[302] — his desertion to the Devas could not efface this Asuric characteristic.

Small livestock was nearly exclusively entrusted to or associated with the Asuras. Particularly Puṣan embodied the divine shepherd and goatherd. He had "woven the woolly garment of the sheep".[303] He made use of "bucks as horses" (*ajāśva*)[304] — his cart was drawn by a he-goat,[305] a locomotion fit for a small stockfarmer, but unfit indeed for long distances, let alone warfare. And a buck was his share in the *aśvamedha.*[306] The ewe was sacred to Varuṇa and Tvaṣṭā,[307] to whom goats[308] and rams[309] were sacrificed. Furthermore the fleece of a sheep symbolized the "birth place of Tvaṣṭā's creatures, because he (Tvaṣṭā) fashioned it as the first form."[310] So pertinent was the connexion of the Asuras with small livestock, that Hinduism still furnished Dakṣa with the head of a ram,[311] and Agni with a *vāhana* in the form of a ram.[312]

The Asuras cultivated their fields very well. Agriculturists of sorts, they were reported as having been capable of ploughing, sowing, harvesting, threshing in one operation.[313] Mitra settled the quarrels over the arable fields (*kṣetrasādhasa*).[314] To him belonged the *nāmba*-plants, a species of wild grain (?), whereas Varuṇa presided over every plant growing on ploughed soil,[315] especially over barley (*yava*), his token crop.[316]

The Ahuras disposed of special emblematic plants too. "Every single flower is appropriate to an Amesha Spenta" — white jasmine to Vohu Manah, sweet marjoram to Asha Vahishta, basil royal to Xshathra Vairya, the musk flower to Armaiti, the lily to Haurvatāt, the *čamba*-flower to Ameretāt, the red chrysanthemum to Sraosha.[317] All the violets belonged to Mithra, the myrtle and jasmine to Ahura Mazda.[318] Vedic Agni dwelt in the trees[319] — a residence becoming of a fire god — or, as their child, in the plants.[320] But Tvaṣṭā's botanical symbol outshone the rest. He was associated with Soma-Vanaspati, the "lord of the forest",[321] he was even reported as residing in the Soma-plant and in the medicinal herbs (*oṣadhi*)[322] and understood to possess profuse amounts of Soma-juice.[323]

The superintendence of the Asuras over the world of vegetation culminated in Soma, the original Asura, or rather in Haoma, his Iranian replica. Soma-Haoma was a plant himself. *Sacrostemma viminale, Asclepias acida,* the Afghan grape, rice, hops,[324] or toadstool (*Amanita muscaria*)[325] have been proposed for the identification of the species. But only the latter mushroom satisfies some conditions concerning the rituals around Soma, namely its purchase and pressing,[326] its colours — white, ruddy, tawny, etc.[327] — and above all its intoxicating and hallucinatory effects.

Soma bestowed immortality (*amṛta*). The divine inspiration it prompted opened the gates of heavens, as it were, and invited identification with the immortals.[328] On the other hand, immortality and its guardianship, attributed to the Āditya's altogether,[329] to Aryaman,[330] or rather to Ameretāt, the "protectrix of the plants",[331] is a property consubstantial with vegetal life. Annual and deciduous plants regenerate after a season of would-be death. Evergreen trees like Ahura Mazda's myrtle, or Soma-Vanaspati's non-blossoming forest trees (*vanaspati*),[332] or plants growing and thriving under conditions hostile to human, animal, even to other vegetal life, on salty soils, in deserts, scorching heat, icy cold, etc., like Varuṇa's barley,[333] harbinger veritable deathlessness. And finally the medicinal herbs vouch for a potential immortality in addition, they save and prolong life. Accordingly Soma-Haoma was the "king of the medicinal herbs",[334] which grew on the island in lake Vourukasha around the foot of the white *haoma*-tree,[335] the "tree of all seeds", the tree "opposed to harm."[336]

The Vedic Asuras and their correlation of functions affirm that the Avestan Ahuras deserved the love and affection of Zarathustra's peace-loving, sedentary communities of tillers and small stockfarmers in trouble about the problems concerning their few cows.

The Vendīdād proclaims:[337]

> Unhappy is the land which has long lain unsown with the seed of the sower, and wants a good husbandman!

And the Earth herself announces:[338]

> O thou man! who dost not till me with the left arm and the right, with the right arm and the left, ever shalt thou stand at the door of the stranger, among those who beg for bread. Ever shalt thou wait there for the refuse that is brought unto thee, brought by those who have profusion of wealth!

The archetypal layman of the Avesta was the husbandman (*vāstrya fšuyant*).[339] According to the two components of his name he lived in permanent settlements (*vāstrya*) and cultivated the fields close by, probably with wheat, the "chief of grains",[340] and raised livestock (*fšuyant*).

Goats appear to have been rather insignificant. They pass nearly unmentioned in the Avesta proper, although Pehlevī writings relating the contents of lost canonical texts considered their milk "the best food of mankind", making a man "healthier and stronger, and even the procreation of children more harmless."[341] But sheep were tended in profuse numbers. Though not figuring prominently in the surviving parts of the Avesta, there must have been plenty of them. Otherwise the shepherd's dog would not have been granted the strict and nearly hysterical protection decreed by the Vendīdād (*supra*), and moreover the frequent sacrificial formula of "100 horses, 1,000 oxen, 10,000 sheep"[342] not have emphasized so high a number. The slaughter of sheep was an unlawful act but for sacrifices.[343] After all the doubts about the importance of sheep in Zarathustrian economy are dispelled by the Dīnkard: Sheep made the "livelihood of mankind".[344] Ahura Mazda had entrusted them to the "diligent and moderate tiller",[345] who, for his careful protection of god's endowment, was elevated to the holy rank of a faithful advocate of the righteous order,[346] and of a "sheep" *expressis verbis* of the shepherd Zarathustra.[347]

There were some cows too. Their meat was exempt from consumption — Yima, the apostate, had conjured up a scandal eating it[348] — but their milk was a victual most welcome, and their urine (*gōmēz*) a purificator most potent in atonements.[349] The "joy-creating"[350] cow was shown due respect, nay sacrosanctity (cf note 740). Ahura Mazda had created the Sacred Kine (Gaus Urvan, Drvaspa) — the mystical, archetypal cow — together with the waters and plants for her subsistence,[351] and bestowed her upon Zarathustra.[352] Or she had chosen the diligent tiller,[353] that he may teach her good tillage,[354] save her from violence,[355] and be elevated to the holiness of a saint[356] furthering Ahura Mazda's righteous faith for his care.[357]

But alas! such pious assertions do not deflect from the problems that cattle raised. The Sacred Kine was rather dissatisfied with her situation. Why had she been bestowed on feeble and "pusillanimous" (*anaeša*) Zarathustra and not on a strong and energetic lord?[358] The prophet himself complained of scarce human and bovine retinue,[359] and the *vāstrya fšuyant* strove for the secret of winning the obviously rare cows for himself.[360]

Of course, cattle might have been scant in the eastern Iranian/western Afghan homelands of the Avesta. Its harsh and arid climate did no harm to sheep, but endangered a cow's life, although it gilded its value. This point of view explains Zarathustra's fervent veneration of the cow.[361]

But his gloomy look might also have had to do with something more than the bad weather alone. After all, the Sacred Kine complained of being exposed to the "assault of wrath, of violent power, the blow of desolation, audacious insolence and thievish might."[362] Cows had become the objects of greedy desires and the bones of contention between the agricultural communities of Zarathustra's followers and some fierce and reckless enemies upsetting their peace again and again. They came, they attacked and "destroyed the settlements of the farmers",[363] they "seized away the gifts of inherited treasures from both household lord and housewife",[364] they "prevented complete harvests from the fields and complete pasture for the cattle",[365] and they "gave the Sacred Kine to rapine", slaughtered cows in their bloody sacrifices.[366]

There is not much doubt about the identity of those boors. The Gāthā's refer to them as Karpans, Daeva-worshippers, Ushij, Kavis, or nomads (*avāstrya*). Perhaps some of them were of Iranian stock other than orthodox Zarathustrian. But their bulk consisted of the ancestors of the Vedic tribes. *They* worshipped the Devas. *They* styled their cattle-obsessed bards *kavi,* and pursued a nomadic way of life dedicated to the welfare of their cattle flocks. *They* sacrificed cows. And *they* reckoned among themselves a clan of half-mythical sacrificers, the Uśij, significantly involved in the archetypal cowraid of the Vala-myth,[367] which may even echo with some reminiscences of historical cowraids waged on Afghan soil, or rather sound the charge for the departure of the Vedic tribes from Afghanistan to India, and for the repetition of the cowraids against the Iranians in Afghanistan, against the *dasyus dāsas* and *paṇis* in India.[368]

In any case, the terms denoting the biped victims of the Vedic cowraids in India are wide enough to cover a triad of enemies of the Indo-Aryans: superhuman and plainly mythical demons[369] modelled after semi-mythical and euhemerized chieftains of actual non-Vedic tribes[370] and their human subjects.[371] However, among the already mentioned distinctive ethnic, linguistic and religious marks of the *dasyu-*, *dāsa-*, and *paṇi*-races (*supra*) only the "noseless" faces admit of an identification with the non-Aryan, Dravidian or Austro-Asian aborigines of India. Their "hostile speech" — everybody would abuse the raiders of his cows — and their non-Vedic cultus do not at all exclude the non-Vedic but nevertheless Aryan provenance of an early RV generation of adversaries called so. Comparing the *dasyu* with Avestan *dahyu* ("province, district"), the *dāsa* with the Dahae of the Caspian Steppes and Herodotus' Turanian Daai or Daoi,[372] and the *paṇi* with Strabo's Parnae, Hillebrandt tried to evince the Irano-Aryan identity of some at least.[373] In this case the RV cowraids would partly refer to the same skirmishes accompanying the

Indo-Iranian schism as the Gāthās, however, seen with the eyes of the victorious aggressors, and not of the defeated victims deprived of their cows.

"The Farmer and the Cowman Should Be Friends"—but they've hardly ever been. Many examples attest their antagonism throughout the world,[374] although Rodgers and Hammerstein, the authors of the musical *Oklahoma* and of its song of the just mentioned come-on title, were certainly not aware of evoking more than the familiar Midwestern brawls between some self-righteous masters of many cows, horses, and chariots in want of waters and pastures, and their weaker and less agressive victims, the farmers, in vain defending their ancestral soil. However, the more so as the plot of *Oklahoma* even casts a homeless Iranian hawker,[375] they have unconsciously hit the nail on the head of the economic circumstances and catalysts rendering midwifery to the Indo-Iranian schism about to be born in Afghanistan.

Considering the heaping of the Indo-Aryans and not of the Irano-Aryans with horses, chariots, cows and their economic correlation, the antagonism between the Indian cowmen and the Iranian farmers admits of some glimpses — at least in terms of a hypothetical attempt however blurred in the twilight of mere conjectures — into the possible prehistory of the Indo-Iranian schism.

Not that horses and chariots would have been absent in the Avesta, but their number shrank in conspicuous contrast with the RV profusion and in proportion with the reduced number of cows. A comparison between Soma and Haoma may betoken the statistic scarcity of horses and horse races in the Avestan communities: about 100 references identify the turncoat Soma with a bay horse or prize-winning racing horse.[376] On the other hand Haoma figures in the context of horses and horse racing only twice, of which one half even relates an ambiguous if not downright negative attitude.[377] Haoma was no turncoat, he reflects the altered conditions surrounding the horse in the Ahura culture of the Avesta.

As an implication of the arid climate and the deserts of the Irano-Aryan territory, the camel appears to have contested the horse's right to the first place among the animals of draught and transport.[378] As though one male camel would outweight ten pregnant mares, Zarathustra himself desired from Ahura Mazda the gift of "ten costly mares male-mated and with them the camel."[379] Even his very name — *he* was the paragon of the tradition after all — may have contributed towards setting this standard. The etymology of Zarathustra denotes "having *zarath* camels"[380] . . . as opposed to the name of his father Pourushaspa, who — only, one could say — was "possessing many horses."

Similar names of the *bahuvrīhi*-compound type ending in *aspa,* "horse" were not uncommon.[381] Their relative popularity, however, does not necessarily admit of inferences about the abundance of horses in the everyday life of the Avestan tribes. Hippophoric names are rather rare among the Indo-Aryan horse-and-chariot drivers of sorts.[382] After all not every George is a "tiller", not every Alexander a "vanquisher of men", not every Jyotindra "having Indra as his light". And likewise not every Pourushaspa or Xshviwrāspa is understood to be a master of many or swift horses. Names are conventions relating to potential or would-be realities, although, of course, a tribal society as the Avestan may guarantee to a greater congruence between names and circumstances.

A congruence taken for granted, the preference given to the hippophoric names above the names containing *ratha,* "chariot" in the same position as horse[383] would mirror the utilization of horses without chariots, or rather the relative unpopularity of chariots in daily life. And indeed, the Iranians had taken up riding on horseback, a technique rather exceptional among the Indo-Aryan charioteers,[384] long before Sassanid or Achaemenian art depicted its royal sponsors given to it in breathtaking expertness.[385] Riding on horseback was obviously advised to the Avestan tribes by the prevalent form of economy and the topographical features of their homeland. Agriculture does not require chariots to the degree of cattle nomadism, moreover fields, pastures, or springs are better defensible on horseback in an area too hilly and rugged, horseable perhaps, but without chariots. The observation that riding figured quite prominently in the context and environment of Ardvī Sūra Anāhita may corroborate these points of view. The Avestan water goddess was worshipped on horseback,[386] each of her 1,000 cells and channels was reported as "extending as much as a man can ride in 40 days riding on a good horse",[387] and in her Yasht even the Daevas attack from horseback.[388]

Chariots were less popular. To be sure, chariot driving was considered the noblest form of locomotion,[389] but it appears as if it was preserved for merely ceremonial purposes of princely representation outside an economic or martial context. With regard to this, the relative rarity of the term *rathaeštar,* "standing on the chariot", the denomination of the Avestan warrior nobility, does not testify to the absence of a warrior class corresponding to the Vedic *ksatriya-kṣatra,* as has been assumed,[390] but simply to a missing link with the everyday reality indicated by the term.

Otherwise, horses, chariots, or horses and chariots figured among the paraphernalia and gifts of several Avestan gods. According to single myths—and to their good or bad qualifications—Verethraghna[391] and Tishtrya (Sirius)[392] transformed into a white horse, Apaosha (Orion)[393] and Ahriman[394] into a black one. Morning was regularly associated with "glittering horses",[395] likewise the Sun and Apām Napāt with "swift horses".[396] Ashi had a "loud-sounding chariot"[397] and bestowed horses "swift and loud-neighing who drive the chariot lightly".[398] Pārendi, the goddess of wealth, drove on her "light chariot".[399] Vāyu bore the epithet "of the golden chariot".[400] And Verethraghna "carried the chariots of the lords ... the lordly ones ... the sovereigns".[401]

We cannot fail to make several observations. As though the question was of mere hints at circumstances different from the ruling mainstream to which horses and chariots were of all but vital relevance, the associations give a rather stereotype and pale impression lacking the everyday experience so striking in the Vedic examples. Moreover they are concerning gods who did not figure very prominently in Zarathustra's reformed pantheon. Otherwise they would not have escaped the renamings and reshapings of his horse-and-chariotless main gods in the frame of the schism and not have direct Vedic counterparts, let alone namesakes — Morning and Uṣas, the sun god, Ashi and *ṛta,* Pārendi and Puraṃdhi,[402] Apām Napāt, Vāyu, Verethraghna-Vṛtrahan.

On the other hand, the attributes do not surprise in the case of the original Devas, Morning-Uṣas, Vāyu and Verethraghna. They held, as it were, the fortress of the Devas within the Asuric environment rather disinclined from horses and chariots. However, Ashi-*ṛta,* Pārendi-Puraṃdhi, and Apāṃ Napāt are real Asuras, and in the Veda destitute of horses and chariots.[403] Does this, perhaps, admit the conjecture, that they originally belonged to a non-Zarathustrian, even preschismatic field of worship, to which horses and chariots were more vital and not just emblematic memories? After all, the gods in question do not figure in the Gāthās, but in the so-called "heathenish" Yashts, which are supposed to antedate Zarathustra notwithstanding their younger language, at least to bear witness of the existence of some less orthodox, non-Zarathustrian, in other words, still rather Indo-Iranian circles among the Irano-Aryans.[404]

No other god speaks more in favour of this state of affairs than Mithra, who—in comparison with the scarcity and accidentality otherwise — abounded in and made vital use of horses and chariots. Mithra was reported as "giving swiftness to horses",[405] as "making them beautiful with chariots",[406] as possessing "good horses and good chariots",[407] as being "carried by white-hoofed horses",[408] as "driving a high-wheeled chariot made of heavenly substance",[409] drawn by "four stallions",[410] or by "white horses",[411] and among them the white stallion Verethraghna.[412]

The liveliness of these references is to be reconducted with the martial arts of Verethraghna and Mithra. Verethraghna, the genius of victory, was "the most victorious in victory...the most glorious in glory *(xᵛarənah).*[413] But Avestan Mithra, the "warrior of the white horse, of the sharp spear, of the long spear, the quick arrows",[414] was a war god downright contrary to peace-loving Mitra of the Veda. His chariot abounded in thousands of arrows, spears, steel hammers, swords, iron maces, clubs, which "go through the heavenly space, fall through the heavenly space upon the skulls of the Daevas".[415]

And above all Mithra, obviously an Avestan Indra, vouched for the correlation of horses' chariots, warfare and cows! Mithra looked "with a health-giving eye on this bright region 'Of the Sounding Chariot' *(x^{v}aniratha)*, the abode of cattle, the dwelling of cattle".[416] He had "pasture fields to give at his will",[417] because he was the "lord of wide pastures".[418] All this implies his rule over a flat country, "where wide-flowing rivers swell and hurry towards ... Mouru, the Gavasughdha and X^{v}āirizm"[419] — Merw, Sogdiana, Choresmia, the vast plains of Middle Asia, in other words, where it was still worthwhile driving chariots, and even the Sacred Kine herself, Drvaspa, whose name signifies "keeping horses in health,"[420] still yoked "teames of horses, who make the chariot turn and its wheels sound".[421]

The evidence of the "classical" RV cattle nomadism versus Zarathustrian agriculture, and of pre- or non-Zarathustrian Mithra and Drvaspa enables us to skeletonize a possible answer to the economic prehistory of the Indo-Iranian schism. Horses and chariots, or rather the effects inherent in them on big stockfarming prepared its way, as it were.

It has been observed that some tribes of Red Indians of the great North American Plains (Mandan, Hidatsa, Arapaho, Cheyenne) changed their way of life and their tribal economy within two-three generations from sedentary agriculture to nomadic buffalo breeding after their first acquaintance with the horse and its domestication mediated by the Spanish in the 17th/18th centuries A.D.[422] What had happened? The swift horse had qualified them for covering greater distances within a shorter time than ever before, for discovering, in other words, yet unknown pastures and waters far off in the prairies, hence for increasing the flocks of big livestock, for controlling their seasonal movements, and finally for adopting rider nomadism to the detriment of agriculture.

With regard to the American paradigm the Russian archeologist Grjaznov has reconstructed a similar process in the case of the Pontian Scythians, a nomadic people of Iranian descent.[423] They had made their appearance around the turn from the 2nd to the 1st millennium B.C. on the northern shores of the Black Sea.[424] Herodotus — and other Greek writers in his succession — wondered at their exclusively nomadic way of life always on the move on horseback controlling their cattle flocks.[425] They too had cultivated their fields before they had learned how to tame and ride horses, and to take up rider nomadism. But they rode into a *circulus vitiosus*. The cows fed them well indeed. However, cows and horses are big eaters themselves, and one cannot say that they handle the vegetation with care. They graze their favourite fodder plants and prevent them from blossoming, dissemination and regeneration. As for the Pontian Scythians the result was an ecological crisis. It overburdened the feeding capacities of their original homeland, of Middle Asia, from which they had to dash away rather abruptly in order not to starve.

There can be no question of pressing the economic concomitants of the Indo-Iranian schism into the model of the Red Indians or the Pontian Scythians by hook and by crook. The Aryans were no rider nomads, but a chariot yoked to a horse — so much the more in an area of vast, flat steppes—may be attributed the same effects on big stockfarming as a horse without a chariot. And that the Aryans, above all the Indo-Aryans had discovered and taken advantage of the possibilities is certain, if we look at the *mariịannu*.

The domestication of the horse was an achievement of the later 3rd millennium B.C.[426] which the Aryans had probably learned from some Mongolian-Tungusian tribes in their neighbourhood,[427] and enriched with their own invention, the spoke-wheeled *ratha*. The new and exciting combination may have conjured up a first split in their unity. The *mariịannu* seceded from the bulk to finally settle in Mitanni, and to introduce horse and chariot into the civilizations of Mesopotamia, Anatolia and Egypt, an assumption corroborated by the Aryan hippological *termini technici* in Hurrian and Hittite texts,[428] by the export and gifts of horses from Mitanni to Egypt,[429] and last, but not least by some of their proper names,[430] including Akkado-Hurrian *mariịannu* and its Egyptian (*mrịn*) and Ugaritian (*mrịnm*) equivalents.

mariịannu denotes "horse chariot fighter" and derives from Aryan *marya-maria* (RV) or *maⁱrya* (Avesta), "youth, young warrior, member of a secret congregation of men", of a Männerbund, which obviously assembled the unmarried youths of the tribes living separate from their parents,[431] because *marya* also denotes the "lover, gallant, or bridegroom".[432] All these significances meet in the horse. The word itself is probably reminiscent of the horse domestication, it may be related with Mongolian-Tungusian *morin,* "horse".[433] The *marya* Soma embodied a prize-winning racing horse (*supra*) and the archetypal bridegroom,[434] who inaugurated a custom still valid, at least in some parts of India, according to which a bridegroom is expected to decorate a horseback on his way to the bride's house. The most typical *maryas* of the RV pantheon, Indra[435] and the Maruts,[436] exceed in the art of chariot fighting, as we have seen, and they may have been the ideal standards of the actual *maryas,* the youths initiated into the Männerbund given to the drilling of the recruits to the early Aryan horse and chariot tradition . . .

. . . and, may be, to jealousies and rivalries within and without its noble precincts. It can be taken for granted, that horses and chariots were immediately recognized as instruments of power casting shadows on the *maryas* and their collaborators — the tamers and breeders of the horses, the chariot-builders, etc. A faction within the *maryas* may have sought for the engrossment of the know-how; or the traditional warriors not initiated into chariot fighting feared diminution of their authority:

> Under such circumstances some *maryas*, fed up with the tensions, and keen on saving their privileges, carried out a conspiratory plan: to take hold of as many horses as possible, of more mares than stallions, because one stallion is sufficient for fertilizing many mares, and of enough chariots, and to dash away before the remaining fellow tribesmen would have recovered from loss and shock, far enough from revenge at first, and then to decide where to proceed further. That way the *mariịannu* came to Gorgan and to Mitanni.

Admitting the trashy sensationalism of this explanation, so dramatic a farewell would conform with the scant number of the *mariịannu* and their wifelessness. Only unmarried *maryas* had arrived, potential bridegrooms, who had to marry Hurrian wives in order to keep their lineage. This initial marriage situation may very well be remembered by the convention of the Mitanni aristocrats to give Aryan names to their sons, though Hurrian ones to their daughters.

Despite their utter scantness the linguistic documents of the *mariịannu* testify to the already Indo-Aryan provenance of their authors. Their language exhibits some prakritisms,[437] which could only have developed within an Aryan dialect having already shifted the points towards the Indian direction. Their personal names give a very Vedic impression,[438] they worshipped gods known from the RV,[439] and — a unique exception from the obsequies of the other civilizations of ancient Western Asia or North Africa, given to interment and mummification, or from the Irano-Aryans who decreed nothing but exposure — they cremated their dead like the Indo-Aryans.[440]

The horse and the chariot, in other words, were the salient points in the development of the Indo-Aryan branch of the Aryan pedigree, and they catalyzed its full autonomy the moment they started to give cattle nomadism a leg up. After the secession of the *mariịannu* the still superficially united Indo-Iranians discovered the effects of horses and chariots on cow breeding in grand style. Both branches about to form pursued it for a while, as the examples of Mithra and Drvaspa show, and while increasing the flocks they gradually extended their territories southwards until they came to Afghanistan — and to the crisis. The Iranians had to content themselves with agriculture, small stockfarming and a few cows kept in the vicinity of their settlements, because the ancestors of the Vedic tribes were nevertheless the traditional masters of the horses and chariots. They had completely engrossed the new economy and gained the lead on the Iranians. Their increasing flocks required ever more water and pastures, and Afghanistan was not exactly the country to fulfil the request. So they grew violent and snatched away the pastures and the water they needed and the cows they found from their Iranian siblings, until, within a short time, the alienation was sealed by the schism.

d. *Mothers and Fathers, Incest and Exogamy*

Once, the Devas and the Asuras organized a linguistic competition, (M 2):[441]

The Devas said one (*eka*), two (*dvau*), three (*trayaḥ*), four (*catvāraḥ*), five (*pañca*). Each time the Asuras countered with the feminine gender, *ekā, dve, tisraḥ, catasraḥ* and lost, because from five onwards Sanskrit desists from forming the feminine of the numerals.

To be sure, the demoniac Asuras of the Brāhmaṇas lost the competition, but nevertheless the little myth settles *in medias res* of an existential antagonism distinguishing the RV Asuras from the Devas already at their very roots. The Devas hinged on the male, the Asuras on the female world to the extent of rendering the two prerequisites of human existence, procreation and birth, and its agents, father and mother, independent from one another, as revealed by the two fundamental methods of creation associated with either group. The unborn Deva-creator, an absolute father, ejaculated or emanated his motherless offspring, whereas the born Asura-creator was subordinate to an absolute mother bringing forth her offspring from fatherless virginal birth. At the same time, the Asuras favoured intricate incestuous relationships, the Devas, however, gaping exogamic alliances.

There are no doubts about the matricentric disposition of the RV Asuras. Tvaṣṭā literally "stuck" to the wives of the gods (*gnā, patnīr devānām*),[442] his typical retinue.[443] Agni was exceedingly often mothered.[444] Savitā was the darling of Aditi, the great mother.[445] The Āditya-brothers derived their name from, and lived together with (cf. M 4b) their mother Aditi. Their metronymy and matrilocality was enriched by a pure matrilinearity. They had no father, because they were born from Aditi's parthenogenesis, (M 3a):[446]

Thrice Aditi had eaten the remains of a sacrificial rice dish (*odana*), thrice she had become pregnant, and thrice given birth to a couple of twin brothers, first to Dakṣa and Aryaman, then to Mitra and Varuṇa, and finally to Bhaga and Aṃśa . . .

The Asuric way of creation *par excellence* was focused on the womb of the maternal principle. The roots *jan* and *sū*, "to give birth", denominated the creative activities, which encompassed two aspects: asexual or virginal birth evincing the absolute predominance of the womb by completely excluding paternal procreation; and sexual birth from incestuous procreation, which nevertheless subjected the participating father to the birth-giving maternal principle determining the forms of the creatures by the womb.[447]

The Asuras dearly embosomed incest. Pūṣan[448] and Agni[449] lay with their sister (Pūṣan) or mothers (both). Dakṣa was not only the eldest brother of the Ādityas, but also their father,[450] or the father of the gods.[451] As Aditi was the mother of the Ādityas and the gods,[452] the question is of an incest preceding their birth. Aditi's and Dakṣa's incestuous entanglements superimposed an incest between sister and brother with two simulataneous incests between mother and son, father and daughter, (M 4a):[453]

Birth is the *prima causa* of being. First of all being was born from the parthenogenesis of not being, then the spaces of the universe and the earth were born from the parthenogenesis of the abstract maternal principle called *uttānapad*. According to a third step in the evolution of the universe it personified by taking seat in — or forming the womb of — the primeval hermaphrodite Aditi (a phallic mother) or Dakṣa (a uterine father). From incest within itself the hermaphrodite became pregnant and polarized its double sex by birth into mother and son, father and daughter:
"From Aditi Dakṣa was born, and from Dakṣa Aditi."
Their incestuous reunion after the polarization led to the birth of the gods and the Ādityas . . .

The many-layered incestuous entanglements of the RV birth creation gave birth, as it were, to paradoxical family relationships.[454] Before the polarization Aditi, the female, and Dakṣa, the male half of the primeval hermaphrodite were like sister and brother. By incest and mutual birth brother Dakṣa fathered himself as son of sister Aditi, his mother now, and sister Aditi brought forth herself as her own daughter fathered by brother Dakṣa, her father now. That way the gods born from their reunion were at the same time the grandchildren and the children of mother Aditi and son Dakṣa, and father Dakṣa and daughter Aditi. These quasi-Merovingian intricacies are enclosed by the womb of the absolute maternal principle. The participation of a procreating father does not at all balk its superiority. It shaped and bore the gods, it polarized their parents by the womb within the hermaphrodite, and even the fixation of the polarization on a father–daughter relationship, subordinating the daughter to the father in terms of agnate kinship, places the womb above procreation: Father Dakṣa always remained the "firstborn" (*prathamajā*)[455] son of the abstract maternal principle preceding him and operating in his incest-creation, too.

Several RV allusions allow the reconstruction of a similar dependence and a similar myth in Tvaṣṭā-Savitā-Viśvarūpa's name. Despite his often emphasized virility,[456] this Asura was subject to his nameless daughter, the great mother, (M 5):[457]

Tvaṣṭā was the "firstborn" (*agrajā*) of the absolute maternal principle. Moreover he was a "bull with three bellies and three udders." From incest within himself the "older bull gave

birth first" — obviously to his daughter, with whom he reunited:
"(I praise Tvaṣṭā), who ardently transforming his forms in the wombs of his daughter has created this our (form)."

Tvaṣṭā transformed his forms after the precedents of his daughter who determined the species of the creatures to be born from her womb. This is evidenced by a Late Vedic myth based upon the aforesaid cryptic strophe, (M 6):[458]

The primeval hermaphrodite Ātman polarized into father and daughter Vāc. From a first incestuous reunion man was born. But Vāc tried to escape Ātman's lascivious advancements by subsequent transformations into a cow, a mare, a she-ass, etc. Each time Ātman imitated her form, became a bull, a stallion, an ass, etc., until all the creatures "from man down to the ants" were born from Vāc's incestuous womb.

The myth forms a link between the physical incest creations of the RV and their abstract Late Vedic variants, the so-called *logos*-creations. According to them the objects of creation are brought forth by mere pronunciation of their names.[459] Vāc, the goddess Speech embodied this power. She obviously developed from the absolute *magna mater* of the Asuras,[460] whence she justly extolled her superiority above the gods, their activities, and the universe.[461]

The matricentric and incestuous disposition of the Asuras would be invalidated without the dramatically antagonistic mirror of the Devas. It focused a world saturated with anti-uterine violence, motherless virility, and anti-incestuous exogamy.

The capital RV myth dealing with Indra's refuted birth and the murder of his incestuous father Tvaṣṭā-Savitā Viśvarūpa[462] set the standards valid in the world of the Devas, (M 7):[463]

Contrary to his elder brothers, the gods, Indra loathed his birth from the incestuous womb of Tvaṣṭā's nameless daughter. In order to avoid the "evil passage" (*durgaha*) of birth, he broke out through his mother's side. She exposed him to great dangers, either for hatred or for precautions against Tvaṣṭā's jealousy at his future power. But Indra grew up very fast, and, forsaken by all gods except Viṣṇu, his faithful friend, killed Vṛtra, the monster, which Tvaṣṭā had created to destroy him, and murdered Tvaṣṭā. But Indra was punished for his parricide. He had to "cook the intestines of the dog" (*śuna āntrāṇi*), and "saw his wife dishonoured" (*amahīyamānā*), until the falcon brought him Soma, and he became the king of the universe.

Several related myths testify to Indra's active or passive disinclination from birth. He was to be born from the parthenogenesis or the incest of the great mother, but only to demonstrate that he, her older sons, or she herself disapproved of this. Indra tore his mother's (Vāc's) womb into pieces, which he threw, so to say, at the head of his incestuous father (Prajāpati), *expressis verbis* in order to prevent further births (M 8).[464] Or the womb of Aditi became the target of bloody violence exerted by the older Ādityas against Indra and Vivasvat-Mārttāṇḍa, (M 3b):[465]

. . .Having given birth to the "real" Ādityas by eating the remnants, Aditi ate the whole sacrificial rice dish. She became pregnant with Indra and Mārttāṇḍa. The twins insulted the Ādityas from within the womb by comparing with them. Enraged, Dakṣa and Aryaman, Mitra and Varuṇa ordered Bhaga and Aṃśa to abort Aditi. From this abortion Indra and Mārttāṇḍa came into existence.

Or Aditi herself was averse to her pregnancy of Indra, because she had tied him up with iron chains within her womb (M 9).[466]

The other Devas conformed with Indra's anti-maternal disposition. To be sure, Uṣas, a girl (*kanyā*) or young woman (*yuvati*) was notorious for her amorous adventures with her own kinsmen and strangers,[467] but her motherhood of Rudra and the cows (cf.M 1a, M 11)[468] was extrauterine and merely nominal. Only when set into an unequivocal Asuric context she gave birth from her womb — identified with Aditi to the gods,[469] or to Rudra identified with Agni.[470] Likewise the "dappled" cow Pṛśni was not the uterine mother of the Marut.[471] She did not give birth to the "three times sixty",[472] brothers "of equal age".[473] Fertilized by Rudra[474] she milked them out from her udder.[475] Or the Marut were self-existent.[476]

The mere avoidance of motherhood was even transcended by the intrinsically Devic way of creation and its protagonist, the absolute great father Prajāpati. He couterbalanced the absolute mother of the Asuras and her fatherless offspring with motherless emanation or ejaculation of the creatures from his semen. Occasionally dubbed "mother and father"[477] and entangled in a quasi-incestuous *logos*-cosmogony with Vāc,[478] Prajāpati's creative activities nevertheless pivoted on nothing but the pure virility of his absolute fathership, (M 10):[479]

Prajāpati was "all this (universe) in the beginning" and completely alone. Fed up with his solitude he desired multiplication and company. He toiled and performed acts of penance (*tapas*), from which he spontaneously emanated (*asṛjata*) the creatures as such (*prajā*), the stones, the stars, the waters, etc.

The root *sṛj*, "to hurl, set free, release, discharge" (missiles, animals, liquids, from a place inside),[480] denominating Prajāpati's creative activities most frequently,[481] discloses the physical model and the fundamental substance of his emanations. Prajāpati anticipated the ascetics of later Indian tradition, whose superhuman creativity was said to be rooted in a profuse, but withheld amassement of semen. His supervirility was repeatedly emphasized: Prajāpati superintended male reproductiveness,[482] the reproductive organ,[483] or *semen virile,*[484] and averted impotence.[485] Regarding this, his emanations may be described in terms of chemical sublimation. Prefigured in his semen, the creatures condense in physical form without the intermediate stage of ejaculation, as ice crystalizes from steam omitting the liquid stage of water.

However, ejaculation made but one, the younger, asexual, abstract aspect of the absolute father's creation. According to a second, more uncouth and archaic sexual aspect, which outside Aryan India is only traceable in the mythology of Ancient Egyptian Heliopolis,[486] Prajāpati ejaculated the gods,[487] or he gleefully masturbated the he-goat called *aja*, "unborn",[488] because ejaculated creatures are not born:[489]

With the *vaiśvadeva*-litany Prajāpati ejaculated (*asṛjata*) the creatures. Ejaculated and not born (*sṛṭṣāprasuṭa*) they ate Varuṇa's barley.

Devic creation started from an "unborn" — and not from a "firstborn" — great father, from "unborn" Prajāpati,[490] who emanated or ejaculated his offspring, or from "unborn" Viśvakarman,[491] who modelled his children in as motherless a fashion by handicraft.

The versions of an important Vedic myth combine the creative ejaculation of the absolute great father with the origin of Rudra-Paśupati, the overlord of cattle, of the cows, the pivots of RV cattle-nomadism, and of the Aṅgiras, involved in the archetypal cowraid of M 1b. This myth was sometimes attached to the RV report of the aforesaid origins, (M 1a):[492]

Dyauṣpitā felt attracted towards his alluring daughter Uṣas. At her sight he prematurely lost his semen, from which Agni or the gods produced Rudra Vastoṣpati, the "guardian of the law or vow" (*vratapā*), the cows, and the Angiras. Hardly come into existence that way, Rudra "shot his arrow at him" (Dyauṣpitā), whereas Vala and the *paṅis* kidnapped the cows, so that Indra and the Aṅgiras had to set out on their campaign of M 1b.

The title *vratapā* probably referred to Rudra's superintendence of the incest taboo which the gods had entrusted to him. Even the slightest transgressions he would not let pass without capital punishment: "Whosoever commits a lapse, you should kill him!' And indeed, he shot his arrow at Prajāpati, when he made advancements to his own daughter."[493] The statement evokes the Brāhmaṇa-versions of M 1a,[494] above all M 11. The myth replaces Dyauṣpitā with Prajāpati, and Rudra's motherless ejaculation of M 1a and M 12 with his motherless piecing together from all the gods existing before him:[495]

Desiring intercourse with his daughter Uṣas or Dyaus (fem.), Prajāpati transformed into a blackbuck (*Antilope cervicapra*). Angry at their father's planned incest the gods united their dreadful (*raudra*) forms to Rudra, and ordered him to kill Prajāpati with his three-pointed arrow. Rudra asked for the supremacy over the cows as a reward and pierced Prajāpati's head. The head became the constellation of Orion (*mṛgaśiras*). Rudra represented the star Sirius (*mṛgavyādha*), and Uṣas the star Aldebaran (*rohiṇī*).
While running after Uṣas Prajāpati had lost his semen. It had fallen to the ground and formed a large lake. Lest it should decay, the Marut and Agni Vaiśvānara kindled it, and

produced the Sun, the solar months, Bhṛgu, the Aṅgiras, Bṛhaspati, the black and ruddy cows, the *gaura* (*Bos gaurus*), the *gavaya* (*Bos gavaeus*), the gazelle (*Gazella gazella*), the ass, and the camel.

Another variant of the myth of Rudra's origin heightened the motive of motherless ejaculation, but weakened the revenge on incest, (M 12):[496]

Prajāpati desired offspring and performed acts of penance, from which Agni, Vāyu, Sun, Moon, and Uṣas sprang forth. The four brothers gave themselves to penance, too, and lost their semen at the sight of Uṣas transformed into a seducing *apsaras*. Prajāpati collected it in a huge golden pot, one bowshot high and wide, from which Rudra emerged with 1,000 eyes, 1,000 feet, and 1,000 strung arrows. But he abstained from shooting his fathers. Instead he extorted nine names from Prajāpati. Otherwise he would starve himself to death.

I have already dealt in detail with the perfectly systematic relations underlying the apparently heterogeneous surfaces of M 7 and M 11 at another place.[497] In our context here only Indra's and Rudra's emphatic inclination towards exogamic matrimonial alliances attract our attention. It results from the strict revenge of both Devas on incest, the climax of endogamy, and exaggerates the gap between the partners welded into wedlock as for their age or social provenance to the degree counterbalancing the intimate closeness of incest. Such exotic exogamy was encoded in Indra's dog cooking and in Rudra's hunting.

The statement requires some preliminary remarks. We have to make a difference between the phenomenon of marriage, with which Aryaman,[498] Mitra,[499] and Bhaga[500] were associated in addition to the generally incestuous bias of the Asuras, and the exogamic weddings prevailing among the Devas. In the case of the three Asuras the legal transactions, the necessity, and the happiness of married life were stressed. But in the case of the Devas the odd provenance of the marrying partners was the salient point. It aimed at the demonstration of conspicuously genuine, even forbidden forms of exogamic alliances. The Devic weddings either united husbands and wives of immense difference of age or of social class. The difference of age inverts the mutual penetration of three generations insufficiently distinguished from each other prevailing in the Asuric creation from incestuous birth (cf. M 4a):[501] Indra, the "bestower of wives",[502] married aged Kakṣīvat to very young Vṛcayā, or blessed the ageing and skin-diseased spinster Apālā with a young husband.[503] Likewise the Aśvin married the old maid Ghoṣā,[504] and more than a hundred years old Cyavana to the young girl Sukanyā.[505]

The difference of social provenance inverts the common origin of incestuous marriage partners locked up in one and the same family, or rather of isogamic marriage partners locked up in one and the same *varṇa*. Isogamy was introduced during the Late Vedic era for the benefit of ritual purity particularly among the Brahmins.[506] The other classes of Indo-Aryan society (Kṣatriya, Vaiśya, Śūdra) eagerly imitated their precedent in a process comparable to modern "Sanskritization" or "Brahminization" of low castes,[507] until Vedic *varṇa*-society gave way to the Hindu hierarchy of castes (*jāti*) at the end of the Vedic period. However, during this passage the texts described two further forms of marriage, namely the *anuloma*-hypergamies, and the *pratiloma*-hypogamies. Both of them served as theoretical models for the integration of non-Aryan Śudra-tribes into Aryan society, because the offspring born from these *varṇa*-mixtures often bore the names of several primitive tribal communities of Indian aborigines.

The alliances called *anuloma* united husbands of higher with wives of lower *varṇas*. They were generally allowed in addition to the first isogamic marriage of the husband.[508] Their offspring was reckoned among the pure mixed castes, with the exception of the Niṣāda. He was born to a Brahmin from a Śūdra-mother,[509] his parents, in other words, disregarded the strict separation of the Aryans from the non-Aryans. The Niṣāda-*anuloma,* however, was invoked in the name of Rudra together with members of other mixed castes living like him[510] on some form of hunting.[511] The association does not admit inferences about Rudra's non-Aryan origin. He was a genuinely Aryan god, however endowed with the special function of integrating non-Aryan elements into Aryan conventions. The most practical expression of Rudra's intrinsic function of bridging gaping differences was his superintendence over the exogamic marriage. Its token was hunting. The hunter Rudra bestowed husbands to unmarried girls.[512] The occupation signified exogamic alliances which would even transgress the customs recognized by the culture, as evidenced by the Niṣāda and other examples from the Vedic and the Hindu traditions.[513]

The *pratiloma*-hypogamies involved wives of higher and husbands of lower social class. They were generally forbidden between the three Aryan *varṇas,*[514] let alone between Aryans and Śūdras.[515] Their offspring was reckoned among the impure untouchables, who had to dwell outside the communities of the pure ones.[516] Their archetype was the *caṇḍāla* (or *cāṇḍāla*), the offspring of a Śūdra-father by a Brahminess.[517] The base rank of his existence was hardly superable. But there also was the *śvapaca* or *śvapāka.* A brahmin mother had born him to a *caṇḍāla,*[518] or he sprang from a more complicated *pratiloma*[519] between an *ugra*-mother — who was born from the *anuloma* of a Kṣatriya and a Śūdra wife — and a *kṣattri*-father—born *pratiloma* from a Kṣatriya princess and a Śūdra.[520] His exogamic provenance leaves nothing to desire. As his name indicates he had to live on cooking dogs — like Indra, who was punished for his revenge on incest with the existence of a dog cooker at the end of M 7.[521]

Other Devas gave themselves to *pratiloma*-hypogamies too. King Soma, a Kṣatriya, is reported as having abducted and raped Tārā, the wife of the divine Brahmin Bṛhaspati. The scandalous event gave a first opportunity to conjure up the dangers resulting from such forbidden transgressions.[522] Moreover, Soma married the divine Brahminess Sūryā Sāvitrī,[523] and so did, according to another variant of the same myth, the Aśvin,[524] veritable Śūdras in Late Vedic mythology.[525] After all, the social *pratiloma* of Late Vedic conventions was already prefigured in the RV on a cosmographical or existential level, namely between immortal goddesses in the place of brahmin wives — who were born into the *varṇa* dubbing itself the "gods among men"[526] — and mortal human fathers in the place of Śūdras. Immortal Uṣas displayed an unequivocal bias towards amourous adventures with mortal men,[527] and Saraṇyū, Tvaṣṭā's immortal daughter, was married to mortal Vivasvat-Mārttāṇḍa. Yama, Yamī, and the Aśvin were born from this alliance.[528] If at all born, the Devas were born *pratiloma,* whence the Aśvin became Śūdras, and Yama occasionally even an untouchable![529]

Consequently Yama was averse to the incest which his lewd sister Yamī had desired to seduce him to (M 13).[530] The Indo-Aryans, of course, followed the examples of Yama, Rudra, and Indra, and took great care not to transgress their meticulously formulated incest taboo, all the more so as the *varṇa*-isogamy of Late Vedic days could easily run the danger of coming too close to forbidden degrees of blood relationship between husband and wife.[531]

Moreover Indo-Aryan kinship organization was patriarchic to the purest degree, as already evidenced by the birth rituals (*jātakarman*), which aimed at the symbolical separation of the new-born son — and the new-born daughter[532] — from the mother by the father. When a Vedic mother lay in, her husband was present in order to receive the child. He animated the newborn with his breath,[533] fed him with a mixture of milk, curds, butter, honey, and water, or ground barley and rice from a golden dish or spoon,[534] secured him intelligence,[535] and long life,[536] cut his navel string,[537] and bathed him in lukewarm water.[538] Only then he placed him in his mother's lap to pass him her breasts which he had washed before.[539]

In gradation of sex (male before female) and age (older before younger) the Indo-Aryan joint family (*kula*) hinged on a patriarch, whose personality was extolled as the standard of tender emotions, wise advice, and circumspect responsibility.[540] Free from greed and threat, the flattering image may be coloured by the idle absolutism of its guardians, and not convince the modern feminists. They could indeed reproach the Vedic order with "male chauvinism", naively admitting — even in terms of Germaine Greer — that women are "smitten and unmanned, they neither own any self nor do they own any heritage".[541] They were excluded from religious activities, except black magic,[542] their world and its implications (metronymy, matrilocality, matrilinearity, mother goddesses) had shrunk into the aforementioned islands of the Asuras and Ādityas within the swollen patriarchic mainstream.[543] But its spring, the father, appears to have been less naughty than his exalted position would imply. After all, a Vedic father took his food only when his subjects, however humble, had already had their fill.[544] And of merciless tyrants there is rather scant mention.[545] If reasons why are given at all, they do not concern the patriarch in full possession of his independence, but insinuate the psychological problems of the matrilinear and matrilocal father — as in the case of Aditi's most remarkable son Varuṇa.[546] Exceptional as his example is, it may be considered the negative complementary affirming the paternal kindness which a patriarchy as pure as the Vedic type was expecting from its paragon.

Like their Indian counterparts the Irano-Aryan Ahuras could be born from a parthenogenesis — at least Ohrmazd (Ahura Mazda) according to Mani[547] — or will be born from a virginal mother — as Zarathustra's messias.[548] To be sure, these speculations may have been fomented by Christian doctrines — but on the Asuric fundamentals of M 3a. In any case Irano-Aryan conventions concerning kinship, law, and education were seasoned with a strong pinch of matriarchy. Its patriarchic surface undenied, like the social organizations of the Jews, Christians, or Muslims, Zarathustrian society concealed an influential mother at its very base. Though bound to be strictly obedient to her husband, a Zarathustrian woman occupied a more honourable position in the community than was sanctioned by any other Oriental religion.[549] The frequent mention of Zarathustra's mother[550] besides his father Pourushaspa, and of his wife Hvovi and her kin[551] are indicative of the latent tendency. Women were entitled to inheritance.[552] Wives were allowed to make legal plaints in the place of their husbands,[553] it is even understood, that "the proficiency of women (and children) acquainted with the law is superior to a full grown, but unacquainted man".[554] Both sexes were initiated into religion with the sacred thread girdle,[555] because both were considered equal in the good work of celebrating the rituals.[556] A woman was at least fit for minor priestly duties among women[557] or children.[558] All these decorations were granted on account of motherhood: "We sacrifice upon the females bringing forth flocks of males".[559] One living son was already enough to make a mother in certain cases guardian over a living father,[560] or head of the family after her husband's death.[561]

So, when a son was born, a midwife, his maternal grandmother perhaps, cut the navel string.[562] And the emotional education of his first five years may have been exclusively supervised and directed by his mother. Herodotus[563] reports from western Iran — from a cultural background strongly influenced by the Yashts[564] — that a boy spent his early years with his mother in the harem, and was not allowed to meet his father before his fifth birthday.

In a man's later years the sentimental education of his youth was interlarded with an overreadiness for incestuous alliances. Ahura Mazda was married to his daughters Ashi and Aramaiti,[565] Yima and Yimak committed the incest (M 14),[566] shunned by their Vedic counterparts Yama and Yamī (M 13), and its imitation was warmly recommended to Avestan mankind. "Next-of-kin-marriage" (*x*^{v}*aetvadatha*)[567] was thought the best shelter against the assault of the evil—and correspondingly exogamic—Daeva-demons, ever alert to deprave the souls, and hence the best warrant for an eternal place in Ahura Mazda's paradise after death. That way an orthodox Zarathustrian could call his father grandfather, uncle, or brother — he was his mother's father, brother, or son — and his mother, grandmother, aunt, or sister — she was his father's mother, sister, or daughter. Numerous references testify to the popularity of incest in Avestan and Pehlevī texts,[568] let alone the remarks of Herodotus, Plutarch, Diogenes Laërtius, and Arnobius.[569]

e. *Heavens and Day, Underworld and Night*

The heavenly light radiating from all Vedic gods could not completely outshine the original cosmographical coordination of the Devas and the Asuras with the two hemispheres of the Indo-Iranian universe. The former inhabited the luminescent upper, the latter, however, the umbrageous lower of the two hemispherical goblets (*camū*) lying edge on edge at the horizon, the earth's and the ocean's surface forming the plane of demarcation inbetween.

The etymology of *deva-daeva* — the "shining or heavenly one" — reveals the celestial abodes of the Devas. The word is closely related with a vast genus of Indo-European appellatives for sky (Hittite *šiuš,* Sanskrit *dyaus, dyo-*), day (Sanskrit *dyaus, dyu-,* Latin *dies*), god (Greek *theos,* Latin *deus, divus*), and gods of the daӯ-sky (Vedic Dyauṣ-pitā, Greek Zeus, Dios, Latin Ju-piter, from *dju-piter,* Germanic Tiu). Accordingly the Devas Uṣas ("Dawn"), Vāyu,[570] the Maruts,[571] the Aśvin,[572] etc. presided over the early morning. Indra (cf. M 1a) and Rudra (cf. M 11) caused the first sunrise of all. Indra presided over the eastern quarter of the sky.[573] Day by day Uṣas,[574] the Aśvin,[575] the Maruts,[576] etc. crossed the firmament in their chariots. Vāyu and Vāta,[577] or Rudra[578] freely roamed in the atmosphere. Most of them handled the weather. Vāyu, Vāta, and the Maruts caused winds and storms.[579] Indra hurled lightnings and rolled thunder, and made the celestial waters fall to the earth in the form of rain[580] — a task also entrusted to Vāta,[581] the Marut,[582] and to Soma[583] — or run from the mountains to the plains in the form of the rivers.[584] Two cosmographical schemes overlapped in the Vedic imagination, heaven-earth, and mountains-plains.[585] That way rain and rivers belonged to the category of celestial waters and celestial Rudra would also be addressed as "abiding in the mountains" (*giriśa*).[586]

Despite the heavenly localization of the whole pantheon, casual references allude to the chthonic, subterranean habitat of the primitive Asuras, as becoming of gods of vegetation. Originally their abodes were laid out at the foot of the cosmic mountain or pillar (*skambha, skambhana*) washed round by the floods of the primeval fresh water ocean (*salila*).[587] As though aspiring to their subterranean residences, the Asuras altogether were reported as digging medicines into the earth.[588] Moreover the adjective *gabhīra,* "deep" distinguished the Ādityas,[589] and Agni, the child of the "deep" Ādityas Dakṣa[590] or (Tvaṣṭā-) Savitā-(Viśvarūpa),[591] originated from the dark depth or bottom (*budhna*) of the subterranean waters.[592]

Varuṇa, the Vedic water god *par excellence,* could at times also command the celestial rains[593] and the rivers[594] of the Devic hemisphere. But on the other hand, and only in Varuṇa's case — a proof of a very old and intrinsically Asuric heritage — the question was of the stagnant abysmal waters. Pool diggers were said to attain Varuṇa's world after death.[595] To Varuṇa belonged the whirlpools which gravitate towards the depths of the earth,[596] or the stagnant fresh[597] and marine[598] waters on the surface, as it were, of the subterranean ocean heaving his "golden chamber",[599] his aquatic abode.

According to the Aryan view night was caused by a nocturnal outpouring or upsurge (RV *ūrmi,* Av. *varəmiš*) of the subterranean ocean over the day-sky, or rather the occultation of the upper and diurnal hemisphere by the lower and nocturnal one rotating upward.[600] Therefore night was consequently called the "undulating one" (RV *ūrmyā*), or the "cover, wrapper" (RV *kṣap, kṣapā,* Av. *xšap*). For this reason night and nightsky made a further essential domain of the Asuras, particularly of Savitā and Varuṇa. Night came up on Savitā's command,[601] and Varuṇa, whose name derives from the root *vṛ* (*vṛṇoti*), "to cover, obstruct, isolate", had not only appointed the stars as his spies,[602] but he also "embraced the nights" (*kṣapaḥ*),[603] obviously like a piece of black cloth,[604] or like the star-spangled mantle and girdle Ahura Mazda wore,[605] the lord of the fixed stars.[606] Avestan Mithra, however, inhabited the depths of the earth.[607]

f. *Avestan Dualism and Vedic Monism*

Apart from these Indo-Iranian relics Zarathustra had otherwise taken great care to invert the pre-schismatic cosmographical coordination, and uplifted the Ahuras from their chthonic realm into the sheer light of air and heavens transfigured to paradise, but banned the Daevas from atmosphere and day sky into the darkness of the underworld sharpened to hell. This happened when he renamed the foremost deities of the two groups. He had good reasons for doing so. The new names covered the old identities and their primitive cosmographical contents, which would not have given expression to the stringently dualist drama of his new religion enacted by nothing but good and radiant Ahuras as against nothing but bad and blackened Daevas.

However, the Vedic tradition shows that not the Daevas, but the Ahuras were the leading protagonists of Zarathustra's rigid Moral Dualism.

One of Varuṇa's etymological namesakes, Vṛtra (Veda), or rather *vərəthra* (Avesta) — the arch "enemy" as the "obstructor" of the vital waters,[608] who was slain by Indra Vṛtrahan (cf. M 7) or Verethraghna – shared some typically Asuric features. He spread darkness,[609] he lived together with his mother Dānu,[610] bore the metronymical name Dānava, "son of Dānu,"[611] could be begotten from parthenogenesis or incest,[612] and was above all identified with the creator Father Asura (M 15). Or Vṛtra had been created by Tvaṣṭā who was jealous at Indra's future power (M 7), or angry at Indra's murder of his second demoniac son, the glutton Viśvarūpa Tvāṣṭra.[613] The latter had passed all sacrificial dishes to the Asuras and starved the Devas,[614] and looked very much like his father. Equipped with three heads, six eyes, and three bellies both, father[615] and son[616] were as like as two peas.

The identification, fatherhood, and physical identity of the otherwise benevolent Asura-creator[617] with or of two monsters as dangerous and exorbitant as Vṛtra or Viśvarūpa Tvāṣṭra gives expression to the essential ambiguity of the whole Asura-group. On one hand *ṛta* the fundamental and inherent law of nature, the cosmic truth, was placed under the guardianship and maintenance of the Ādityas,[618] of Mitravaruṇa,[619] and above all of Varuṇa alone.[620] A responsibility that loftly pledged them to obedience to the universal "law" (*vrata*)[621] and the "duty or order" (*dharman*),[622] and it is in this context that Mitra and Varuṇa distinguished between right and wrong,[623] and punished untruth, sins, and sinners,[624] whom they caught and fettered with their "nooses" (*pāśa*).[625]

But on the other hand particularly Varuṇa was ready to counteract and undermine his awe-inspiring moral principles himself. He "inflicted whatsoever distress one undergoes here on earth."[626] He was allied to, even identified with Vṛtra.[627] He was reported as being "jealous at the sacrifice" (*yajñavanas*),[628] full of wrath (*heḍa, heḍas*),[629] and fraud (*dhūrti*).[630] And above all he exerted *māyā*,[631] which was sort of his signboard,[632] but practised by the other Asuras — *the* Asura,[633] the Ādityas,[634] Tvaṣṭā,[635] and Pūṣan[636] — let alone the evil demons and monsters,[637] too.

The notion of *māyā* is no easy one. The word derives from the root *mā*, "to measure, calculate, construct, make visible", and the question is of a superhuman magic power and its designs oscillating between the miracles of creation,[638] trickery, cunning and not really sincere, but — the end justifies the means — an efficient weapon, particularly in the hands of Indra, against the demons,[639] and downright dirty tricks and noxious sorcery[640] which was "godless" (*adevī*).[641] In any case *māyā* produced the impression of polymorphic illusion,[642] the reason why it came to occupy such a central position in both Hindu (Vedānta) and Buddhist (Mādhyamika) philosophy later on.

Crafty, crooked, and deceptive, *māyā* was at variance with the firm straightforwardness of the *ṛta*. Endowed with these two antagonistic powers by nature,[643] the essence of the Asuras was torn and split between two opposite poles evoking one another, because good and moral qualities can only be determined by their bad negatives of equal weight. Without bad there is no good, and vice versa. This, however, is the salient point and the reason why the Ahuras of the Avesta have to be called the fomentors of Zarathustra's already Gāthic Moral Dualism.[644] The doctrine caged the world within the two complementary and accordingly absolutely interdependent, but unbridgeable principles Good and Bad embodied in the Ahuras and the Daevas. Their indispensable equilibrium pervaded Zarathustra's whole concept of creation in ruthless consistency, because any good creation immediately enchained its bad countercreation. Had Ahura Mazda created the fixed stars, Ahriman had answered with the planets.[292] Had Ahura Mazda brought forth the good Amesha Spentas, Ahriman had opposed their evil counterpoises.[645] Had Ahura Mazda preceded with the 16 provinces of Iran, Ahriman had followed with a set of diseases, perversions, and spells.[646] Had Ahura Mazda called the magpies, dogs, ichneumons, hedgehogs, and cocks into existence, Ahriman had confronted them with the noxious locusts, wolves, snakes, corn–carrying ants, and the wizards, because "the conclusion is this, that of all beasts and birds and fishes every one is created in opposition to some noxious creatures".[647] This state of affairs even attracted the attention of Plutarch who dealt with it in De Iside et Osiride.[648]

The RV Asuras kept faith to themselves, they were ready to bear and endure their split nature. The Ahuras of the Avesta, however, disposed of their negative abyss and imposed it upon the Daevas, who made good scapegoats on account of their intrinsically amoral — and not moral/immoral — attitude towards the course of the world, calling the validity of the good/bad-limitation in question (*infra*). As they gnawed the fundamentals of Asuric existence that way, the Ahuras could easily burden them with all sorts of bad qualities imaginable, and impute the dualist cleft to them. Pious hopes, so to say. If the Daevas weren't so evil — or have grieved for and rejected the allegations — the Ahuras would not be so good, they would suffer from an identity crisis questioning their right of existence. After all the dualist Ahuras maintain the gap. *They* will not be able to defeat the Daevas until the end of our present age. Only then an eschtological battle will take place, after which Ahura Mazda will purge the world in a stream of liquid metal.[649] But even then Good and Bad, Ahuras and Daevas, will not be compatible. The two principles and their supporters will only dismiss the close contacts ensuing from their coexistence in time. The good souls will forever rejoice in Ahura Mazda's "abode of songs" (*garonmānem*), the paradise. And the bad souls will forever suffer in Anghra Mainyu's hell.[650]

The situation was rather different in Vedic India under the sway of the Devas. *They* — or rather Indra in place of them altogether — had already defeated the Asuras at the beginning of our present age, (M 15):[651]

Obviously swallowed, Varuṇa, Agni, and Soma (in order of decreasing age) were hidden in the darkness of Father Asura-Vṛtra's belly. Promising them a share in the sacrifice and his new kingdom, Indra had to lure them out. After some consideration of Father Asura's friendliness, Agni and Soma, and the turncoats from the Asuras to the Devas, readily followed Indra's invitation. But Varuṇa hesitated, and deprived of his power, had "to release the waters" (the rivers), when Indra (Agni and Soma) killed the Father Asura, daylight and atmosphere came into existence, and the present era of Devic sovereignity started.

M 15, M 7, M 1a, b, and M 11 form a group of myths to be interpreted in terms of the rudimentary Vedic doctrine of the four ages of the world (*yuga*).[652] The group deals with the passage from the (three) former age(s) to the present age, or rather from darkness and night to day and light, from incest to exogamy, from the sway of the great mother to the sway of the great father, from vegetal life and self-existent agriculture[653] to cattle nomadism, in a word, from the older Asuras to the younger Devas.[654] In their name Indra (and Rudra) supervise the parental, matrimonial, economic, etc. orders vital to the Vedic Indo - Aryans. These had been established at the beginning of the present age, when diachronic time came into existence replacing the timelessness of the Asuras and their characteristic marks.[655]

All Devas are gods of diachronic time. Indra "temporally arranged the expanded timeless darkness with the sun",[656] for he released Uṣas (dawn), the Sun God, and Soma (moon) from the darkness of Vala's cave, caused, in other words, the archetypal daybreak (Uṣas), and the first rise of the sun and the moon (M 1b).[657] Rudra's parricide resulted in the origin of the sun and the solar months (M 11).[658] The sun, however, "arranges days and nights",[659] the basic elements of diachronic time. Or Indra "arranged the series of the days with the nights",[660] or "delineated day from night",[661] whereas the Aśvin, Vāyu, Vāta, and the Maruts, presided over the early morning of each single day,[662] not to mention Uṣas, who "made" (*kṛ*) time (*vayuna*)[663], regularly alternating with her twin sister night.[664] Even the Deva-creator Prajāpati, otherwise above all implications of time, was not destitute of the characteristic. He was identified with the year (*saṃvatsara*)[665] which in its turn represented Death.[666]

There is no death without diachronic time. Day and night being the "embracing arms of death",[667] Indra[668] and Uṣas[669] — although ageless and eternally youthful themselves — "made old" (*jaraya*, both), and "curtailed the life of the mortal"(Uṣas). Yama was the first mortal and became the Vedic god of death *par excellence* — since he refused the incest with his sister Yamī (M 13), and procreated offspring on some unknown, but certainly exogamic wife.[670] His father Vivasvat-Mārttāṇḍa had already set the standard. His *pratiloma*-marriage to Saraṇyū[528] was the cause of his death, as suggested by the sequel of M 4a, (M 4b):[671]

Eight are the sons of Aditi born from her womb. With seven she went to the gods, Mārttāṇḍa she cast out. With seven sons Aditi entered the first age. Mārttāṇḍa she took back again, that he may procreate and die soon (*prajāyai mṛtyave*).

Incest[655] and abstinence from procreation[672] vouch for the immortality of Mārttāṇḍa's elder Āditya-brothers. Procreation, however, and its matrimonial frame, so much the more of the impure *pratiloma*-type, cause death. This is why the *āśvinaśāstra* which had been composed for the *pratiloma*-wedding of Soma or the Aśvin and Sūryā[523–524] was originally used for the piling up of the funeral pyre.[673] The price of marriage and offspring — and of cattle and the rest of the orders under the guardianship of the Devas since the beginning of the present age — was the short life.

Contrary to the Ahuras always on the alert to exclude and deprave the unconquered Devas, the victorious Devas treated the defeated Asuras with kindness and reverence. They were generous by nature, and for this reason the lines of demarcation between the two groups are at times hardly discernible. They allowed the Asuras to assemble many of their own intrinsic attributes, and vice versa availed themselves of the opportunity of their victory, and would occasionally lay claim to some typically Asuric loans. That way even Devas could be addressed — or endowed with — the honorific title *asura*, "lord", or be distinguished by *asurya* or *asuratva*, the awesome lordly power of the Asuras — like the Devas altogether,[674] Dyauṣpitā,[675] Uṣas,[676] the Marut,[677] Rudra,[678] or Indra.[679] There is no doubt that this decoration was a consequence of Indra's triumph over the Asuras. On occasion of a dispute between him and Varuṇa the latter boasted of having been the first god to be destined for *asurya*,[680] whereas Indra was understood to only have inherited it — and the power of Dyaus and all the gods — after he had slain Vṛtra with the help of Viṣṇu (cf. M 7).[681]

The Devas had not only inherited the lordly power of the Asuras, but also taken possession of their *māyā*. Occasionally the Marut,[682] even the Aśvin,[683] but above all Indra exerted the Asuric trickery. Having defeated the Asuras, he was most justified to employ this spiritual booty of his victory in quite practical a fashion, namely against his demoniac enemies in order to pay them off in the same coin,[684] or to mysteriously stop a river's flow,[685] and last but not least to transform himself at his liking.

As already indicated above *māyā* would also serve the purpose of evoking the illusion of manifoldness and polymorphism. Tvaṣṭā, whose characteristic mark was the superintendence over the various forms of the creatures and objects of creation (cf. M 5 and note 130), was reported as "knowing the illusory transformations" (*māyāḥ*).[686] Capable of transmutation (*māyinaḥ*), [687] the Maruts clad themselves in clouds by means of *māyā*. [688] And of Indra we learn that in quite playful a fashion he, the generous one,[689]

rūpaṃrūpam maghavā bobhavīti
māyāḥ kṛṇvānas tanvam pari svām|

"transforms into any form undertaking transformations of his own body",....

however, without ever concealing his one true form, because[690]

rūpaṃrūpam pratirūpo babhūva
tad asya rūpam praticakṣaṇāya|
indro māyābhiḥ pururūpa īyate
(*yuktā hy asya harayaḥ śata daśa||*)

he has adjusted to any form, but this (his true) form can be recognized (in all forms). By means of his illusions Indra moves along as one of many forms, (for ten hundreds of bay horses are harnessed for him).

Manipulated by the Devas, in other words, *māyā* loses its Asuric (and Vedāntic) duality, and dissolves the multiplicity of its designs into that constant and incorruptible oneness forming the most essential mark of Devic existence. Like a magnet, as it were, or like the gravitational collapse of an astrophysical singularity they attract opposite energies, and condense or implode the illimitable diversity of creation into the undivided unity of its primeval source. The *coincidentia oppositorum* of the Devas manifested in various ways.

On a most practical level the conspicuously exogamic weddings under their aegis welded into wedlock partners of gaping difference of age, social background, and existential provenance, very old husbands and very young wives, or vice versa, Aryans and non-Aryans, mortals and immortals (*supra*). It is noteworthy in this context that the whole created universe was summoned to unite for attending the *pratiloma* - wedding of Vivasvat and Saraṇyū,[691] or rather for compounding the dowry and the oxcart of Soma's (or the Aśvin's) *pratiloma*- bride Sūryā.[692]

Moreover the *pratiloma*-origin of the Aśvin was supplemented on a merely cosmographical level. According to another genealogy one of the identical twins [693] was reported as being the son of Dyaus, his alter ego, however, the son of a certain Sumakha,[684] Consequently the Aśvin were born at different places, namely in heaven and on earth, [695] run into one another as though their visible difference would not exist.

Indra was produced by all gods[696] assisted by heavens and earth.[697] Hence he was " all the gods",[698] and his earthly replica, the king, was said to incarnate the eight *lokapālas*, the guardians of the directions (Indra, Agni, Yama, Nirṛti, Varuṇa, Vāyu, Soma or Kubera, Iśāna), the moon, the sun, and fire.[699] Or his *vajra* was fashioned from an implosion of all creation.[700]

The implosive tendency culminated in Rudra. All the gods had united their dreadful forms in order to piece him (M 11), or his hypostasy Śarva together.[701] Agni, Vāyu, and the sun, the representatives of earth, atmosphere, and heavens,[702] and the Moon had mixed their semen in order to form him (M 12). Or the year (Prajāpati) and the Seasons (Prajāpati's offspring) had begotten him on the Break of Day (Uṣas).[703] For these reasons he was justified to extort nine names from Prajāpati corresponding to nine elements of nature: Rudra (fire or moon), Śarva (water or fire), Paśupati (plants or wind), Ugra (wind or plants), Aśani (lightning), Bhava (rain or waters), Mahandeva (moon or sun), and Iśāna (sun or food). These eight names and their elements, however, coincided in Kumāra, the "boy", Rudra's ninth and all-inclusive name.[704]

Oneness within the illimitable polymorphism of creation reached the dimension of an apotheosis in Rudra's name in the so-called *śatarudriya*-litanies of the Yajur Veda, to be solemnly recited in front of the just piled-up fire altar. Here thousands of Rudras of multiple abodes throughout the universe are celebrated without ever losing one and the same Rudra's oneness, the bond and the elementary power within the duality of creation, out of sight. He is omnipresent[705]

in the directions, the spaces, on earth, in the air, in the sky, copper-coloured, reddish, tawny, red, dark red, blue-black, white, golden-armed, green-haired, in sound, in tone, in the ear, in the echo, he sits, lies, sleeps, wakes, stands, runs, fast, speedy, fleet, hasty, tall, small, short, dwarfish, high, higher yet, grown, adult, oldest, youngest, born before, born afterwards, middle, aborted, last, deepest, in the waves, in the river, on the island, in the amulet, on the paths, in the field, on the threshing floor, in the forest, in the thicket, in the kettledrum, in the roll of the kettledrum, on the ways and roads, in the hole, by the foot of the mountains, in the ditch, in the lake, in the stream, in the waterpot, in the well, in the pit, in the rain, in the cloudburst, in the cloud, in the lightning, in the clear sky, in the heat, in the wind, in the storm, at the ford, on the shore, in the flood, on this side of the river, at the landing place, in the foam, in the sand, in flowing water, in barren places, on wide roads, in small stones, in still water, in the harbour, in the byre, in the house, in bed, in the residence, in the deepest places, in the pond, in the whirlpool, in the dust, in dry leaves, in the copse, in the green, in the soft grass, in the submarine fire, in the channels, in the foliage, in the refuse ...

Likewise the Deva-creator, the absolute great father, harmonized and transcended the dualist differences inherent in his creation. Prajāpati was "one alone",[706] and "all the gods".[707] He had fathered the Devas and the Asuras (of Brāhmaṇa-mythology),[708] but impartially refrained from interfering with their contests like his Hindu successor Brahmā, or his RV predecessor Viśvakarman.[709] In Prajāpati the mortal and the immortal, the determined (*nirukta*) and the undetermined (*anirukta*), the limited (*parimita*) and the unlimited (*aparimita*) rested together.[710]

The Devas are the source and the estuary of Vedic Monism flowing in an ever increasing stream from the first presentiments — or the *soma*-drunk insights into the supreme identity[328] — of the RV via the all-embracing speculations of the Brāhmaṇas towards its final philosophical representation in the Upaniṣads. Its absolute, the onefold (*ekam*) *brahman* or cosmic soul, self-existent (*svayambhu*),[711] unborn,[712] and not being born,[713] omnipresent and all-pervasive, is the impersonal abstraction of the One (*eka*), the unborn absolute father of the Devas and the Asuras. "What is the One (*eka,*) in form of the unborn (*ajasya rūpe*) who has lifted the six spaces?", the RV asks,[714] to answer the question in a hymn dedicated to Viśvakarman:[715]

Him the waters conceived as the first embryo, in whom all the gods united. In the navel of the unborn the One (*ekam*) lies hidden wherein abide all things existing.

Similarly Prajāpati was said to have emanated (*srj*) the *brahman*. having emanated him in its turn.[716] He was of *brahman*'s nature, or identified with it.[717]

Or he embodied the *ātman*, the individual soul, which, according to the central axiom of Upaniṣadic Monism, is essentially identical with the cosmic *brahman*. Having recognized and experienced this supreme identity, the individual is forever redeemed. The BĀrUp proclaims:[718]

'I am verily *brahman*.' Therefore he (the *ātman*) became all (this universe). Whosoever among the gods comprehended it, he alone became it. Thus whosoever among the seers, whosoever among men ... Whosoever knows this *brahman* also in this time in the said manner: 'I am *brahman*', even the gods are not able to prevent him from its possession. For he becomes the soul of them.

And the TUp expounds that whosoever has comprehended it:[719]

Him indeed does not afflict (the thought): 'Why have I omitted what is good?' — 'Why have I committed sin?' A person who thus knows considers them both (good and bad) as the soul (*ātman*). For he who thus knows considers them both as the soul.

Moral decisions caged by the inseparable interdependence of good and bad are irrelevant to the *ātman* who has reached his goal of supreme identity. He may do whatever he prefers — play with relatives, dally with women, or visit an exhibition of vehicles (*yāna*).[720] The absoluteness of Ahura Mazda may justly be doubted, as a true absolute has to be free from the mundane duality of good and bad, even free for it. After all good and bad are two correlated aspects of its own creation.

But within creation good and bad are on no account qualities of the objects considered so. Their seat is the limited subject, the ego, deciding upon the qualifications. Everyday experience teaches that one man's meat is another man's poison. Likewise the collectives of limited subjects, groups, clubs, cultures, whole cultural fields, often diverge from one another in the face of evaluating classifications: the good and pure animals of the Irano-Aryans were bad and impure to the Indo-Aryans, and vice versa. The incest, so cherished by the Asuras and the orthodox Zarathustrians was drastically punished by the Devas and forbidden by the Indo-Aryan legislators.

The statement is of immediate impact on the dualist or monist types of redemption. A Zarathustrian could never be really sure of his place in Ahura Mazda's eschatological paradise, he might have committed some wrong and ill-considered acts which condemned him to hell. For example he might have killed a bitch or fed a shepherd's dog with bones too hard (*supra*). Or he might have dropped "on the ground a bone of a dead dog or a dead man as large as the top joint of a forefinger."[721] In these cases he was at least allowed to expiate his sin under the merciless lashes from the two abovementioned whips which Ahura Mazda had decreed for the punishment and the benefit of the sinners, or by killing various noxious animals. Nevertheless he was not safe from — at least a temporary stay in — hell, which, however, was understood to last forever, had he accidentally killed a beaver, or masturbated, [722] or "thrown clothes on a dead body, even so much as a maid lets fall in spinning".[723] The pressure of proving unavailing and the fear of eternal damnation was particularly stringent inasmuch as each soul was ascribed one earthly life only.

On the other hand the monist type of redemption does not recognize heaven(s) and hell(s) but as temporary transit camps on the path of each soul's growth to maturity, its countless reincarnations crowned with the experience of supreme identity. Nobody, the gods and the seers included — their transient existence only reaps the merits from former lives — is perfect until he knows that he is *brahman*. The insight releases from any determinable creation, or rather incorporates the whole universe within the soul. And it happens here and now, in this life on earth, irrespective of moral restrictions. If supreme identity is concerned, the end justifies the means. The individual is basically at liberty to follow its intuitions which are not caged by moral considerations.

However, this does not admit a Californian interpretation of everyday life. Good and bad are not invalid within the world. But in any case the Indo-Aryans handled their implications with far less an unbending rigidity than Zarathustra and his successors. They ever had to be on the alert of not being trapped by the assault of evil, whence the Vendīdād, their lawbook, bristles with incontrovertible edicts. On the contrary, the Indo-Aryan lawgivers were much more aware of the limited value of good and bad, and replaced Zarathustra's generalizations with flexible prescriptions. Manu, for example, forbade the consumption of meat in some ordinances. But a closer look reveals that other rules only dissuade from certain species of animals, or from certain circumstances, while other species and other occasions are permitted without restrictions. Such a vacillation does not admit the philological argument according to which the Manusmṛti was pieced together from the writings of different authors of different times and traditions. This may be correct to a certain extent, but it misses the genuine spirit of Manu's — and other — lawbooks. The ambiguity rather testifies to an attitude abstaining from moral generalizations and leaving the decisions to the individuals themselves. One man's meat is another man's poison, and one might not mind going to hell for a while, and being reborn as a *caṇḍāla,* while another hopes for some peaceful days in Kṛṣṇa's *goloka*-paradise, and for his rebirth as a Brahmin. None of them is perfect, but either may reach the final goal in his respective form of existence on earth.

Not only the property of reuniting the dualist oppositions of creation predisposed the Devas to the rise of Vedic Monism, but also their certain lack of moral austerity. To be sure, Uṣas,[724] the Maruts,[725] the Aśvin,[726] and Indra[727] may casually be associated with the *ṛta,* the *vrata,* or the *dharman* of the Asuras. These principles formed a part of the booty conquered after the defeat of the Asuras, as it were. But they handled them the way they handled the Asuric *māyā,* accidentally by and large. On the other hand particularly Indra turns out to be a decided opponent of the *ṛta* [728] But unlike Varuṇa he did not undermine his own principles. The association of the Devas with *ṛta* and *māyā* was not obligatory but facultative, based on availability. Their freedom was illimitable. Destitute of moral considerations they did whatever they liked to do, did not omit what is good, and committed sins, too, without getting stuck to either routine, nor having to suffer from qualms of conscience: they were amoral, that means not liable to the cleft and the interdependence of good and bad, but basically free for both sides.

Not that they could be called unscrupulous hedonists. But the

Maruts[729] and Uṣas were notorious for their boundless and sexually very attractive eroticism, which even would transgress the borders of the permissible in the cases of Soma raping Tārā, the *pratiloma* hypogamies and the licentiousness of the Aśvin, Vāyu, Yama, and Indra.[730] Moreover the Aśvin[731] and above all Rudra[732] cruised around among people of dubious reputation, doctors, robbers, highwaymen, pickpockets, swindlers, and cut-throats — company becoming of a son who did not shrink from killing his own father for cows (M 1a, M 11). Indra was compared with a robber or a highwayman,[734] and embosomed many illicit desires.[735] And the gods charged him with a long list of crimes[736] — among them his murder of Vṛtra and Viśvarūpa Tvāṣṭra, which burdened him with the sin of brahmin slaughter (*brahmahatya*)[737] — in order to justify his exclusion from the sacrifice. He shared this destiny with Rudra[738] and the Aśvin.[739]

The exclusions from the sacrifice are rather interesting. They paradoxically converted Indra, Rudra, and the Aśvin into profane gods, or rather opposed them in terms of the binomial sacred, holy/profane, unholy to the sacred rest of the holy gods. They behaved like Brahmins refusing the commensality of the sacrifice to non-Brahmins, especially to Śūdras. On the other hand, however, there are some convincing footholds suggesting that the caste of the Brahmins was modelled after the precedent of the RV Asuras.[740] From this point of view the exclusive gods behaved like the Avestan Ahuras against the evil and unholy Daevas. However, what the self-righteous holiness of the Ahuras — and of the Vedic gods — coveted to punish by exclusion, was not so much the badness or unholiness of the Daevas — or of Indra, Rudra, and the Aśvin — as such, rather their indifference to goodness and badness, holiness and unholiness — their amorality, in other words. It called the general validity of good and bad, holy and unholy, the fundamentals of Zarathustra's Moral Dualism — and to a certain extent of the holy Brahmins — in question, and made the Ahuras on their lofty throne seat tremble with fear of deprivation.

There is yet another prerequisite to the origin of Vedic Monism in the Devas, namely their easy accessibility. Only Rudra appears to establish the exception from the general rule — at least in the eyes of the mortals approaching him on the defensive.[741] Otherwise a similar awe only marked Varuṇa's aura for reasons of his moody incalculability. One never knew, of course, if Rudra would lay it on, or not, but the anxiety he inspired was less rooted in a cunning trickery of Varuṇa's dimensions, which undermined his own moral principles, than in his utter autonomy. It did not hold out unkept promises, but was — like pure consciousness — merely reactive for the various circumstances of existence. So Rudra's alleged inaccessibility was less a problem of his own, but of his hesitant worshippers overwhelmed by his overdosed freedom.

Otherwise the situation was less complicated. Uṣas freely granted her alluring favour to mortal men.[527] the Aśvin roamed around among men,[201] and saved them from distress again and again. Agni lived among men,[301] and Indra, the best friend of all anyhow,[742] visited their homes day by day, got drunk as usual — and overbearing perhaps — and was politely urged upon returning to his dear wife.[743] That way men and gods were given opportunity to become acquainted with and learn to love each other, to deepen their ties of kinship, and to jointly approach their great father Viśvakarman that he may answer their existential questions in his unsurpassable wisdom.[744]

However, the mutual permeation of gods and men, irradiating the RV and the Brāhmaṇas with so golden, tender, and fearless a light, is flowing from the unconcern of the Devas about moral or holy pretexts. It desisted from excavating those bridgeless moats of idealized goodness and holiness, which shielded the Ahuras from the spontaneous comprehension of men. After all moral order and holiness made up the two fundamental elements of Zarathustra's religion.[745] The Ahuras were simply too holy and good — or the bulk of mankind too frail — to be accessible or acceptable. Their holiness guarded them against curious existential questions. Instead Ahura Mazda asked the human race the holy questions (*spento frasna*) — concerning, of course, the correct moral conduct. This may content most of us, who are more predisposed and willing to embrace various types of Dualism than the sole Monism. Our fear of freedom overshadows our love for it. But yet, the existential fears raised by Dualism oppress more than the confrontation with and the conquest of the fear of freedom required by the monist type of redemption. That is why the Avesta, grandiose though, is so rigid and gloomy here and there, and Zarathustra not infrequently full of grief.

g. *Cremation and Exposure*

To sum up: a vast set of complementary oppositions rooted in the prehistorical Aryan culture made the life of a paragonal Indo-Aryan computable by simple inversion, as it were, from the life of a paragonal Irano-Aryan, and vice versa. The Indo-Aryan was born into an entirely patriarchal family. As a child he was taught to avoid contacts with asses, pigs, dogs, crows, ravens, and cocks, but to honour ants, frogs, and tortoises. With his kinsfolk and tribe he ranged the vast plains of northwestern India on oxcarts and horse chariots. He was fond of horses and horse racing, and lived on the many-headed cattle flocks of his parents. He married into a non-consanguineous family. And he worshipped the morally unconcerned, rather profane, and very spontaneous Deva-gods, who offered him the chance of recognizing his supreme identity with the all-pervasive cosmic spirit. No matter if he was not yet mature enough to reach this ultimate goal. After some temporary stay in heaven or hell decided by his earthly merits or mistakes his soul was reborn and given the chance to accomplish again. On the other hand the Irano-Aryan was born into a family patriarchal only on the surface, but concealing some strong matriarchal undercurrents. He was taught hatred and contempt for tortoises, frogs, and ants, but reverence for cocks, ravens, crows, dogs, pigs, and asses. His way of life was settled, he stayed at home in his village, and helped his father to cultivate the fields, and to raise sheep, some cows, and perhaps some horses. Of horse and chariot races he might have only heard. He was expected to marry into his own consanguineous family, and he worshipped the (originally) chthonic, holy, morally very concerned, and somewhat formal Ahura-gods, who offered him the chance to either resurrect in their eternal paradise, or be condemned to the eternal hell of the Daevas.

The antagonism in life and eschatology pertained to the obsequies, too. The dead Indo-Aryan was cremated, whilst the dead Irano-Aryan had to be exposed in a *daxma* under any circumstances.

To be sure, the early Veda appears to have admitted several types of funerals. The RV mentions bodies "burnt in the fire" (*agnidagdha*), and "not burnt in the fire" (*anagnidagdha*),[746] the AV even adds "cast out" (*paropta*) and "exposed" (*uddhita*) corpses.[747] But cremation was likely to be the prevailing type, ousting the other methods in the Late Veda, at least with regards to "normal" dead persons. Children under two years had to be buried,[748] a custom advocated by theHindus too, who moreover bury outcasts and saints dying in *samādhi*.

The rituals accompanying a Vedic cremation are described by Āśvalāyana in full detail,[749] and in full conformance with the funeral hymns of the RV:

Hair, body hair, beard, and nails were removed from the dead body. Then men and women, but not going together, carried the three sacrificial fires (*ahavanīya, gārhapatya, dakṣiṇa*) and the sacrificial vessels and implements of the dead, and the body to the funeral pyre, which was to be heaped up at a place from which the water could flow off to all sides. The dead body was covered with a slaughtered she-cow or she-goat. The wife of the dead was asked to take place to the north of the pyre. In the case of a dead Kṣatriya a bow was added. Then a brother-in-law, a pupil of her husband, or an old servant caused her to rise from that place, with:

"Rise, wife, to the world of life"...(RV X.18.8), and "Taking the bow out of the hand of the deceased"... (ib. 9).

Then the bow was broken and thrown on the pyre, and the dead body covered with the sacrificial implements. The omentum (*vapā*) of the cow (or the goat) was put on his head and mouth, with:

"Put on the armour (which will protect thee) against Agni by (that which comes from) the cows"... (ib. 16.7).

The cow's kidneys were placed in the hands of the dead with:

"Escape the two hounds (of Yama), the sons of Saramā" ... (ib. 14.10).

The heart of the animal was put on the heart of the deceased. Then four oblations were offered, to Agni, Kāma (the god of love), the world, and Anumati (a goddess embodying the "favour" of the gods). A fifth oblation followed, with:

"From this one verily thou hast been born. May he now be born out of thee, N.N., to the heaven-world *svāhā*!"

Now the pyre was lit with the three holy fires. If they reached the body at the same time, it signified highest luck. While the body was burning the following verse was recited:

"Go on, go on, on the ancient paths" ... (ib. 14.7).

Then, to the north-east of the *ahavanīya*-fire a knee-deep pit was dug and a water plant (*avakā, śīpāla*) deposited in it. From this pit the soul was supposed to soar up to the heavens. After the recitation of:

"These living ones have separated from the dead" ... (ib. 18.3), the relatives turned round the pyre from the right to the left and went away without looking back. They had to take a bath in a standing pool, put on other garments, and wait till the stars appeared. They were not allowed to cook food during that night, but requested to subsist on bought or ready-made victuals. For three nights they had to abstain from saline food, and for twelve nights to avoid the distribution of gifts and the study of Vedic texts, if the dead was a chief *guru*.

After the lapse of ten lunar days (*tithi*) aged persons of an odd number were to gather the bones, and put them in a male or female urn. The urn was put into a pit dug at a place were the waters did not flow together, except rain, with:

"Go to thy mother Earth there" ... (ib. 18.10).

Then earth was thrown into the pit, with:

"Arch, o Earth do not oppress him" ... (ib. 11), and

"Arching the Earth should stand firm" ... (ib. 12).

Finally the pit was covered, with:

"I raise earth upon thee" ... (ib. 13), and the relatives went away, without looking backward, took a bath, and performed a first *śrāddha* for the deceased.

Death was much more problematic in Iran. To bury a body was a sin without atonement.[750] It defiled the earth, although it might have been practised by the Achaemenids. To drop a corpse into the water was a deadly sin, too. It polluted the water. And cremation was a sin without atonement, it defiled the holy fire. It had been designed by Anghra Mainyu in order to compensate Ahura Mazda's creation of the two provinces Harax^v aiti and Cakhra.[751] Coming across a "corpse burning fire, wherein a corpse is being cooked", a worshipper of Ahura Mazda was obliged to kill the man committing the crime, and to "take off the cauldron and the tripod".[752] Eating the corpses of dogs and men was an inexpiable sin, too. The home of the perpetrator "shall be dug out, his life shall be torn out, and his bright eyes shall be put out."[753] Zarathustra had good reasons for being on the alert. Necrophagia might have been practised within his horizon. The Issedones, a people of Iranian descent (?) inhabiting the area between the Alai Tau and the Altai are understood to have regaled on their dead fathers in lurid banquets. Herodotus reports:[754]

Some knowledge of the practices of the Issedones has come through to us. For instance, when a man's father dies, his kinsmen bring sheep to his house as a sacrificial offering. The sheep and the body of the dead man are cut into joints and sliced up, and the two sorts of meat, mixed together, are served and eaten. The dead man's head, however, they gild, after stripping off the hair and cleansing out the inside, and then they preserve it as a sort of sacred image, to which they offer sacrifice. Son does this to father, just as the Greeks observe ancestral commemoration.

A fear of pollution from corpses far deeper seated than in India embarrassed the Iranians. The corpse-seeking demonness Nasū obviously lay in ambush everywhere to "rush upon the corpse as soon as the soul has left the body", and to defile and infect everyone and everything close by with "infection, uncleanness, and pollution". Of course the contaminations subsided after an exactly established time and the obligatory purifications of men and objects, among them the house of the dead — it could even be broken down — and the path, on which the body had been carried away.[755]

Death in the house was not at all avoidable. If the corpse could not be removed at once — as in rain, snow, darkness or winter — a special chamber or hut (*aka*) had to be erected to receive it, until "the birds begin to fly, the plants to grow, the floods to flow, and the wind to dry off the waters from the earth."[756] In the house or the *aka* the most indispensable ceremony to be performed was "the look of the dog" (*sag dīd*) — a dog was ordered to gaze at the corpse,[757] while (parts from) the Avesta were recited.[758] Then a breach was broken into the wall, through which the body was carried away[759] by two (professional) bearers wearing special clothes.[760] One man alone was not requested to do it. he would have run danger of falling victim to Nasū and other fiends attending the occasion. If he set the prohibition at naught, he was to be imprisoned in an enclosure, clad with the "most worn-out clothes", and fed with the "coarsest of food" for the rest of his life. Then a "strong, vigorous, and skilful" man was asked to "flay the skin off his body and cut the head off his neck on top of the mountain." Now he had at least repented his sin.[761]

Accompanied by the relatives up to a certain point, the two bearers carried the corpse to the *daxma,* a stone structure erected on the highest summits, "where there are always corpse-eating dogs and corpse-eating birds",[762] and "wherein the rain waters cannot stay."[763] Here they fastened the dead body "by the feet and the hair, with brass, stones, or lead, lest the corpse-eating dogs and the corpse-eating birds shall go and carry the bones to the waters and to the trees."[764] Then they sat down, three paces from it, and washed their hair and their bodies with the urine, held in readiness, of oxen, sheep, or the nearest kinsman/kinswoman of the deceased.[765] Meanwhile the relatives at home had started to perform the "three nights ceremony" (*satūih*). It was dedicated to Sraosha. He assisted the soul in passing to the other world without delay. During this period meat was not to be eaten. In the early morning of the fourth day, however, a sheep was slaughtered, and the ceremonial for the righteous guardian spirit performed. Afterwards the tenth-day, the monthly, and the annual ceremonies followed.[766]

The word *daxma* is paraphrased — with a creepy touch for Western tourists to Bombay — as "Tower of Silence". The question is of a round pit, about six feet deep, built up and paved with stone. It is surrounded by an annular stone pavement, about six feet wide, for the deposition of the bodies. The place is enclosed all round by a stone wall, some 20 feet high, with a small door on one side for taking the body in. The pit is communicated with three other pits at a distance, into which the rain washes out the liquids and the remains of the dead bodies.[767] A *daxma* was the first structure to be built, whenever Zarathustrians settled in a new area.[768] The exposure of corpses was the most striking practice of their prophet's faith, and its adaption was the sign of conversion, as Procopius reports.[769]

h. *Short Linear Time and Long Cyclic Time*

It remains to say that, according to the Iranian view, the history of the world does not last more than 12,000 years. Time moves in entirely rectilinear a fashion from creation to the eschatological battle, and is composed of four periods of 3,000 years each. During the first three millennia creation remained undisturbed in a merely spiritual state. During the next three Anghra Mainyu appeared from his hell, but flew back to it again in confusion. During the next three, when man appeared on earth, he attacked creation and kept it in a constant state of tribulation. And during the last three, nowadays, his power, having attained the maximum, will be gradually weakened close to the end. The Saoshyant, Zarathustra's yet unborn son, will be born from the parthenogenesis of a virgin,[548] lead the final battle which will destroy Anghra Mainyu and his evil retinue, forever fling them and the unworthy souls they have captured back to hell, and establish Ahura Mazda's "house of songs", wherein the worthy souls rejoice, forever.[770]

In India, however, time is incomparably extended. According to the Hindu view a day of Brahmā, a *kalpa,* lasts 4,320,000,000 years of mortals, measuring the duration of the world. These are divided into 1,000 *mahāyugas* of 4,320,000 years each. A *mahāyuga* encompasses four *yugas, kṛta* or *satya* (1,728,000 years), *dvāpura* (1,296,000 years), *tretā* (864,000 years), and *kali* (432,000 years), during which creation and humanity gradually decline from their former perfection. We are living in the *kaliyuga* now, the worst age, as everybody knows. It started some 5,000 years ago, and will still last some 427,000 years. Then the world will be temporarily destroyed by Śiva or Kalkin (Viṣṇu's 10th *avatāra*), and sink into a stage of decomposition. But it will start again according to the same schedule, until the whole *kalpa* will have been accomplished, and Brahmā will fall asleep for his night of 4,320,000,000 years. But he will wake up again to initiate a new *kalpa.*

Time is long and sufficient in India, as long and as sufficient as a soul probably needs for passing through the cycle of reincarnations (*saṃsāra*). And it moves along in a cyclic fashion, like a spiral. A man of the *satya-yuga* is reported as having lived 6,000 years — as long as two periods of Zarathustrian world history — let alone the 8.4×10^{14} years of a man in the golden age of the Jainas.[655] The *yūga*-doctrine of the Hindus, however, developed from Vedic prefigurations,[652] and already in the Veda long periods of time, for instance one of 100,000 years, had been recognized.[771]

III Aftermath

The reality of the Aryan Schism established, some remarks about its opponents will not be misplaced. It is hardly necessary to dwell on the alchemists among them, the adherents of the comparativist school and of the ideal that "all be the same". Veda and Avesta, Aztecs and Romans, Papuas and Silesians they melt down in their crucibles for reasons of merely superficial identities, moreover separated from their generic contexts, in order to mould their *idée fixe* of ostensible sameness in durable gold. But they soon lose themselves in cant verbosity.

However, two arguments produced by the more serious contradictors deserve attention: that some Devas of the RV bear the title *asura* and are endowed with *asuryam* or *asuratvam,* and that the so-called Daeva-edict of Xerxes testifies to the necessity for forcibly suppressing Iranian Daeva-cults as late as in the 5th century B.C.[772] As we have seen, by nature the Devas reunite dualist contrasts, even between themselves and their already conquered opponents, the Asuras. This enables them to adopt some Asuric features *ad libitum.* On the other hand the Ahuras emphatically exclude and vilify their lethal enemies, the not yet conquered Daevas. By nature they uphold duality and dualism, as they would suffer from an identity crisis without the projection of a foe. This is the reason why Iranian Daeva-cults did exist. Any dualism as rigid and thorough as the Avestan needs and provokes heretics within its own precincts to asseverate its right to be. Looking out it will ever find them, and dedicate considerable alertness and attention to them, as, for instance, the Vendīdād.

Medieval Catholicism demonstrates similar circumstances with great transparence. The moment it started paying enhanced watchfulness to Satan and damnation (14/15th centuries A.D.), the inquisition — having been instituted for the purpose — found ever profuser opportunities to thrust its tongs into the flesh of witches and satanists. They had actually mushroomed in proportion with the request. Some 200,000 are supposed to have expired on the pyres between 1450 – 1750 A.D. Every Jeanne d'Arc will find her Gilles de Rais. But one cannot say the cults of the witches, or satanists of Gilles' calibre, or the Iranian Daeva-worshippers were more than subsidiary sectarian phenomena within the Catholic or Zarathustrian mainstreams of the medieval or Avestan cultures.

Another instance brings us closer to modern times — and to the cradle of Zarathustra's Dualism, to Iran. The strident outcries against the "great devil" America serve the Ayatollah very well to underpin the validity of his impact and the continuity of his Fundamentalist Islamic Revolution. He often sounds like Ahura Mazda in the Vendīdād, even makes use of the same wordings, *à son insu*, of course, but as the unconscious recipient of clandestine echoes that appear to have impregnated the air in Iran since Zarathustra's days.

And more yet. Islam itself, and Christianity, and their common cradle, the Old Testament and Judaism, may be considered the spheres of influence and the unconscious heirs to Zarathustra's Moral Dualism, or rather, in a wider sense, to the Asura-tradition. Professing the least dualist creed among the three western religions though, Judaism had prepared its two scions for easily receiving Zarathustrian undercurrents. Israel had cultivated close friendship with Persia before and after the Babylonian Exile, and readily adopted various typically Zarathustrian concepts, ranking from creation — Yahweh's six-day creation and Ahura Mazda's six-day creation — to Satan's independence from God. In the Book of Job he still was a member of the celestial court surrounding Yahweh. He functioned as a roving chief prosecutor who afflicted the faithful, testing their virtue. But he was neither evil himself nor opposed to God. Enter the Devil, however, as a powerful figure in his own right — as the fallen angel Lucifer flung to hell for having tried to imitate God (Monism!) — and developed under the influence of Avestan Moral Dualism in the apocryphal scripts of the Old Testament that appeared in Palestine between the 2nd century B.C. and the second after — at the right moment, as it were, to infiltrate the Catholic Religion about to set out on its world career.

Satan's alleged impact helped to dogmatize the already prefigured doctrine of resurrection and eternal redemption of the good souls in paradise as against the eternal damnation of the bad ones in his ninefold hell. No orthodox Catholic ever doubted the truth and validity of this doctrine and — at least not until the last century — its established temporal frame. The destiny of the world was taught as accomplishing within a few thousand years of rectilinear time. Having started in the 6th millennium B.C. — an inception calculated from the Old Testamentarian genealogies[773] — it was to end in the near future with the return of Christ (Saoshyant!) and the Apocalypsis. The fear of the end — or rather its consequences — was sometimes very great. It gave rise to a mass hysteria when Apocalypsis was expected for the first time on the turn from the 1st to the 2nd millennium A.D. And it led to the congregations of weird penitents — the Flagellants and the Dance Maniacs — in the 2nd half of the 14th century A.D. under the pressure of the great plague and the Catholic Schism (Rome/Avignon) when the Last Judgement appeared to be imminent, and even Christ, the Saviour himself, was represented with sword-protruding mouth.

It is not to be wondered at that Gregory of Tours thought Zarathustra-Zoroaster, the "Living Star" to be Chus, the son of Noah's son Ham. From him the Persians are understood to have acquired their habit of worshipping the fire.[774] As Zarathustra had ever occupied the European mind as a paragon of simple and noble wisdom — although most of his admirers had no exact idea about what he really taught until Anquétil Duperron presented his French Avesta translation in 1771[775] – Israel was not the only mediator of Avestan influences upon Catholicism. For instance in the Dark Ages they penetrated via Mani's gnostic Avestan-New Testamentarian syncretism, which St. Augustine had professed before converting to Christianity and strengthening its dogmatic framework with some Manichaeoid principles.

Moreover Manichaeism survived its North-African/Mediterranean heyday in the Dark Ages in the sectarian and heretic underground of the Catholic High Middle Ages. The sect of the Catharists and Albigenses was based on it. Their cruel persecutions by the Church blackened the still radiant 13th century in France. But they could not entirely uproot the doctrines. The secret congregations of the cathedral architects and artisans (Dombauhütten), the predecessors of the masonic lodges, have handed them and Zarathustra down to us. It has even been postulated that Wolfgang Amadeus Mozart, a fervent freemason, was poisoned, having disclosed some guarded Zarathustrian secrets in his *Zauberflöte* (The Magic Flute), exactly spoken in the tonal symbolism of the opera's music, not so much in Emanuel Schikaneder's libretto, which opposes Sarastro-Zarathustra's realm of eternal light and wisdom with the black and ignorant kingdom of the Queen of the Night.

Islam embraced the doctrines of Satan's autonomy, of eternal damnation *or* eternal redemption, of hell *or* paradise, and of short rectilinear time, too. But among the three western religions Christianity, the westernmost and most successful, is the most Zarathustrian — as evidenced by its downright Asuric mythological symbolism. Christ was born from the parthenogenesis of the Virgin — Varuṇa and Mani's Ohrmazd were born from the parthenogenesis of Aditi and the Mother of All Life. Christ's virginal birth was supplemented with a *logos*-creation[776] rooted in Yahveh's Old Testamentarian *logos*-creation of the Genesis[777] — according to the Veda the abstraction of the Asuric incest cosmogony. Christ worked as a carpenter's apprentice — Tvaṣṭā's name derives from the root *t(v)akṣ,* "to carpenter".[778] Many women followed Christ and were present during his crucifixion[779] — Tvaṣṭā's typical retinue were the wives. Christ was compared with a lamb or a shepherd — small livestock was placed under the guardianship of the Asuras. Christ was sometimes represented wearing a star-spangled robe[780] — Ahura Mazda and Varuṇa represented the nightsky.

On the other hand Christ's symbolism was influenced by gods from his eastern Mediterranean environment. They displayed the same symbols in the same contexts as the Asuras and may be considered their closest consanguineous (Indo-European) and non-consanguineous (Semito-Hamitic) relatives. Greek Ouranos, the virgin-born nightsky, and etymological namesake of Varuṇa, belonged to them, and virgin-born Phrygian Attis, who wore a star-spangled cap, and the other gods of his type,[781] the so-called Vegetation Gods (Frazer) — DUMUZI-Tammuz (Sumer-Babylon), Adon (Canaan, Cyprus), Osiris (Egypt), Telipinus-Sharruma (Hittite). They embodied life after the model of plants, as demonstrated by their characteristic death and resurrection, or disappearance and reappearance. They superintended the chthonic waters. They introduced agri- and horticulture, and tended small livestock. They were born from incest, or committed incest with their sisters and mothers, the (partly even parthenogenetic) great mother goddesses of their cultural fields, — INNANA-Ishtar, Astart, Isis, the Sun Goddess of Arinna, Kybele (Attis). And they represented duality in some form, as absence/presence, dearth/abundance, heavens/underworld, or moral judgement leading to resurrection or damnation.

Christ, whose flesh and blood transubstantiate into bread (corn) and wine (grapes) may be considered as their outmost sublimation, and from this point of view his Asuric symbolism needs not to be directly derived from the Asuras. It had been prefigured in the Vegetation Gods, to catalyze, however, the Zarathustrian influences upon Christianity. Like an Asura he may nevertheless be reflected in the inversive mirror of the Devas.

As for this I may sum up my article (Deppert II) dealing with the invariable parallels and transformations between the Asuras, the Vegetation Gods, Jesus Christ, and their myths. They obviously derive from one prehistorical prototype rooted in the Neolithic Revolution (7th–5th mill. B.C.), i.e. in the discovery of systematic cultivation (millet, barley), domestication (dogs, goats, sheep), and in this context consequently of astronomy, the observation of the night sky or rather its correlation with the sun and the seasons. This is the primordial reason why the Asuras

Varuṇa and Ahura Mazda, or Ouranos, Attis, and Jesus Christ combine vegetal life, small livestock, and night sky, or why the (genuine) Asuras Tvaṣṭā-Vṛtra (M 7) and Father Asura (M 15), the imitators of their typical incest, Dyauṣpitā (M 1a) and Prajāpati (M 11), as well as their non-Indo-European replicas DUMUZI-Tammuz and Osiris encode the constellation of Orion and their myths refer to the vernal equinox in it (7th–5th mill. B.C.). During the millennia to follow the dawn of civilization the precession of the vernal equinox was taken into account, and the astronomical event (the sun in Orion) either adapted to the proper season — to the summer as in the case of the Vedic Orion-gods[658] and of DUMUZI-Tammuz and Osiris — or Orion's mythology transferred to the constellations of the subsequent vernal equinoxes — as in the case of Attis to Taurus and Aries, or in the case of Jesus Christ to Pisces concealed in his acronym *ichthys* ("fish"), or I(esos) CH(ristos) TH(eou) (h) Y(ios) S(otēr).

That way Orion's original symbolism and the most typical feature of his life, namely his death, were handed down to posterity. His death was inflicted by a god of the *deva*-type (hunter, warlord, presiding over wind and weather, diacronical time and death) in the frame of a tragic family conflict. DUMUZI-Tammuz was killed by his hostile brother NER.GAL (NIN. IB = Sirius, Osiris by his hostile brother Seth (= Ursa Maior). Tvaṣṭā, Father Asura, Dyauṣpitā, Prajāpati were murdered by their hostile youngest son Indra or Rudra (= Sirius). Jesus Christ, however, the only son of God, lost his life with the consent—at least not against the disinclination —of his omnipotent, but indifferent father.

My article establishes an invariable transformative formula governing the passage from the Vedic to the Western form of the conflict. In spite of symbolic identity fathers and sons exchange or invert their position according to the pattern

Veda — West

(youngest) SON:FATHER :: FATHER: (only) SON

An example concerning the Vedas and the Hittites may demonstrate the operation of the pattern. It encompasses a whole set of associations:[782] Indra, the king of the heavenly gods (the Devas), is the youngest son of Tvaṣṭā (M 7). He produces lightning, thunder, and rain. He bears a club (*vajra*). He kills the giant serpent Vṛtra and his father Tvaṣṭā (M 7). His animal is the eagle or falcon (M 7). Tvaṣṭa is a hermaphrodite and commits incest with his daughter (M 5, M 7). His retinue are the "wives of the gods", and he bears an axe (*vāśī*).[783] The "king of the plants" also called Vanaspati, "lord of the forest", i.e. evergreen tree, is in his possession. Bucks and sheep are sacrificed to him, and the fleece of a sheep is the "first birthplace of his creatures".[310] The statement refers to his superintendence over fertility.

Maintaining the same symbolism the relation inverts in the Hittite pantheon:[784] Telipinus-Sharruma is the only son of the Weathergod of Heavens (Teshub, Tarhunt, Taru, Adad). He bears an axe, the emblem of Hittite hermaphrodites. He lives in quasi-incestuous relationship with his mother. His retinue are the wives of the gods (Yazılıkaya). His tree is the tree of life, the evergreen tree called *e̯ia(n)* (boxwood). On it the "fleece of a sheep is suspended, (into which) long life is put together with plentiful offspring, sons and daughters". The statement refers to Telipinus' superintendence over fertility,

The Weathergod of the Heavens is the King of the heavenly gods. He produces lightning, thunder, rains, and wind (D_{IM}). He bears a club. His animal is the falcon or eagle. He kills the giant serpent Illuyankas, in which context he also kills another only son.[785]

A second example is to be added. It is even more intricate, inasmuch as it is set into the context of several systematical inversions corroborating that Christ *is* reflected in the inversive mirror of the Devas, in Rudra of M 1a and M 11.

Rudra, sometimes compared with a player at dice,[786] is the youngest and most significant son of Dyauṣpitā or Prajāpati, the creator. He is not born, but ejaculated (M 1a) or pieced together (M 11). A nominal "mother" (Uṣas), however, is present while this happens. She causes the ejaculation of the father, who is transformed into a grown up and sexually active antilope, a horned animal of nature. Rudra kills his father, the creator, who dies of head injuries. This happens in the early morning before sunrise (passage night – day). Christ, the only son of God, the creator, is born only. He is not procreated, but a nominal "father", God, has caused his virginal birth. He is compared with a not grown up and sexually inactive lamb, a horned animal of culture. He is killed and dies from body injuries (heart, hands, feet). His father, who has forsaken him[787] may be responsible for his death. He does not make use of his omnipotence to save him. Christ's killers, the Roman soldiers, throw dice for his robe.[788] This happened between the 6th and the 9th hour of the day, in the afternoon, when darkness falls upon the land (passage day – night).[789]

The Aryan Schism did not only engender the antagonism of the Vedic and the Avestan cultures. It also produced after-effects on the religious and philosophical history of the West, starting west of India, and the East, starting east of Iran. There is hardly any monist redemption or thought west of India, barring the visions of some mystics (e.g. Meister Eckhard) or the doctrines of some philosophers (e.g. Spinoza, Fichte). Their knowledge, however, is confined to small sandbanks and avoided, misunderstood, if not downright depreciated by the masses swimming in the dualist mainstream.

On the other hand dualist thought was not very successful east of Iran. Zurvanism, a further development of Zarathustra's faith, probably left some impact on Kālacakra. Otherwise the Parsis may have helped to influence the plots of popular Hindi-films, so Zarathustrian in their endless confrontation of good guys and girls with bad guys and girls. But they did not influence the Monist mainstream of traditional Indian thought, which was wide and tolerant enough to house some dualist systems without being outshone by them.

And yet, all is not gold that glitters. It seems as though Monism is too impracticable not to flare up only once in a while, even within the Indian culture fostering it. The Aryan fire has since long stopped burning. The caste of the Brahmins has seized upon the Veda and given it an interpretation according to its own rules of conduct – caste, commensality, *ahiṃsā*, etc. In this context the simple Monism of the Upaniṣads was transformed into Vedānta Philosophy, the official Hindu ideology. This transformation, however, established Upaniṣadic Monism in the Asuric origin of the Brahmins.[740] Since Śaṃkara Vedānta has been defending its monist (*advaita*) claim with reference to the entirely onefold absolute. But *brahman* and *ātman* have forfeited their essential unity with the world, separated from them by *māyā,* the mother of objective creation. Deprived of the dualist-non-dualist (*dvaitādvaita, bhedābheda*) quality it once had in Indra's hands (*supra*), *māyā* has turned to nothing but dualist (*dvaita*) and moreover unreal illusion now.

The question arises why such a crypto-dualism has happened. A hypothetical answer is possible. Two antagonistic sets of symbols correlated with each other have served us to describe the essential difference between the Asuras and the Devas. The set of the Asuras — corroborated by the Vegetation Gods, and Jesus Christ — correlates underworld, chthonic waters, night-sky, etc. with parthenogenesis, incest, mother and birth, short rectilinear time, and Dualism, as against the set of the Devas correlating sky, day, etc. with exogamy, father and procreation, long cyclic time, and Monism.

The focus of each set is the salient point. The representatives of Monism are procreated only and not born, whereas the representatives of Dualism are born and not procreated, and if at all from incest. In other words, father and procreation appear to betoken Monism, mother and birth, however, Dualism. From this point of view Śaṃkara had to advocate a concept of dualist *māyā.* Although aware of the end of birth and reincarnation and correspondingly of caste at the moment of redemption, Vedānta nevertheless was rooted in the most exalted form of birth possible in Hinduism, in the "birth" (*jāti*) of the Brahmins, or at least as a member of the Aryan *varṇas.* The *adhikāra,* a criterion of access to the doctrine and the redemption it promised, would not permit members of other castes to take part. They were simply not born enough.

We have to consider that everything takes place in human consciousness. Man, however, is in any case procreated by a father and born by a mother. That means the two indispensable prerequisites to human existence are rooted deep down in consciousness — on the threshold, as it were, which consciousness itself has to pass over when it comes to the world it reflects. Here it associates procreation with Monism and creates gods of the Deva-type. This is a matter of the ecstasy of ejaculation. And here it associates birth with Dualism and creates the Asuras. This is a matter of the pain of birth, the first taste of the wordly dualities.

The Vedic seers had made up their mind about this very well. They recognized the correlation between birth and Dualism, but went deeper into the mysteries of existence, and discovered the secret of procreation and Monism. They reconducted the *brahman* with the unborn absolute father and with semen. He ejaculated or emanated it from his semen, and it ejaculated or emanated him (*supra*). For the semen, originating in the heart,[790] was the essence of man.[791] It comprised the *ātman* transmitted during procreation,[792] whence semen passed as *brahman* into the body overseen by Prajāpati,[793] and any genealogy returned via father and forefathers to the *brahman svayambhu,* the self-existent, unborn, absolute consciousness.[794]

Śiva, Rudra's Hindu successor, and his family preserve the secret of Devic existence. Śiva ejaculated Skanda, *his* son. And Pārvatī or Śakti, Śiva's wife, did not give birth to Gaṇeśa, *her* son, but formed him from mud and breathed life into him. Her hypostases are no uterine mothers either. Durgā is a virgin, and Kālī, normally represented with skeleton-like body, emaciated breasts, and protruding tongue, a mother in a merely nominal sense, if not at all an anti-mother, as suggested by her looks.

A genuine monist doctrine of Tantric, whence non-orthodox Hindu outlines flaring up in the 9th/10th centuries, was Kashmir Śaivism, also known as *svātantryavāda,* "doctrine of freedom", namely of Śiva's freedom to deliberately confine himself and forget his own identity in Śakti's creation, or as *pratyabhijñā,* "(doctrine of) recognition or rediscovery", namely of Śiva himself by Śakti. According to it Śiva is absolute consciousness conceived as the absolute subject simply called I (*aham*), timeless, spaceless, yonder duality, entirely transcendend. Śakti is his awareness I am (*aham asmi*), through which he knows that he is in the world, becomes immanent, and makes use of his illimitable possibilities realized by Śakti.

Śakti is endowed with three qualities, language, perception, and causality. Whatever Śiva wants to be, she creates it. She manifests the world as correlation between limited subjects, their limited means of perception, language, and causality, and the limited objects they can recognize. Śakti is *māyā,* but of dualist-non-dualist (*bhedābheda*) properties as in the hands of Indra. She hides Śiva under her superficially dualist creation, but projects the objects perceived by the limited subjects according to the axioms of limited[121] awareness into their true but forgotten identity Śiva, the all-reflecting mirror of consciousness. The world never separates from its source. The duality is nothing but a fancy enacted by Śiva-Śakti for their own fun, that they may lose their close contacts for a while now and then, and, for instance, experience the life of all limited subjects on earth, in hell, and in paradise. And each of them may rediscover that he/she is Śiva, irrespective of caste, race, nation, colour, moral stains, and not be prevented by moral considerations, if supreme identity is concerned.

Kashmir Śaivism may very well be rooted in the Devas and some theories of the Upaniṣads. This, however, is the subject of another investigation. A statement of Abhinavagupta, the brightest star of Indian Monism in the fashion of Kashmir, may be quoted in conclusion. In his short autobiography at the end of the Tantrāloka, his *summum opus,* he lets us know:[795]

tasmātmajo 'bhinavagupta iti prasiddhaḥ
śrīcandracūḍacaraṇābjaparāgapūtaḥ/
mātā vyayūyujadamuṃ kila bālya eva
daivam hi bhāviparikarmaṇi saṃskaroti//
mātā paraṃ bandhuriti pravādaḥ
sneho 'tigāḍhikurute hi pāśān/
tanmūlabandhe galite kilāsya
manye sthitā jīvata eva muktiḥ//

His (Narasiṃhagupta's) son was known as Abhinavagupta. He was purified by the pollen of the lotuses of Śiva's feet. His mother died when he was a child. That way fate prepares for future works.

Kinship, so the proverb says, is above all the mother, for her love ties the nooses (of existence) too tight. Is this fundamental fetter solved, redemption in life, so I think, is a matter-of-fact.

NOTES

1. My original contribution to the seminar was entitled "Hittite Gods and Aryan Myths". It dealt with the identical symbolism of and several conspicuous systematic inversions between Tvaṣṭā-Savitā-Viśvarūpa and Indra on the Vedic side, and Telipinus — Sharruma and the Weathergod of Heavens on the Hittite side. I did not want to publish it here. It was based on some older informations about the Hittites which I had already collected some years ago in Germany. But my intention was to be completely up-to-date, and no Indian library could supply me with the books necessary for relating the latest stand of the research into the Hittites and the Aryan aristocrats of Mitanni, who, in my opinion, were responsible for the amazing parallels I described in my lecture.
2. RV I.100.18, cf. VIII.46.31.
3. An epithet of Sūrya (RV X.37.9), Savitā (ib. 139.1), and Agni (ib. III.2.3). In their case it refers to the rays or the brilliance of the sun and the fire. In the case of Indra (ib. X.96.5.1), however, the question is of the embodiment of the ideal Aryan male, all the more so as Indra had a golden beard (ib. 8.), too.
4. RV I.130.8/II.12.4/20.7/VI.47.21.
5. RV V.29.10.
6. ib./VI.6.3.
7. Their religion was "without rituals" (*akarman,* RV X.22.8), "not sacrificing" (*ayajvan,* I.33.4/VIII. 70.1), "lawless" (*avrata,* I.175.3/VI.14.3/X.22.8), "of different laws" (*anyavrata,* VIII.70.11/X.22.8), "not loving the gods" (*adevayu,* VIII.70.11), "despising the gods" *(devapīyu,* AV XII.1.37), "without Indra" (*anindra,* RV VII.18.16), etc.
8. Accordingly only the name of the own tribe denotes "human being".
9. The Indo-European languages (and accordingly their supporters) appear to have developed in three successive waves from the simplest to the most complicated stage of their main characteristic, inflection (conjugation, declension):
   a. Pre-inflectional Indo-European, probably spoken by the so-called Old Europeans of Bessarabia, Rumania, and the Balkan (c. 4400 – 4200 B.C.). Remnants of their language are probably preserved in the "Old European" water names in Europe (cf. H. Krahe, Unsere ältesten Gewässernamen, Wiesbaden, 1964).
   b. Monothematic inflection, the suffixes being attached to one inflectional stem only, as in Luvian and Hittite (c. 3400 – 3200 B.C.).
   c. Polythematic inflection, the suffixes being attached to more than one stem, either to two — as in Celtic, Germanic, Italic, Slavic-Baltic, Thracian-Macedonian, Illyric, Phrygian, etc. — or to three — as in Greek and Aryan (from 3000 B.C. onwards).
   cf. F.R. Adrados, Arqueología differenciación del indoeuropeo, in: Emerita 47 (Instituto de Filologia Antonio de Nebrija, Madrid), pp. 261 - 82.
   From this point of view Sanskrit is much younger than German and Indian Romanticists would claim.
10. This trend was instituted in the name of the Aryans by Dayananda Sarasvati, the founder of the Arya Samāj. Nowadays P.N. Oak's Institute for Rewriting Indian History (N-128, Greater Kailash-I, New Delhi 110048) leads it *ad absurdum* in the name of Hinduism. In the Annual Report of 1980 we learn (pp.43 - 45) that "the term Christianity is the Sanskrit term Chrisn-nity. The two extra vowels, i and a, in the term Christia only signify a peculiar mode of intonation. Therefore the term Christ-nity is the Sanskrit word Chrisn-nity meaning the mode of life exemplified or propounded by lord Krishna". Hence, the Pope "as the archpriest or head of Christendom needs to be advised and educated about the Sanskrit-Hindu origin of the religion over which he presides".... because "it was that Hindu god, Lord Shiva, whom the Hindu Papa alias Pope used to worship in his Vatica (alias Vatican), i.e. hermitage in Roma (the city of

Rama)", until in the 4th century the Emperor Constantine became "in a weak moment inveigled into accepting Christianity . . .and Roman troopers crushed the vestiges of Hinduism under their high heels."

11. cf. E. Meyer, Geschichte des Altertums II.1, Stuttgart-Berlin 1928, pp. 44ff. J. Lechner, Neues über Pferd und Wagen in der Steinzeit und Bronzezeit, in: Mannus 25 (1933), pp. 123-136 W. Helck, Überlegungen zur Geschichte der 18. Dynastie, in: Oriens Antiquus 8 (1969), pp.281 - 327.
12. P. Bosch-Gimpera, The Migration Route of the Indo-Aryans, in: Journal of Indo-European Studies I (1973), pp. 13 - 17.
13. Darkness still shrouds their seccession from the trunk and their arrival in Mitanni. The lack of Aryan loan-words and names in the written documents of Mari, Chagar Bazar, and Alalah VII does not, however, exclude an arrival as early as *c.* 2000 – 1750 B.C. In this case the Cassites (Zagros) could have laid claim to the military support of the Aryans for their assault of Babylon which dethroned king Samsu-iluna shortly after the death of his father, the great Hammurabi (*c.* 1740 B.C. cf. A. Kammenhuber, Hippologia Hettitica, Wiesbaden 1961, pp. 15ff.). Moreover Aryan mercenaries might have assisted the Hurrians (Mitanni) and (Amurru-) Semites (Naharin) to the success of the Hyksos-campaign into Egypt (not later than 1730 B.C., as suggested by the so – called "Stela of 400 Years" which was exacavated at Tanis-Auris, the site of the Hyksos capital on the Pelusian mouth of the Nile). A rich literature has been discussing the *pros* and *contras* of a possible Aryan participation in the Hyksos-campaign (cf. M. Mayrhofer II, 147). Nevertheless the *mariįannu*-Aryans did not become visible in Egypt until the end of, and against the Hyksos-rule (*c.* 1580 B.C.). Mercenaries taking the path ot money and glory, pharaoh Ahmes (Amosis), the founder of the XVIII dynasty and of the New Kingdom, is reported as having chased the Hyksos with the help of his *mrin̯* (Egyptian for *mariįannu,* oral information by Dr Paul Yule, Bonn)—probably back to Northern Mesopotamia, where the Aryans are identified now with certainty for the next barely three centuries, above all in connexion with the rise, heyday, and decline of the Hurrian-Aryan kingdom of (the) Mitanni. From *c.* 1520 onwards (Mayrhofer II p.31) it was ruled by an Aryan dynasty until it fell under the re-emergence of the Hittites as a world power (king Shuppiluliuma I, c. 1366 – 1332 B.C.), Hittite-Egyptian quarrels (which led to the battle of Qadesh, *c.* 1288 – 1286 B.C.), and finally under the blows of the Assyrian conqueror Shalmanashshar (*c.* 1240 B.C.).
14. The toponym Middle Asia was coined by Russian historical anthropologists. The area is not to be mistaken for Central Asia (Sinkiang-Tokharistan, Inner Mongolia, Tibet), as the art historians do.
15. R. Girshman, L'Iran et la migration des indo-aryens et des iraniens, Leiden (Brill), 1972, pp. 10ff.
16. e.g. the mention of vernal equinoxes in Taurus (the asterisms *kṛttikāḥ* and *rohinī c* 3400–1400 B.C.) in Orion (the asterisms *mrgaśiras-invāka* and *ārdrā, c.* 5500–3400 B.C.), and probably even in Canis Maior (*Sirius-mṛgavyādha, c.*8000–6500 B.C.), referred to by Veda and Avesta. cf. L.B.G. Tilak, The Orion, or Researches into the Antiquity of Vedas, 4th Edition, Poona, 1955, and Deppert I, pp.174–205.
17. Mainly the Nuzi-tablets (Yorgan Tepe), Kikkuli's Hippological Treatise (Boghazköy), the Mattiwaza-treaty (dto.), and the Amarna-letters (Tell-el-Amarna), besides various inscriptions.
18. Let us not forget that the Indo-Aryans were nomads carrying their drinking water in leatherbags instead of clay pots. Pottery is no reliable source, all the more so as it does not appear until Late Vedic days. The words for pots (*ghaṭa, kumbha, etc.*) are lacking

in the RV — and B.B. Lal may be wrong.

19. The present form of the RV and of the AB appear to have been "edited" under the vernal equinox in the asterism *apabharaṇīḥ* (35, 39, 41 Arietis c. 900 B.C.). To be sure, this asterism is not mentioned by name, but implictly alluded to by several myths introducing its tutelary god Yama in the context the tutelary gods of past and future equinoxes, e.g. of Agni (*kṛttikāḥ*), Uṣas (*rohiṇī*), and Aśvin (*asvayujau*, Hamal and Sheradan in Aries), cf. RV X.51–53 and AB IV. 7–9. The latter myth is particularly interesting as Uṣas and Agni lose a race meeting from Agni, the lord of the house, to the sun, which Yama had organized, against the Aśvin. The myth may be interpreted in astronomical terms as the precession of the vernal equinox from Taurus to Aries, cf. Deppert I, pp. 178ff.
20. cf. H. Kulke and D. Rothermund, Geschichte Indiens, Stuttgart (Kohlhammer) 1982, p.39.
21. VA p.247.
22. AV V.22. 5, 7, 9.
23. VI II, p.63.
24. Kurram=Krumu (RV V. 53.9/X.75.6), Kabul=Kubhā (ib.), Gomal = Gomatī (V.61.9/VIII.24.30/X.75.6), Swāt = Suvāstu (VIII.19.37).
25. Jhelum=Vitastā (X.75.5), Chenab=Asiknī (VII.20.25/ib.), Ravi=Paruṣṇī (VII.18.8, 9/ib.), Beas=Vipāś (III.33.1/IV.30.11), Sutlej = Śutudrī (III.33.1/X.75.5).
26. The Sarasvatī was the holiest river of the RV. Referring to RV VI.49.7 Hillebrandt (VM I.pp.99f and III, pp. 372–378) identifies it with the Avestan Harax^{v}aiti (modern Arghandab, a tributary of the Helmend). The bulk of the references, however, leaves no doubt about the identification of Vedic Sarasvatī with the modern Sarsūti into which the Ghaggar debouches SW of Patiala. One of the most conspicuous landmarks of Late Vedic geography was the "disappearance" of the river in the sands of the northern Thar desert at the place called Vinaśana (PB XXV.10.6/JB IV.26).
27. Yamuna mentioned RV V.52.17/VII.18.19/X.75.5, and Gaṅgā VI.45.31/X.75.5.
28. As for the localization of these lands cf. VI II, pp. 125ff.
29. RV VII. 18, cf. also VA, pp. 249f. and *passim*.
30. ŚB I.4.I 10ff.
31. VA, pp. 258ff.
32. ib., pp. 261, 264ff.
33. Rau, p. 20.
34. The Kuru-Pañcāla appear to have emerged from a fusion of RV tribes — Pūru, Bharata, Kuru, Sṛñjaya, and Pañcāla cf. VA, pp. 256.
35. Isogamy and commensality within one and the same *varṇa*. Regarding the exclusion of the Śudras from the Vedic religion, cf. R.S. Sharma, Śūdras in Ancient India — A Survey of the Position of Lower Orders down to c. 500 A.D., Varanasi-Delhi (Motilal Barnasidass), 1958, p. 69.
36. During the RV age the membership to a *varṇa* was not yet hereditary, but decided by abilities and inclinations.
37. While writing the present paper, I found an article in the Times of India (Ancient Tribe in W. Asia Fears Genocide, December 8, 1982) according to which the Parsis of Iran are in the Ayatollah's grip now.
38. C.R. Pangborn, Zoroastriansim — A Beleaguered Faith, Delhi (Vikas), 1982, p.xiv.
39. Gāthā I = Y XXVIII - XXXIV, G.2 = Y XLIII - XLVI, G.3 = Y XL VIL - L, G.4 = Y LI, G.5 = Y LIII.
40. e.g. the Gāhs, Sīrozahs, Āfrīgan, etc.
41. The redaction was finished under king Shapur 11 (309–380 A.D.)
42. E. Meyer, Geschichte des Alterums III, Darmstadt, 1953 (2nd Edition), p. 110, n.3.

43. Cambridge History of India, I. p. 76.
44. Atropatene (Ekbatana) in Media was specified, cf. SBE IV, pp. XL VIIIff.
45. Y XIX. 18.
46. Vend XIX, 4, 11
47. SBE IV, p. XLIX.
48. VA, p. 222.
49. Vend I. The enumeration starts with 1. Aíryana Vaegho, the mythical "Aryan Land". The following six provinces cover an area bordered by the Jaxartes, western Afghanistan, and eastern Iran (Seistan): 2. Sugdha (Sogdiana), 3. Mouru (Merw), 4. Bākdhi (Bactra), 5. Nisaya (?), 6. Haroyu (Aria), and 7. Vaekereta (Kabul ?). Then the enumeration continues with 8. Urva (Isfahan) and 9. Vehrkana (Gorgan) in the (north-) west of modern Iran. The rest is arranged in the form of a spiral retrograding to 10. Harax^{v}aiti (Arachosia) and 11. Haetumant (Helmend), but revolving round a centre in 12. Ragha (Raï), 13. Cakhra (?), and 14. Varena (Elborz or Kerman), to finally swing its arms in embrace of the territory of the Achaemenian Empire between its easternmost and westernmost fringes, 15. Hapta Hindava (Punjab) and 16. Rangha (Mesopotamia). The identification of the provinces after J. Darmesteter, SBE IV, p. 2.
50. Bund XIX. 1–10.
51. Epistles of Mānūshcihar I.8.3.
52. Yt X.70, 125/XIV. 15.
53. Fox (*raopi*), young dog (up to four months old), stray dog (*vohunazga*), house dog, shepherd's dog, cf. Vend XIII.
54. Lynx, weasel, fox (again), hedgehog, and beaver are classified among the dogs, cf. Vend. XIII. 16. The beaver was the holiest among them. The hedgehog was the "dog" of Ahura Mazda, Vend. ib. 1–4.
55. ib. XV. 46–49.
56. ib. 20–45.
57. ib. *passim*.
58. ib. 12, 20–24.
59. SBE IV, p. XLVI n.
60. Vend VII. 6–9, 34.
61. SIS II.3/Vend VII. 34.
62. Bund XIX. 22.
63. The raven was particularly holy to Verethraghna, Yt XIV. 19.
64. ib. 35–36.
65. Vend VII. 34.
66. Bund XIX. 33.
67. Vend. XVIII. 14–29.
68. RV I.29.7.
69. AV V. 31.2.
70. AB II.15.
71. Viṣṇu LXXX1.9.
72. ĀpDhS I.5.17.32/GDhŚ XVII.29/Vas XIV.48/Manu V.12.19.
73. e.g. the "heavenly vultures flying over the waters" (RV I.118.4), or the Aśvin are "like two vultures (coming) to the tree" (ib. II.39.1).
74. AV V.23.4.
75. ib. VIII.4.22/RV VII.104.22.
76. AV XII.3.13/XIX.57.4.
77. ib. XII.3.
78. GDhŚ XVII.10.

79. ŚB XIV.1.1.31.
80. Watchdog (RV VII.55.3–5), hunting dog (ib. X.86.4), a gift of 100 dogs (ib. VIII.55).
81. TS IV.5.4m - p/VS XVI.27c.
82. Indra's bitch Saramā, e.g. RV X.108.
83. Two dogs, ib. X.14.10–12.
84. ib. VII.104.22/AV VIII.4.22.
85. RV IX.101.1.
86. PGS II.8.3 Moreover touching a dog rendered impure (BDhŚ I.5.11.39), and Veda-studies were to be interrupted in their presence (ĀpDhS I.3.10.19/GDhŚ XVI.8/ŚGS IV.7.33 etc).
87. ŚB XII.4.1.4.
88. Viṣṇu LXXXI.9.
89. ĀpDhS I.5.17.29/GDhŚ XVII.29/Manu V.34.
90. ŚB VI.4.4.12/PGS III.16.6.
91. e.g. BDhŚ II.1.1.31/GDhŚ XXIII.17–18/Vas XXIII.1. Otherwise an unchaste Kṣatriya was requested to shave with the urine of an ass (Manu VIII.390), or an unchaste woman exhibited to the bemused crowd on an ass (Vas XXI.1ff).
92. ApDhS I.3.10.19/GDhŚ XVI.8/PGS II.11.6/Manu IV.115/Viṣṇu XXX.12.
93. e.g. ĀpDhS I.5.17.29.
94. AV VI.100.1.
95. ib. VII.56.
96. Kauśikasūtra XXV.7.
97. M. Bloomfield, Seven Hymns of the Atharva-veda, in: American Journal of Philology VII, pp. 482ff.
98. AV VI.100.1–2.
99. TĀr V.1.4.
100. RV VII.103.
101. AV VII.116.2.
102. Vaitānasūtra XXXIX.13.
103. RV X. 16. 14.
104. ŚB IX.1.2.20/KS XVIII.17/XVIII.1/MS II.9.9,10/TS V.4.4.2/VS XVII.1.16.
105. ŚB VII.5.1.1.
106. ib. 9.
107. ib. 5.
108. ib. VI.1.1.12.
109. ib. VII.5.1.1.
110. ib.2.
111. Vend XIII.5.
112. The translation is perhaps questionable, cf. SBE IV, p. 153 n. 2.
113. Bund XVIII. 2–3, cf. SBE IV, p. 59 n. 4.
114. Gabriel du Chinon, a French visitor to the Parsis in the 17th century, remarks: "Un jour que j'étois surpris de la guerre qu'ils font aux fourmis, ils me disent que ces animaux ne faisaient que voler par des amas des grains plus qu'ils n'étoit nécessaire pour leur nourriture." Quoted SBE IV, p. 167 n. 3.
115. SD XLIII.7.
116. ib. 2. cf. Gabriel du Chinon: "Pour les grenouilles et crapeaux ils diśent que ce sont ceux (sic!) qui sont cause de ce que les hommes meurent, gâtans les eaus où ils habitent continuellement." Quoted SBE IV, p. 167 n. 2.
117. Vend XIV.5.
118. I thank Paul Thieme for having marked the misspelling of the name (Lévy-Strauss) in my thesis, which he criticized *con bravura* (ZDMG 1982). I admit that structuralism

and German philology are unbridgeable, and I still don't believe in the omniscience of etymologies.

119. C. Lévi-Strauss, Le cru et le cuit (Mythologiques I), Paris (Plon), 1964, pp. 233–45.

120. In Abhinavagupta's sense awareness (*caitanya, vimarśa, pratibhā*) is objective consciousness, or consciousness of objectivity, as distinct from the subjective consciousness (*bodha, cit, prakāśa*) of the absolute which is nothing but pure I (*aham*).

121. In Hegel's sense seen through the eyes of Abhinavagupta at least. Awareness is completely fettered by internal (thoughts, phantasies, dreams) and external (heard, touched, seen, tasted, smelled) objects of perception. Otherwise it is not aware of itself nor of the world — as in deep sleep, swoon, or death. On the level of the absolute the object of awareness is the subject of consciousness itself, which deliberately abandons its absolute fullness in order to become aware of itself ("I am"). On the level of everyday life the initial self-negation of the absolute subject manifests in the form of duality between the limited subjects and the limited objects filling their limited awareness, and between the limited objects themselves: each "something" perceived is not, what the rest of perceivable objects is, or rather is, what the rest is not. This general delineation from notness encloses a special case in myths and systems of myths in which the ancient cultures are rooted. They select a limited number of special, archetypal objects (symbols) from the theoretically illimitable objectivity of the world for reasons of everyday utility and ideally redundant intercommunicability. The latter results from a generic complementary partner determining the positive significance by negative inversion: the mythical symbols are or are not, what their negative partners are not or are. That way every myth can only co-exist with its inversion within or without its cultural field, and myths may fit together like a jigsaw puzzle even if they come from different cultural fields and different continents.

122. C. Lévi–Strauss, Le totemisme aujourd' hui, Paris (Presses Universitaires de France), 1962.

123. cf. n. 1. My original contribution to the seminar dealt with the phenomenon, for which the Hittites appear to place striking examples at our disposal. The paradoxical and burlesque oddities of the Hittite Illuyankas-myth, e.g., may very well be explained as aware inversions of Seth's combat with Apep (Egyptian), of the Humbaba-sequence of the Gilgamesh epic (Sumerian-Akkadian), and of Indra's fight with Vṛtra or Śuṣṇa, let alone the systematic inversions between Tvaṣṭā-Savitā-Viśvarūpa and his son Indra, and Telipinus-Sharruma and his father Teshub-Taru-Tarhunt (the Weathergod of Heavens).

124. Akhenaton's monotheist reform caused a sort of civil war in Egypt, which in its turn caused the decline of the XVIII dynasty. The Arian schism resulted in bloody prosecutions of the Catholics particularly in Spain under the Visigoth kings, who followed the Arian confession, and of the Arians particularly in France under the Catholic Merovingian kings. cf. Gregory of Tours, HF II.2, II.37, III.1, etc.

125. Likewise other Indo-European pantheons were divided into two opposed groups, e.g. Ass and Vanir in the Germanic pantheon, god and goddesses in the Hittite pantheon (e.g. in Yazılıkaya), Titans (and other pre-Olympians) and Olympians in the classical Greek pantheon, or, at least rudimentarily, Fir Bolg-Fomore and Tuatha De Dánann in the Irish pantheon.

126. Prajāpati, one of the favourite gods of the Brāhmaṇas, replaced the older creator gods of the RV of both, the Devic and the Asuric type. He figured as the father of all Devas and (demoniac) Asuras, but did not take part in their quarrels.

127. The Aśvin are the children of Vivasvat and Saraṇyū (RV. X. 17.2), although other genealogies are also given.

128. Agni is an Asura (RV III.29.11/V.12.1/15.1/VII. 6.1). Soma is not called Asura, but there are no doubts about his Asuric provenance: according to RV X. 124 (M 15) he left his Father Asura together with Agni on Indra's instigation.
129. Asura according to RV III. 38.4
130. Savitā is a sun god with "golden hands" (ib. I. 22.5/35.9/III.54.11/VI.85.8/71.4 etc.), a feature comparable with the "beautiful-handed" (III.54.12/VI.49.9) and unsurpassingly skilful (X.59.3) artistic creator Tvaṣṭā, who supervises the forms and the forming of the creatures (I.13.10/188.9/II.55.19/V.42.13/X.184.1). Therefore Tvaṣṭā is called Viśvarūpa, "having all forms".
131. Their number is 3 (RV II.27.8), 6 (II.27.1), 7 (X.72.8) or 8 (ib./MS I.6.12), and later on even 12 (AB III.34). However in the latter case they are identified with the 12 solar months.
132. Asuras according to RV VIII.27.20, cf. also III.56.8 and II.27.4.
133. Asura as Āditya.
134. Asura according to RV V.42.1.
135. Asura according to RV VIII.19.23/42.1/X.132.4, cf. also IV.42.2.
136. Asura together with Varuṇa according to RV I.151.4/VII.65.2/VIII.25.4. cf. also V.66.2/VII.65.1/66.2/VIII.25.3.
137. Asura as Āditya.
138. Not *expressis verbis,* but as Āditya and by his identification with Savitā (RV V.42.5/ VII.38.1.6, etc.).
139. Asura according to RV IV.53.1/V.49.2. Āditya according to VIII.18.3, cf. also VII.38.4.
140. Apart from his identification with Savitā great closeness between Bhaga and Savitā.
141. Asura according to V.51.11.
142. Asura according to II.35.2.
143. A hexad e.g. Yt IV.1/X.92, a heptad e.g. ib. XI.14. In the latter case Sraosha is included, cf. Y LVII.11.
144. Yt XIX.34ff./DD XXXIX.16–17.
145. Vend XIX.43/Bund XXVIII.7–13/Epistles of Mānūshcīhar I.10.9.
146. cf. VI I, s.v. *gauḥ*.
147. TS II.5.2.6.
148. RV X.62.7,8/102.5,9/VIII.5.37.
149. ib. IX.58.3
150. ŚB XIII.5.4.7.8.
151. Rau, p. 24, p. 111.
152. RV VI.47.26/75.11/X.27.22.
153. ib.X.17.6.
154. ib.II.7.5/VIII.43.11.
155. TB III.4.16.1/VS XXX.18.
156. TB II.7.11.1/PB XX1.14.5.
157. ŚB III.1.2.21.
158. The Vedic animal sacrifice (*paśubandha*) irritated the *ahiṃsā*-doctrine anyhow.
159. AB I.15/ŚB III.4.1.2/Manu V.41–42/Vas IV.5.6–8.
160. RV X.85.13/ cf. A.B. Keith HOS 32, p. 374. The wedding feast was an occasion comparable with the guest reception.
161. *tūpara* denominates any type of hornless domestic animal normally carrying horns, but particularly the hornless goat.
162. TB III.4.9.1/VS XXX.11
163. RV VIII.67.3/X.75.8.
164. ib. IX.109.16, cf. VM I, p. 203.

165. RV I.126.7.
166. A gift of 100 dogs is mentioned in one breath with sheep by RV VIII.55.3.
167. First the Kṣatriyas were refused genuine Soma (AB VII.28.1) and had to content themselves with substitutes.
168. KS XVI.17/MS II.7.17/TS IV.2.10.1–4, etc.
169. ŚB XII.4.1.4/II.5.2.15/JB I.51.4.
170. Sheep's milk forbidden according to ĀpDhS I.5.17.23/GDhŚ XVII.24. Goat's milk allowed according to TS IV.1.6.1/V.1.7.4.
171. AB II.8.1–8. The myth is a first milestone on the way towards vegetarianism and *ahiṃsā*, cf. n. 158.
172. RV I.23.15/176.2/IV.57.4,8/VIII.20.19/22.6/X.34.13/117.7.
173. RV I.23.15/66.3/117.21/135.8/II.5.6, etc. Here *yava* may denote both, *Hordeum hexastichum* or *H. vulgare,* and grain in general.
174. Barley is associated with the winter season, cf. ŚB III.6.1.8–10 and VM III, p. 35 n. 2. Moreover the season of warfare after the harvest started in the 2nd half of the month *phālguna* (February—March, cf. TB I.8.4. On the other hand spring (KB IV.13) and summer (TS VII.2.10) are specified as seasons of barley harvest.
175. 6 oxen (AV VI.91.1), 8 (KS XV.2).
176. As for the many crops cultivated during Late Vedic times, cf. VI I, p. 182.
177. VA, p. 467./RV VII. 89.I.
178. Comparable to the modern Gujars. They reoccupy their clay dens on the higher altitudes of Kashmir when they return from the plains for the summer.
179. Rau, p. 20.
180. ib., pp. 51ff.
181. A compact wheel consisted of three horizontal layers of wood, cf. Kātyāyana Śrauta Sūtra.
182. RV X.85.10.
183. There are c. 130 – 140 references to horse racing in the RV.
184. The third horse was called *praṣṭi,* cf. RV I.39.6/VIII.7.28/ŚB V.1.4.11, etc.
185. RV II.18.8/ŚB V.4.3.17.
186. MS II.6.3/KS XV.2.
187. According to the RV the *ratha* was carpentered from different species of wood (III.53.19). The parts of its box were tied together with cow leather strings (IV.47.26,27). The same way the box was fixed on the axle *(akṣa,* I.166.9/TS VII.2.9). The two wheels (*cakrau*) had a hub (*nabhya, nābhi,* I.164.48/VIII.41.6), four, six, or more spokes (*ara,* I.164.11/VIII.20.14/X.78.4), a rim (*nemi,* II.5.3/X.61.16), and an outer metal cover (*pavi,* I.88.2/V.52.9/V.58.6). A nail (*aṇi,* I.63.3/VI.43.8/X.22.11) prevented the slipping off of the wheel from the axle.
188. Three seats are mentioned particularly in connexion with the chariot of the Aśvin, cf. I.34.5,9/47.2/118.1/157.3/183.1/VII.69.2/71.4, etc.
189. *yantā* (RV I.162.19/X.22.5), *rathī* (I.25.3/II.39.2/III.3.6 etc.), *rathin* (I.122.8/V.83.3/VI.47.3/VIII.4.9), *sārathi* (I.55.7/I.144.3/II.19.6/VI.20.5, etc.
190. RV I.143.7/II.2.1/34.4.
191. ib. I.173.4,5/II.17.3/VI.21.1/22.5/29.1, etc.
192. cf. the terms *savyaṣṭhā* (AV VIII.8.23), *savyaṣṭhṛ* (ŚB V.2.4.9/V.4.3.17–18), *savyastha* (MS IV.3.8), *savyeṣṭha* (TB I.7.9.1), "standing on the left".
193. ŚB V.1.4.3/4.3.3, both references in the context of the *vājapeya-* or rather the *rājasūya*-rituals which provided for chariot races. cf. also RV VI.75.8.
194. cf. W. Ruben, Über die frühesten Stufen der Entwicklung der altindischen Śūdras, Berlin (Sitzungsberichte der Deutschen Akademie der Wissenschaften zu Berlin, Klasse für Sprachen, Literatur und Kunst, Jahrgang 1964, Nr. 6), 1964.

195. *gaviṣṭi* as normal expression for warfare, cf. RV I.91.23/III.47.4/59.7, etc. cf. also the related term *gavyā* e.g. VII.18.7/VIII.46.10.
196. RV I.36.8/IV.40.2 (here with the famous horse Dadhikrā)/V.63.5/IX.76.2/X.61.23, etc. cf. also the term *gavyū rathaḥ* (IV.31.14), or *gavyantaṃ ratham* (VIII.2.35), or *gaveṣaṇaṃ ratham* (VII.23.3, etc.).
197. Impure according to ĀpDhS I.6.18.18/GDhŚ VII.17, etc.
198. VS XVI.2.17,19.
199. TS IV.5.1.1–11 *passim*/MS II.9.2-9 *passim*/ KS XVII. 11–16 *passim*.
200. RV I.3.3/VIII.22.1,14/X.39.11.
201. As doctors, cf. ŚB IV I.5.8/TS VI.9.1.2
202. AB VII.15.1d.
203. VS XVI.3.24.
204. TS IV.5.1–11 *passim*.
205. RV V.42.1, cf. VII.46.1.
206. KS IX.7/MS I.4.10/VS III.6.1.
207. cf. AV XI.2.24–25.
208. Cattle belongs to Rudra (*raudra*), cf. ŚB VI.3.2.7.
209. AV V.24.2/PB VII.9.19/XXI.14.13/ŚB V.3.3.11.
210. PB VI.9.8–9.
211. PB I.8.3/TB 1.11.5.8–9, cf. particularly the *śūlagava*-ritual, ApGS VII.20/PGS III.9, etc.
212. Origin of title Paśupati cf. AB III.33–34 (M 11).
213. c. 33 references in RV to horses, otherwise bulls (I.182.1/VII.71.3), asses (I.34.9/116.2), eagles (VIII.57), falcons (I.119.1,4), geese (IV.45.4), bull and crocodile (I.116.18), birds (c. 14 ref.).
214. More than 180 references to their chariot in RV.
215. RV I.118.3/VI.63.8/VIII.5.9,10.
216. ib. I.124.5/IV.52.2,3/V.45.1,6/VII.77.2, cf. also M 1a and M 11.
217. ib. I.71.1/V.45.1/VI.65.5/VII.75.7, etc.
218. Uṣas' chariot(s) cf. ib. I.48.7/49.2/113.14/IV.14.3/VII.75.6/78.1,4. Her red horses cf. I.92.15/113.14/III.61.2/IV.51.5/VII.75.6/78.4. Her bulls VI.64.3,5. With regard to the latter often also a cart driver, cf. II.15.6/IV.30.11/VIII.91.7, etc.
219. ib. I.134.4/135.8.
220. Vāyu's chariot(s) cf. II.41.6/IV.48.1/V.41.6/VI.49.4. His bay or ruddy horses cf. I.134.1,3/IV.48.5/VIII.26.20,23. There are c. 18 references to his *niyut*-horses. cf. also the 6 references to Vāta's horses.
221. c. 25 references to the horses of the Maruts. Otherwise c. 20 references to their antilopes.
222. c. 27 references to their chariots.
223. RV VIII.7.35.
224. ib. V.55.5/VIII.7.13. cf. also notes 471 – 475.
225. c. 20 references to Indra's unspecified horses.
226. c. 5 references to Indra making use of Vāyu's *niyut*.
227. c. 150 references to Indra's two *harī*.
228. c. 60 references to Indra's chariot.
229. I.101.4/III.30.21/IV.30.22, etc. often together with *aśvapati*, "lord of horses".
230. c. 110 references to Indra's generosity in RV.
231. RV VIII.61.8
232. e.g. I.10.8/33.1/53.2/X.19.2/98.4/133.7/, etc.
233. e.g. III.30.21/IV.22.10/VI.23.4/VIII.24.20/45.19, etc.
234. cf. X.99.4.

235. c. 20 references to the lances of the Maruts in RV.
236. c. 14 references to their other weapons.
237. c. 70 references to their warlike qualities.
238. e.g. I.10.2/101.9/II.31.3/III.32.2,4/35.9/VI.52.11, etc
239. I.101.6/II.12.8.
240. c. 400 references to Indra's warfare.
241. IV.23.7/VIII.45.5.
242. II.30.5/IV.22.1/VII.104.19.
243. Indra's *vajras* (pl.) cf. I.80.8/X.27.21. His *vajra* (sng.) referred to c. 110 times.
244. Indra's *vajra* was wooden because it was carpentered (roots *takṣ* or *vṛt*) by Tvaṣṭā, cf. I.32.2/52.7./85.9/121.3/V.31.4/VI.17.10. Another type was brazen, cf. I.52.8/X.113.5. Yet another type resembled a cudgel, with 100 spikes (1.80.8/VIII.6.6) or 1000 spikes (I.80.12). Or it had 4 edges (I.152.2/IV.22.2).
245. I.153.4,5/II.17.3/VI.21.1/22.5/29.2/VIII.4.13/33.14/IX.97.14. No other god bears the epithet.
246. I.56.4/IV.17.13/42.5.
247. c. 60 references to Indra crushing forresses in RV.
248. c. 52 references to their fortresses in RV.
249. VII.23.3/III.44.5.
250. c. 90 references to the Valamyth in RV.
251. II.11.19/X.8.8–9/42.2/99.6/ŚB I.6.3.1–5/TS II.5.1.
252. e.g. RV V.6.1,2,6,7/I.140.4/VI.2.2.
253. c. 27 references to Agni's warfare in RV.
254. VIII.19.23.
255. I.36.8/74.2.
256. c. 42 references to Agni's horses in RV.
257. c. 21 references to Agni's chariot in RV.
258. III.7.2.
259. V.3.3.
260. V.2.4,5.
261. II.7.5.
262. AB I.15.
263. RV IX.91.5/107.9/62.24.
264. c. 700 references to Indra's and Soma's friendship.
265. c. 100 references in RV.
266. V.62.4/VII.60.2.
267. I.122.15.
268. I.151.5/153.4/V.62.2,13/69.2/VI.67.7. Here the two gods are only mentioned in the context of cows.
269. X.64.10/93.7.
270. I.141.10/III.49.2.
271. I.141.10/II.38.10/VII.41.5/VIII.31.11/IX.101.7.
272. I.35.2–5/VII.45.1.
273. I.162.3,19.
274. ŚB V.1.4.5/V.3.1.5/VIII.4.3.13. Association with *aśvamedha* horse not *expressis verbis,* but with horses as such or one-hoofed animals, because the horse was supposed to have originated in the water, Varuṇa's realm.
275. ŚB V.4.9.1/VS IX.8/AV VI.92.2.
276. RV I.84.15.
277. V.5.9.
278. I.188.9/AV IX.4.6/TB II.5.7.4.

279. RV II.3.9/III.55.19/VII.34.20, etc.
280. Once the seeds are reported as being the gift of the Maruts (RV V.53.13).
281. cf. RV IV.42.
282. VII.12.5,6.
283. III.59.1,5/VII.36.2.
284. I.21.3/V.40.7.
285. V.3.2.
286. ŚB VI.8.1.1.
287. RV V.64.3.
288. V.63.1.
289. X.64.5/105.6.
290. e.g. VII.65.3.
291. cf. VI I, p. 37.
292. e.g. Bund III.25/V.1/Mkh VIII.19/XXIV.8/XXXVIII.3/, etc.
293. RV III.54.20, cf. VII.35.8.
294. IV.13.3, that the Ādityas are meant is inferable from str. 2.
295. V.72.2.
296. VII.88.7, here *dhruvāsu kṣitiṣu.*
297. cf. also Kuiper 1960, 1964 *passim.*
298. ib. cf. RV VII.89.1.
299. RV III.48.2 (*gṛha*)/IV.18.3 (*dama*).
300. VIII.29.3.
301. I.73.4.
302. X.46.3, cf. also Agni's frequent epithet *gṛhapati,* "lord of the house", e.g. I.12.6/36.5/60.4, etc.
303. X.26.6.
304. VI.55.4/IX.67.10/X.26.8.
305. I.138.4/VI.55.3,6/57.3/58.2.
306. I.162.3,4.
307. ŚB VII.5.2.20.
308. TĀr III.10.3/ Kātyāyana Śrauta Sūtra VIII.9.1.
309. ŚB VI.2.5.1.
310. ib. VII.5.2.35/VS XIII.50.
311. Beheaded by Śiva Vīrabhadra Dakṣa was revived with a ram's head, cf. e.g. Mahābhārata XII. 283.
312. As *lokapāla* of the SE.
313. ŚB I.6.1.3.
314. RV VIII.31.14.
315. ŚB V.3.3.8.
316. e.g. KB V.3 (beginning) and other texts referring to the *varuṇapraghāṣāḥ*-rituals.
317. Bund XXVII.24.
318. ib.
319. c. 30 references in RV.
320. c. 25 references in RV.
321. In the so-called *āprī*-hymns of the RV.
322. Bhaviṣyapurāṇa 1.74.14/Sāmbapurāṇa IV.12.
323. cf. RV III.48/IV.18.3/TS II.5.2.1/ŚB I.6.3.6.
324. cf. VI II, p. 475.
325. R.G. Wasson, Soma, Divine Mushroom of Immortality (Ethno-Mythological Studies, I), 1968 (limited edition), reprint London 1971.
326. Soma was received at the sacrificial site like a guest (e.g. AB I.15). This implies the

non–Indian origin of the *soma*-plant which the Indo-Aryans had brought along from Middle Asia. Later on they had to import it from there, since *Amanita muscaria* does not grow in India, cf. Wasson, ib.

327. White (RV IX.74.9/97.15, etc.), bay (IX.92.1/65.8,etc.), reddish, VII.98.1/X.94.3, etc.), tawny (IX.33.2/63.4,6, etc.). The colours refer to the plant and its sap.
328. Particularly RV VIII. 48.
329. I.122.11,cf.VIII.18.18,22 (long life).
330. X.93.4.
331. Y III.1,20/IV.1,3/VI.17/VII.20/Bund IX.2, etc.
332. Particularly of the *Ficus*-genus, like *Ficus glomerata* (*udumbara*), *F. infectoria* (*nyagrodha*), etc.
333. cf.ŚB III.6.1.10.
334. RV X.97.18,19,22/AV VI.96.1/VIII.1.17/ Bund XXIV.18.
335. e.g.Vend XX.4.
336. Yt XII.17/Bund XVIII.1–4/XXVII.4, etc.
337. Vend III.24.
338. ib. 25.
339. cf.Y XXIX.6/XLVIII.9/XIII.2,3/XIX.17, etc.
340. Bund XXIV.19/Mkh XVI.13.15/LXI.11.
341. ib. XVI.4.9 – 12.
342. Yt V.25,29,45,108,112/IX.3, etc.
343. Dk IX.18.2/VIII.29.11/30.12.
344. ib.IX.65.2.
345. ib.53.13.
346. ib.15.
347. ib.3.
348. Y XXXII.8.
349. Vend V.56/VII.14.74/VIII.11,13,37,39, etc.
350. Y L.2/XXXI.9/XLVII.3/LI.7, etc.
351. ib. XLVIII.6/LI.7.
352. ib. XXXIX.6.
353. ib. XXXI.10.
354. ib. 1.
355. ib. XII.2.
356. ib. LVIII.4/cf. Visperad I.9.
357. Y XXXIV.14.
358. ib. XXXIX.9.
359. ib. XLVI.2.
360. ib. LI.5.
361. cf. G.C. Cameron, Zoroaster the Herdsman, in: IIJ X (1967/8), pp. 261–281.
362. Y XXIX.I.
363. ib. XXX. 9, 10/XLVIII. 10/L.3/LII.2/IX.8, 18.
364. ib. XXXII. 11.
365. ib. LI. 14.
366. ib. XLVI. 20.
367. RV VII. 90.4/X.45.11.
368. Mention of Afghanistan (*Paktha*) in the frame of the Vala-myth RV X.61. Moreover movement of Uṣas to the south (ib. 8) and location of the (mythical) river Rasā, i.e. of Vala's rock cave, in the farthest south: India is south of Afghanistan.
369. e.g. Vṛtra I.32.11 (*dāsa*)/ŚB 1.6.3.13 (*dasyu*), or Vala as *paṇi par excellence* (RV X.108), or Śuṣṇa IV.16.9/VII.19.2 (*dāsa*), etc.

370. e.g. Śambara IV. 30.14/VI.31.4/47.21 (*dāsa*), or Varcin IV.30.15/VI.47.21 (*dāsa*).
371. Wealthy *dāsa*-tribes I.176.4/IV.30.13/VIII.40.6/X.69.6, wealthy *dasyu* V.7.10, etc.
372. Herodotus I.126.
373. VM I, pp. 83ff.
374. C. Lévi-Strauss, L'origine des manières de table (Mythologiques III), Paris (Plon), 1968, p. 308.
375. In Fred Zinnemann's film version the part was played by Eddie Albert.
376. cf. note 265.
377. Positive according to Y IX.22: "Haoma grants racers who would run a race with span both speed and bottom." Ambivalent-negative according to Y XI.2 (the curse of the cow, the horse, and Haoma): "The horse cries to his rider thus: 'Be not a spanner of the racers, stretch no coursers to full speed, do not stride across the fleetest, thou, who dost not pray me swiftness in the meeting thick with members, in the circuit thronged with men!'"
378. cf. Vend IX.37 – 38 (camel, stallion, bull, cow, ploughing cow, draught cow, lamb). The order of camel and horse may also be reversed, e.g. Yt XIV.11.
379. Y XLIV.18.
380. The significance of *zarath* is not clear. It may be related with Vedic *hari*, "bay, yellow".
381. e.g. Vishtāspa, Habāspa, Frīnāspa, Tūmāspa, Xshviwrāspa, Dazgarāspa, etc.
382. e.g. Āśvaghna (RV X.61.21), Aśvamedha (V.27.4-6), Aśvattha (VI.47.24), not more. But cf. Aśvin, "having horses". Mark the different position of aśva.
383. e.g. Aghraeratha, Xvaniratha, Frāyatratha, etc.
384. Rider = *sādin*, cf. RV I.162.17/163.9/V.61.3/AV XI.10.24, cf. *aśvasādin* in VS XXXI.13.
385. Particularly frequent in Sassanid art, if. the silver plates.
386. Yt V.53.
387. ib. 4, 101.
388. ib. 50.
389. cf. the formula "walking and running and riding and driving", e.g. Vend VIII.73.
390. e.g. by B. Schlerath, Die Indogermanen, Das Problem der Expansion eines Volkes im Lichte der sozialen Struktur, in: Innsbrucker Beiträge zur Sprachwissenschaft, Vorträge Nr. 8, Innsbruck 1973, p. 27. Moreover there is a terminological balance. Vedic *kṣatriya-kṣatra* denominates the human warrior class mainly, but Avestan *xshathrya-xshathra* the divine sovereignity only, whereas Avestan *rathaeštar* denominates the human warrior class, and Vedic *ratheṣtha*, *ratheṣṭhā* Indra only. cf. n. 245.
391. Yt XIV.9.
392. ib. VIII.20,21,26,27,30, etc.
393. ib., *passim*.
394. In form of a black horse Ahriman was ridden by Yima's brother Takhma Urupa. Afterwards he swallowed his rider, cf. Yt XV.12 and Mkh XXVII.32.
395. e.g. Gāh Usahin 3,4.
396. Sun according to Sīrōzah I.11/II.11,30/Y IV.16/VII.13/XVI.4/XXII.24/Yt VI.I, etc. Apam Napāt according to Sīrōzah II.7/Yt XIX.51, etc.
397. Yt XVII.1.
398. ib.12.
399. ib. X.66/Sīrōzah I.25.
400. Yt XV.57.
401. ib. XIV.39 (as white horse).
402. Puraṃdhi appears to have personified the *dakṣiṇā*.
403. Except Apāṃ Napāt, cf. RV II.31.6/II.35.1/VII.47.2.

404. Christensen, pp. 214ff.
405. Yt X.3.
406. ib. 30.
407. ib. 56.
408. ib. 47.
409. ib. 67.
410. ib. 125.
411. ib. 136.
412. ib. 70, 102.
413. Yt XIV.2,3, etc.
414. Yt X.102.
415. ib. 128 – 132.
416. ib. 15, 67.
417. ib. 60.
418. ib. 1, 3, 4, 5, 9, 39, 40, 41, 42, etc.
419. ib. 14 - 15.
420. Yt IX.1, 2, 4, 5, 6, 9, 11, 15, etc.
421. ib. 2.
422. J. Jablow, The Cheyenne in Plains Indian Trade Relations, 1795 – 1840, in: American Ethnological Society Monographs, 19, New York, 1951, pp. 1 – 10.
423. M.P. Grjaznov, Etapy razvitija chozjajstva skotovodčeskich plemem kazachstana i Junoj Sibiri v epochu bronzy, in: Kratkie soobščenija instituta archeologii, XXVI, Moskva 1957, str. 21 - 28. Or: Vostočnoe Priaral'e Srednaja Azija v ėpochu kamnja i bronzy, Moskva-Leningrad, 1966, str. 233 – 238 etc.
424. Their arrival probably induced the Mass Migration, which came to a halt only in the early Catholic Middle Ages, at the gates of Charlemagne's Frankish Empire.
425. Herodotus IV.2,11,47.
426. The history of the horse domestication raises some problems. The earliest indisputable evidence (2nd half of 4th mill. B.C.) is from the Neolithic Sredni Stog culture in the Dnieper and Don basins, where the domesticated horse played a large role in economy as a meat (and perhaps milk) animal. It may also have been ridden, for herding at least, because of antler objects, which have been found, resembling later cheekpieces of bits (Littauer-Crouwel, p. 25). Nevertheless it is not clear, whether the domesticated horse was known to the leading civilizations (of Elam, Mesopotamia) of the early 3rd mill.B.C. The basic early dynastic (ED) Sumerian term ANŠE appears to have been the generic term for equids like ass (*Equus asinus*) and hemione (*Equus hemionus*, ib. pp. 26ff.). The real horse (*Equus caballus*) made its (still very rare) appearance only in the later 3rd mill.B.C., when texts from the UR III, Akkadian, and Jamdat Nasr periods are occasionally referring to ANSE. LIBIR, ANŠE. ZI. ZI, and ANŠE. KUR. RA (ib. p. 43). Then, however, the horse was introduced to Mesopotamia from outside as domesticant (ib. p. 35). cf. also next note.
427. The ethnic origin of the horse domestication is rather problematic, too. The ethnic identity of the Sredni Stog people is not known. The Indo-Europeans may have had an important finger in the affair, but not have been the first domesticators of the horse. Their predecessors in the achievement may have been of Mongolian-Tungusian origin, and have inhabited the areas east of Middle Asia, which supply some osteological evidence for domesticated horses from the middle of the 3rd mill. B.C. (cf. F. Zeuner, A History of Domesticated Animals, London, 1963, and TIME-LIFE Book about Eurasia). Some details of the Germanic and particularly of the earliest Aryan horse terminology support the conjecture of Mongolian–Tungusian origin. cf. also note 433.

428. e.g. *iššua* (Hurrian), "horse", from Ved. *aśva*. *aššusanni* (Kikkuli), "equerry", from Ved. *aśva-śam*, "to train horses". *u̯ašanna* (Kikkuli), "racing course, stadium", from Ved. *vahana*, orig. *vaźhana*. *aika-*, *tēra-*, *panza-*, *šatta-*, *na* (+ *u̯a*)-*u̯artanna* (Kikkuli), "a racing course with one, three, five, seven, nine turning points", and Ved. * *eka-*, *tri-*, *pañca-*, *sapta-*, *nava-vartana*. *asuu̯aninni* (Alalah), "leading of horses", and Ved. * *aśva-nī*, "to lead horses". *babrunnu*, *paritannu*, *pinkarannu*, *zirannu* (Nuzi), "a horse of tawny, grey, reddish colour, a speedy horse" and Ved. *babhru*, *palita*, *pingala*, *jīra*. cf. Mayrhofer II, pp. 16ff.

429. Littauer-Crouwel, p. 83, as evidenced by Tell-el-Amarna and Hittite letters.

430. e.g. Tu(i)š(e)ratta, "having a fast chariot", *cf. RV tveṣaratha*. Birii̯aššuu̯a "fond of horses" cf. Ved. *priyāśva*. Or Aššazzana, "taking delight in horses" cf. Ved *aśvacanas*, etc. cf. Mayrhofer II, p. 21.

431. A *marya* obviously lived in his own house, cf. RV I.91.13/IX. 97.18. In both cases the *marya* is Soma, the bridegroom (about to marry) *par excellence*.

432. cf. Mayrhofer I, s.v. *marya*.

433. A. Salonen, Hippologia Accadica, Helsinki 1956, p. 210.

434. cf. RV X.85/AB IV. 7–9.

435. RV I.77.3/173.2.

436. ib. I.64.2/III.54.13/V.53.3/V.59.6/VII.56.1/X.77.2,3/78.1,4. The Maruts are the divine equivalents of the human *maryas*, cf. S. Wikander, Der Arische Männerbund, Studien zur Indo-Iranischen Sprach-und Religionsgeschichte, Lund, 1938, p. 83.

437. As in Pālī and other types of Prakrit clusters of consonants are replaced by geminations directed by the second component, e.g. *šatta* (Kikkuli), "seven", and Ved. *sapta*, or Aitaggama (a prince of Qadesh) and Ved. *iṭat/aiṭat* + *kāma/krama*. Bibliography concerning the prakritisms in Mayrhofer II, Sachregister p. 149.

438. The personal names make a particularly rich mine of comparisons. At least one name invokes a common ancestor. RV X.171.1 mentions a certain Iṭat ("speeding up"), whose name forms part of the aforesaid name Aitaggama (cf. n. 437), which may be translated as "descendant from Iṭat's clan" (*iṭat/aiṭat* + *krama*). Other personal names literally occur in the RV, e.g. Indaruta and Indrota-indraūta (RV VIII. 68.13), "upheld by Indra". Or Šubandu and Subandhu (X.59.8, 9/60.7, 10), "having a noble family". Or Tugra and Tugra (I.116.3/117.14/VI.20.18 etc.). A third group of Aryan names from Western Asia served as epithets to RV men or gods, e.g. Zitra and *citra*, "variegated, colourful". Or Šutatarra and *sudatra*, "bestowing good gifts", like Agni (VII.8.3), Tvaṣṭā (VII.34.22), or Sarasvatī's breasts (I.164.49). Or Kurtiu̯aza (Mattiu̯aza) and *gūrtavacas(tama)*, "softest-spoken", a characteristic of king Tūrvayāṇa (X.61.1, 2, 15). Or Šauššattarand *sukṣatra*, "ruling well", an epithet of the gods altogether (I.19.5), of Mitra (III.59.4), of Indra (V.38.1) etc. Again other names are so RV in spirit that they would not attract exotic attention were they to actually appear in the hymns, e.g. Artatama and *ṛtadhāman*, "abode of truth". Or Kirta and *kīrta*, "glorified", or Zirdamii̯ašda and *citramedhā* (from * *miyazdha*), "having a manifold sacrifice", etc. etc. Some even are of Hindu character: Šattiu̯aza (Mattiu̯aza) may be *śaktivacas*, "whose speech is (induced by) Śakti".

439. e.g. Mitra, Varuṇa, Indra, Nāsatya (Mattiu̯aza-treaty), Akni/Agni (Hittite texts), Surii̯aš/Sūrya, Maruttaš/Marut, Bugaš/Bhaga (Cassite), Šunaššura/*śunaḥśūra*/Indra "hero of the dog", cf. M 7, Kizzuwatna). Otherwise, of course, the Mitanni-Aryans took part in the Ancient Oriental syncretism, and also worshipped endemic Hurrian (Tešub, Šarruma, Hepat) or conquered Assyrian gods. The latter is testified by king Šuttarna's noble decision to send the idol of Ištar of Niniveh to Thebes, that it may cure his ailing son-in-law, pharaoh Amenophis III.

440. cf. E. Strommenger-Nagel, Reallexikon der Assyriologie 3, 1957 – 1971, p. 592.
441. ŚB I.5.4.6–12.
442. RV I.161.4, the verb is *nyañj-*, "to stick to".
443. ib. I.22.9/II.1.5/31.4/36.3/VI.50.13/VII.35.6.
444. c. 50 references in the RV.
445. RV VII.38.4.
446. MS I.6.12.
447. *jan*-creations cf. Deppert I, p. 1ff.
448. RV VI.55.4,5.
449. ib. I.141.2, 5.
450. ib. VII.66.2.(of Mitra and Varuṇa).
451. VI. 50.2.
452. I.113.19.
453. X.72.1–5/5.7 (Dakṣa hermaphrodite)/I.89.10 (Aditi hemaphrodite).
454. As Dakṣa's son Agni conceived his own father (III. 27.9), or became father of his father in the womb of his mother (VI. 16.35), or produces his mothers (I.95.4.).
455. X.5.7.
456. "Bestower of semen" (*retodhā,* MS IV.13.2), "having good semen" (*suretas,* VS XXVIII.32), "semen" (*turīpa,* MS III.11.11), moreover addressee of a ritual masturbation (KB XIX.6.).
457. RV IX.5.9. ("firstborn")/III.38.7/56.3 (hermaphrodite)/III.38.5. (older bull giving birth)/V.42.13 (incest with daughter).
458. BĀrUp 1.4.1–4.
459. The *logos*-creations are the base of highly philosophical Hindu speculations.
460. The river goddess Sarasvatī figures as Tvaṣṭā's daughter (?RV V.42.12), with whom he commits the creative incest (ib. 13). In Hinduism Sarasvatī takes the position of Vāc (as goddess of learning and speech). She, too, is involved in an incest, namely with Brahmā (e.g. Matsyapurāṇa III.32 – 49).
461. RV X.125.
462. Tvaṣṭā definitely is Indra's father, cf.RV II.17.6. in the context of I.32,2/52.7/61.6/121.3.
463. RV IV.18.
464. ŚB III.2.1.25–28.
465. MS I.6.12.
466. ib. II.1.2.
467. RV I.124.6. Uṣas libertine sexuality is often emphasized, cf. ib.7/VII.80.2/81.3, etc.
468. cf. n. 216.
469. RV I.113.19.
470. ŚB VI.I.3.7ff.
471. The Marut are *pṛśnimātaraḥ,* "having P. as mother" (RV I.23.10/38.4/85.2, etc.)
472. ib. VIII.85.8.
473. I.165.1/V.59.6/60.5, etc.
474. VI.66.3, cf. Rudra as father of the Marut I.114.6,9/II.33.1.
475. II.34.2/VI.66.1,4/VII.56.4
476. I.168.2. cf. also Hindu myths according to which the Marut came into existence as an abortion, after Indra had cut Diti's embryo into 49 pieces (Viṣṇupurāṇa I.21).
477. e.g. ŚB V.1.5.26.
478. e.g. ib. VI.1.2.1–13.
479. Cosmogonies of this type are rather frequent in the Brāhmaṇas, cf. ŚB II.2.4.1/5.11./VI.1.3.1ff./KS 11.5.
480. It may also denote the process of speaking words.

481. Related roots are *(vi-)kṣar-*, "to pour" (AV XIII. 3.2), or *si(ñ)c-*, "dto." (RV I.184. 1/KB XIX.6). As for the *sṛj-* creation of. Deppert I, pp. 26ff.
482. ŚB V.1.3.10.
483. Manu XII.121/Anugīta XXVII. 26.
484. e.g. ŚB VII.2.1.6/X.4.1.2/HGS 1.7.25.2, etc.
485. AV IV. 4.2.
486. Râ-Atûm ejaculating Shu and Tefnut.
487. AĀr II.1.3.1cf. ib. I.3.5.
488. ŚB VI. 2.2.6.
489. KB V.3 (beginning).
490. That is why he is associated with *aja,* the "unborn" he-goat, cf. ŚB III.3.3.8/V.2.1.24.
491. RV X.82.6, cf. I.67.5/164.6/VIII.41.10 (in the latter case Varuṇa is identified with the unborn creator by handicraft).
492. cf. RV I.71/III. 31.1–3/X.61.3–8.
493. JB III. 261–262.
494. e.g. ŚB I.7.4.1–4/II.1.2.6–10.
495. AB III. 33–34. As for the astronomical, seasonal, and zoological codes cf. Deppert I, pp. 100ff. 186-191.
496. KB VI. 1–9.
497. Deppert I, pp. 153ff., Deppert II, pp.37f.
498. RV X.68.2/V.3.2.
499. ib.
500. X.68.2.
501. cf. note 454.
502. RV IV.17.16, cf. V.32.2/X.32.1. Note also that Indra's wife is mentioned more often than the wives of other gods.
503. ib. VIII.91 (Apālā)/I.51.13 (Kakṣīvat). "100 years old" Kakṣīvat (IX. 74.8) was rejuvenated later on (cf. X.143.1).
504. X.39/40.
505. ŚB IV.1.5.1–15, cf. RV I.116.10/117.3/118.6, etc. Like Kakṣīvat Cyavana was rejuvenated.
506 cf. ĀpDhs II.6.13.1ff/BDhŚ II.9.16.3/GDhŚ IV.29, etc.
507. The term was coined by M.N. Srinivas, cf. his Caste in Modern India, London, 1962, particularly the chapter entitled a Note on Sanskritization and Westernization.
508. BDhŚ 1.6.16.1–5/Manu III.12ff.
509. GDhŚ IV.16/Manu X.8/Vas XVIII.8, cf. ApDhS I.18.19/Manu IV.215, etc.
510. A Niṣāda was supposed to live on fishing, aquatic hunting, cf. Manu X. 48.
511. Various types of hunters including the Niṣāda are invoked in Rudra's name in the so-called *śatarudriya* litanies of the Yajurveda, e.g. TS IV.5.4m–p/VS XVI.27 etc. Moreover it is noteworthy that other mixed castes like the Pukkasa or Paulkasa (cf. Manu. X.18), the Meda (ib. 36) etc. should live on hunting animals living in holes (ib. 49), or wild beasts (ib.48), etc.
512. During the rituals of the *tryambakahoma,* cf. ApŚS VIII.17.1 – 18.10.
513. cf. Deppert I, pp. 34 – 40, 102f.
514. Vas XXI.2/GDhŚ IV.25.
515. Vas XXI.I/ApDhS II.10.27.9ff., etc.
516. The so-called *niravasita*-Śūdras, the untouchables.
517. BDhŚ I.9.17.7/GDhŚ IV.17,18/Manu X.18/Vas XVIII.1/cf. also VS XXX.21. The Caṇḍāla had to live on executing criminals, cf. Manu X.56.
518. cf. Monier-Williams, Sanskrit Dictionary s.v. *śvapaca.*
519. Manu X.19.

520. ib.12/8/GDhŚ IV.16.
521. Indra's dog cooking may also conceal an astronomic code, namely the dogstar (Sirius), cf. Deppert I, p.199.
522. RV X.109/AV V.17.
523. AB IV.7–9/cf. RV X.85
524. RV I.116.17/117.13/119.3,5/IV.44.1,etc.
525. cf. TS VI.9.1.2 and G. Dumézil, L'idéologie tripartite des Indo-Européens, (Latomus XXXI), Bruxelles, 1958, p. 86.
526. e.g. TS I.8.10.2/TB I.7.4.2/6.4, etc.
527. RV.I.30.20.
528. ib.X.17.1–2.
529. cf. Deppert I. pp. 107f.
530. RV X.10.
531. ŚB I.8.3.6/ApDHS I.25.2/GDhŚ XXIII.8–11/Manu III.5/ IX.237/XI.172/Viṣṇu V.3–7/XXXIV.2, etc.
532. The rites are obligatory in the case of sons, but facultative in the case of daughters.
533. ŚGS 1.24.2.
534. ib.3/ApGS VI.15.1ff/AśGS I.15.1/GGS II.7.4.
535. ib. 20ff./AśGS I.15.2/HGS II.1.3.9/PGS I.16.4.
536. ib. 5ff.
537. GGS II.7.22.
538. HGS II.1.3.10.
539. ib.4.3ff./ApGS VI.15.5ff./GGS II.7.22.
540. cf. RV II.26.2/VI.9.2/VII.32.26/AB VIII.13.
541. ŚB IV.4.2.13.
542. ApDhS II.11.29.12.
543. Only few exceptions otherwise, e.g. metronymy in the case of Aitareya (from Itarā), or of Aupasvatī-putra, "son of a female descendent of Upasvat.
544. VA, p. 512.
545. e.g. Bhujyu exposed by his father (Tugra) on the ocean (RV I.119.19), or Ṛjrāśva blinded by his father (I.116.16/117.17–18).
546. Varuṇa exposes Vasiṣṭha on the ocean and punishes him — rather arbitrarily evidently – with dropsy (RV VII.86–89). He sends his (adopted) son Bhṛgu to hell (ŚB X.6.1.1–3) JB I.42–44). cf. also AB VII. 13–18. Varuṇa appears to be psychologically tormented and split in many respects, cf. Deppert II, p. 36.
547. Christensen, p. 308
548. Yt XIII.142/Dk VII.10.15–18.
549. SBE V, p.367 n. 1.
550. Her name was Dughdhava (Dūkdak Dūkdav̄ etc.), cf. SIS X.4/XII.11/Dk VII.2.39ff./ 3.4./Bund XXXII. 10, etc.
551. ib.9/Yt XVI.15,etc.
552. Dk VIII.7.20.DD LIV.1ff.
553. Dk.VIII.20.11.
554. ib.22.21.
555. SD X. 1ff.
556. ib.V.5/SIS XII.30.
557. ib. X.34ff./Dk VIII.29.6.
558. SBE V, p. 332 n.6.
559. Y I.6/II.6/Yt XIII.139–144, 148/Sīrōzah II.7/Gāh IV.2.
560. DK VIII. 43.18.
561. DD LIV.9.

562. Dk VIII.25.9.
563. I.136.
564. Christensen, p. 238.
565. References in Duchesne-Guillemin, p. 216f.
566. Bund XXXI. 1.4.
567. Earliest reference Y XIII.28.
568. cf. E.W. West, The Meaning of Khvētūk-Das or Khētūdād, in: SBE. XVIII, p. 389–430.
569. Herodotus III.31/Plutarch, Artaxerxes XXV/Diogenes Laërtius, Prooemium VI/Arnobius, Adversus Nationes.
570. RV I.134.3–5/VIII.46.26/I.122.3 (Vāta).
571. RV V.54.10.
572. I.184.1/III.39.3/IV.45.2,6/VII.69.5/71.1/72.4, etc.
573. As *lokapāla.*
574. RV VII.75.4.
575. III.58.8/V.50.3/74.8/VIII.26.6, etc.
576. I.168.5/V.58.5.
577. X,65.1,2/I.161.14 (Vāta).
578. X.136.
579. V.58.7/I.64.5/VIII.7.3,4,17.
580. Lightning and thunder with his *vajra,* rain according to IV.19.7/26.2.cf. also the Buddhist rain god Sakka=Śakra=Indra.
581. VII.40.6, cf. also Vāta and Parjanya, the rain god, side by side X.65.9/66.10.
582. c.95 references to Marut and rain in RV.
583. IX.49.1,3/97.17.
584. Indra's release of the rivers is the special message of the RV Vṛtra-myth, cf. I.32.
585. cf. IV.54.5.
586. Also *girisuta, giriśanta, giricara,* TS IV.5.Ic–e,36.
587. Kuiper 1960, 1964.
588. AV II.3.3/VI.109.3.
589. RV II.27.3.
590. ib. III.27.9,10,14 (in latter place Dakṣa is *the* Asura).
591. I.45.2,5/III.7.4/X.2.7/49.9.
592. e.g. IV.1.11.
593. V.85.3,4.
594. VII.34.10,11/VIII.41.2.
595. Viṣṇu XLI.2.
596. ŚB XII.9.2.4 (whirlpool is V's son or brother).
597. ib. V.3.4.12.
598. RV I.25.7/161.14/184.3/VII.87.6/AV IV.16.3, etc.
599. AV VII. 83.14.
600. Kuiper 1960, 1964.
601. RV I.35.2, 5, 9,10/II.38.3./V.81.4/VIII.27.10.
602. AV IV. 16.4.
603. RV VIII.41.3.
604. cf. ŚB V.2.5.17.
605. Yt IX.26/XIII.3.
606. Y I.11/XLIV.3.
607. Yt X.25.
608. Vṛtra has swallowed the rivers (RV 1V.17.I/V.32.2.), or lies around the rivers (II.11.2.9/III.32.11/33.6/IV.17.7, etc.). He has the form of a serpent (*ahi* I.32.4/51.4/

80.1/IV.19.2, etc.).

609. e.g. V.32.5,6/X.73.5.
610. I.32.9/III.30.8.
611. II.11.10/V.29.4, etc.
612. Since monsters are born from incest, cf. ŚB III. 2.1.25–28. On the other hand virginal birth is possible, on account of metronymy, matrilocality, etc.
613. cf. note 251.
614. TS II.5.1.1.
615. RV III.56.3 (three bellies and three udders).
616. RV X.8.8/99.6/ŚB I.6.3.1/TS II.5.1.1. (three heads, six eyes).
617. e.g. Tvaṣṭā bears the epithet *suśaraṇa,* "granting good shelter", RV V.42.13/VII.34.22.cf. M 15.
618. V. 67.4/VI.51.5/VII.66.6/VIII.27.14.
619. I.151.3, 4, 6/152.1/V.41.1/63.1/66.2/68.4/69.1/VII.64.2./66.13, cf. also their attribute *ṛtavṛdh* (I.2.8/23.5/, etc).
620. II.28.4/VI.42.4/V.66.1/VII.40.4./83.9, etc.
621. X.64.5 (Dakṣa)/I.22.6/II.38.2, 3, 6/X.10.5 (Tvaṣṭā-Savitā-Viśvarūpa)/II.3.9/III.59.2, 3 (Mitra)/I.24.10/25.1/II.28.8/III.55.18 (Varuṇa).
622. VIII.52.3 (Mitra)/V.63.7/72.3/X.65.5 (Mitravaruṇau)/VII.89.I5/IX.107.I5/X.167.3 (Varuṇa).
623. e.g. I.139.2/X.124.5.
624. I.24.9, 13, I5/V.85.7, 8/VII.60.5/88.6/89.5, etc.
625. I.24.15/25.21/II.27.16, etc.
626. ŚB IV.5.7.7f.
627. cf. M 15 and VIII.41.7.
628. IV.1.2.
629. I.24.14/IV.1.4/VII.62.4/84.2.
630. I.128.7.
631. V.85.5, 6/VIII.41.3/IX.73.9 (Varuṇa)/I.151.9/III.61.7/V.63.3, 4, 7 (Mitravaruṇau).
632. VI.48.14/VII.28.4/X.99.10/X.147.5. One exerts *māyā* like Varuṇa.
633. V.63.3, 7/IX.73.9/X.124.5/177.1.
634. II.27.16.
635. X.53.9.
636. VI.58.1.
637. I.11.7/56.3/IV.16.9/V.31.7/VI.20.4/X.138.3, etc.
638. e.g. III.61.6/V.63.3,4, 7/85.5, 6/VIII.41.3/X.73.9, etc.
639. I.11.7/51.5/80.7/II.17.5/IV.30.12/V.30.6.
640. Particularly in the hands of the demons or human sorcerers.
641. V.2.9/VI.20.4/46.9/VII.1.10/98.5/99.4, etc.
642. I.64.7/III.53.8/V.63.6/VI.47.18/58.1/X.53.9.
643. Duchesne-Guillemin, p. 27.
644. For the first time in Y XXX.
645. e.g. Dk VIII.9.2–3/Mkh VIII.1–39/DD XXXVII.44–57, etc.
646. Vend I.
647. Bund XIX.24–33.
648. 46ff.
649. cf. A.J. Carnoy, Iranian Mythology, New York 1964, p. 23.
650. cf. Vend VII.21.22/23–26.
651. RV X.124
652. The plants grew first, three ages (*triyuga*) before the gods (RV X. 97.1). Aditi entered the first age with her Āditya-sons (X.72.9, M 4b). cf. also AB VII.15.

653. cf. ŚB. VII.2.4.26/TS V.1.7.3. Formerly the plants ripened fruit thrice a year, nowadays only twice. The same idea in Greece and Rome: in the Golden Age the earth ripened fruits and plants by herself, if. Ovid, Met. I.1.
654. cf. M 7: Indra is the youngest among the gods. According to M 3b he and Mārttāṇḍa are the youngest among Aditi's children. According to the Brāhmaṇas the Asuras were the older brothers of the Devas.
655. Plants, incest, and very long life correlated in the Hindu and Jaina theories of the Golden Age. According to Hindus brother and sister live together, the earth ripened the plants, they lived for 6,000 years (Vāyupurāṇa VIII.22ff.). According to Jainas a brother-sister couple, supplied by wishing trees, even lived 8,400, 000, 000, 000, 000 years.
656. RV VI.21.3.
657. This in the frame of an astronomical/seasonal code. As Uṣas represents Aldebaran (cf. M 11) and Vala Orion (cf. Deppert I, p. 193) the question is of the sunrise in Taurus. In the year 1000 B.C. this event took place towards the end of April. However, the myth preserves reminiscences of a vernal equinox in Taurus (3400 – 1400 B.C.) , even in Orion (6000 – 3400 B.C.), because the passage night – day which it describes corresponds to the passage from *pitṛyāṇa* (autumnal – vernal equinox) to *devayāna* (vernal – autumnal equinox, cf. ib. pp. 177ff.).
658. M 11 encodes the same astronomical message as M 1a and M 1b. It even appears to commemorate a vernal equinox in Canis Maior (8000 – 6000 B.C.) inasmuch as Rudra represents Sirius (cf. n. I6). That does not mean that the present version of the myth is as old. It dates back to the vernal equinox in *apabharaṇīḥ* (beginning of Aries), and considers the precession of the equinoxes. Their typical astronomical events — the conjunction of the sun with Sirius, Orion, or Taurus — take place in April – June now, in other words in the hot and arid summer of Northern India, as referred to in the form of *Gazella gazella,* ass, and camel coming into existence at the end: these three animals typify aridity and are repeatedly associated with the summer season (Deppert I, pp. 100f, 190ff.). Nevertheless M 11 remains attached to the vernal equinox, because the blackbuck (*Antilope cervicapra*), into which Prajāpati transforms in order to commit incest in the beginning, mates between mid-February and mid-March (ib.).M 7 may also preserve reminiscences of former vernal equinoxes. Indra may represent Sirius (cf. n. 521), and Tvaṣṭā-Vṛtra represent Orion (ib. pp. 194ff). But a seasonal correlation with the vernal equinox is lost. Instead the myth takes the precession of the equinoxes into consideration. It refers to the end of the summer season close to the beginning of the monsoon. This may at least be inferred from the two mentions of the rain god Indra (RV IV.19.7/26.2) immediately attached to the hymn (IV. 18) dealing with M 7. (cf. also ib. p. 199). The independent Vṛtra-myth appears to corroborate the conclusion. Its oldest variants, still closer to the vernal equinox in Orion, speak of real rivers released from the grip of Vṛtra-Orion (= the thaw in the mountains). Later on these rivers change into celestial waters, and finally, when the conjunction of sun and Orion coincides with the beginning of the monsoon season, into rain.
659. KB XIX.3.
660. RV II.19.3.
661. ib. IV.30.3.
662. cf. notes 570–572.
663. RV I.92.2, 6.
664. ib. I.113.2, 3/III.55.11/X.61.4.
665. ŚB VII.2.1.18/3.2.8/7.1.8, etc.
666. ib. X.4.3.1ff./6.5.1ff.

667. KB II.9.
668. RV II.16.11
669. ib. I.92.10.11/124.2.
670. cf. Deppert I, p. 107.
671. RV X.72.8–9.
672. KS VIII.4
673. AB IV.10.15.
674. RV III.55.1.
675. III.53.7/X.67.2.
676. X.55.4.
677. I.64.2.
678. I.122.1/II.1.6/33.9/V.42.11/VIII.20.17.
679. I.174.1/VIII.90.6/X.99.2, 12/105.11.
680. IV.42.2.
681. VI.60.2/cf. VI.36.1.
682. V.58.2/63.6.
683. X.24.4.
684. I.11.7/51.5/80.7/IV.30.21/V.30.6.
685. IV.30.12.
686. X.53.9.
687. I.64.7.
688. V.63.6.
689. III.53.8.
690. VI.47.18.
691. X.17.1.
692. X.85.6–12.
693. III.39.3.
694. I.184.1.
694. I.184.1.
695. ib.4/V.73.3.
696. X.48.11.
697. III.49.1.
698. ŚB I.6.3.22.
699. Manu V.96/VII.4.
700. II.17.6.
701. JB III.26.2.
702. ŚB XI.2.3.1/VI.1.2.1–4.
703. ib. VI.1.3.7–8.
704. ib. 18/KB VI.2–9.
705. TS IV.5.1–11.
706. KB XXIX.7, cf. M 10.
707. TS II.1.4.3.
708. ŚB I.2.5.1/5.3.1/9.2.34, etc.
709. RV X.85.5.
710. ŚB IV.5.8.2/VI.5.3.7/VII.2.4.30.
711. AB I.19.1/KB VIII.4.
712. BĀrUp IV.4.20.
713. Kāṭha Upaniṣad II.18.
714. RV I.164.4.
715. ib. X.82.6.
716. ŚB VI.1.1.8/II.2.9.1.

717. ib. XIII.6.2.7–8/Bṛhaddevatā I.62.
718. BĀrUp I.4.10.
719. TUp Brahmānanda Vallī 9.
720. ChUp VIII.12.3.
721. Vend VI. 12–13.
722. ib. VIII.27–28.
723. VII.21–22.
724. RV I.113.12.
725. ib. I.44.14.
726. I.47.1, 3, 5.
727. VI, 59.4 (with Agni).
728. G. Dumézil, in: Revue des Etudes Latines, 32, pp. 139ff.
729. RV V.52.3, 6, cf. also c. 50 reference to their grooming, ornaments, etc.
730. e.g. he had seduced Menā (MS II.5.5/RV I.51.13/121.2/Ahalyā (ŚB III.3.4.18), etc.
731. The Aśvin were doctors (RV I.157.6.). The profession was despised (cf. TS VI.9.1.2). cf. also Deppert I, p.96.
732. Rudra was a doctor, too (RV II.33.4). As for his association with thieves, robbers, etc. cf. TS IV.5.3b–d/VS XVI.20cd/21, etc.
733. RV I.12.3/103.6.
734. ib. V.34.4–5.
735. X.99.5.
736. AB VII.28.1.
737. TS II.5.1–5.
738. ŚB I.7.3.1–8. cf. also Deppert I, pp. 109ff.
739. ŚB XIV.1.1.18–25/cf. RV I.116.12/119.9/117.22.
740. There are many indications for the Asuric roots of the caste of the Brahmins. Indra was accused of Brahmin slaughter having killed Viśvarūpa Tvāṣṭra. He, however, was a *purohita* (cf. TS II.5.1.1.). As the *purohita*-office was restricted to Brahmins only and hereditary within the *varṇa* of the Brahmins Tvaṣṭā must have been a Brahmin too. Moreover Mitra and Varuṇa represented the *brahman*-class among the gods, as G. Dumézil has demonstrated in his books. Practically all the hallmarks of brahminical life are prefigured in the Asuras. Viśvarūpa Tvaṣṭra sets the standards of commensality — he feeds the Asuras only and starves the Devas. The first critique in the consumption of alcohol, prefiguring the teetotalism of the Brahmins, is pronounced in a hymn dedicated to Varuṇa (VII.86.7). Brahminical vegetarianism is prefigured in the agriculture of the Asuras. The protection of the Brahmin's cow, first pronounced AV V.I8, conforms with and appears to be rooted in Zarathustra's Ahura religion (cf. text). The isogamy (endogamy) of the Brahmin-caste is anticipated by the incest of the Asuras. Moreover their creation by birth prefigures the emphasis on birth so typical of the Brahmin caste. And let us not forget that the whole system of brahminical values is a system of moral obligations.
741. cf. RV II.33.
742. RV I.62.9/101.1/178.2/129.4/173.9/II.20.3, etc.
743. ib. III.53.4–6.
744. X.82.3.
745. J. Darmesteter SBE XXIII, p.41.
746. RV X.15.14.
747. AV XVIII.2.34.
748. PGS III.10.2-4.
749. Aś GS IV.1.1–5.
750. Vend III.38–39.

751. ib. I.13, 17.
752. ib. VIII.73–74.
753. ib. VII.23–24.
754. Herodotus IV.25.
755. Vend VII.2, 7, 11 etc. (Nasū)/VIII.1–3 (purification or destruction of the house)/ib. 14–22 (purification of the way, which was quite complicated and depended on the willingness or unwillingness of two dogs ordered to walk on it).
756. ib. VIII.4–13/V.10–14.
757. VII.3 (this passage is from the Vendīdād Sādah).
758. SD XCVI.3/cf. ib. XLV.9 (the *ashem vohū*-formula is put into the mouth of the deceased).
759. Vend VIII.10.
760. The text reads: "Having stripped off their clothes". The commentary says: "As they are exchanged for the special clothes in which they carry corpses".
761. ib. III.14–21.
762. VI.45.
763. ib. 50, but cf. V.15–18. Here Ahura Mazda says that he sends the rains down (from lake Vourukasha) to cleanse the *daxmas*.
764. ib.46. If they don't they are flogged — twice 200 lashes, so Ahura Mazda says (48).
765. VIII.11–13.
766. SIS VIII.6/XVI.1–6.
767. Vend VIII.10 (a building of "clay, stones, and mortar"). Description according to SBE IV, p.xli n. 5.
768. ib. Under the Achaemenians the practice appears to have been restricted to the priests only. The rest of the Persians buried their dead after coating them with wax (Herodotus I.140).
769. De Bello Persico I.12.
770. Bund I.8, 18, 20, 22/III.1/XXXIV.1–9.
771. TB III.12.9.2.
772. Sukumar Sen, Old Persian Inscriptions, pp. 148–156.
773. HF I.4 (from Adam to Noah)/7 (from Shem to Abraham)/8–9 (from Isaac to Joseph and Jobab)/10 (from Abraham to departure of Israel from Egypt)/12 (from Abraham to David)/15 (from David to Babylonian Exile)/16 (from Exile to birth of Christ).
774. ib. I.5.
775. As for the classical and Renaissance reception of Zarathustra cf. SBE IV, pp. XIIff. Half the learned world doubted the authenticity of Anquétil's translation. A book full of such "silly tales, of laws and rules so absurd, of descriptions of gods and demons so grotesque could not be the work of a sage like Zoroaster." (ib. p. XVI) ... This, however, might only have been the surface of the shock. It rose from unconsciousness, perhaps, recognizing the origin of Christian Dualism.
776. Gospel of St. John I.1–3: "When all things began, the Word already was. The Word dwelt with God, and what God was, the Word was. The Word, then, was with God at the beginning, and through him all things came to be; no single thing was created without him." Luther's German translation is more precise (and closer to the Greek original) regarding Jesus Christ: "Im Anfang was das Wort, und das Wort was bei Gott, und Gott war das Wort. Und das Wort ward Fleisch und wohnte unter uns, und wir sahen seine Herrlichkeit, eine Herrlichkeit als des eingeborenen Sohnes vom Vater, voller Gnade und Wahrheit." That means: The Word became Flesh, became Christ on God's command.
777. Genesis I.3: "God said: 'Let there be light', and there was light." The same with the vault of heaven, the waters, plants, etc.

778. And probably denotes the "carpenter". In addition to his incest creation Tvaṣṭā, the "most skilful" (cf. n. 130), carpentered (*takṣ-*) Indra's *vajra* (cf. n. 244). According to the Nirukta *tvakṣ* is identical with *takṣ*, but emphasizes the creative power.

779. Gospel of St. Matthew XXVII.55: "A number of women were also present, watching from a distance; they had followed Jesus from Galilee, and waited on him."

780. e.g. on the Crucifix of St. Imerward (12–14 century) at Braunschweig. cf. Die Zeit der Staufer (Catalogue of the Stuttgart exhibition 1977), no. 462.

781. The names Ouranos and Varuṇa derive from the Indo-European root *u̯er*, "to cover, obstruct, isolate". Varuṇa presides over barley, and Ouranos is castrated on Gaia's instigation with a sickle. He is, in other words, cut like ripe corn. Attis is castrated too, and Varuṇa impotent (Śāṅkhāyana Śrauta Sūtra VI. 18.18/AV IV.4). Together with virginal birth these castrations give expression to an absolute maternal predominance. Both exclude paternal or male participation in creation. This view appears to be corroborated by Vṛtra, who is castrated (RV I.32.7), born from parthenogenesis (?), and living too close to his powerful mother Dānu (cf. notes 610–612). It may also be supported by the ritual castrations in the cultus of Hierapolis and Kybele. Both goddesses are conceived as virginal mothers. On the other hand the castrations conform with the vegetal life which the respective deities—even Vṛtra who is compared with reed (RV I.32.8) — embody. Vegetal life regenerates asexually. That is why the gods are born from parthenogenesis as if sprouted from their mother earth. And they are castrated as if to demonstrate that mother earth is not even dependent on incestuous fertilization. In cest, however, is the only form of sexuality associated with vegetal existence: the plants regenerate from their own flesh and blood, as it were, like members of one and the same family regenerate from incest.

782. Several other examples testify to the validity of the transformative formula. For example: Rudra is a doctor (cf. n. 732), the mole (*ākhu*) is his typical animal (cf. ApŚS VII.17.3). His son Gaṇeśa-Vinayaka presides over poetry (in Hinduism at least) and rides on a mouse. Within the same symbolism the parental relationship inverts in Greece: Apollo embodies poetry, his sacred animal is the mouse (cf. Apollon Smintheus). His son Asklepios is a doctor, his sacred animal is the mole (*skalops*), cf. H. Grégoire (avec la collaboration de R. Goossens et de M. Mathieu), Asklèpios, Apollon Smintheus et Rudra — Études sur le dieu à la taupe et le dieu au rat dans la Grèce et dans l'Inde, Bruxelles 1949.

   Moreover, according to M 15, Father Asura has swallowed his children embodying fire (Agni), ocean (Varuṇa), and grain or plants as such (Varuṇa, Soma). His oldest son Varuṇa may be castrated (cf. preceding note). Varuṇa's Greek namesake Ouranos is castrated, and his youngest son Kronos has swallowed his children, among them ocean (Poseidon), corn and agriculture as such (Demeter) and fire (Hestia).

783. RV VIII.29.3. *vāśī* is the carpenter's axe. Its activity is described with the root *takṣ* (cf. n.778 and X.53.10/101.1). But occasionally also the battle axe (e.g I.37.2/87.6).

784. cf. Deppert II, pp. 42ff. Literature concerning Telipinus: É. Laroche, Le dieu anatolien Sarrumma, in Syria, Revue d'art oriental et d'archéologie, XL, Paris 1963, and H. Otten, Die Überlieferungen des Telipinu-Mythos, in: Hethitische Texte, in Umschrift, mit Übersetzung und Erläuterungen, Heft VII, Leipzig 1942.

785. The "only son" is a mythological type figuring as such in single myths. In a system of myths several "only sons" may appear. That way the Weathergod of Heavens is the father of the only son Telipinus — according to the myth of T.'s wrath and disappearance — and of the only son rescuing him in the younger version of the Illuyankas-myth. Both sons are most important, T. for the welfare of the gods, men, animals, and plants. They starve, thirst, and whither when he vanishes. The son of the Illuyankas-myth, however, had been begotten by the Weathergod in order to regain his father's

eyes and heart, which Illuyankas had snatched away. He was successful because he married Illuyankas' daughter, and desired to be killed together with Illuyankas. Regarding the Vṛtra-myth and the Illuyankas-myth some inversive parallels may be added: Tvaṣṭā is the parent of Vṛtra (parental relation with the serpent) and killed against his will; the Weathergod's son is the son-in-law of Illuyankas (matrimonial relation with the serpent) and killed of his own accord. Tvaṣṭā is incestuous—the Weathergod's son born from a gaping exogamy (of his father, a god, and the daughter of the man "Poor"). Last but not least Indra is intoxicated with Soma and forsaken by all the gods apart from Viṣṇu when he kills Vṛtra — but all the gods help the Weathergods to kill Illuyankas who is drunk with liquor (according to the older version of the myth).

786. On occasion of the *ratnahavīṃśi* of the royal consecration the king offers a *caru* of *gavedhuka*-seeds (*Coix barbata*) to Rudra in the house of the royal "thrower of dice" (*akṣavāpa*) and the butcher (*govikartana*), cf. ŚB V.3.1.10.

787. Gospel of St. Mark XV. 33–35: "At midday a darkness fell over the whole land, which lasted till three in the afternoon: and at three Jesus cried aloud, *'Eli, Eli, lema sabachthani?'*, which means, 'My God, my God, why hast thou forsaken me?' " cf. St. Matthew XXVII.45–46.

788. St. Mark XV.24: "They divided his clothes among them, casting lots to decide what each shoud have." cf. St. Luke XXIII.35.

789. cf. note 787.

790. BĀrUp III.9.22.

791. ib. VI.4.1.

792. AUp II.1.

793. AV XI.8.29–30, in a hymn dedicated to the creation of man, the abode of all the gods and the whole universe.

794. ŚB X.6.5.9.

795. Tantrāloka XXXVII.56–57.

BIBLIOGRAPHY AND ABBREVIATIONS

Books quoted only once are mentioned in the notes)

AĀr	Airtareya Āraṇyaka, translated by A.B. Keith, New Delhi (Master Publishers),1981 (reprint).
AB	Aitareya Brāhmaṇa, translated by A.B. Keith, HOS XXV.
ĀpDhS	Āpastambīya Dharma Sūtra, translated by Georg Bühler, SBE II.
pGS	Āpastrambīya Gṛhya Sūtra, translated by H. Oldenberg, SBE XXX.
ĀpŚS	Āpastambīya Śrauta Sūtra.
ĀśGS	Āśvalāyana Gṛhya Sūtra, translated by H. Oldenberg, SBE XXIX.
AUp	Aitareya Upaniṣad, translated by R.R. Mitra, E.B. Cowell, and E. Roar, in: The Twelve Principal Upaniṣads, Delhi (Nag Publishers), 1978.
Av.	Avestan.
AV	Atharva Veda, translated by R.T.H. Griffith, Chowkhamba Sanskrit Studies LXV-LXVI.
BĀrUP	Bṛhadāraṇyaka Upaniṣad, translated by F.M. Müller SBE XV.
BDhŚ	Baudhāyana Dharma Śāstra, translated by G. Bühler SBE XIV.
Bund	Bundahish, translated by E.W. West, SBE V.
Ch Up	Chāndogya Upaniṣad, translated by F.M. Müller, SBE I.

Christensen	A. Christensen, Die Iraner, in: Handbuch der Altertumswissenschaft. Dritte Abteilung, erster Teil, dritter Band, dritter Abschnitt, erste Lieferung, München, 1933.
DD	Dādistān-ī Dīnīk, translated by E.W. West, SBE XVIII
Deppert I	J. Deppert, Rudras Geburt — Systematische Untersuchungen zum Inzest in der Mythologie der Brāhmaṇas, Wiesbaden (Steiner), 1977 (Beiträge zur Südasienforschung 28).
Deppert II	J. Deppert, Der Vater in der vedischen und seine Transformationen in der westlichen Mythologie, in: H. Tellenbach (Editor), Vaterbilder in Kulturen Asiens, Afrikas und Ozeaniens, Stuttgart (Kohlhaammer) 1979.
Dk	Dīnkard, translated by E.W. West, SBE XXXVII.
Duchesne-Guillemin	J. Duchesne-Guillemin, La religion de l'Iran ancien, Paris (Presses Universitaires de France), 1962.
GDhŚ	Gautama Dharma Śāstra, translated G. Bühler SBE II.
GGS	Gobhila Gṛhya Sūtra, translated by H. Oldenberg SBE XXX.
HF	Gregory of Tours, Historia Francorum, translated by L. Thorpe, Penguin Classics.
HGS	Hiraṇyakeśin Gṛhya Sūtra, translated by H. Oldenberg SBE XXX.
HOS	Harvard Oriental Series, edited by C.R. Lanman, Cambridge (Mass.).
IIJ	Indo Iranian Journal.
JB	Jaiminiya Brāhmaṇa, translated by W. Caland, Verhandelingen der koninklijke Akademie der Wetenschappen te Amsterdan, Afdeelung Letterkunde, Niewe Reeks Deel 19.4.
Kuiper 1960	F.B.J. Kuiper, The Ancient Aryan Verbal Contest, in: IIJ IV, 1960, pp. 217–281.
Kuiper 1964	F.B.J. Kuiper, The Bliss of *asha,* in: IIJ VIII, 1964, pp. 96 – 129.
KB	Kauṣītaki Brāhmaṇa, translated by A.B. Keith, HOS XXV.
KS	Kāṭhaka Saṃhitā.
Littauer-Crouwel	M.A. Littauer and J.H. Crouwel, Wheeled Vehicles and Ridden Animals in the Ancient Near East, in: Handbuch der Orientalistik, Siebente Abteilung, 1. Band, 2. Abschnitt, B – Vorderasien, Lieferung 1, Leiden-Köln (Brill), 1979.
M	Myth.
Manu	Manusmṛti, translated by G. Bühler SBE XXV.
Mayrhofer I	M. Mayrhofer, Kurzgefasstes etymologisches Wörterbuch des Altindischen, Heidelberg (Winter), 1956ff.
Mayrhofer II	M. Mayrhofer, Die Indo-Arier im Alten Vorderasien, Wiesbaden (Harrassowitz), 1966.
Mkh	Dīnā-ī Maīnōg-ī Khirad, translated by E.W. West SBE XXIV.
MS	Maitrāyaṇī Saṃhitā.
PB	Pañcaviṃśa Brāhmaṇa, translated by W. Caland, Calcutta (Biblioteca Indica 285), 1931.
PGS	Pāraskara Gṛhya Sūtra, translated by H. Oldenberg SBE XXIX.
Rau	W. Rau, Staat und Gesellschaft im Alten Indien nach den Brāhmaṇa-texten dargestellt, Wiesbaden (Harrassowitz), 1957.
RV	Ṛgvedic, Ṛgveda, translated by K.F. Geldner, HOS XXXIII – XXXVI.
ŚB	Śatapatha Brāhmaṇa, translated by J. Eggeling SBE XII, XXVI, XLI, XLIII, XLIV.
SBE	Sacred Books of the East, edited by F.M. Müller, reprinted by Motilal

	Barnasidass, 1965, 1970, 1977.
SD	Sad Dar, translated by E.W. West SBE XXIV.
ŚGS	Śāṅkhāyana Gṛhya Sūtra, translated by H. Oldenberg SBE XXIX.
SlS	Shāyast Lā-Shāyast, translated by E.W. West SBE V.
TĀr	Taittirīya Āraṇyaka.
TB	Taittirīya Brāhmaṇa.
TS	Taittirīya Saṃhitā, translated by A.B. Keith HOS XVIII - XIX.
TUp	Taittirīya Upaniṣad, translated by F.M. Müller SBE XV.
VA	R.C. Majumdar (editor), The Vedic Age, History and Culture of the Indian People, vol.I, Bombay 1971.
Vas	Vasiṣṭha, translated by G. Bühler SBE XIV.
Vend	Vendīdād, translated by J. Darmesteter SBE IV.
VI	A.A. Macdonell and A.B. Keith, Vedic Index of Names and Subjects, Delhi-Varanasi-Patna (Motilal Barnasidass), 1982 (reprint).
Viṣṇu	Viṣṇu's Institutes, translated by J. Jolly SBE VII.
VM	A. Hillebrandt, Vedische Mythologie, Band I - III, Breslau, 1891, 1899, 1902.
VS	Vājasaneyi Saṃhitā.
Y	Yasna, translated by L.H. Mills SBE XXXI.
Yt	Yasht, translated by J. Darmesteter SBE XXIII.

Urban Centres of Western India and the Western World

R.N. MEHTA
Baroda

To commemorate Dr Hermann Goetz, who spent most of his time in Baroda in India, it was thought that in this *śrāddha,* the *tarpaṇa* should be an account of the region where he worked. With such a feeling, the subject the Urban Centres of Western India and the Western World would be appropriate and adequate *añjali.*

The choice of the subject rests on the understanding of two concepts: one of them is "Urban" and the other is "The Western World". The term urban simply means a fortified habitation in its original sense, but the tendency to extend its meaning by contrasting it with rural, suggests that urban habitation has non-agricultural connotations. This extreme classification in economic terms is not observable in practice because there are agricultural centres with many non-agricultural workers living in them and in the so-called urban centres, agricultural activities can also be witnessed. To circumvent this situation, census authorities define the term on the basis of population. On a global scale, countries use different standards, so the minimum number of people constituting an urban centre is more than 200 and the maximum number is more than 5000. Thus, it is seen that the term has many shades of meaning and therefore, in the present context, urban centres are understood as the habitats, where clear evidence of the activities of imports is available.

Similarly the idea of the Western World also requires analysis. *Kaṇāda* explains that direction is a relative term. From an Indian point of view the areas from Iran to the Atlantic ocean and beyond could be classified as the Western World. If the Islamic practice in India is followed, Arabistan, Syria, Iraq and other countries will have to be defined as West, because all Muslims in India offer their prayer by facing west.

From the viewpoint of the countries from Portugal to Germany, the area from Poland to the Pacific becomes east, and therefore they talk of "Ost Probleme" (Eastern Question), etc., when they deal with countries in Eastern Europe and beyond. Many of them from an Indian viewpoint are in the West. Under this condition, as we are meeting in India, it is better to follow the Indian viewpoint while discussing the urban centres of Western India and the Western World.

The subject under discussion belongs to bygone ages and therefore one has to rely on oral tradition, literary sources and archaeological remains for a clear understanding of the activities. In the present paper the archaeological sources are given prominence because of the special consideration of the contribution of Dr Goetz in the field of Indian studies.

It could be pointed out that art historical discussions in India prior to the contributions of Dr Goetz generally endorsed the view of the static, unchanging nature of Indian art. This view that Indian art was tradition bound and did not change for centuries, was effectively challenged by Dr Goetz and he emphasized that like European art, Indian art has also changed according to time and place. This dynamic view of art presented in the art-historical studies was further strengthened by him specially in the study of the cave temples of Ellora by indicating stratigraphic changes that proved that the work was undertaken at different times.

This viewpoint of dynamic changes with the passage of time is well known to archaeologists, who explore and excavate the material remains of past human activities. These activities in Western India have revealed two types of antiquities that help in understanding the contacts with the Western World. One type of antiquities are small portable ones that could be easily imported or exported. The second type covers larger structures that are in different stages of preservation.

The first type of antiquities includes bronze objects, stone objects, metals and ceramics, whereas the other type includes prayer halls, houses, churches, cemeteries, etc. A study of both types of antiquities indicates that the contacts of the Western World in the centres of Western India could be chronologically classified into the following groups:

1. Chalcolithic contacts—*circa* 3000 - 2000 B.C.
2. Contacts with the Graeco-Roman World—*circa* 6th century B.C. - 6th century A.D.
3. Contacts with the Arab World—*circa* 7th century A.D. to present day.
4. Contacts with Europe—*circa* 15th century to present day.

A perusal of the contacts of the chalcolithic period that were available at the centres like Lothal and in West Asia suggests that during this period, the areas of contact were around the cities of West Asia. The indications of common techniques of ceramics known as Black-Topped Wares or Black and Red Wares, and of the crested ridge for stone blades are significant and possibilites of contact at least up to the Mediterranean could be visualized. However, these indicators require further work to expand the hypothesis of contacts. These contacts slowly withered away after about the middle of the second millenium B.C.

With the rise of the Iranian Power and its link with the Greek cities on one side and the Indus on the other, contact was established with Eastern Europe. This has led to knowledge of the Yavanas in India and that of Indians to the Greeks. Specially the Iranians had dispersed the Greeks in Central Asia, and from these centres, the Greeks came in closer contact with India. This Indo-Greek contact was known in the cities of Punjab and U.P., but was not extensive in Western India. Their coins are found in centres like Hathab in Saurastra or Kadiadunger mines near Bharuch. On the basis of the few references and antiquities the picture of large Indo-Greek kingdoms developed by scholars like Tarn would however require further proof before acceptance.

In this context, an interesting point is the appointment of Yavanaraja Tusaspa by Aṣhoka in Western India. He was responsible for the construction of channels at the famous Sudarśana lake (Fig. 1) of Junagarh. This tank was developed by Puṣyagupta the Vaiṣya minister of Candragupta, who had defeated Seleukos Nikator. The later Greek contact had contributed the legend on coins that are found from many sites of Western India.

Extensive evidence of contact with the Roman World is obtained from the towns of Western India. Significantly, the first Roman antiquity obtained from archaeological work was found at Ankoṭṭaka, a district headquarters near which modern Vadodara began developing as a suburb and later on engulfed it. In this process, the ancient Ankoṭṭaka turned into Akota, a suburb of Baroda or Vadodara. The mounds representing this town revealed the presence of a trefoil neck and a curved handle of bronze (Fig. 2.). The lower end of this handle carried a decoration of Cupid on a boat playing with a car. This motif was identified by Dr H. Goetz and the antiquity was published in the Bulletin of the Baroda Museum and Picture Gallery by its discoverer Shri M.D. Desai.

This discovery of the antiquity from the Roman World helped to push the chronology of Ankoṭṭaka to an earlier period of about 1st/2nd century A.D. and give indications of further work in this town.

The explorations of Ankoṭṭaka led to the discovery of the Jain bronzes that had important bearings on Art history. Excavations at this site brought to light the terracotta seals with prancing horses (Fig. 3) and other objects, structures and helped in the study of the ancient history of this area.

These discoveries helped to prove one of the ideas of Dr Goetz. He was of the opinion that Western India had its own art tradition. This opinion was shared by another distinguished scholar Dr U.P. Shah. The study of the images discovered in the Sabarkantha district, and those of Vasant Gadh reinforced this thought. But the discovery of the Jain bronzes at Akota ultimately helped to prove the point, and gave further impetus to the study of sculptures of pre-Cālukyan period in the region.

The discovery of Roman bronze was highly significant as it indicated that some of the ports that were described by the anonymous Greek navigator not only imported the materials from the Western world, but also transmitted them to the hinterland. If this process were accepted and studied, it might help in tracing the habitats and routes that existed in this area, and would help in chronological studies also.

Following this line of thought, in the forties of the present century Sir Mortimer Wheeler, Director General of Archaeology, was also active in South India. He knew the Roman antiquities well, and therefore he was surprised to find them at Arikamedu. This discovery was taken up by him in his excavations at Arikamedu. It was pointed out that from the Roman world amphorae, and terra sigillata, aretine ware, came to India. Thus the repertory of import from the Roman world included coins, bronze objects, ceramics. These were important tools for investigation at Western Indian sites.

The investigations at Karvan, at a distance of about thirty kilometers to the South of Ankoṭṭaka, revealed the existence of a cameo of a patrician lady from the Roman world (Fig.4). This fine specimen of the Lakulīśa cult indicated that materials from Roman ateliers probably came to Barygaza or Bharuch, situated at a distance of about fifty kilometers to the south of Karvan. The site of Timbarva between Bharuch and Karvan yielded contemporary ceramics and thus suggested the existence of a land route, that was vaguely known to literature.

The Karvan settlement of about 500 x 500 meters was later on studied by Dr Margabandhu, who recovered intaglio also from the Roman world. The explorations of Bharuch led to the discovery of the contemporary antiquities. These discoveries helped in understanding the chronology and parts of the trade routes and centres like Timbarva, Karvan and Ankoṭṭaka.

This line of inquiry was pursued and it was found that the site at Ajabpura on the Mahi revealed the presence of amphora-sherds, along with coins of the Kṣatrapas. This site connected the Narmada Valley and the Mahi Valley. The discovery of Kṣatrapa coins from Tarsang on the Mahi suggested that this route might have been used. From a large site of Jalat near Doha also, similar antiquities were obtained. All these centres suggested that from Bharuch the imported materials moved inland on a route. Similarly the discovery at Sathod, an important settlement near Dabhoi, of the Roman amphora suggested that the route had bifurcated in other directions, probably in the Narmada Valley. Probably these were the centres on the famous Ujjain-Bharukacch route known to literature.

Along with these features, a very interesting discovery of an amphora was made in the excavations at Devnimori. There from outside of a Mahavihara, amphora sherds were obtained. This Mahavihara existed near Mahastupa (Fig.5) in which relics of Dasabala were installed. This circumstantial evidence led to the inquiry of the laity of the Buddhists that might have supplied the materials to their monks. There was some black material sticking to the sherds. Upon examination it was discovered that the material was resinous. Thus indications of the import of possibly wine were ascertained. Whether it was consumed by the monks or was served to the laity is a moot point.

This Roman material suggested that the urban centre of Shamalaji might have supplied this material to the Suburban *mahāvihāra*. Fortunately the excavations at Shamalaji, a site on the opposite side of the Meshvo, supported the suggestion. At Shamalaji during its period of prosperity, the Roman material arrived and from there, it went to Devnimori and other sites. Shamalaji was a true urban centre with its fort walls of bricks, and seemed to be strategically situated on the route connecting the coastal plain of Gujarat with the interior region of Udaipur and beyond. But, the problem about the entrepot of the Roman goods required solution.

The Sabarkantha district is on the east of Kheda district that abuts the sea. With the indication of the involvement of the Buddhists as one of the parties engaged in foreign trade, the explorations at Nagara, where a sand-stone figure of Buddha was known, proved meaningful. From Nagara, a settlement of about 1st millenium B.C., amphora sherds (Fig.6) were discovered. A clay seal with a figure of an owl was another indicator.

Nagara was a flourishing open town, which was prosperous and started importing Roman goods. From the excavations, conducted at this site, charcoal was discovered and analysed for 14_c. It was calculated at 1945 ± 90 and 2030 ± 105 years. Thus the indication of the import of the amphora found in the same layer suggests the period of 2nd/1st century B.C. as the beginning of this sea-borne trade on the Western littoral.

The excavations revealed another fact, that the site showed marked prosperity from this period. Good houses, large hearths for mass cooking were seen to begin from this period and continued for some time. This prosperity was commercial, and it began shrinking after about 7th/8th century A.D. The reason for this shrinkage was the drying up of the local water channel. This led to the search for a better port, which was located and developed at Cambay, situated in the vicinity of Nagara.

After the development of Cambay at a distance of about five kilometers to the south of Nagara, it was often mentioned by Arab and European travellers while Nagara does not find a place in these travelogues though it continued to exist as a suburb of Cambay, but in local records it is noted in inscription. Inquiry at Nagara provided the necessary background for tracing the route on which the Roman goods moved to Shamalaji. The settlements at Tarapur, Dehgan, and Kathlal provided some useful data. Thus another route was traced. It connected the Western Indian Urban settlements to the materials from the Western World. Another route from this centre possibly turned to the north and perhaps connected Kheda, Dholka from which contemporary materials including the Red polished ware, other Indian ceramics, and Kṣatrapa objects were found. From these sites the Roman goods moved towards Modhera and Vadnagar which were important urban centres. At Modhera amphora sherds were obtained, while at Vadnagar the Red polished ware and clay bullae were obtained. Modhera has a large mound of about a square kilometer; the same situation exists at Vadnagar where the area outside the fort is much larger. Vadnagar was visited by Hsuien Tsang who described it as a large town. If one takes the suburban area around the nucleus into consideration the information supplied by the Chinese pilgrim in the 7th century would seem to be valid.

From Vadnagar, possibly the routes ran towards the North and East. On the East further work is necessary to identify the Roman material. Till this day only the evidence of Buddhists is available. But in the North an important settlement of Shrimala or Bhinnamala exists in Southern Rajasthan.

Bhinnamala also known as Shrimala, was a large urban centre. From this urban settlement amphora and Red Polished ware were discovered. This important settlement had supplied a number of ministers to the Cālukyas, and the great Sanskrit writer Māgha was from this place.

It was interesting to see that the entrepôts of the materials from the western world on coastal Gujarat were active. Bharuch, Nagara, Variav, Kamrej were such important centres. But the urban centres of Saurastra peninsula also, it was thought, might be active. Some indications of Saurastra were given while noting the inscription at Junagadh.

Junagadh was surveyed recently. On the bank of the Sonarekh, the *Suvarṇasikta* of the inscriptions, at several places amphora sherds were discovered. These sherds indicate along with the Red polished ware that into this famous capital of western India goods arrived from the Western World. Geographically it is an inland town and therefore the goods might have moved from some entrepôt on the coast.

Fig. 1 The Earthwork at Sudarśana Tank, Junagadh.

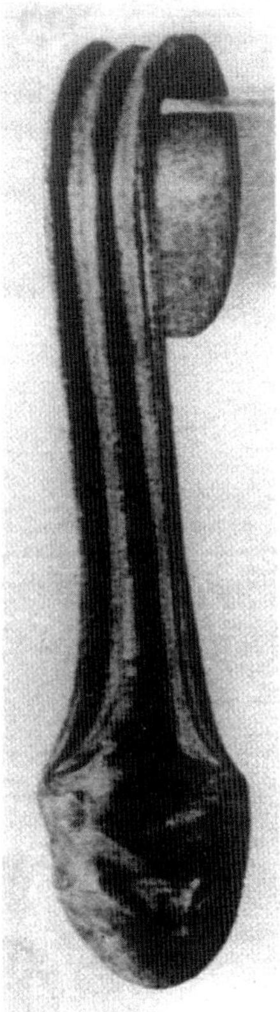

Fig.4 Cameo from Karvan.

Fig.2 Bronze handle from Aṅkoṭṭaka.

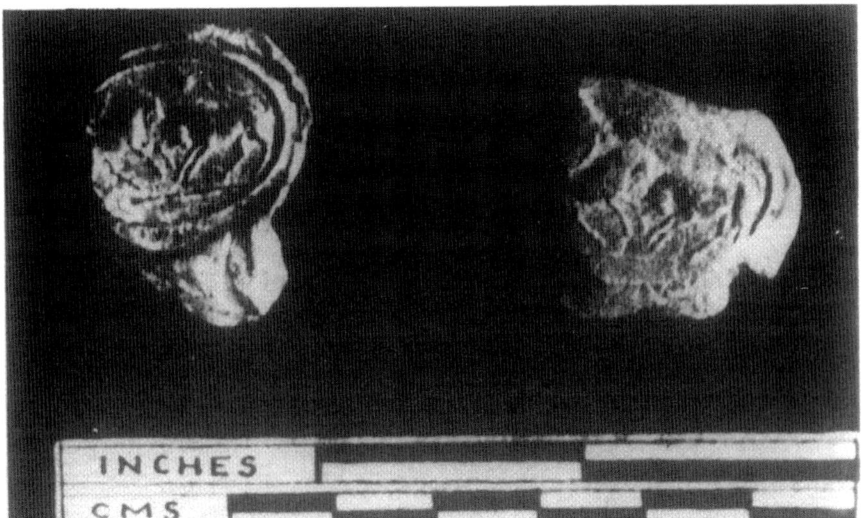

Fig.3 Terracotta seals with prancing horses.

Fig.5 Mahastupa at Devnimori.

Fig.6 Lower part of an amphora from Nagara.

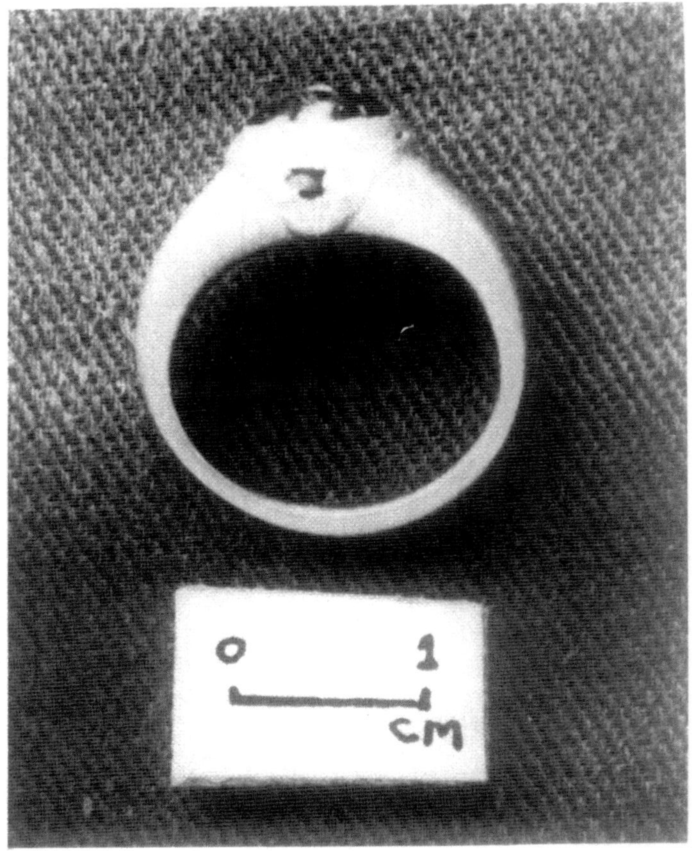

Fig.7 Hollow gold ring from Valabhipur with intaglio of garnet.

Fig.8 A Christian Prayer Hall at Champaner.

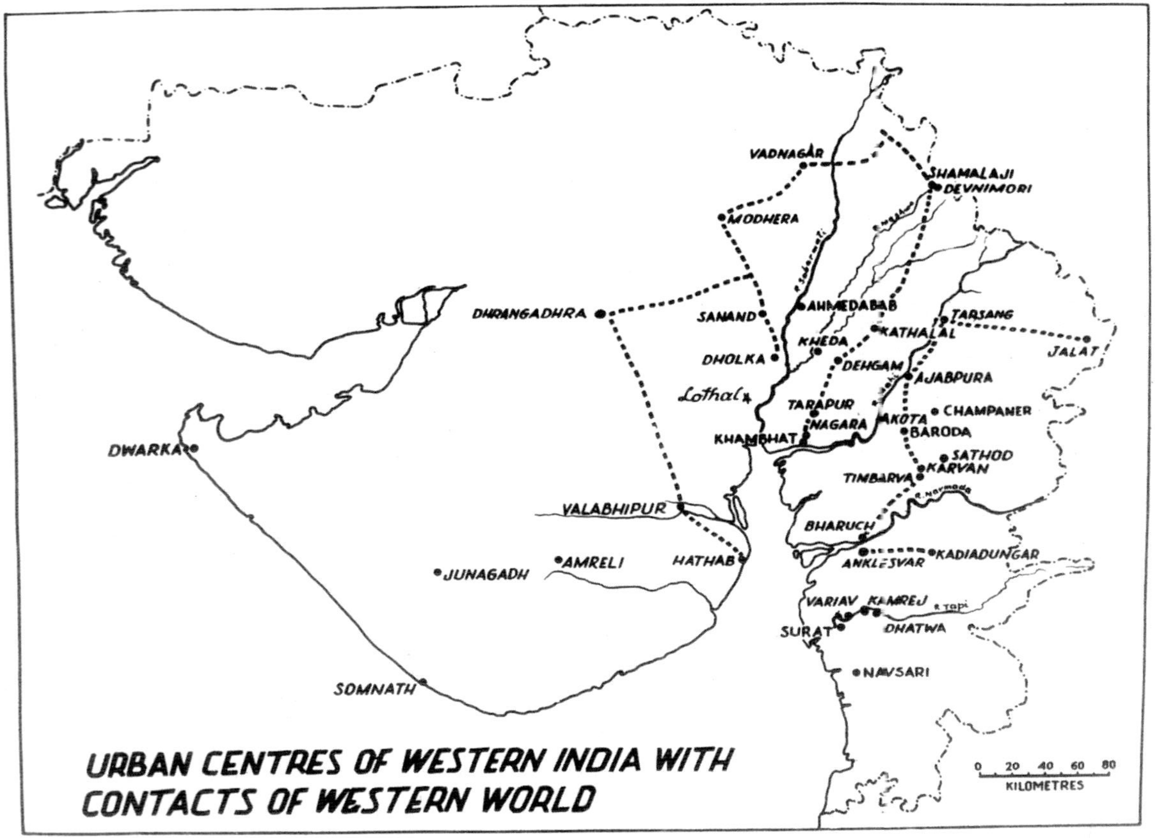

URBAN CENTRES OF WESTERN INDIA WITH CONTACTS OF WESTERN WORLD

Fig.9.

Fortunately several coastal cities like Valabhipur, Somnath, Dwarka indicated these contacts. Out of these cities the evidence from Valabhipur sheds much light on the politico-social conditions of this area. It is well known that after the collapse of the Gupta power, the Maitrakas became powerful in this area. Their copper plates indicate that their capital was Valabhi. The opening lines of these copper plates indicate that Senāpati Bhattarka received military assistance from the *maula, bharta* and *śreṇi bala*. Here the important term *śreṇi* indicates the security force of the trading guilds. From which area of Saurastra would such a force be collected?

It is clear that the Maitrakas preferred Valabhi as a capital. Investigations at Valabhi proved very useful because the site yielded a rich harvest of amphorae, intaglios as well as a hollowgold ring (Fig.7) with an intaglio of garnet representing a running horse. Systematic excavations at this site also proved that the Roman material was available at the base on the natural earth. About it there were sufficient deposits on which the layers of Maitraka period were laid. This excavation was on the periphery of the site, so it indicates that the town had at least expanded with the Roman trade. There were *sārthavāhas* and traders on the sea at Valabhi and Hathab if the evidence of literature be taken into consideration. This archaeological and literary evidence suggests that the *śreṇi bala* that helped the Maitrakas was provided by the merchant *śreṇis* of Valabhi region. The assistance might have led to the transfer of the capital of Western India from Junagadh to Valabhi.

Interestingly the commercial interests supported the political power that suited them, but the later records suggest that the commercial interests of Valabhi were responsible for inviting the Arabs to attack it in the 8th century A.D. Thus this urban centre points to the changing relationship between the commercial and the political power.

The decline of the central administration of Rome, the growth of the Eastern Roman or Byzantine Empire and the development of Islam in Arabia contributed to the slow collapse of this important phase of the contact with the Western world and the beginning of a new phase in which the Iranians and Arabs played a major role. Significantly in the Arab world, cities like Hatra, Petra existed. In the latter town Dr Goetz had identified structures with Indian affinities. The sculptures discovered from these settlements in the Arab world indicate that Indian communities had settled in this region. From tombs in Arabistan at Jawan, north of Ratif, material from India, Parthia and the Roman Hellenistic world was obtained from deposits of *circa* 500 years before *hijra* era — about second century A.D. These evidences suggest long-standing contact with the Arab world. After the growth of Basrah, the sea route became very important and was known at Bakhailal to Indian navigators. These contacts led to the growth that is reflected in the Arab world in which the acceptance of Indian numerals, stories of Pañcatantra and some aspects of medical knowledge, indicate that the contacts with the Western world in the period from about 7th century to the 15th were a continuation of earlier contacts.

On the other hand the merchants of the Arab world used to come to the ports of Western India. The references indicate their presence at towns like Cambay, Ghogha, Somnath, where even their masjids existed.

In the 8th century these Arabs attacked the cities of Western India, but Avani Janaśraya Pulakeśirāja defeated them at Navasari, an important town of South Gujarat. Their successors the Rāṣṭrakuṭas brought the territories conquered by the Arabs under their control. The Chichini plates indicate that Rāṣṭrakuṭas had recruited some of their officers also from this regionn

These contacts with the Western World continued to exist from the port towns of Western India. From cities like Cambay and Surat many pilgrims used to go to Mecca. Gujarat had wide contacts with Mecca and therefore the Sultans of this part used to send their treasures also to the holy city for protection. This mutual relationship was shattered towards the close of the 15th and the beginning of the 16th century by the Portuguese.

The perusal of this phenomenon indicates that the political powers of Western Indian and Egypt put up a joint resistance. But the collapse of the local administration in Gujarat after 1536 was responsible for the stable control by Div and Daman by the Portuguese. In this period the Portuguese were defeated in the battle of Chaul and some of them were captured after their ship was wrecked at Bassin.

These captives were brought to Champaner where an interesting monument exists. Champaner was a very large settlement with its suburban area spreading to about ten kilometers from its centre. In this town a prayer hall (Fig.8) was built, possibly by Malek Gopi, perhaps at the order of Mehmid Begda for the Christian Portuguese. This monument indicates the Indian spirit of religious tolerance and respect for other cultures.

The activities of the Portuguese in India and those of Spain and England in other parts of the world indicated that they were marked by intolerance, destruction of other cultures, enslavement of other groups and often wanton slaughter. This Euro-centric attitude was resented and different countries reacted in different ways. In India, the European contact that was renewed from the 16th century was essentially commercial in the beginning. The urban centres like Surat, Ahmedabad, Baroda, Champaner and others used to supply manufactured goods to Europe. These industries existed in India up to the 18th century and their traditions were preserved in many Indian states, where the destructive economic policies of the British were felt to a limited extent.

The collapse of the Indian political power in the 18th century and the struggle for supremacy during that century also resulted in the use of the *śreṇibala* of the English, much like its use during the time of the Maitrakas. But mercantile exploitation was the chief motive of the Europeans like the British, French and Portuguese. This had world-wide repercussions in their mutual wars and cruel treatment of others. In India the British *śreṇibala* succeeded in parts of the country. They moved from 1740 to about 1848 — a period of about a hundred and eight years — to conquer India, mainly for economic exploitation. The East India Company of the English tried to perpetuate its power through the education policy framed around 1832 A.D. This led to a lot of contact with the Western world for Indian towns and people.

However, after 1885 India had to wage political struggle for about sixty-two years to achieve the objective of political freedom. But it was essential to secure cultural freedom also.

In this struggle for cultural freedom Indian and European scholars like Rammohan Roy, Ananda Coomaraswamy, E.B. Havell, Vasudeva Saran Agrawala, and Dr Hermann Goetz played their own role in the sphere of art history and archaeological studies. These studies indicate that the contact of the urban centres of Western India with the Western World was long standing. This contact was strong when there were powerful centres in the West and in India, and was beneficial to both the groups, but when heavy exploitative attitudes were taken there was equally strong resistance and better sense was also prevailing in certain circles.

At the end, I should like to say that Dr Goetz contributed substantially to the idea of cultural freedom by demonstrating through his writings that Indian arts experience was similar to European experience and was equally self sufficient. Similarly the archaeological search of the urban centres of Western India (Fig.9) and its contact with the Western world indicates that the rise and fall of the urban centres also depended on the interplay of socio-economic forces not only in India but also on a much larger scale everywhere and showed independent growth.

BIBLIOGRAPHY

1. Rao, S.R., Lothal and the Indus Civilization, 1973.
2. Mehta, R.N., Excavation at Nagara, M.S. University Archaeology Series No. 10., 1967.
3. Subba Rao, B., Baroda through the Ages, M.S. University Archaeology Series No. 1, 1953.
4. Shah, U.P., Akota Bronzes, Bombay.
5. Mehta, R.N., Sudarshan Lake, in: J. of the Oriental Institute, Vol. XVIII, No. 1 and

2, 1968.
6. Shah, U.P. and Mehta, R.N., A few early sculptures of Gujarat in: J. of the Oriental Institute Baroda. Vol.1, No.2, 1941.
7. Wheeler, Sir Mortimer, Arikamedu. An Indo-Roman trading station on the east coast of India, in: J. Ancient India, 2, 1941.
8. Mehta, R.N., Khambhat (Cambay) topographical archaeological and toponymical perspective, in: J. of the M.S. University of Baroda, Vol. XXII No. 1, 1873
9. Subbarao, B. and Mehta R.N., Excavatiion at Vadnagar, in: J. of the M.S. University, Vol. IV, No. 1. March, 1955.
10. Parmar, Bhabhutimalla, Srimala Purana, A cultural study, A thesis submitted to M.S. University for degree of Ph.D.
11. Shastri, H.G., Maitrak kalin Gujarat.
12. Mehta, R.N., Urban Surat as archaeological topographical and toponymical perspective, in: J. of the M.S. University of Baroda, Vol. XXIV, 1975.
13. Mehta, R.N., A Christian prayer hall at Champaner, in: Indica, Vol. 14, 1977, Heras Institute of Indian History and Culture, Bombay.
14. Mehta, R.N., A Roman cameo from Karvan, in: J. of the M.S. University of Baroda, Vol.1, No.2, 1951.
15. The Museum of Archaeology and Ethnography, Riyadh, Saudi Arabia, A handbook of visitors. I am grateful to Dr. S.A. Hashim for this reference.

Hellenistic Echoes in the Legend of Kṛṣṇa

LOKESH CHANDRA
New Delhi

A vast corpus of legend has gathered around the person of Kṛṣṇa, crystallizing forgotten personalities into His picturesque figure of *līlā-puruṣottama*. It is no easy task to separate the multiple strata that have gone into its formation from time to time. Various strands merge together in the Purāṇic traditions of Kṛṣṇa into an indivisible harmony of One Supreme. We shall have to bear this in mind to understand that parts of the Kṛṣṇa cycle betray nuances of the Graeco-Bactrian world which played a unique role in the radiation of Hellenistic elements to the Indian mainland. The work of Prof. Heinrich von Stietencron on the Sun-cult of India, entitled Indische Sonnenpriester: Sāmba und die Śākadvīpīya-Brāhmaṇa[1] has led me to investigate the relationship of the Kṛṣṇa-Kaṃsa sequence to the Hellenised Northwest of India. The Purāṇas inform us that Sāmba, a son of Kṛṣṇa, was afflicted by leprosy. He could be cured only by worshipping the Sun-God. There were no Brahmins in India well-versed in Sun-worship. The Sun-God advised Sāmba to invite Maga priests from Śākadvīpa. Sāmba brought with him 18 Maga families from Śākadvīpa to India. He constructed a temple at the Mitravana grove on the banks of the Candrabhāgā river (modern Chenab) and consecrated an image of the Sun. The 18 Maga families settled down here, in the township of Sāmbapura named after its founder Sāmba. This aspect of the life of the son of Kṛṣṇa assumes importance when we find some sidelights pointing to cultural interflow between Mathurā and the Hellenised kingdoms in the northwestern or *udīcya* region. This is an area wherein Balkh and Bamian, Multan and Mathurā have seen a constant interflow of ideas and forms, trade and power. Arnold J. Toynbee points out that "The region between Oxus and Jumna has been the theatre of decisive events in mankind's history. It is perpetually demanding the historian's attention. For years it has been a lodestone to me. In the early centuries of the Christian Era it was bestridden by the Kushan Empire".[2]

Kaṃsa the king of Mathurā was killed by Kṛṣṇa. He was an incarnation of an asura called Kālanemi. He is widely held to be the son of Ugrasena, but another legend has it that he was born to the wife of Ugrasena by a *gandharva.*[3] Thus the parentage of Kaṃsa had not been beyond doubt in the Indian tradition. In view of the introduction of Sun-worship and Maga priests from Śākadvīpa by Sāmba, it may be interesting to point out that the Jātakas[4] and the Petavatthu commentary lll refer to Kaṃsa as the King of Kaṃsabhoga whose capital was Asitañjana.[5] Kaṃsabhoga was a division of Uttarāpatha or Northwest of India. Kaṃsa was killed by Vāsudeva, one of the Andhakaveṇhu-(dāsa)-puttā or the ten sons of Devagabbhā and Upasāgara, brought up by the maid of Devagabbhā and the maid's husband Andhakaveṇhu. When Vāsudeva had cut off the head of both king Kaṃsa and his brother the viceroy Upakaṃsa, the populace begged Vāsudeva and his brothers to be their guardians. Thereupon they assumed the sovereignty of Asitañjana.[6] What was the exact location of Asitañjana? We know from the Manorathapūraṇī commentary of the Aṅguttara-nikāya 1.207 that it was the birthplace of the merchant-brothers Tapassu and Bhallika. Bhallika means "a resident of Bhallaka, that is the kingdom of Balkh/Bactria".[7] Thus Asitañjana was the metropolitan city of Bactria. It was at Asitañjana that the two merchants had constructed a *stūpa* on Buddha's hair and nail-pairings. Hsüan-tsang places the two Hair-Relic Stūpas 50 *li* northwest from the city of Balkh.[7] The Pāli version of the Kṛṣṇa legend points to the Bactrian origin of Kaṃsa, and Pāli seems to preserve an earlier version of Purańic legends, For comparative study we have reproduced it at the end of this paper from Malalasekera's Dictionary of Pāli Proper Names. The evolution from the Pāli version to that of the Purāṇas indicates a period when there were close contacts between Bactria and Mathurā.

Kṛṣṇa is famous for his *hallīṣaka* (*-saka*)dance. According to Nīlakaṇṭha's commentary on Harivaṃśa it is *rāsa-goṣṭhī* (quoted in Śabda-kalpadruma 5.525). It consists of singing and dancing by one male and 7, 8, or 10 female performers. It is a circular dance performed by women under the direction of a man. No etymology is given in Monier-Williams' Sanskrit-English Dictionary or in Sanskrit lexica. This word may be cognate to Hellas "Greece", and the dance-form may be traced back to Hellenistic models. The dress of the Rāsa dancers and the folk-dancers of Greece bear close resemblances. *hallīsaka* (with the dental sibilant) also recalls to us the ancient city of Eleusis, famous as the site of the Eleusinian mysteries, with its Kallichoron well ("of beautiful dances") mentioned in the Homeric hymn to Demeter. To the west of Eleusis lay the Rharian plain where Demeter sowed the first seeds of corn. Kṛṣṇa as the Gopāla also represents agrarian traditions. *Hallīsaka* can go back to the Eleusinian mysteries or to the cult of the Thracian Nature-God Dionysus (alias Bacchus) "which gave a dominant role to women, and it provided a vent for the irrational passions of the subconscious depths of the psyche."[8] A Bacchanalian group has been discovered from Mathurā wherein the drapery of the *yakṣīs* is Greek.[9] The Dionysiac mysteries were founded by Orpheus who was a priest of Dionysos. He was a seer, and a marvellous musician. His superhuman skill in music and song was connected with religious functions. Orpheus was killed in a Bacchic orgy. "His head with his lyre, still singing, floated to Lesbos, where an oracle of Orpheus was established. The character of Orpheus, particularly his lyre-playing and song, make him an Apolline figure, a missionary of the Hellenic spirit."[10] The divine lyre of Orpheus recalls the soul-stirring flute of Kṛṣṇa. Whether it is a parallelism or influence needs further study.

Kṛṣṇa says in the Bhagavad Gītā 9.19: *sad-asac-cāham* "I am both good and evil". So also the Orpheic tenets hold that man is "a creature of mixed origin, containing a divine principle (Dionysos) and an evil one (the Titans)".[11] Orpheus was torn to pieces by women possessed by Dionysian frenzy. So also Kṛṣṇa was cursed to death by Gāndhārī. The association of Kṛṣṇa with Yavanas is apparent in his killing of the powerful *asura* Kāla Yavana.[12] The depth and extent of Indian contacts with the Hellenistic world need extensive investigation. An amphitheatre with pronounced Graeco-Roman characteristics has been excavated at Nagarjunakonda in Andhra Pradesh. An apsidal temple has been exhumed at Sonkh near Mathurā on the site of a modern *nāga*-temple: does *nāga* stand for a foreigner, a Greek ?

A comparison of thePali version with the Bhāgavata and other Purāṇas indicates the composite character of the Kṛṣṇa legend and its diaphanous Hellenistic strains carry us away beyond memory. The intricacies of *līlā-puruṣottama* Kṛṣṇa reduce us to silence in the tumult of the lost.

APPENDIX 1

Pali Version of the Kṛṣṇa Legend (reproduced from Malalasekera, 1960, 1.108-109)

Andhakaveṇhu-(dāsa)-puttā. Ten brothers, sons of Devagabbhā and Upasāgara.

As it had been foretold at Devagabbhā's birth that one of her sons would destroy the lineage of Kaṃsa, each time a son was born to her, fearing lest he be put to death, she sent him secretly to her servingwoman, Nandagopā; the latter had married Andhakaveṇhu and, by good fortune, daughters were born to her at the same time as sons to Devagabbhā; these daughters she sent to Devagabbhā in exchange for the latter's sons.

The ten sons were named Vāsudeva, Baladeva, Candadeva, Suriyadeva, Aggideva, Varuṇadeva, Ajjuna, Pajjuna, Ghatapaṇḍita and Aṅkura.[13] They had also a sister, Añjanadevī. When they grew up they became highway robbers, seizing even a present sent to their uncle, King Kaṃsa. Thus they became notorious as the Andakaveṇhudāsaputtā. The king, having learnt of their true descent, devised various plans for their destruction. Two famous wrestlers, Cānura and Muṭṭhika, were engaged to have a public wrestling match with them. The brothers accepted the challenge and looted several shops for clothes, perfumes, etc., to be used for the occasion. Baladeva killed both the wrestlers. In his death-throes Muṭṭhika uttered a prayer to be born as a yakkha; his wish was fulfilled and he was born as such in the Kāḷamattiya forest. When the king's men attempted to seize the brothers, Vāsudeva threw a wheel which cut off the heads of both the king and his brother the viceroy, Upakaṃsa.

The populace, terrified, begged the brothers to be their guardians. Thereupon they assumed the sovereignty of Asitañjana. From there they set out to conquer the whole of Jambudīpa, starting with Ayojjhā (whose king, Kāḷasena, they took prisoner) and Dvāravatī, which they captured with the help of Kaṇhadīpāyana.

They made Dvāravatī their capital and divided their kingdom into ten shares, for getting their sister, Añjanadevī. When they discovered their mistake, Aṅkura gave her his share and took to trade.[14]

In course of time the brothers had many sons and daughters, the average human age at that time being 20,000 years. Later their sons annoyed the sage Kaṇhadipāyana by dressing up a lad as a woman and asking him what child she would bring forth. "A knot of acacia wood," he answered, "with which will be destroyed the line of Vāsudeva."

They laughed at the sage and kicked him. On the seventh day the lad voided from his belly a knot of acacia wood which they burnt, casting the ashes into the river. From those ashes, which stuck near the city gate, an *Eraka*-plant sprang up. One day, while disporting themselves in the water, the kings, with their families and followers, started a sham quarrel and plucked leaves from the *Eraka*-plant to use as clubs. The leaves turned into weapons in their hands, and they were all killed except Vāsudeva, Baladeva, Añjanadevi, and their chaplain, all of whom fled in a chariot. Thus were the words of the sage fulfilled.

In their flight they reached the Kāḷamaṭṭiya forest in which Muṭṭhika had been born as a yakkha. When Muṭṭhika saw Baladeva he assumed the shape of a wrestler and challenged him to a fight. Baladeva accepted the challenge and "was gobbled up like a radish-bulb."

Vāsudeva proceeded on his way with the others and at night lay in a bush for shelter. A huntsman, mistaking him for a pig, speared him; when Vāsudeva heard that the huntsman's name was Jarā (Old Age) he reconciled himself to death. Thus they all perished except Añjanadevī,[15] of whose later history nothing is mentioned.

In the *Kumbha Jātaka*[16] it is suggested that the Andhakaveṇhus[17] were destroyed as a result of indulging in drink. This story was evidently well known to tradition as it is so often referred to.[18]

APPENDIX 2

Excursus on Prof. Stietencron's Indische Sonnenpriester

MAGA. Prof. Stietencron p. 279 says: "In some Puraṇic passages, three particularly famous places of Sūrya worship are mentioned. One of them was the sun-temple of Konarka

(Konarak), the idol of which was called Muṇḍira or Muṇḍīrasvāmin. The second was Kālapriya on the banks of the Yamunā river, and the famous sanctuary Mūlasthāna, i.e. modern Multan, was the third". The name Muṇḍīra is attested in the name of the village Munirka in South Delhi. It is close to the present village of Mehrauli or Mihirapalli "the village of Mihira or Sun". There may have been a number of Sun temples around the Yamuna river. Yamuna is the daughter of the Sun (Yamunā-janaka "father of Yamunā" = Sun-God).

Prof. Stietencron p. 280 says: "The Sūrya temple Mūlasthāna whose name became the name of the ancient town, driving into oblivion the older designation Kaśyapapura, was famous at the latest in the beginning of the 7th century A.D. But it seems to me, that it did not yet exist when the Sāmbapurāṇa was composed, as the name Mūlasthāna does not occur in the text". Prof. Stietencron is right in surmising that Mūlasthāna means the Sun Temple. The central attraction of the town was its Sun Temple. By semantic extension, Mūlasthāna came to mean "(The City of the) Temple". Mūlasthāna primarily means a temple. In Tamil, this word occurs as *mūla-t-tā nam* "sanctum sactorum of a Temple" (Tamil Lexicon). *Tiru-mūlattānam* refers to the sacred shrine of Tiruvārūr (Tamil Lexicon p. 1913). In Srilanka too *mūla* = *ārāma* "monastery" (Encyclopaedia of Buddhism 3.22, 24). In the Inscription of Sri Kahulunnan dated Saka 764 = A.D. 842 from Indonesia *kamūlan* refers to the sanctuary constructed by the Sailendra monarch. The author of the Sāmba-purāṇa must have known the town as Kaśyapapura and *mūlasthāna* as a denotation for a temple. He must have found it redundant to nickname the city as Mūlasthāna in lieu of its appropriate name Kaśyapapura. The transition of *mūlasthāna* "the temple" to Mūlasthāna "the city of the temple" must have been from popular parlance. It seems to have been brought into widespread use by foreigners. The word Kāśyapāḥ (plural) denotes "a class of semidivine genii connected with or regulating the course of the sun" (AV. 15.1. 23, TAr. 18, PārGr. 2. 9. 13). Kaśyapa is an ancient sage who was the author of several hymns of the Ṛgveda, husband of Aditi and twelve other daughters of Dakṣa (MBh.1.2598, Mn.9.129); by Aditi he was the father of the Ādityas. (cf. Kāśyapaya)TS., SBr. and of Vivasvat, R.(MW). The toponym Kaśyapa-pura clearly indicates the ancient connection of the town with Āditya "Sun". The town should have had a temple dedicated to Āditya long before Sāmba constructed here Maga's first temple to the Sun.

BHOJAKA. Prof. Stietencron 1966:280 says: "The other group of sun-priests with foreign religious traditions arrived much later in India than the Maga did. They called themselves Bhojaka which does not mean "the one who feeds the deity", as later Indian etymologies would have it, but is to be deduced from a Middle-Iranian form **bōžak*, healer, saviour (compare arm. *bužakan,* healing, rescuing; **božišn*, cure, liberation; mp. *božišn,* idem.) . . .But the Bhojaka claimed their descent from Zarathustra and remained faithful to the Avesta holy scriptures".

The Bhojaka were both healers and saviours and they observed scrupulous cleanliness according to prescriptions of the Vidēvdād. The hygiene and medical skill of people from the Northwest was well known since early antiquity. The Tibetan histories of Ayurveda say: Jīvaka was born as the son of king Bimbisāra and a trader's wife. Grown up, he saw a group of *white-clad* men and he asked his father: "Who are they?" He said: "They are called doctors and they protect people from diseases". Jīvaka was filled with the wish to become a doctor. He asked his father for permission to study under Ātreya the famous doctor of Taxila. King Bimbisāra sent him to Taxila with a letter to its king.[19] The white clothes are an indication that the doctors wore the dress of Zoroastrian priests. That Zoroastrian doctors travelled as far as Bihar in Eastern India and as early as the period of Bimbisāra is noteworthy.

The Buddhist cult of Bhaisajyaguru is another point of contact with the **bōžak*, and it is of an early date. Bhaiṣajyaguru is the Buddha of Healing. He cures physical illness and dispels spiritual darkness. His sutra was translated into Chinese five times. The earliest translation by Śrimitra dates to A.D. 317-322. In his paradise dwell innumerable bodhisattvas chief among whom are Sūrya-vairocana and Candra-vairocana. They are also known as Sūryaprabha and Candraprabha. Bhaiṣajyaguru has Twelve Great Yakṣa Generals (*dvādaśa mahāyakṣa-senāpatayaḥ*)[20]. Bhaiṣajyaguru developed in an age when an Iranian term like *bešāz*[21] "healing" was correctly understood as *bhaiṣajya* "medicine, healing". The two bodhisattvas Sūryaprabha and Candraprabha are the counterparts of the Iranian Rašnu (Skt. Rājña) and Sraoša (Skt Śrauṣa), companions of Mithra. The Twelve Generals are the 12 Ādityas as solar aspects.

NOTES

1. Wiesbaden, Otto Harrassowitz, 1966.
2. Between Oxus and Jumna, London, Oxford University Press, 1961, p.vi.
3. V̄ettam Mani, Purānic Encyclopaedia, Delhi, Motilal Banarasidass, 1975, p. 382a.
4. Jātaka, ed. Fausboll, 4.79.
5. G.P. Malalasekera, Dictionary of Pali Proper Names, Luzac & Co. Ltd. London, 1960, I, p. 467.
6. ib. I, pp. 108-09.
7. Lokesh Chandra, Three Iranian Words in the Buddhist Tradition, International Academy of Indian Culture, New Delhi, 1979, pp. 6-7.
8. Arnold Toynbee: a selection from his works, ed. E.W.F. Tomlin, Oxford University Press, 1978, p. 278.
9. W.W. Tarn, The Greeks in Bactria and India, Cambridge University Press, 1951, p. 252 n.9.
10. Encyclopaedia Britannica, 1965,16.1116b.
11. H.J. Rose, Thrace, in Encyclopaedia of Religion and Ethics, 1921, 12, p. 328a.
12. V̄ettam Mani, 1975, p. 425, no. 13.
13. Cowell sees in this story the kernel of a nature-myth (Jātaka, trans. iv. 51 n.); cf. with this the Kṛṣṇa legend in the Harivamsa; see also Wilson's Visṇu Purāṇa (Hall's Ed.), V. 147 f.; and the article on Kṛṣṇa in Hopkins' Epic Mythology, pp. 214f.
14. Aṅkura's later history is found in PvA,p. 111 ff. See S.V. Aṅkura.
15. J.IV. 79 ff.
16. J.V.p.18,
17. Andhaka Veṇhu is Andhaka Vṛṣni in Sanskrit. According to A Pali Dictionary, Copenhagen 1924–48, p. 255 *Andhaka-Viṇhayo was replaced by Andhaka-Veṇhuyo. Veṇhu is Viṣṇu. Hence the singular Andhaka Veṇhu.
18. E.g., in the *Sankicca Jat.* (v.267) and in Vv., p. 58.
19. Rechung Rinpoche, Tibetan Medicine, Berkeley (University of California Press) 1973, p. 12.
20. Nalinaksha Dutt, Gilgit Manuscripts, Srinagar 1939: 1.29.
21. D.N. MacKenzie, A Concise Pahlavi Dictionary, London (Oxford University Press), 1971), p. 18.

Abbreviations

J. = Jātaka, ed. Fausboll, 5 vols.
PvA. = Petavatthu Commentary (P.T.S.)
Vv. = Vimānavatthu (P.T.S.)

Interrelations between East and West in the Light of Newly Discoverd Gāndhāra Sculptures

KLAUS FISCHER
Bonn

Hermann Goetz contributed to the understanding of the originality of Indian art and to the various fruitful interrelations between the Eastern and Western art schools. In an outstanding article he showed the possibilities of Indian sculptors enriching their vocabulary by motives from Roman art.[1] I should like to pay my respects to the memory of Hermann Goetz by drawing attention to recently discovered Gāndhāra sculptures[2] emphasizing his earlier remarks. We select episodes from the legendary biography of the Buddha, taken from accounts of the youth of the Bodhisattva.

When prince Siddhārtha had to show his athletic skill he defeated his adversaries in all competitions, for example in sword-fighting, boxing, wrestling, archery and in the use of elephants, horses, chariots, bows and spears.[3] Until recently no early Indian sculptures were known displaying prince Siddhārtha's victory in sword-fighting; the first example of this iconography was published after a fragment from Haḍḍa in the Kabul Museum and interpreted as a model for later Central and Eastern Asian art. These remarks can now be corroborated by two other fragments whose owners have kindly permitted me to make them known to the public. One piece is said to have been found in the environs of Taxila (Fig.1). To the right are two juvenile fighters brandishing their swords, and to the left two boys in a wrestling-match before two observers. In both panels the sportsman portrayed frontally towards the viewer is distinguished from his adversary by a nimbus, and in the left portion of the fragment he is marked as a winner by lifting the contestant from the ground. The other example is supposed to have been acquired near Haḍḍa (Fig.2). Eight princely clad persons with turbans on their heads look at two adolescents who brandish their swords at each other. Stylistically all these three scenes (Figs 1, 2.) show close affinities to late Hellenistic and early Roman sculptures and contribute new details to our studies of interrelations between East and West. During this period easily transportable models from the Mediterranean world may have inspired Indian artists to enrich Buddhist legends by classical forms, or Mediterranean artists may have migrated to the East and served as masters or craftsmen in Gāndhāran workshops.[5] Accordingly we recognize aesthetic ideals and sculptural formulas of Hellenistic-Roman art in the actions and attitudes of the sword-fighters with their arms in front of the upper parts of their bodies.[6] In correspondence with the traditions of the Classical West, the chest and back of the sword-fighters are anatomically well defined. In this respect they contrast with ancient Indian conventions where artistic ideals did not require the representation of bones, veins or muscles.[7] The back-views of the Gāndhāran sportsmen even display anatomical details, for example the spine and dorsal vertebra (Fig.1 left—the boy lifted from the ground, and right—the left sword-fighter; Fig. 2—again the left fighter), and let us see the action of the musculus latissimi dorsi.[8]

We shall now turn to the fragment with the wrestling-match (Fig.1 left). Every new discovery or excavation in the Gāndhāra country will supply new material for comparative art studies and allow us to evaluate interrelations between Western models and their transformation according to the requirements of Eastern iconography.[9] The same is true with sculptural patterns of wrestlers in classical antiquity and their reflections on Indian art during the Kuṣāṇa epoch in the beginning of the 1st millenium A.D. In the majority of all reliefs hitherto known the two wrestlers are interlocked in various ways, but both have their feet firmly on the ground.[10] Some years ago I was able to publish a fragment from Kunduz in Northern Afghanistan in which the Bodhisattva is turning his adversary upside down.[11] Whilst the texts narrating the episode of the Bodhisattva's victory in the wrestling-match contain very few particulars the Kunduz relief may tentatively be interpreted in the light of a passage in the Lalita Vistara according to which the Bodhisattva whirled the young Devadatta three times through the air.[12] But recently the Italian excavations in Pakistan taught us that another variation of the wrestling-match, in which one contestant separates the other from the ground, can be definitely understood as an independent iconographic pattern of Mediterranean origin: the portrait of Hercules in the act of suffocating Antaeus.[13] With regard to the much debated question of classical models

Fig.1 Fragment, schist, private property, supposed to be found in the environs of Taxila. Wrestling scene and sword-fighting.

Fig.2 Fragment, schist, private property, supposed to be found in the environs of Haḍḍa. Sword-fighting.

for Gāndhāran imagery,[14] Taddei has clearly shown that a sculpture in the round, presumbly a bronze statuette, was actually present in a Gāndhāran atelier.[15] There the two wrestlers were seen from different points of view: the victorious athelete from Butkara I viewed from the side,[16] and that from Saidu Sharif I from the back.[17] Our new illustration of a Kuṣāṇa Bodhisattva as the victorious wrestler in the "Antaeus-raised-from-the-ground-motif" (Fig.1 left) adds a new perspective to Taddei's most important considerations.[18] When he reminds us (i) that classical reliefs invariably represented the winner (of a wrestling-game, etc.) full-face or almost so, and (ii) that Gāndhāran artists usually took pains to introduce the Bodhisttva in as visible a way as possible (frontally or at any rate in a position of hierarchical pre-eminence) we have now before our eyes (Fig.1 left) a composition fulfilling both rules. Wherever possible Indian artists emphasized the figure of the Bodhisattva—the prince Siddhārtha—the future Buddha, by a halo behind his head.[19] When this proved to be difficult in profile views of the Exalted One the latter was turned full-face to the spectator, for example in the well-known iconography on his death-bed[20] or frontally on a chariot drawn by horses in profile from right to left.[21] In wrestling scenes contestants rendered in profile do not show traces of a nimbus,[22] whilst the victorious Bodhisattva seen from behind carries his halo in a way artistically not very satisfying.[23] At Kunduz the Bodhisattva is given three times full-face: riding on a quadruped in profile from right to left and turned towards the spectator; at school in the writing lesson; and in hierarchical frontality during his victory in the wrestling-match.[24] The sculptor of our relief (Fig.1 left) has succeeded in carving a vivid wrestling action after a classical model as well as in drawing our attention to the main figure of the frontally rendered Bodhisattva with his halo. In the sense of Taddei's interpretation one might suppose that this piece and the above-mentioned reliefs from Saidu Sharif I and Butkara I were modelled after the same bronze statuette by one (Mediterranean, migrating?) artist, or in the same atelier, or after a group of such art-works distributed over the workshops of Swāt and viewed by the local craftsmen from various angles.

NOTES

1. H. Goetz, Imperial Rome and the Genesis of Classic Indian Art, 1, 2, in: East and West, N.S. 10,3, 1959, and 10,4, 1959.
2. K. Fischer, Zu erzählenden Gandhāra - Reliefs, Allgemeine und vergleichende Archäologie - Beiträge, Bd. 2, 1980.
3. The Mahāvastu, tr. J.J. Jones II, London, 1952, p.71. Le Lalita Vistara, trad. Ph. Ed. Foucaux I, Paris, 1884, pp. 128, 139–141. On further notes, especially the Divyāvad-

āna, see A. Foucher, La vie du Bouddha d'après les textes et les monuments de l'Inde, Paris, 1949, pp. 15, 75-79, 83-86; p. 79 remarks on the fact that Gandhāran artists preferred to illustrate the wrestling match and the contest in archery.

4. B. Dagens, Monuments préislamiques d'Afghanistan, Paris, 1964, p. 15 with n. 31 and pl. I, 6.
5. M. Wheeler, Romano-Buddhist Art, in Antiquity 23, 1949. A. Sopor, The Roman Style in Gandhāra, in: Amer. J. of Archeology 55, 1951.
6. A.H. Borbein, Zur Bedeutung symmetrischer Kompositionen in der hellenistisch-italischen und spätrepublikanisch-römischen Reliefplastik in: Hellenismus in Mittelitalien, 1976, Pl.11,14.
7. A.N. Tagore, Some Notes on Indian Artistic Anatomy, Calcutta, 1940, p.1.
8. W. Tank, Anatomie der Körperformen für Künstler and Sporttreibende, 1948, K. Tittel, Beschreibende und funktionelle Anatomie des Menschen, 1976, pl, 17, 20.
9. K. Fischer, Current Reviews on Publications in Gandhāra Art, in: Gnomon, 31, 1959, p. 269; 34, 1962, p. 403; 38, 1966, p. 279; 48, 1976, p. 290.
10. A. Foucher, L'art gréco-bouddhique du Gandhāra, Paris, 1945–51, figs. 171b, 172a. H. Ingholt, Gandhāran Art in Pakistan, New York, 1957, pls. 27-30. J. Marshall, The Buddhist Art of Gandhāra, Cambridge (U.K.), 1960, fig. 105. M. Taddei, II mito di Filottete ed un episodo della vita del Buddha, in: Archeologia Classica 15, 1963, pp. 198-218 and pl. LXX. A.H. Dani, Excavation at Chatpat, in: Ancient Pakistan 4, 1968-69, pl. 59b, nos. I and II. Thareli, Buddhist Site in Pakistan, ed. Seiichi Mizuno and Takayasu Higuchi, Kyoto, 1978, pl. 105, 1 left.
11. K. Fischer, Gandhāran Sculpture from Kunduz and Environs, in: Artibus Asiae 21, 1958, p. 235, panel I, fig. 2, no. 3.
12. cf. n. 3, Lalita Vistara, p. 138.
13. M. Taddei, On a Hellenistic Model Used in Some Gandhāran Reliefs in Swat, in: East and West, N.S. 15, 1965, pp. 174-78 and figs. 1 detail 4 (from Saidu Sharif I) and 2 (from Butkara I) with references to classical bronzes n. 4.
14. For extensive bibliography see n.5 and 9.
15. cf. n. 13, Taddei, p. 177.
16. l.c. fig. 2.
17. l.c. fig. 4 (where the nimbus can be clearly seen appearing on the background of the relief).
18. l.c. p. 178.
19. Gandhāra. Buddhistische Kunstwerke des 1-5. Jahrhunderts aus Pakistan und Afghanistan, Museum für Indische Kunst, Berlin, 1980, p. 7.
20. cf. n. 10, Ingholt, pls. 137-41.
21. cf. n. 11, Fischer, and n. 2, Fischer, Abb. 15.
22. cf. n. 10.
23. cf. n. 17.
24. cf. n. 2, fig. 2, nos. 1-3.

Westerners beyond the Great Himalayan Range

Rock Carvings and Rock Inscriptions in the Indus Valley near Chilas

KARL JETTMAR
Heidelberg

Since 1979 thousands of rock-carvings and hundreds of inscriptions have been discovered in the mountain valleys north and northwest of Pakistan. One important concentration is in the famous Hunza valley, but the most impressive findings were made in the western part of the Diamir District, i.e., along the Indus River below Chilas. Some sites are situated in the Kohistan District which includes the left bank of the Indus east of the great bend of Sazin. With the help of my old friend, the late Ismail Khan, former Deputy Commissioner of Chilas, I got the chance to be the first visitor with scholarly interests to see and record most of the rock-carvings and inscriptions. Several preliminary reports appeared in the meantime.[1] Since 1980 a joint Pak-German team headed by Prof. Dani[2] and myself took over the difficult and almost infinite task of preparing scientific documentations fit to be published.

As for the inscriptions, they are in Kharoṣṭhī, Brāhmī, Proto-Śāradā and Śāradā, but there occur many Sogdian texts too, and even some in cursive Bactrian letters. So far, four Chinese inscriptions were located. I think, such findings have never before been made in the Indian Subcontinent (cf. map, Fig. 1).

The material is of no less importance to specialists of Buddhist art. Last summer our team noted 530 elaborate drawings of stupas, certainly most of them of the first millennium A.D. Some of them represent Central Asiatic types. We found 43 drawings of Buddhas or Bodhisattvas, often inserted in multi-figurative scenes. Many of them are connected with inscriptions of religious content mentioning eventually artist and sponsor. In this way the chronology of the art historian can be controlled by datings of the palaeographer.

Since the last campaign we know that this rock art has had a long prelude. The earliest carvings were done by Stone Age hunters stimulated by the desert varnish on the smooth rocks near the river, where even by simple pecking impressive pictures can be made visible from a great distance. Later on came herdsmen from the periphery of the Near Eastern Neolithic. Their drawings reflect the influence of painted pottery. We don't know whether the bearers of this tradition were Aryan tribes, but earlier or later Dardic, i.e., Northwest Indian languages were spread throughout the area. Only in the Gilgit valley and beyond, the pre-Indo-European Burushaski was prevalent.

Buddhism appeared here in the 1st century A.D., evidently brought by a garrison of semi-barbarian warriors who had been posted in the lowlands before.

Inscriptions and drawings of the time of the Great Kushans were observed exclusively in places situated on the direct road from Kashmir to the Tarim Basin (Alam Bridge, Hunza-Haldeikish).[3]

Petroglyphs of astonishing artistic perfection were made between the 5th and 8th centuries A.D. In this period the (present) Northern Areas were ruled by the Paṭola Ṣāhis.[4] The name of their kingdom was Bolor as we learn from Chinese sources.[5] The Ṣāhis were fervent Buddhists who had many foreigners in their service. Their official language was Sanskrit. Bolor included the Burushaski speaking area, and here the famous Gilgit Manuscripts were written and finally deposited inside a hollow stupa.[6] By expanding to the North, Bolor controlled all important passes protecting trade and pilgrimage. Connections with Swat, Uraśa (=Hazara), and Kashmir were intense, and even influence of the art of the Gupta Empire reached this remote region. The invasion of the Tibetans during the 8th century could not entirely destroy the traffic system, but Buddhism was submitted to local transformations and later on merged with ideas derived from the Hindu revival in the plains.

Finally, Islamization of the area happened in a slow process which was finished only in the 9th century by pious Muslim officers of the Dogras.[7]

Certainly the most fascinating aspect of the petroglyphs is that we learn so much about connections with Central Asia and the Far East. Between the so-called Silk Roads and what is now Pakistan there was a sort of short-cut. Many travellers using this dangerous highroad have left their marks on the rocks — messengers and missionaries, merchants, artists and pilgrims.

But our material is so rich and so divergent that it can also serve as a basis for a contribution to a conference devoted to a quite different

Fig. 1 Situation of newly discovered clusters of rock-carvings and inscriptions in North Pakistan:

1. Hunza-Haldeikish, 2. Chilas I, 3. Chilas II, 4. Shatial Bridge, 5. Thor/Northern Bank, 6. Hodar, 7. Thalpan.
The rock-carvings at Alam Bridge are marked x.

Fig.2 "Strutting animals". Rock-carving in Achaemenid tradition at Thalpan, Altar Rock.

Fig.3 Fantastic animal at Thalpan, Altar Rock.

Fig.4 Fantastic animal at Thalpan, Altar Rock (stylistically later).

Fig.5 Marching warrior with spear. Thalpan, Altar Rock.

Fig.6 Man, ready to slaughter a goat. Thalpan, Altar Rock.

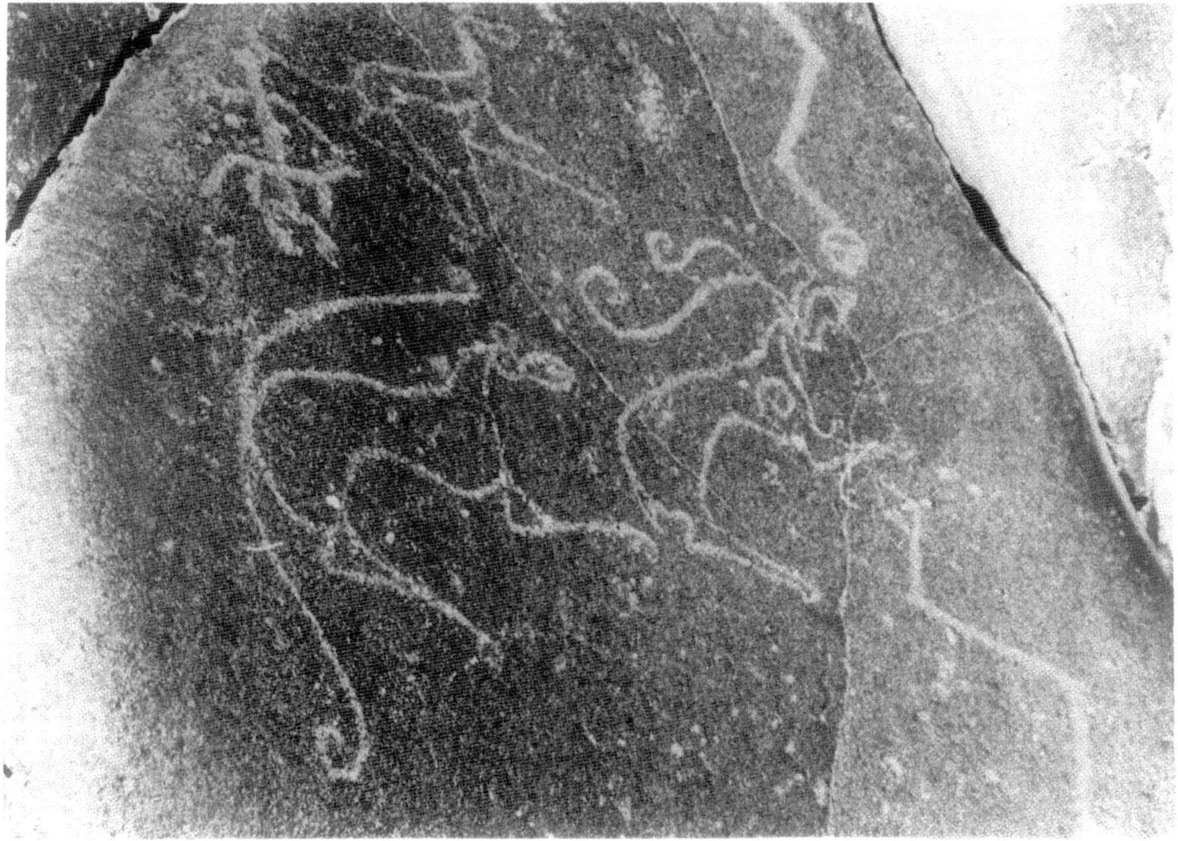

Fig.7 Animal Style carvings on the Altar Rock, Thalpan.
Horned animal pursued by beast of prey. The attacking snakes are later additions.

Fig.8 Horned animal, near the mouth of the Minar-gah, west of Chilas.

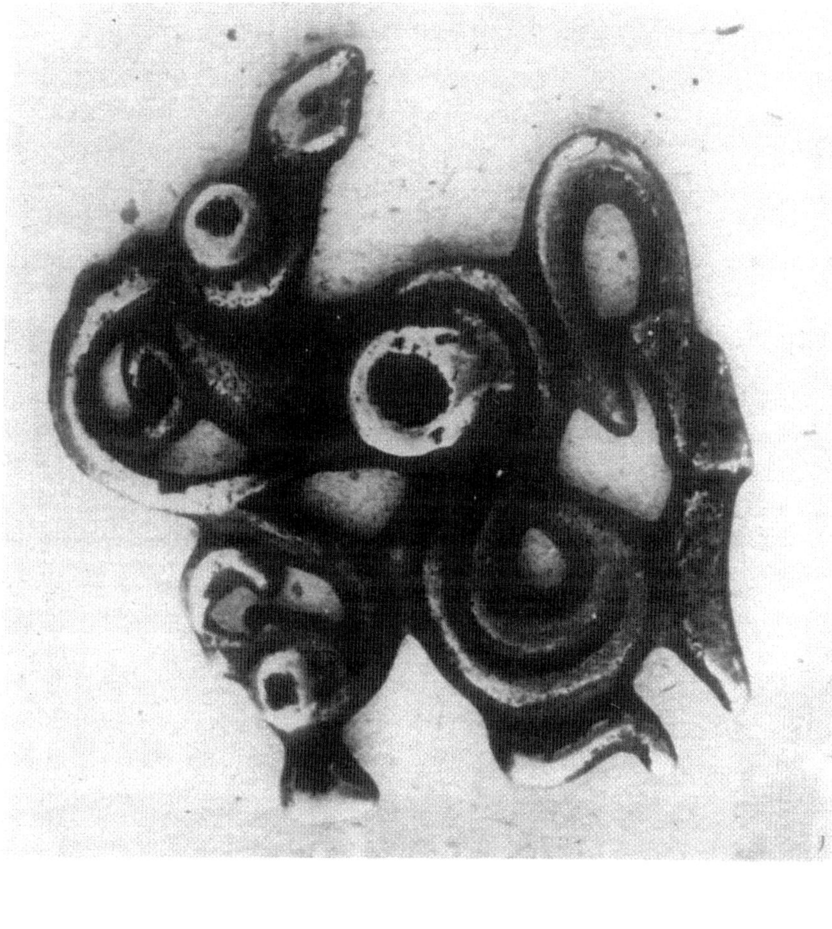

Fig.9 Bronze plaque, acquired in Kandia, Indus-Kohistan. 4,8 cm (from tail to nose of the animal).

Fig. 10. Man in Sogdian dress venerating a stupa (Ziarat II).

problem, that is to say, the relations between the Subcontinent and Western Countries.

Arguments for such connections during an early period, namely, the time when the Persian Empire extended up to the Indus, are to be found opposite of Chilas near the village of Thalpan. Here a sandy plain sloping to the river is dominated by bulwark-like rocks almost sure to have been used as a pre-Buddhist sanctuary. The spot where the altar stood is still recognizable. The smooth surfaces below and to the sides of this "Altar Rock" are decorated with many carvings. Only a few of them belong to the Buddhist period. A Kharoṣṭhī inscription, the only one found on the right bank of the Indus River, belongs to this complex.

In a prominent position, however, we saw animal drawings of a distinctive form of stylization. The figures are filled in by peckings, but shoulders and buttocks are exempted resulting in comma-shaped decorations. The neck is stressed by a similar figure. One front-leg is always advanced indicating a majestic pace. What we see here is clearly a simplified sample of the official art of the Achaemenid court. The comma-shaped designs correspond to inlays on metal objects or appliqué work known from preserved textiles (Fig. 2).

Achaemenidic art was extremely syncretistic absorbing most of the tendencies of peoples included in the large empire. Several of them used a device which we call in German "Knielauf", i.e., one shank of the walking figure is bent backwards at an angle of 90 degrees.

"Knielauf" can be seen, for instance, in an Urartaean wallpainting in a fortress excavated in Soviet Transcaucasia[8] (Fig.3). The same stylistic element occurs repeatedly in the rock-carvings at Thalpan. And here too we have the body markings which already are identified as being of western origin (Figs 3, 4).

On the same rock, three human figures are depicted, one moving a strange variation of the "Knielauf", the next one is a marching warrior, breast and shoulders seen frontally, head as well as feet from the side. The man holds a spear pointing downwards (Fig. 5). This is a typical Near Eastern motif, and the dress belongs to the same context. Below a belt his robe ends in many tassels, leggings are fixed to the shoes by straps. Edith v. Porada informed me that such figures might belong to the Late Parthian period, but there is no perfect congruence with the wellknown statues or reliefs.[9] The third figure holds a large knife in one hand ready to slaughter a goat hanging down from his other hand. The posture is known from Near Eastern seals. Marks on the body of the goat point in the same direction (Fig. 6).

The sources of the different elements are quite clear while the dating remains controversial. We may put this complex into the first centuries A.D., but in this case the petroglyphs must have been made by members of a tribe or military unit preserving Achaemenid traditions. Some peculiarities of the dress (e.g. the broad belt) point to Transcaucasian representations made not later than the first half of the first millennium B.C. We have to consider that only a few miles off rock-carvings and inscriptions of the 1st century A.D. were found, i.e., certainly contemporary with the Parthian period. The warriors depicted in those carvings wear a different dress.

Let us face the question: Who made such archaic pictures in such a remote area? A romantic idea would be to explain them as produced by soldiers of a Persian detachment posted on the eastern frontier of the Empire and retreating during the invasion of Alexander the Great into the sheltering mountains. Or we could assume that such a unit was posted later on along the upper course of the Indus because from this area came the gold which was an essential tribute of the easternmost provinces.

The situation is complicated by the fact that on the same Altar Rock, less than one metre off, there are linear carvings featuring a horned animal apparently a stag followed by a beast of prey with two tails. The shoulder of the stag is decorated by a spiral hook. Its nose is bent downwards resembling the snout of an elk (Fig. 7). Here we are surely confronted with typical samples of the so-called Scytho-Siberian Animal Style, the art of the nomads between Eastern Europe and the borders of China. It must be mentioned that no deer as seen here is found in the local fauna.

We might get an easy explanation for the appearance of Animal Style, if we could date the drawing into the 2th century B.C. or later. This was the time when the Sakas, called Sai by the Chinese, marched from Central Asia southwards into India where they founded several principalities. According to the same source they went over the "hanging passages" which certainly means that they used the straight route through the Karakorum, crossing the Indus River somewhere near Chilas.[10]

Unfortunately the stylistic peculiarities of other Animal Style drawings which we found in the meantime do not allow such a smooth explanation. A horned animal seen by us west of Chilas is depicted with long stretched legs as if standing on tiptoes (Fig. 8). This posture is frequent in the 7th and 6th centuries B.C. The Animal Style of Chilas, in the meantime documented by approximately a dozen carvings, was evidently influenced by several consecutive impacts from the Steppes.[11]

One argument more for my thesis is the astonishing fact that I could acquire a bronze plaque, a masterpiece of Animal Style Art, in Kandia, in fact the remotest corner of Indus — Kohistan (Fig. 9). It shows a crouching ibex. The body is twisted into an S-spiral. On the shoulder there is an empty round embedding as meant for a precious stone. A part of the antlers is transformed into a bird's head. The proto-type was a plaque in the shape of a crouching deer as known from the Pamirs. There the feet of the animal are rendered in the same manner. The plaque, now handed over to the Department of Archaeology and Museums, was cast between the 5th and 3rd centuries B.C., hardly later.[12]

Some of the nomads may have remained in the mountains using the same place for sanctuary as the Achaemenid warriors, namely, the Altar Rock. During this coexistence the inherited motives and stylistic tendencies were perpctuated in a rather superficial — we could say, heraldic — way, may be for centuries. So we have Animal Style drawings without the former elegance on the one hand, and rather clumsy "Achaemenoid" pictures on the other one (cf Fig. 4).

If we include Sogdiana into the countries of the West, a much later group of carvings must be mentioned. Many ideas and technical traditions common in the Near East were brought along the Silk Road to China. The chief operators of the Silk Roads however were the Sogdians, the people living in the oases of Transoxania. Samarkand, the Maracanda of Alexander's time, was their capital. Sogdian traders spread the great religions: Buddhism, Christianity and Manichaeism.

In recent years we have learnt that they made use of many elements of Indian iconography up to the 8th century A.D., shortly before they were subjugated by Arab armies and forcibly converted to Muslim faith. In the palaces of their nobility excavated by Soviet scholars there were found wallpaintings with Indian motives showing Indian deities, e.g., a dancing Shiva and the god Veshparkar identified by his name written below.[13]

Since the discovery of rock-carvings in the Indus Valley we may guess by which route Sogdians reached India even at the time when the normal routes through Tukhāristan were blocked by the Muslims. Following a track via Chitral, the Shandur pass, Ghizr, Tangir they went down to the Indus. The spot where they crossed the river near Shatial is marked by a sanctuary where hundreds of Sogdian inscriptions were found. These tell us the names of the travellers. Some were Buddhists, but their names are derived from Iranian deities. Forty miles up the river, in the site Ziarat II, I saw a composition showing the veneration of a stupa by a man in Sogdian dress. Evidently the artist had used his sketch-book very skilfully. The incense burner in his right hand was perhaps originally something else — a flower or a wine cup (Fig. 10).

In conclusion, we may say that foreign influences in the rock-carvings of the remote Chilas area give us a surprising insight in political and cultural contacts during the pre-Buddhist periods of the Subcontinent revealing some hitherto unknown western impacts.

NOTES

1. Jettmar, 1980a, 1980b, 1980c, 1980d, 1982.
2. Dani, 1981.
3. cf. Fussman, 1978, pp. 54-56.
4. v. Hinueber, 1979, 1980.
5. Jettmar, 1980e.
6. Jettmar, 1981.
7. Biddulph, 1880/1971, pp. 113-25.
8. Truhtina, Hodžaš, Oganesjan, 1968.
9. Ghirshman, 1962, pp. 78-107.
10. Hulsewé, 1979, p. 105.
11. Šer, 1981, p. 246.
12. Litvinskij, 1972, pp. 60-68, 113.
13. Belenickij, Maršak in Azarpay, 1981, pp. 26-35.

REFERENCES

G. Azarpay, 1981: Sogdian Painting — The Pictorial Epic in Oriental Art. Contributions by A.M. Belenickij, B.I. Marshak and M.J. Dresden. Berkeley and Los Angeles.

J. Biddulph, 1880/1971: Tribes of the Hindoo Koosh, Calcutta, reprint Graz.

A. H. Dani, 1981: Karakorum Highway Unfolds the Romance of the Past, Islamabad.

G. Fussman, 1978: Inscriptions de Gilgit, in: Bulletin de l'École Française d'Extrême Orient, LXV, pp. 1–6, pls. I–XXXII.

R. Girshman, 1962: Iran, Parther und Sassaniden, München.

O. von Hinueber, 1979: Die Erforschung der Gilgit-Handschriften (Funde buddhistischer Sanskrit-Handschriften, I).Nachrichten der Akademie der Wissenschaften in Göttingen, I. Philol.-hist. Klasse, Jahrg. 1979, Nr. 12, pp. 329–359, Göttingen.

——1980: Die Kolophone der Gilgit-Handschriften. Studien zur Indologie und Iranistik, ed. o. von Hinueber, G. Klingenschmitt, A. Wezler und M. Witzel, Festschrift Paul Thieme, H. 5-6, pp. 49–82, Reinbek.

A. F.P. Hulsewé, 1979: China in Central Asia. The Early Stage: 125 B.C. - A.D. 23. Sinica Leidensia, Fol. XIV, Leiden.

K. Jettmar, 1980a: Felsbilder und Inschriften am Karakorum Highway, in: Central Asiatic Journal, XXIV/3–4, pp. 185–221.

—1980b: Bolor-Zum Stand des Problems, Zentralasiatische Studien, 14/2, pp. 115–32.

——1980c: The Visitors' Book of a Silk Road. Rockcarvings and Inscriptions in Northern Pakistan. German research reports of the Deutsche Forschungsgemeinschaft, 2–3/80, pp. 6–9.

——1980d: Neuentdeckte Felsbilder und-inschriften in den Nordgebieten Pakistans. Allgemeine und vergleichende Archäologie-Beiträge, Bd. 2, München, pp. 151–99.

——1980e: Bolor and Dardistan, Islamabad.

——1981: The Gilgit Manuscripts: Discovery by Instalments, in: Journal of Central Asia, IV/2, pp. 1–17.

——1982: Rockcarvings and Inscriptions in the Northern Areas of Pakistan, Islamabad.

B. A. Litvinskij, 1927: Drevnie kočevniki "kryši mira", Moskva.

J. Šer, 1981: Petroglifi Srednei i Central'noj Azii, Moskva.

N. S. Truhtina, S.I. Hodžaš K.L. Oganesjan, 1968: Rospisi Ėrebuni. Soobščenija Gos. Muzeja Izobr. iskusstv. im.A.S. Puškina, IV, Moskva.

Vijayanagar and Portuguese Chronicles

VASUNDHARA FILLIOZAT
Pondichery/ Paris

When we say Vijayanagar, many problems are thrown up. The first and the foremost is about the name of the empire; almost all the historians, including myself, have made the same mistake, i.e. calling the empire by the name of the capital. While going through late Dr M.H. Sharma's work The History of Vijayanagar Empire[1] it struck my mind that the Saṅgamas and their successors, according to the inscriptions, were ruling Karnāṭaka with their residence at Hampi-Vijayanagar.

Between 14th and 16th centuries, Vijayanagar was the name given to Hampi, a modern tiny village on the southern bank of the Tungabhadrā in Hospet *tāluk,* Bellary district, Karnatak state, when the sons of Saṅgama, a petty chieftain, took powers in their hands. Though traditionally 1336 is accepted as the date of the foundation of the empire, we have proved elsewhere 1345 as the commencement of the rule of Karnāṭaka (Vijayanagar) kings.[2]

Of the three dynasties which ruled the Karnāṭaka (Vijayanagar) empire, the Saṅgamas were the first (1346–1485), followed by the Sāḷuvas (1485-1505) and the Tuḷuvas (1505-1565-roughly upto 1580).

Harihara I was the first ruler of the Karnāṭaka (Vijayanagar) empire. Bukka I joined hands with his eldest brother in the administration as his elder brother Kampa I died prematurely in 1349. During the rule of Harihara I the region of Goa was governed by his younger brother Mārappa. Then Mādaras was his minister.[3]

In the time of Harihara II (1337–1404) the whole of Koṅkana was conquered and governed by the same minister Mādaras. He should not be confused with Mādhava, brother of Sāyaṇa, the famous commentator of the Vedas. Mādaras, the governor of Goa, rendered his services to the emperors of Karnāṭaka till the end of his life in 1392. A grant issued by this minister Mādaras engraved on copperplate, was the first Sanskrit text to be translated into a European language, i.e. Portuguese.

The territory of Goa remained undisturbed under the sway of the Saṅgamas till 1470. After the death of Devarāya II in 1461 the power of the Sangamas began to shake due to the weakness of the rulers.

The Bahmanis, the Muslim sultans who came to power in 1347[4] and were ruling from Gulbarga as their capital, began to encroach on the Karnāṭaka empire. Gulbarga is situated approximately 200 kms north of Hampi-Vijayanagar and the rulers were hostile to the Hindu kings. Constant wars were fought between these two kingdoms. The Bahmanis were also trying to establish their supremacy over the seaports because of the trade with foreign countries, specially in horses. Horses were imported to India from Persia and the Arabs were the sole merchants. The Bahmanis conquered Goa in 1470[5] from Kaṉṉaḍa kings and Goa was lost to Karnāṭaka for ever.

In Europe this was a period of discovery of sea routes. Portuguese vessels began to navigate towards the East. When the Portuguese landed at Goa, Sāḷuva Narasiṃha II was ruling from his capital Vijayanagar. The Portuguese called the kingdom Narasynga and the capital "Bisnaga" for Vijayanagar.[6]

The Portuguese began to have contacts with the Indian kings for trade. Soon they learnt the importance of the horse trade with Hindu and Muslim sovereigns of South India. The Portuguese merchants who went to the capital in this connection were impressed by the wealth and glory of Vijayanagar and have left their reminiscences. "... for I know that no one goes there (Bisnaga) without bringing away his quire of paper written about its affairs" writes the Portuguese informant who was posted in Goa for collection of documents on Indian history.[7]

These chronicles are very important for rewriting the history of Vijayanagar but should be used cautiously. Some of these chroniclers were very good historians but, unfortunately, not all. Tome Pires,[8] Barbosa,[9] Domingo Paes,[10] Fernao Nuniz, were the Portuguese who provided much information about the Kaṉṉaḍa capital, though it is valuable to supplement their remarks from other foreign and local sources. So we have made use of other chronicles by Abder Razzak,[11] a Persian ambassador who was in the capital during 1440s; and Nicolo dei Conti,[12] Vartema,[13] Cesare Frederici,[14] all Italians. Cesare Frederici was in the capital in 1567-68, two years after the downfall of the Hindu kings. He had witnessed the contemporary chaotic conditions and the gradual desertion of the town by the nobles and the seigneurs. Lastly, there is the map of Hampi prepared by Colonel Mackenzie in 1800.

The chronicles of Paes and Nuniz provide most valuable information about the history, social and economic conditions. They were in the capital in 1520 and 1535 respectively. The former saw the glory of the empire whereas the latter saw the extravagant life led by the Vijayanagarians.

Since no Indian documents furnish any information about the military architecture of the capital nor are the scanty remnants in situ helpful, only foreign accounts are available.

"Seven citadels and the same number of walls enclose each other" says Abder Razzak.[15] But Paes writes, "at the end of it you have another gate with its wall, which wall goes to meet the wall of the second gate of which I have spoken, in such sort that this city has three fortresses, with another which is the kings' palace".[16] Further Paes while describing the other fortwalls remarks "So that, returning to the city of Bisnaga, you must know that before you arrive at the city gates there is a gate with a wall that encloses all the other enclosures of the city and this wall is a very strong one and of massive stone work".[17]

From these two contradictory statements, it is not easy to imagine the shape of the Vijayanagar fortress. At present, in Hampi we are able to trace out only five fort walls, and those not fully.[18]

The "circumference of the city" according to Vartema was "sixty miles",[19] whereas Abder Razzak states, "The distance between the opposite gates of the outer fortress north and south is two parasangs, and the same east to west".[20] Sewell roughly calculates that the distance between the gates is seven miles.[21] Because of the destruction of these fort walls nothing can be verified nor ascertained. We are obliged to leave the matter in doubt.

According to Abder Razzak the area occupied by the seventh and central fortress which enclosed the king's palace was ten times larger than the market place of the city of Herat. Paes remarks that the area of the king's palace was greater than all the castles of Lisbon.

No Indian documents furnish any information either about the population or the dwelling houses. Nicolo Conti writes, "in this city there are estimated to be ninety thousand men fit to bear arms".[22] Barbosa writes the "king is in possession of 900 elephants and 20,000 horses. The total number of men in the army reaches ten lakhs".[23]

Prof. G.S. Dikshit arrives at a tentative conclusion that there were 500,000 inhabitants in the capital, basing his views on the statements made by Paes that in the capital there were 100,000 houses.[24]

All the chroniclers are unanimous in their statements that the houses were built of wood with thatched roofs, unlike the religious monuments. Cesare Frederici relates that Muslims plundered and burnt the capital after their victory over the Hindu king.[25] But according to a letter written in 1585 "the capital was burnt by the Hindu kings"[26] for the succession to the throne after the battle of Tāḷikōṭa in 1565. It is difficult to judge whose statement is correct because neither of them witnessed the facts. Moreover, many statements made by Cesare Frederici are subject to question.

A few statements can be quoted here from Paes and Nuniz, the most important chroniclers for rewriting Vijayanagara history, but at the same time historians should be very critical while studying them.

Paes describes graphically "going along the principal street, you have one of the chief gateways, which issues from a great open space in front of the king's palace; opposite this is another which passes along to the other side of the city."[27] The present conditions of the ruins in Hampi and the modern tar roads piercing through fort and palace walls prevented us from tracing this main road which used to issue from the front yard of the king's residence. Luckily, a map of Hampi was prepared by Colonel Mackenzie in 1800 on which a long road is shown, which, probably, must be the main street. In all probability, the entrance mentioned by Paes must be the Hoysala gate or the gates at either end of Dēvērī road. At the southern end of Dēvērī road there is a gate through which one could join the main road which led to the open space in front of the palace.

The king's palace which is at the end of this main road is now called the "audience hall". Perhaps here the "Dasara festival activities" used to take place.

The ferry service on the river Tungabhadrā near Anegondi gate is another interesting point which Paes mentions. "... city called Nagundym; it has only three gates, namely one by the river, which they cross in boats embarking just here at this gate".[28] Elsewhere, he expresses his astonishment about the fabrication and capacity of these boats; "boats which are round like baskets; inside they are made of cane and outside are covered with leather; they are able to carry fifteen or twenty persons, and even horses and oxen can cross in them if necessary, but most part these animals swim across".[29] Even today, the boats have the same appearance and cross at the same place. Epigraphs engraved on nearby boulders confirm the statement made by Paes.

Vivid descriptions about various festivals by Paes shed much light on socio-economic conditions of the epoch. Paes mentions that there were many temples in the capital but the most important were outside the city walls;[30] "on the north there are three very beautiful pagodas one of which is called Vitella, and it stands over against this city of Nagundym; the other is called *Aeoperdianar,* and this is the one which they hold in most veneration, and to which they make pilgrimages." Of course, the first is Viṭṭhala, the most beautiful and the masterpiece of Vijayanagara architecture. *Aeoperdianar* is the Portuguese deformation for Virūpākṣa the most ancient temple in the capital which still attracts thousands of pilgrims every year. Though Paes does not mention the third temple, we think that it must be the one dedicated to Lord Kṛṣṇa.[31]

The genealogy and the duration of the reign of each king of Vijayanagar from the foundation as given by Nuniz is not reliable. Nuniz being a foreigner was confused while enumerating the names of the kings and their ministers, for the simple reason that many times several persons bore the same name, e.g. Devarāya I (1406-1422) had a minister called Lakṣmaṇa. Devarāya II (1424-1446) too had a minister called Lakṣmaṇa also known as Lakkaṇṇadaṇḍēśa. He was a grandnephew of Lakṣmaṇamantrī of Devarāya I.

Nuniz relates a story about the king Pinarao son of Deorao, grandson of Visarao. In fact, Visarao is identified with the king Vijayarāya, father of Deorao alias Devarāya II. But Nuniz ignorant of the fact that Pinarao and Deorao are the names of one and the same person, relates a story that "this king was killed by treason by the hand of a nephew whom he had brought up in his house like a son, who thus caused the death of the king."[32] More or less the same story is told by Abder Razzak too.[33]

It is to be noted that neither of them were in the capital to witness the facts. Abder Razzak was then in Malabar where he heard about the story of an attempt made on the king's life. Nuniz repeats the same story a hundred years later. Both are wrong. An inscription in Hampi itself records that one day some miscreants made an attempt on the life of King Devarāya but his minister Lakṣmaṇa took them by surprise and saved the king's life. This epigraph is dated 1410.[34]

According to another inscription[35] the king Dēvarāya II was suffering from heart disease and after all possible remedies were tried there was no improvement in his health. Finally, the king resolved to send a brahmin on pilgrimage to all holy places to perform sacrifices as prescribed in the Vedic texts. The brahmin accordingly went to places like Gaya and others and executed the king's orders. The king finding himself in better health, thanked the brahmin for his services and granted him the free enjoyment of an *agrahāra* near Bēlūr, Hassan district, Karnāṭak state. Descendants of this family till today enjoy the *agrahāra*.

When the throne of Karnāṭaka fell vacant the Sāḷuva Narasiṃha took the powers in his hands and ruled as a representative of the dead king. Nuniz calls him a "usurper" of the Karnāṭaka throne. Though the study of epigraphs proves that the transfer of power was gradual and progressive, modern historians unfortunately mistake Nuniz's unhistorical statement for authentic fact.

While Sāḷuva Narasiṃha II was on the throne he was assisted by his minister Bhujabala Narasiṃha alias Tuḷuva Narasiṃha II. Nuniz calls him Busbalrao. On the death of Sāḷuva Narasiṃha, Tuḷuva Narasiṃha II proclaimed himself king but ruled for only four years and abdicated the throne in favour of his younger half brother Kṛṣṇadevarāya the Great. But Nuniz often relates hearsay accounts[36] which are contradicted by the epigraphs.

In Chapter XVIII Nuniz tells another story that during his lifetime, king Kṛṣṇadevarāya raised to the throne his own son who was only six years old. The child died due to poison administered to him by Sāḷuva Timma and his son. Sāḷuva Timma, according to the contemporary literature and inscriptions, was the closest minister to the king and highly esteemed by him. Many inscriptions also confirm the statement of Nuniz about the enthronement of the young prince and his premature death. But epigraphs do not confirm the punishment imposed on the minister and his family. Inscriptions issued after the death of this prince mention the grants made by the minister and his family.

Nuniz makes many statements about events which he had not witnessed. As a result, it is not safe to rely upon many facts which he mentions. At the same time his chronicle is important for information about the revenues of various regions, the change in the mode of life, the extravagant amounts spent on religious edifices and other fine arts. Contemporary architectural and iconographic evidence of ecclesiastic buildings corroborate his statements. Paes's chronicle is more reliable and profound.

Though historians may not rely upon these chronicles and travelogues to re-write Vijayanagar-Karnāṭaka history, they nevertheless cannot afford to ignore them.

NOTES

1. Though Dr Sharma suggests that the empire was called Karnāṭaka he had entitled his book "Vijayanagar Empire". Ed. M.H. Gopal, Popular Prakashan, Bombay, 1978, Vol.I, p.1.
2. L'Epigraphie de Vijayanagar du début à 1377, Ecole Francaise d'Extrême Orient, Paris, 1973. See introduction.
3. Mysore Archaeological Reports, 1929, No. 90.
4. M.H. Ramasharma, The History of Vijayanagar Empire, Vol.I, p. 24.
5. *Ibid.*, p. 74
6. Dames, Mansel Longworth, The Book of Duarte Barbosa. Haklyut Society, London, 1918 Vol. I, pp. 200-01.
7. Dr (Mrs) Vasundhara Filliozat, The Vijayanagar Empire, National Book Trust, New Delhi, 1977, p. 13.
8. Donald F. Lach, India in the Eyes of Europe, Chicago, U.S.A., 1968.
9. Dames, *op. cit.*
10. Filliozat, *op. cit.*
11. R.M. Major, India in the Fifteenth Century, Deep Publications, New Delhi, 1974.

12. Robert Sewell, A Forgotten Empire, Publications Division, Delhi, 1962.
13. Lach *op. cit.*
14. H.L. Nagegowda, Pravāsi Kaṇḍa India. Vol. 2. Mysore.
15. Major, *op. cit.*, p. 23
16. Filliozat, *op. cit.*
17. *Ibid.*, p. 34
18. V. Filliozat, The town planning of Vijayanagar, Art and Archaeology Research Papers, 102 St. Paul Street, London, No. 14, p. 57.
19. Major, *op. cit.*, p. 6.
20. Sewell, *op. cit.* p. 87.
21. *Ibid.*, p. 87.
22. Major, *op. cit.*, p. 87.
23. Nagegowda, *op. cit.*, p. 294.
24. G.S. Dikshit, Economic Conditions under Vijayanagar, Six Centenary Commemoration Volume, Dharwar, 1936, p. 215.
25. Nagegowda, *op. cit.*
26. Heras, "Jesuit Influence in the Court of Vijayanager", in Quarterly of Mythic Society, XVI, p. 160.
27. Filliozat, Vijayanagar Empire, p. 35.
28. *Ibid.*, p. 68.
29. *Ibid.*, p. 40.
30. *Ibid.*, p. 40.
31. There are actually four big temples outside the city walls along the river. Paes is not wrong in mentioning only three because the fourth, Tiruvaṅgalanātha (so-called Acyuta) temple was built after his visit to the capital. But Dr G. Michell is wrong in dividing the capital into two parts: religious and secular. Read his articles in Marg, "Homage to Vijayanagar", Bombay, 1981.
32. Filliozat, Vijayanagar Empire, p. 83.
33. Sewell *op. cit.*, p. 61.
34. South Indian Inscriptions Vol. IV, No. 267.
35. Epigraphia Carnatica Vol. V, Belur, 305.
36. Filliozat, Vijayanagar Empire, pp. 85-95.

Jahangir and the Angels: Recently Discovered Wall Paintings under European Influence in the Fort of Lahore

Ebba Koch
Vienna/New Delhi

I

The student of Mughal painting is well aware of the contemporary literary evidence for Mughal paintings depicting European and in particular Christian subjects. This literary documentation — especially prominent in the reign of Jahangir (1605–1627) — is provided by European sources as, for example, the descriptions of Jerome Xavier, William Finch, Sir Thomas Roe or Fra Sebastian Manrique.[1] The evidence these authors provide ties up with that in Mughal painting where European and Christian subjects appear as a favorite architectural decoration on the walls of secular buildings, especially of palaces.[2]

However, so far no wall painting was known to exist matching undisputedly any of these descriptions and representations. Though we learn already from Montserrate that Akbar had hung up pictures of Christ, Mary, Moses and Muhammad in his dining hall,[3] none of the hardly surviving wall paintings in Fatehpur Sikri have so far been identified with certainty to depict Christian themes.[4] The frescoes in the gateway of Mehr Banu (Agha) near Humayun's tomb in Delhi — according to his inscription "an old [servant] of Jahangir Shah"[5] — are not well enough preserved to allow us to make any definite statement about their iconography although in one of the painted panels of the transition zone a male figure with a haloe and a female figure can still be made out (Fig.1). These fragments have even occasioned the misinterpretation of this building as a Christian church[6] in spite of its clear Muslim orthodox inscriptions and its obvious function as a gateway to the adjoining sarai.

Thus it was with considerable excitement that I saw during my last visit to the Fort of Lahore[7] in December 1980 the frescoes on the vault of the Kala Burj which had been uncovered recently from their British white-wash by the Department of Archaeology.[8] These frescoes — depictions of angels, birds and stars — are so far the best preserved instance of Mughal wall paintings showing indisputably European-Christian influences in style of representation and in the choice of the figures. They confirm the literary accounts of the contemporary European observers and show that the representations in Mughal miniature paintings were not merely a convention of architecture in painting but a reflex of the architectural decoration in real buildings.

We shall, however, see that the European forms were given the liberty to escape from their original context in order to express a concept deeply rooted in the Islamic tradition of rulership.

II

The so-called Kala Burj, the second residential tower from the West, projects as a half-octagon from the northern front of the Fort[9] (Fig.2). The palace buildings originally overlooked on this side the river Ravi. The fort wall and its projecting towers are here decorated with the famous figurative tilework in accordance with the north part of the West front.[10]

As to the interior of the palace the Kala Burj forms the head of a residential wing that separates two courtyards. The central room of the tower, a vaulted chamber nearly 7 m high, is not octagonal as the outer appearance of the tower suggests but square, about 6 m by 6 m. It is enclosed by double-storied, partly open galleries that give the tower its polygonal outer appearance. The interior organisation of the central vaulted room reflects its double storied encasement in such a way that its wall is divided horizontally by an uninterrupted cornice. Above the cornice rises the vault like a baldachin from the transition zone that is formed by eight deep arched niches and squinches (Fig. 9). The brick structure of the actual vault is completely concealed behind a complex decorative plaster shell. Above the points of the squinches and the spherical triangles over the niches of the transition zone — all structured in themselves by arched panels and fragmentary faceted vaults — rises a system of stars arranged in concentric circles. These stars form the knots of the complicated network of the vault that consists of straight lines cutting out fan- and kite-shaped concave compartments of different sizes (about 40-60 cm). In the centre of this concentric system is a medallion (about 2 m in diameter) of the figure of an eight-pointed star formed by a network of intersecting arched ribs (Fig.9). It appears like an ornamental reduction of an early Mughal vault form, namely the flat saucer dome sitting on an identical network of intersecting arched ribs that integrates the arches of the transition zone.[11] This earlier vault form has been reduced and inserted as the central figure in the design of the vault of the Kala Burj.

Originally, the whole vault, including the transition zone, was covered with paintings which survive only as fragments in the central area of the vault. The programme of the paintings corresponds to the concentric organization of the vault: it consists of birds in the stars that form the knots of the network, angels in the fan-shaped compartments arranged in circles and two fighting *simurgh*-s (mythical Persian birds) in the central medallion. The facets that enframe these figurative paintings are filled with arabesques, flowers and flowery ornaments.

Structure and painting of the vault are conceived as a unified whole in which only the bigger concave forms are actually modelled out of the plaster. The details of the network are indicated by slightly incised painted lines. The paintings and the plaster vault, therefore, must be contemporary.[12]

I have not been able to discover a date on the paintings, and the Kala Burj belongs to those buildings of the Lahore Fort for which no convincing chronology has been established so far. Therefore, before we deal with the paintings in detail, it will be useful to compare the structure of the vault with dated vaults related in character in order to use every available evidence to assign a date to the paintings.

The earliest dated Mughal example of such a painted net vault developed from fixed points in concentric circles that is known to me is found in Lahore itself. It is the central vault of the Mosque of Maryam al-Zamani now called Begam Shahi Masjid (Fig.6). This mosque lies outside the eastern gate of the fort and, according to the inscriptions over its eastern and northern gate was constructed in 1020/1611. This vault represents a simplified version of the vault of the Kala Burj with a less complex transition zone of eight clearly defined arches. Its central medallion[13] appears like a reduction of the central star figure of the Kala Burj, which itself, as we have seen, can be interpreted as a reduction form. The paintings of this vault are not figurative but ornamental. The polylobed medallions that take the place of the stars are however inscribed with several of "the most beautiful names of Allah". It seems that here by means of calligraphy, the same intention is realized as in the Kala Burj by means of figural painting, namely "to let the vault speak". The paintings which cover the vault have been restored lately to the extent that the original colours are lost. The motifs of the flowery ornaments on the facets are, however, similar to the corresponding facets of the vault of the Kala Burj.

The later development of this vault type can be observed in the central ground floor chamber of the tomb of I'timad al-Daulah at Agra, dated by inscription to 1036 - 37/1626 - 27.[14] The general structure is similar to the vault of the Kala Burj but the network is divided into a greater number of facets which are, therefore, flatter and smaller. New is the introduction of curvilinear lines in the central figure. These features point towards the future development of this type of vault in the architecture of Shah Jahan's reign where a thin network of stucco is spread over the whole vault between the fixed points in such a way that the connecting lines create the impression of continuous curves.[15]

The features of the Kala Burj vault, in other words, the plastic modelling of the structure, the big facets, the archaic centrepiece and the straight lines connecting the fixed points, place it early in this group of vaults. We can, therefore, date it as contemporary or slightly earlier than the vault of the Begam Shahi Masjid of 1611.

III

This date coincides approximately with Jahangir's statements about his alterations in the Lahore Fort. These he mentions in the Tuzuk for the first time in 1612 A.D. when he remarks that he sent Khwaja Jahan Khwaja Dust Muhammad to Lahore *"ba-jihat tarh-i 'imarat-i daulat khanah-i Lahur"*.[16] This has been translated by Alexander Rogers as "in order to lay the foundation of a palace of Lahore"[17] but, according to Mughal terminology, it clearly means "for the design of the building of the Lahore palace".[18] The building activities in the Lahore Fort are again mentioned later in 1612, 1617 and 1619.[19] On 5th Muharram 1030 A.H. (30 November 1620) the emperor solemnly entered the palaces which had been brought to completion by Ma'mur Khan.[20] Jahangir approved greatly what had been done. He mentions, especially, that the buildings were all painted (*munaqqash*) and decorated with pictures (*musawwar*) by the work of outstanding masters (*ustadan-i nadirah-kar*). The dates given there are corroborated by the only inscription of Jahangir so far traceable in the Lahore Fort on the gate of a little courtyard now called Makatib or Maktab Khana which served, apparently, as a forecourt to the palaces north of it (Fig. 2). The inscription commemorates the completion of the *daulat khanah* in "the twelfth year of the blessed accession of His Imperial Majesty [1617] the shadow of God, a Solomon in dignity, Kayomarth in state, Alexander in arms, the asylum of the caliphate, the emperor Nuru-d-din Jahangir . . ."[21] Yet it seems that Jahangir's alterations of the palace of Lahore were begun prior to his mentioning them for the first time in the Tuzuk. For William Finch who visited Lahore in February 1610, gives a detailed account of wall paintings in different parts of the palace, representing Jahangir, his ancestors, sons, *mansabdar*-s and also some Christian subjects.[22]

So far the only wall-paintings discovered to tally with this description are the angels of the vault of the Kala Burj. It is difficult to bring Finch's description of the Lahore Fort in accordance with the surviving buildings.[23] He seems however to be clearly referring to the Kala Burj when he speaks of a "small Gallery, at the end of which, next the River, through a small window, the King looks forth at his Dersanee [*darshan*] to behold the fights of wilde beasts on the meadow by the River . . . at the end is a small Devoncan [*diwan khanah*], where the King useth to sit [Fig. 2] . . . In the Gallery where the King useth to sit, are drawne over head many Pictures of Angels, with Pictures of Banian Dews, or rather Divels, intermixt in most ugly shape, with long hornes, staring eyes, shagge haire, great fangs, ugly paws, long tailes, with such horrible difformity and deformity, that I wonder the poor woman are not frightened therewith . . ."[24]

Part of the "many Pictures of Angels" which Finch had seen "drawne overhead" survive in the central area of the vault but for the moment we are left to wonder what he meant with the "Banian Dews" of which no trace is left. They are going to play an important role in our later argument.

We can, therefore, deduct from the description of Finch that the paintings date earlier than 1610. This would still accord with the evidence we have gathered from stylistic comparisons regarding the structure of the vault. They must have been executed sometime between 1605, when Jahangir entered the Lahore Fort for the first time as emperor after the successful pursuit of his rebellious son Khusrau, and February 1610, when Finch saw them.[25]

IV

As pointed out earlier, only fragments of the paintings survive in the central area of the vault. The theme of the frescoes is in correspondence with the surrounding architecture. They interpret the vault of the room as a heavenly vault of concentric spheres demarcated by stars and populated by winged beings of the celestial regions. The golden stars contain different flying birds, most of them only partly preserved. In the area of the three innermost circles ten flying angels and two winged angel-heads are still recognisable in various states of preservation. Their fan-shaped compartments are set off by blue colour and by little clouds as sections of heaven. In the central medallion two *simurgh*-s partly damaged, are engaged in fighting with a definite touch of reality.

What is left of the paintings impresses by its quality. The angels belong to the most original and lively creations Mughal art has brought forth in this genre. They do not follow the traditional Iranian-Mughal type of the winged being dressed in a long floating garment[26] but are clearly derived from a European prototype namely the boyish (half) nude putto image which had been revived in the Italian Quattrocento in conscious imitation of classical models[27] (Figs 14, 15). In the sixteenth and seventeenth century art of Europe it was a popular image as angel in religious and as putto in secular representations. The latter were mostly of an allegoric or symbolic nature. The putto angel had been introduced into Mughal art through the pictorial material brought to the court by the Jesuit missions from about 1580 onwards, mainly engravings from Antwerp printers specially produced for Jesuit requirements in Counter Reformation and mission activities.[28]

The winged child-angel head, a form reduced from the concept of the cherubim who has wings instead of arms,[29] entered Mughal art for the first time through the same sources.

The European type of the adolescent angel which goes back to early Christianity and the Middle Ages,[30] was also taken over from these engravings. Similar in concept he was particularly qualified to fuse with or to supplant the traditional Iranian-Mughal version which, as a matter of fact, largely gave way to the three European types in the reign of Jahangir. First the European angels were copied in their original context (Fig. 14).[31] Later they either took the place of the Iranian-Mughal angel or *pari* figure in traditional programmes,[32] or, they appeared especially as puttos in a Mughal pictorial environment modelled upon the pattern of their original ambiente. This new genre — the Mughal allegory — was created by Jahangir and his artists.[33] I have shown elsewhere that it is a characteristic Mughal hybrid expressing visually Jahangir's literary concepts of rulership by means of composition techniques derived from European allegories.[34] To this end European forms are used which have undergone a Mughalization together with Mughal forms realized with European stylistic techniques.

The angel cycle of the Kala Burj is a vivid demonstration of this process. It shows, simultanously, all the above-mentioned stages of angel depiction, from the only slightly transformed Mughal copy of European models to Europeanized Mughal images, all characteristic products of the creative dialogue between Mughal and European art in the time of Jahangir.

Among the preserved angels the most faithful copy of a European model is the angel holding a red scroll with *nasta 'liq* characters in the innermost circle (Fig. 12). The type of the putto angle with bent legs is close to the one flying in the top centre of the Mughal copy of a Descent from the Cross (1598 A.D.) (Fig. 14).

According to Robert Skelton it is based on a Flemish print that combines Last Judgement scenes with a missing composition of a Descent from the Cross by Raffael preserved through an engraving of Marcantonio Raimondi.[35] The angel has retained the chubbiness of its European prototype. His body is strongly modelled and his short green skirt flies in soft folds around his thighs. The carefully observed naturalistic details of the feathers of his wings, though only partly preserved, recall the best creations of this genre in Mughal painting, namely the bird studies of *ustad* Mansur and his circle.[36] Even without knowing the exact European prototype we realize that his large eyes and their intense took are also a Mughal contribution to the original concept as are the *nasta'liq* characters on the scroll. So far the text could not be deciphered by any of the authorities consulted.[37] Apparently it gives no coherent meaning and, as Dr Ziyauddin A. Desai suggests, was intended only to indicate the character of the scroll as a carrier of writing, since pseudo-writing is a common practice of calligraphic decoration in Islamic art. (The height of the vault and the size of the letters would have made a reading impossible in any case.)

Clearly based on the same model in regard to position and treatment of their legs and skirts but departing from this prototype in the upper part of their bodies, are two more of the preserved angels. One is to the right of the angel with the scroll (Figs 7, 16), the other beneath him. He is the only one surviving in a recognizable shape in the third circle (Figs 3, 4, 5, 9). He flies in the opposite direction and carries a bowl with eatables that cannot clearly be identified but look like fruits.

Closely patterned after a European original but more estranged by his accessories than the angel with the scroll is, in the second circle, the angel with earrings and a European hat (Fig. 13). This headgear though European is not at all used by his European counterparts. A potential source for this angel is found on an engraving known to have been in the possession of the Mughal emperors, namely the second frontispiece of the famous Antwerp Polyglot Bible, presented to Akbar (1556–1605) by the first Jesuit Mission in 1580. It is the flying putto who holds a laurel wreath and a palm branch over the head of the Pietas Regia, the personification of the piety of Philip II of Spain, the sponsor of this Bible edition[38] (Fig. 15).

The Mughal version of this putto is however more athletic, the upper part of his body being even stronger modelled than the one of the angel with the scroll. The enormous pink wings show minute distinctions in texture and in the pattern of the different feathers.

The angel's arms in front of his body and the position of his fingers indicates that he was supposed to hold something like a string. This original design however has apparently not been carried out as his hands are empty. The composition is very fine and the most complete among those which are preserved. The whole background with the sky and the little clouds is still visible. The sophisticated palette uses different shades of pink and grey for the body, the clouds and the wings; purple for the skirt and the ruby of the earring that is set between two pearls. The complimentary colour to this purple appears in the sharp green of the angel's hat.

This angel served as a basic model for a group of four other angels in different states of preservation. In each case however the pattern was used only for the pose of the body (in particular the legs) upon which angel images of a different character were grafted. One is juxtaposed to the angel with the European hat but separated from it by a compartment with a winged angel head (Fig. 16). He alone among the surviving angels wears a thin garment in soft folds reaching down to his ankles. The original colours of this angel can still be seen on the head in profile covered by a red cap and on the black wings. The rest of the body survives only as drawing. He carries an object that seems to be similar to the (fruit) bowl carried by the fragmentary angel in the third row.

The other fully preserved angel who adopts the posture of the angel with the European hat but abandons the original nature of his model completely, is the dark angel with the flower wreath in the innermost circle (Fig. 8). In his hands he holds a turban of the distinctive shape worn by emperor Humayun and his royal brothers.[39] This "Hindu-angel", as we might as well call him,[40] is dressed in a diaphanous *jamah* indicated in brownish-red lines, hardly visible against the dark body. It is tied over the short skirt out of which stick the legs that have kept the chubbiness of their European source. The wings are shaded in grey, black and white.

Two fragments, one at the lower right of the Hindu angel, the other in the western part of the innermost circle, seem to have been derived also from the model of the angel with the European hat.

The two remaining angels in the innermost circle vary from this pattern in the pose of their arms. Instead of holding an object with both arms in front of their bodies they raise the right arm to the height of their heads. Their fingers clutch something that looks like green feathers or stems. Both angels represent again the athletic type with strongly-modelled bodies. One wears a crown-like cap (Fig. 11), the other a pointed cap with a wide brim (Fig. 10).

There remains to be discussed the *saqi* angel in the second circle who holds a long-necked bottle and a cup (Figs. 8, 11). Of all the angels preserved he is the one with the least outlandish appearance. The youthful Mughal cupbearer — here raised to the status of an angel — is however given a new physical presence by his nude, well-modelled torso. The sophisticated palette is limited to three colours. The greyish golden tan of the flesh colour is also used for the wings, the warm red of the skirt appears again on the cap. Its wide brim, the bottle and the cup are indicated in gold. These colours are characteristic of Govardhan and we find a close relative of this angel in the young *faqir* among a group of *faqir*-s resting in a landscape, attributed recently to Govardhan but dated much later to 1625.[41]

The two winged angel heads that are still preserved in the second circle, represent again a purely European concept that has no precedent in the Islamic tradition of painting (compare Fig. 14 with Figs 11 and 16). They became great favourites with Jahangir. They appear especially in miniatures directly related to the emperor, as for instance in the well-known political allegory of Jahangir embracing Shah 'Abbas of about 1618–20.[42] There winged angel heads not only support the great sun and moon halo of Jahangir but also appear as a golden ornament on his green waistcoat. In the durbar scene of the Keir collection, dated around the same time, winged angel heads function as capitals of Jahangir's throne, European angels of the adolescent type appear in the lunettes.[43]

The central medallion of the Kala Burj creates the illusionistic impression of an opening of the vault to the blue sky where a pink and a green *simurgh*, both with long gold, green and red tail feathers, are engaged in a struggle (Fig. 9). (All these colours dominate the palette of the vault.) This dynamic concept hardly fits into the frame of the balanced natural history drawings of the circle of *ustad* Mansur. The whole concept and the style come closer to Mughal marginal drawings — *hashiyah*-s — which are a traditional domain of the aggressive *simurgh*.[44]

Or do we, perhaps, understimate the versatility of Jahangir's miniaturists when working in a different genre and medium?

V

Frescoe painting certainly involves techniques different from miniature painting but there is no evidence that Jahangir employed specialized artists for the murals of his palaces. From the passage of the Tuzuk referred to earlier we obtain only the information that they were *ustadan-i nadirah-kar* (outstanding masters).

On the other hand there is literary evidence of at least one instance prior to Jahangir's reign that Mughal miniaturists decorated palaces with murals. Shaikh Farid Bhakkari mentions in the Dhakirat al-Khawanin, compiled in 1061–61/1650, that 'Abd al-Samad had painted "with his own blessed hand (*ba-dast-i mubarak-i khud*)" the private appartment (*khilwat khanah*) of the house of Khan-i A 'zam in the Red Fort of Agra.[45]

We maintain, then, that Jahangir's miniaturists were also charged with the decoration of his palaces. The high quality of the frescoes in the Kala Burj certainly suggests a cooperation of his best masters available around 1610. This also agrees with his own statement in the Tuzuk. Because of the different medium (frescoe) and the determining influence of the European sources we would not like to venture any definite attribution. May we, all the same, suggest tentatively that Jahangir's experts in dealing with the adaption of European sources for his picture programmes, Abu'l Hasan and Bichitr, may well have contributed?

Close to the concept of the Kala Burj angels is the illustration of the Diwan-i-Hafiz of the British Library of about 1610, where a boyish European angel is introduced for the first time into a Mughal court scene, namely the emperor's departure for hawking[46] (Fig. 17). Thus a metaphor of Hafiz is visually related to Jahangir.[47] As to the birds and angel wings, the authorship of *ustad* Mansur and his circle has already been suggested whereas the *saqi* angel points towards Govardhan though here the comparable material dates from a later time.

VI

Leaving the problems of style and attribution to further discussion we shall endeavour to answer another question. Was the frescoe cycle of the Kala Burj not meant to express a more specific idea than the obvious one, namely, to characterize the *diwan khanah* of Jahangir's private appartments as a heavenly palace? This, in any case, would have been the most traditional way to denote the dwelling of a Muslim ruler.[48] The problem arises in view of several features of the representation that cannot be explained by this general interpretation, for instance the eccentric headgears of the angels and the specific activities in which they seem to be engaged. If a more specific programme was expressed in these frescoes, then we may ask further whether the fact that they were realized with predominantly European forms has a special significance, given Jahangir's pronounced interest in European themes and ways of representation?

The evidence in surviving monuments and representations of palace building in miniature painting shows that angels or winged beings, birds and *simurgh-s* belong to the traditional stock of images used for the decorum of an Islamic ruler. These images appear either as individual motifs or feature in picture programmes that may also include fights of real or mythical animals and birds, beasts or birds of prey descending on their respective victims, or beasts of prey and their potential victims in peaceful coexistence. The tradition of these motifs and themes as symbols of rulership and the paradisical setting of the ruler has been investigated recently, for Iran and its area of influence, by Ingeborg Luschey-Schmeisser in connection with her study of the tile cycle of the Hasht Behisht pavilion in Isfahan of 1670.[49] Luschey-Schmeisser has interpreted winged beings in connection with Muslim rulers as symbols of victory and power going back to the victories of classical times.[50] She views them further as an expression of rulership in search of the blessing of the angels and as winged beings who protect and serve the ruler.[51] Thus her interpretations remain as general as the reading that offered itself as the most obvious interpretation of the function of Jahangir's angels and birds in the Kala Burj. We have seen that Jahangir has a general inclination to be depicted in the company of (European) angels.[52] His angels in the Kala Burj however were actors in a more specific setting. Being as deeply embedded in the tradition of the mythology of Islamic rulership it had become, like the notion of the heavenly palace, a cliche by the time of Jahangir. No other Islamic ruler beside Jahangir however had given this well-worn concept such a naturalistic and individual expression.

The key for our interpretation is provided, though unintentionally so, by William Finch who, as we remember, expressed his astonishment about the "Banian Dews or rather Divels" populating the vault together with the angels.[53] (As no trace of them is left they must have been set in the compartments of the outer circles or the panels of the transition zone.) From Finch's reaction we can deduct that they must have been represented as naturalistically as the angels for he was amazed that the "poor woman" of the *zananah* were not frightened by the view of such monstrous images. Not familiar with the symbolic images of the mythology of Islamic rulers Finch did not realize that far from being a cause of horror these depictions on the contrary were a source of elation and reassurance to the female inmates of the palace. For Finch's "Banian Dews" were of course no other than the *dew*-s or *djinn*-s of Sulayman bin Dawud, the archetypal ruler of the Qur'an, the prophet king who by divine assistance rules over the seen and unseen world.[54] Countless myths and legends had developed around the Qur'anic figure. All sources elaborate the fact that he was granted command over the demons or *djinn*-s which he controlled with the divine seal on his ring and the assistance of the angels, who disciplined the unruly ones or put them in irons.[55]

Among the animal subjects of Solomon the birds are especially prominent, with the Qur'anic *hudhud* (hoopoe) as his messenger.[56] Based on these Qur'anic passages and legends a special Solomonic iconography developed in painting. The most frequent representation is that of Solomon on his throne surrounded by the angels who have acquired the position of his servants, the subjected *djinn*-s, the birds led by the *simurgh* (*shah-i murghan*) and his other animal subjects.[57]

A variation of this theme, particularly relevant in our context, is Solomon on his flying throne[58] (Fig. 18). With him carried through the air by angels and *djinn*-s are the requirements of Solomon's princely household and those animals which cannot fly like the deer or the ibex, as well as the ones which cannot fly very well like the house duck (goose) and the peacock. The birds with the *simurgh* and the *hudhud* complete Solomon's flying retinue. In the decoration of palaces, real buildings and painted architecture, we often find individual winged beings who apparently have been taken out of this pictorial context. They still carry their respective fruit bowls, ibexes, peacocks and the like that acquire now the quality of attributes to denote their carriers as Solomonic angels[59] (Fig. 21).

Each Islamic ruler compared himself with Solomon to the extent that "an automatic association with Solomon developed for all themes, myths and ideas which pertained to the life of the prince and to its setting".[60] The Mughal emperors and among them Jahangir were no exception. The poets celebrate Jahangir as Solomon and Nur Jahan as Bilqis, the queen of Sheba.[61] In his only inscription in the Lahore Fort Jahangir is addressed as another Solomon (*Sulayman jah*).

These literary associations with Solomon were also expressed in visual images. No literary metaphor can be as particularized as a picture must be, hence the same theme can be illustrated in many different ways. This consideration is particularly relevant in our context because Jahangir or the persons responsible for his artistic programmes used the same Solomonic theme not only in the interior of the palace but also on its outer side.

It has not been noticed so far that the famous tile decoration of the Lahore Fort contains clear Solomonic allusions. The tile panels that must have covered originally the whole Northern front and the northern part of the Western front survive only in fragments. The preserved panels depict scenes of Mughal court life in the particular historical period together with the ahistorical symbols of rulership such as mythical animals, beasts of prey descending on their victims and the like, as already briefly discussed.[62] In the spandrels of the arched openings or blind arches of the upper zone we find angels with Solomonic attributes and subjected demons (Fig. 19). They give these representations the significance of the court of a *shah Sulayman hasham* (a ruler with the retinue of Solomon).[63]

This proves that Finch's observation in regard to the *dew*-s was accurate. We can, therefore, use the other representations in particular and the iconography of Solomon and his flying retinue in general to explain the enigmatic features of the angels in the Kala Burj.

The Solomonic angels on the outer fort wall are realized in a more conservative medium (tile) and style. Most of them are derived from the traditional Iranian angel type with a crown-like cap and long floating

Fig.1 Gate of Mehr Banu Agha's sarai south west of Humayun's Tomb, Delhi, 1021/1612, interior, north east corner, transition zone, wall painting after a European (Christian) model. (Photograph E.Koch.)

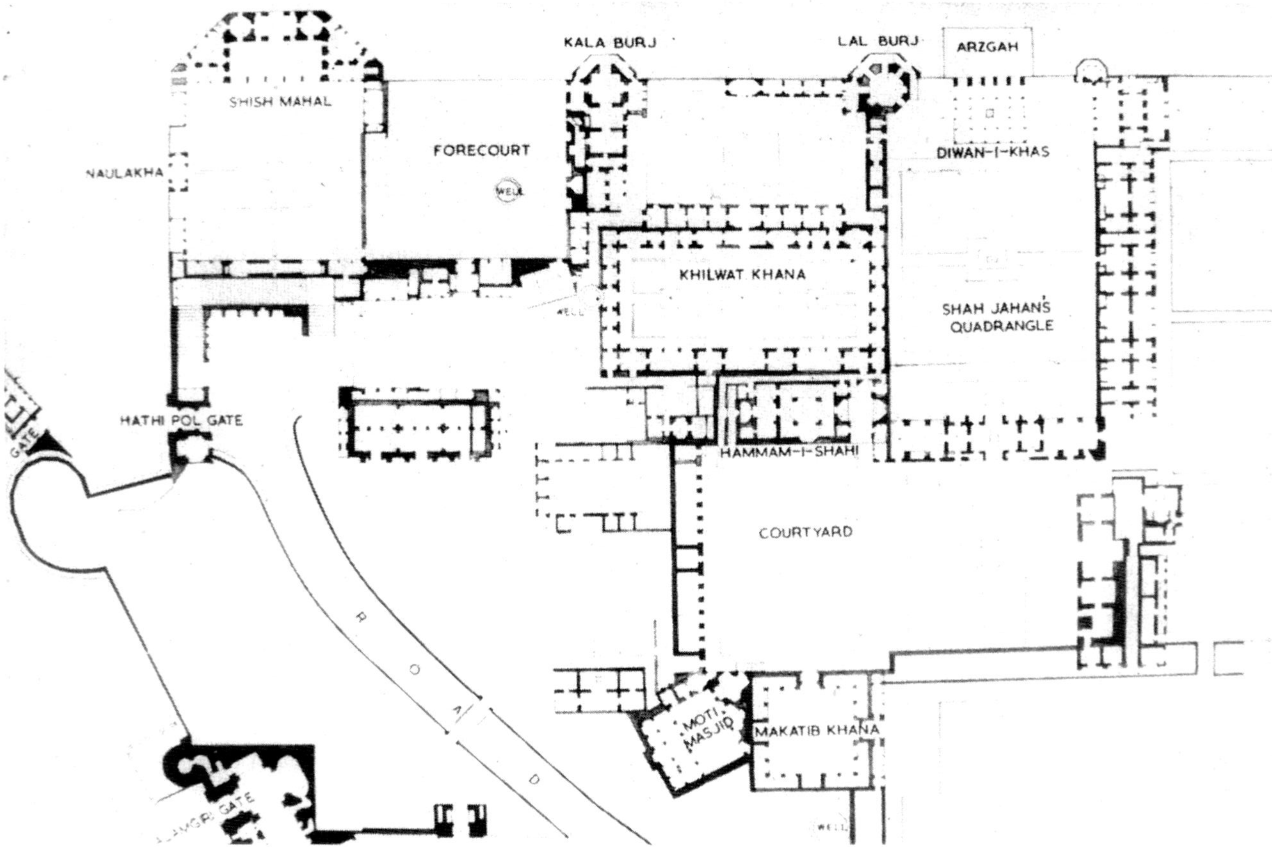

Fig.2 Plan of Lahore Fort, (drawn by Mohammad Anwar Siraj), detail of north west corner, Department of Archaeology, Western Pakistan Circle, Lahore. (Photograph E.Koch.)

Fig.3 Kala Burj, vault from north. (Photograph E.Koch.)

Fig.4 Kala Burj, vault, southern part, detail. (Photograph E.Koch.)

Fig.5 Kala Burj, vault, eastern part, detail. (Photograph E.Koch.)

Fig.6 Begam Shahi Masjid or Mosque of Maryam al-Zamani, Lahore 1020/1611, central vault, north west corner. (Photograph E.Koch.)

Fig.7 Angel with raised arm, Kala Burj, vault, innermost circle. (Photograph E.Koch.)

Fig.8 *Saqi* angel and "Hindu" angel with flower wreath holding a Humayuni turban, Kala Burj, vault, innermost circle. (Photograph E.Koch.)

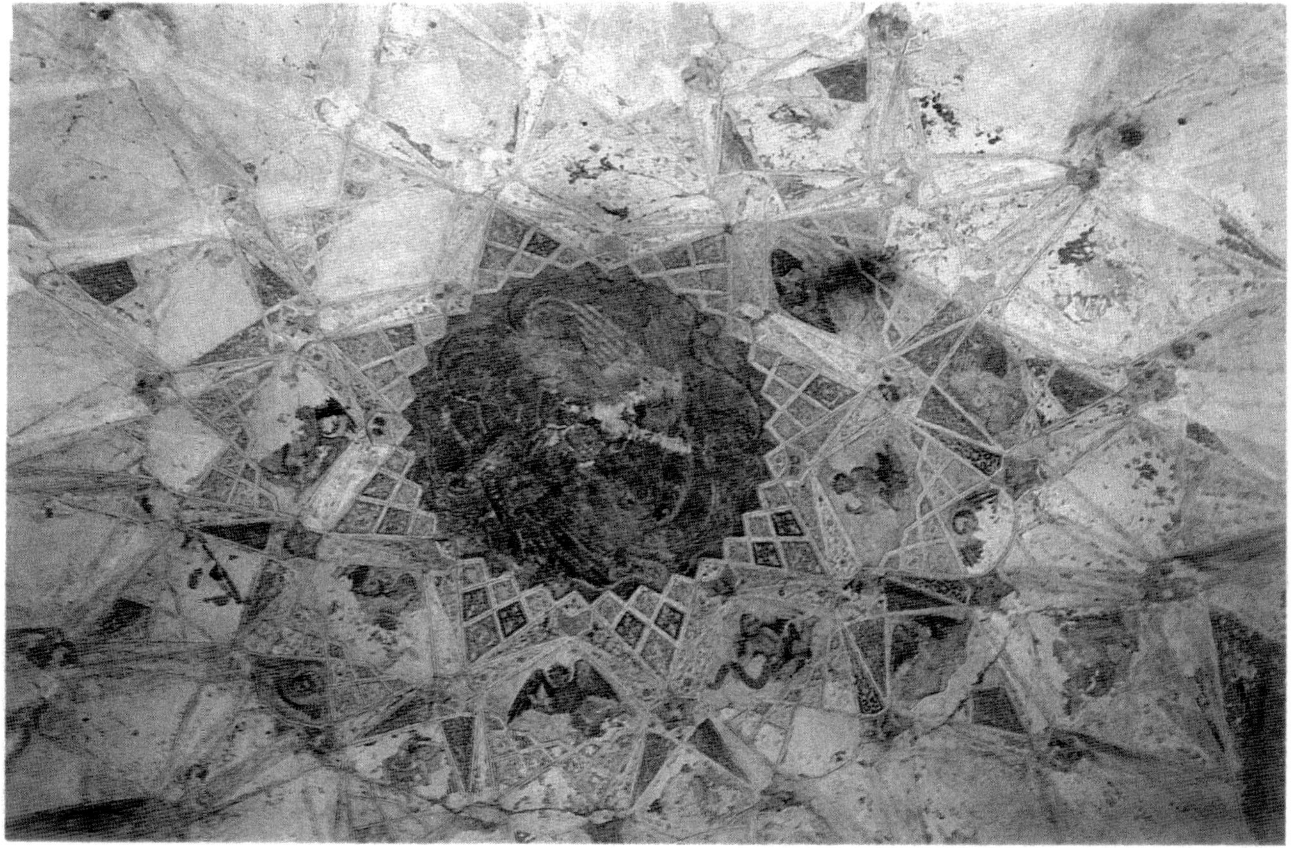

Fig. 9 Kala Burj, Lahore Fort, vault, 1605–1610. (Photograph E. Koch.)

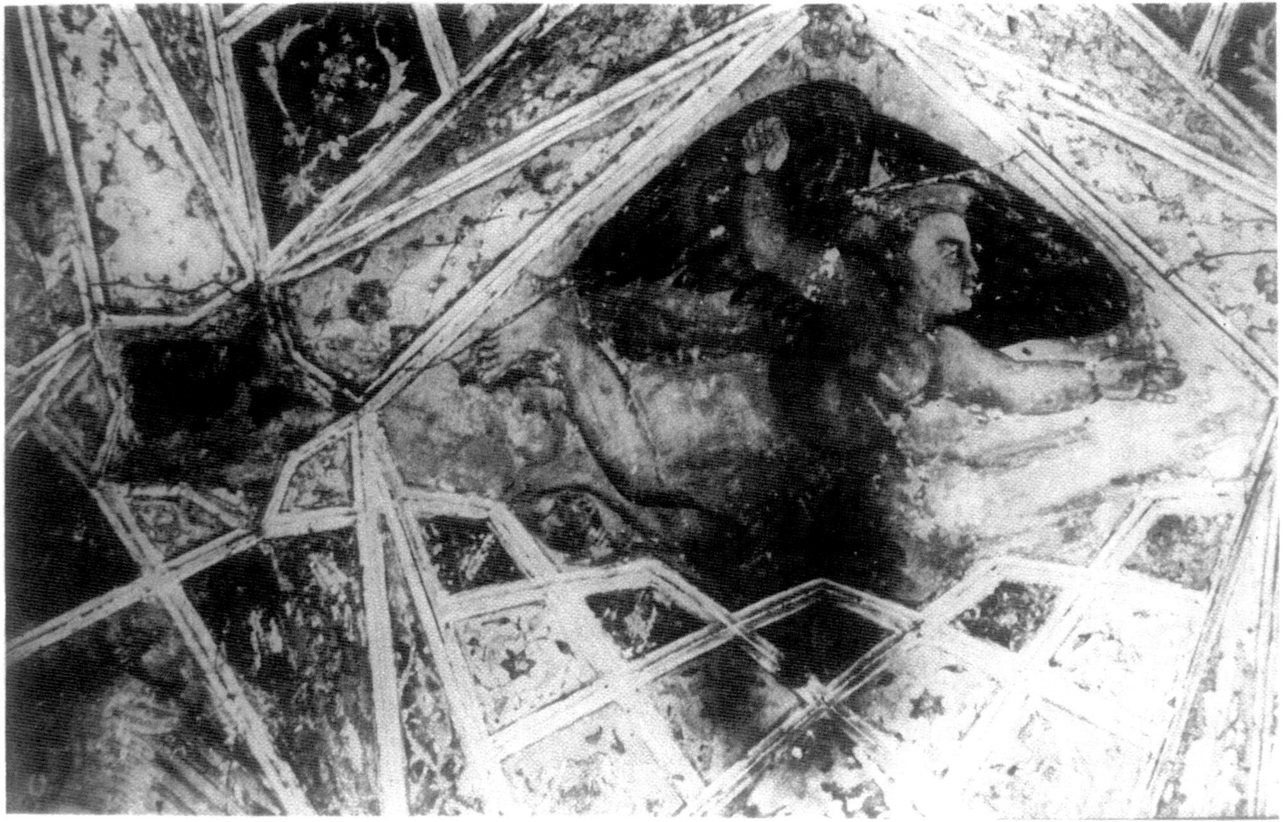

Fig.10 Angel with raised arm, earrings and pointed cap, Kala Burj, vault, innermost circle. (Photograph E.Koch.)

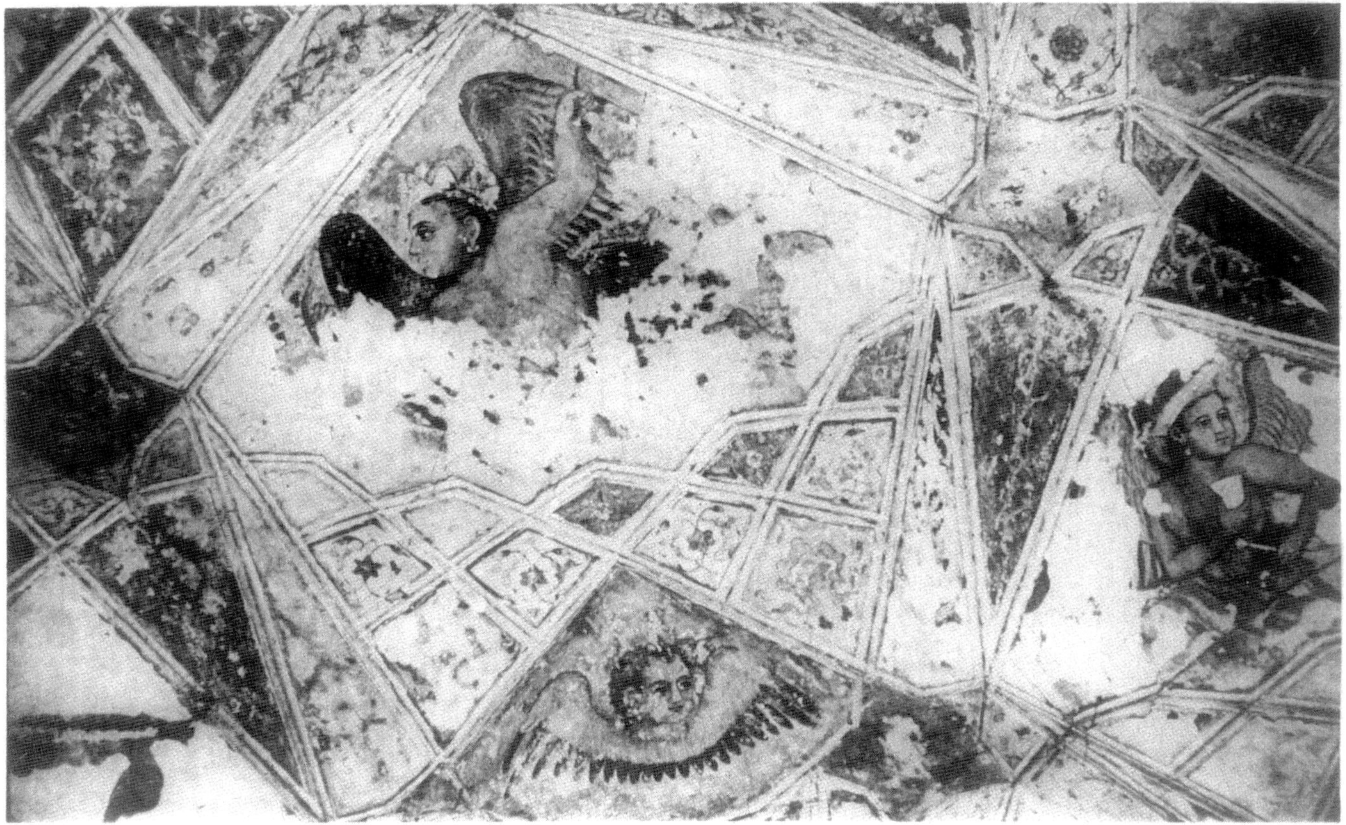

Fig. 11 Angel with raised arm, earrings and crown-like cap; winged angel head and *saqi* angel, Kala Burj, vault, innermost circle. (Photograph E. Koch.)

Fig. 12 Angel holding a scroll with *nasta'liq* characters, Kala Burj, vault, innermost circle. (Photograph E. Koch.)

Fig. 13 Angel with earrings and European hat, and partly preserved hoopoe in the star to the left, Kala Burj, vault, second circle. (Photograph E. Koch.)

Fig. 14 The Descent from the Cross, detail, Mughal, 1598. Victoria and Albert Museum (I.S.133–1964, f.79).

Fig. 15 Putto holding a laurel wreath and a palm branch over the head of *Pietas Regia,* the personification of the piety of Philip II of Spain, detail of the second title page of the first volume of the Antwerp Polyglot Bible, 1568. Vienna, Oesterreichische Nationalbibliothek (I.B.2).

Fig.16 Kala Burj, vault, eastern part, detail. (Photograph E.Koch.)

Fig. 17 Jahangir whilst out hawking meeting an angel, *circa* 1610, illustration to a Diwan-i Hafiz, British Library. (By permission of the British Library.)

Fig.18 Solomon on his flying throne, first half of the 16th century, Tabriz School. (Courtesy of the Freer Gallery of Art, Smithsonian Institution, Washington, D.C.)

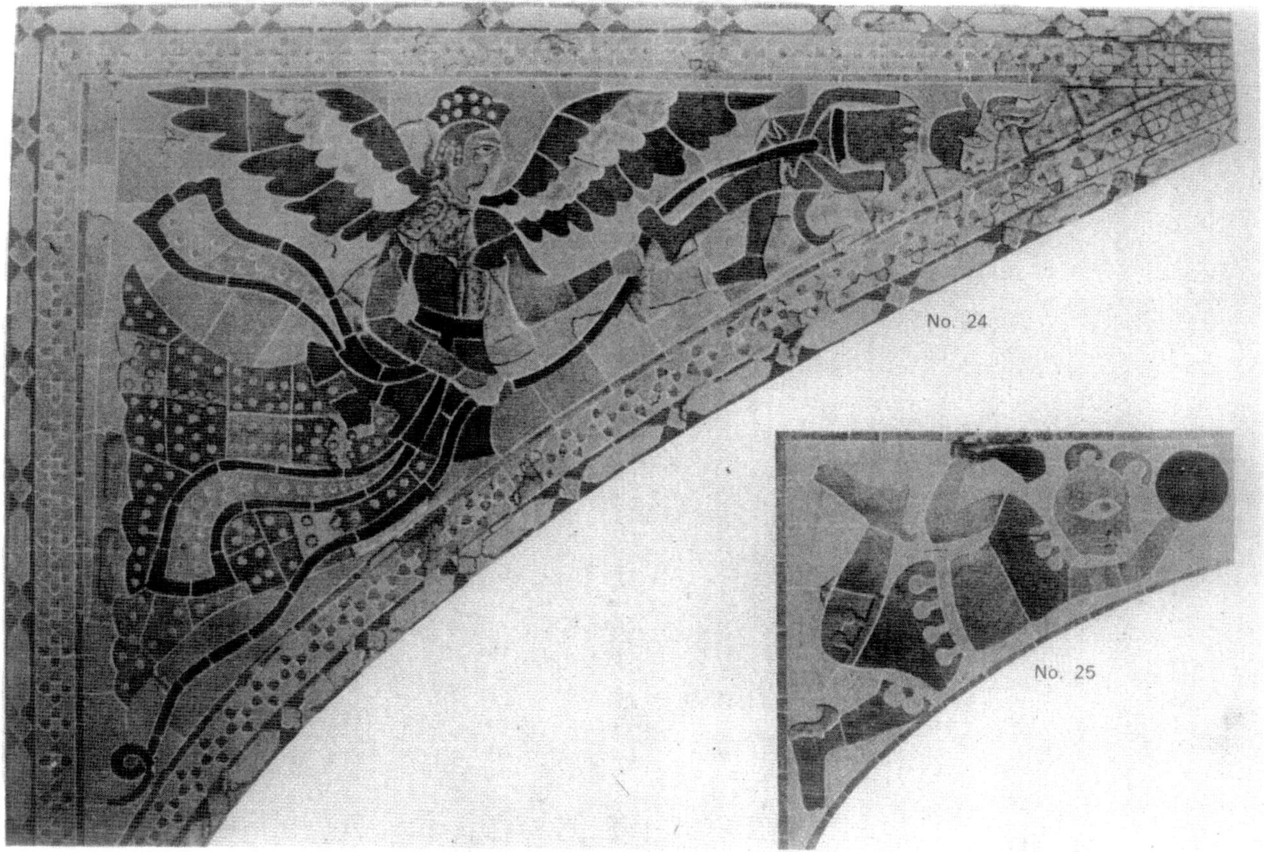

Fig. 19 Solomonic angel leading a subjected *djinn;* dancing *djinn;* Lahore Fort, outer west wall. (after Vogel.)

Fig.20 Rambagh or Bagh -i Nur Afshan, Agra, south pavilion, vault painted with birds and winged beings, southern part, completed in 1030/1621. (Photograph E.Koch.)

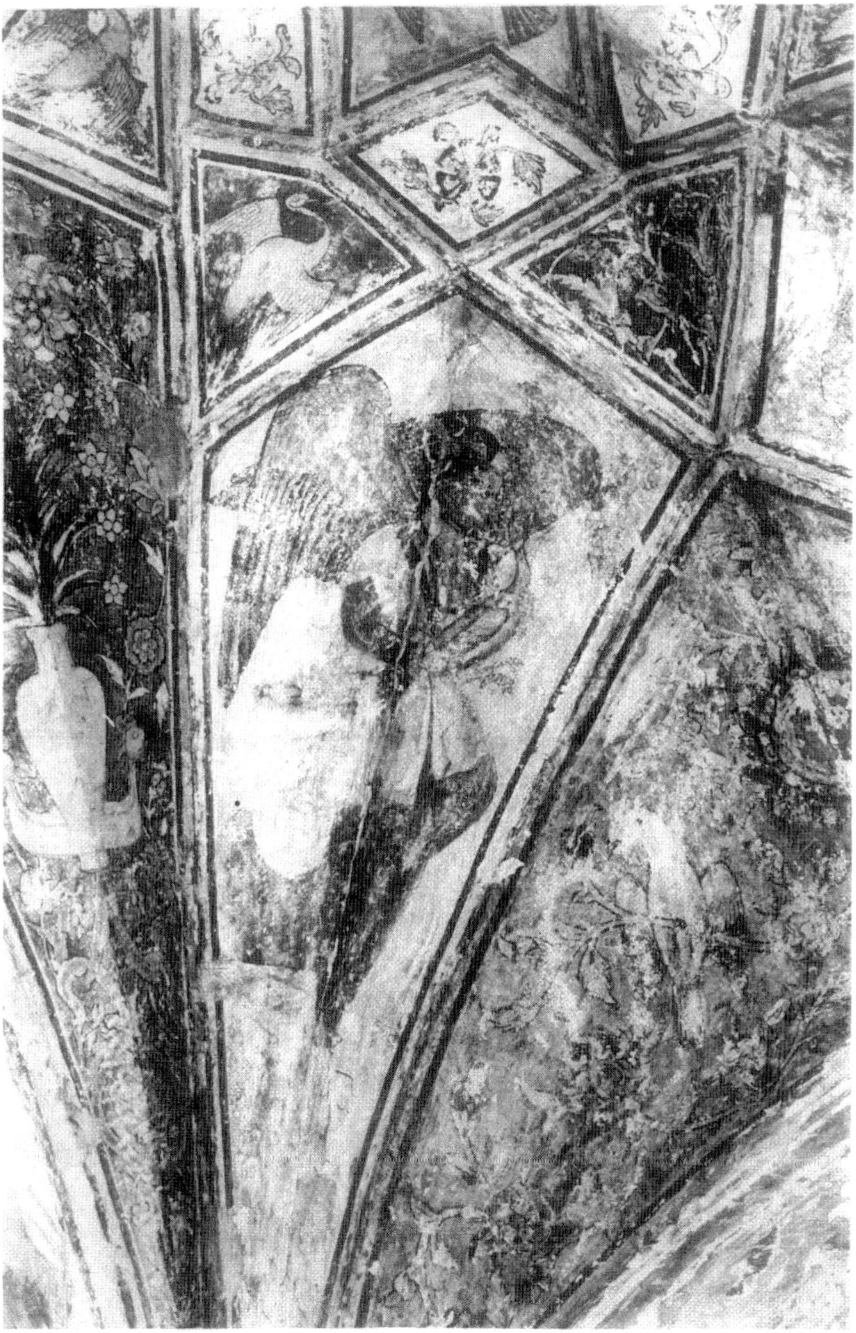

Fig.21 Solomonic angel holding a peacock, Rambagh or Bagh -i Nur Afshan, Agra, north pavilion, arched alcove, soffit of the northern haunch of the arch, completed in 1030/1621. (Photograph E.Koch.)

Fig.22 Allahabad, tomb of Sultan Khusrau, 1031/1621–22, porch, half vault. (Photograph E. Koch.)

Fig.23 Bairat, Mughal palace, first half of seventeenth century, half floor, north western corner room, transition zone over north west corner showing *djinn-s* holding birds. (Photograph E.Koch.)

garment. They carry sunshades, branches with fruits, lambs, and are surrounded by birds and old-fashioned Chinese clouds, in other words they are characterized as the carriers of the flying household of Solomon.[64] On the Western front under the so-called Naulakha Pavilion they lead on chains little blue *djinn*-s with horns. Nearby two little *djinn*-s dance to the sound of their tambourins[65] (Fig. 19). A concession to Jahangir's taste in this traditional setting are certain Europeanisms, like the turned-up feet of some angels to suggest a perspective view from above[66] and the introduction of his favourite cherub heads.[67] There is also a *saqi* angel who, however, being fully dressed wears a cap similar to the one of his counterpart in the interior.[68] Eccentric head coverings including leaf bunches are a characteristic — though not exclusive — feature of Solomonic angels[69] (Fig. 18). The flower wreath worn by the "Hindu angel" and the European hat (*kulah-i firangi*)[70] of the angel whom we named after this unusual headgear seem to be a modern expression of this established iconographic tradition. Though it is not clear in every instance which objects the angels of the Kala Burj are carrying we recognize the traditional (fruit) plate (Figs 3, 4, 5, 9). The green stalks in the hands of the angels with the raised arms might have been flowery twigs or the like (Figs 10, 11). Knowing Jahangir's inclination to materialize his symbolic settings[71] it is tempting to conjecture that real (gold) chains were fixed to the hands of the angel with the *firangi* hat to make him lead one of the *djinn*-s (Fig. 13)

We may therefore conclude that the paintings in the vault of the Kala Burj represent the flying retinue of *Jahangir Sulayman jah*. Conforming to the iconographic tradition of Solomonic angels, his angel servants wear eccentric headgears, some of them styled after the latest *firangi* taste of the Mughal court. They carry (fruit) plates and other objects of the Solomonic household and may even have led the now lost *djinn*-s with golden chains. The birds including his messenger *hudhud* (Fig. 13) complete Solomon's winged subjects. Their leader the *simurgh* undertakes as it were an excursion into another iconographic tradition by doubling up and engaging himself with his dark alter ego in the symbolic fight which had become long since a symbol of the rulers' victory and power.[72]

There remains the question why in contrast to the traditional angels derived from the Persian type on the outer fortwall angels after a European prototype were chosen for the interior of the palace? The outer representations were meant to appeal to a much wider and conservative public than the ones in the private reception hall of the emperor. Here Jahangir's taste as a connoisseur of painting had to be satisfied with the latest achievements of his painters, the adaptation of European prototypes to Mughal taste and symbolic function. The attraction the European prototypes had in this context for the emperor was certainly their potential of reality. Jahangir's interest in the pictorial documentation of natural phenomena is well known but in this context the use of the European form as the most naturalistic form available seems to have had the function to invest the symbol with the greatest possible degree of reality in order to, we may use Abu'l Fazl's words, "lead the ones who consider only the outside of things to the place of inner meaning".[73] Jahangir's painters succeeded. They created for the emperor such a vivid Solomonic atmosphere that even the *firangi* Finch succumbed to the immediacy of its *djinn*-s and credited them with the power of being taken for real.

These naturalistic pictorial expressions of a ruler's asserted reality are Jahangir's own contribution to Mughal painting. The earliest other examples of Solomonic vaults known to me date from his reign. We find the idea expressed in the painted vaults of the pavilions of the Rambagh at Agra that belonged as Nur Afshan garden to the establishment of Nur Jahan[74] (Figs 20, 21). Here the vaults are populated by birds, winged beings holding peacocks, fruit plates, etc.[75] A provincial reflex of Jahangir's Solomonic vaults is found in the painted vaults of the palace in Bairat which dates from the first quarter of the seventeenth century. These representations include also images of winged *djinn*-s holding birds[76] (Fig. 23).

Such frescoe programmes apparently decorated most of Jahangir's palaces.[77] They might have been one of the factors that brought about Shah Jahan's strong reaction against the buildings of his father, at the beginning of his reign.[78] Shah Jahan then reverted to the Law-ful plant decoration in his palaces,[79] like three centuries before him Firuz Shah Tugluq of whom his historian Shams Siraj 'Afif says " . . . and breaches of the Holy Law were all forbidden. One of these was the painting of portraits in the private apartments of kings. It was held right among the monarchs to have painted chambers to gratify their eyes in retirement, but Firoz Shah, in his fear of God, prohibited the painting of portraits as contrary to the Law, and directed that garden scenes should be painted instead".[80]

The miniature painters and poets, however, continued to draw from the stock of these images. The *jharoka*-s of Shah Jahan and the walls from which they are projecting are still occasionally decorated with angels and birds.[81] Abu Talib Kalim, Shah Jahan's court poet, enriches his traditional allusions to heaven in praise of an octagonal palace building with these metaphors: "Angels are under its roof like pigeons... the *huma* of prosperity lives on its threshold and never remembers its nest".[82]

And in the third quarter of the seventeenth century the Rana of Udaipur Raj Singh decorates the ceiling of his marble replicas of the Mughal pavilions in Ajmer with angels, birds and a *simurgh* among a heaven of Hindu gods.[83]

NOTES:

1. All quoted by Edward Maclagan, The Jesuits and the Great Mogul, London, 1932, pp. 237 ff. with further references.
2. Examples are discussed by Richard Ettinghausen, New Pictorial Evidence of Catholic Missionary Activity in Mughal India (Early XVIIth Century), in: Perennitas, Münster, 1963, pp. 385-96, esp. Figs 1,2; see also the representation of Jahangir in durbar, Museum of Fine Arts, Boston, *c.* 1620, where angels are painted on the brackets of the *jharoka* and a picture of the Virgin on the wall behind. Illus. in Milo Cleveland Beach, The Grand Mogul, Imperial Painting in India 1600–1660, Williamstown, Massachusetts, 1978, No.14.
3. The Commentary of Father Montserrate, S.J., trans. J.S. Hoyland, ann. S.N.Banerjee, Oxford University Press, 1922, p.29.
4. The question arose with regard to the unidentified subjects of the wall paintings of the so called Maryam ki Kothi or Sunahra Makan, in particular the so-called Annunciation above the northernmost doorway of the west front. See Edmund W. Smith, The Moghul Architecture of Fathpur-Sikri, Part 1, 1894; rpt. Delhi, 1973, pp. 33 ff; S.K.Banerji, Mariam-ki-Kothi or Sunahra Makan of Fatehpur Sikri, in: J. of the United Provinces Historical Society, XVII, 1944, pp. 103-10; and Athar A. Rizvi and Vincent Flynn, Fathpur-Sikri, Bombay, 1975, pp. 54-6; The scene better preserved in the sketch of Smith (see above Pl.CIX, Fig.1) certainly does not depict the Annunciation but two winged beings, one of them seated on a throne. For a short discussion of related subjects in Iranian art see Ingeborg Luschey-Schmeisser, Engel aus Qazvin, Frühsafavidische Kachelbilder, in: Archaeologische Mitteilungen aus Iran, NF, Band 9, 1976 pp. 299-311, esp. Tafel 56. The representation does show some European influence in regard to the seated figure. A similar winged being derived from a European model appears in a painting of the collection of Edwin Binney, 3rd, Indian Miniature Painting from the Collection of Edwin Binney, 3rd, The Mughal and Deccani Schools, Portland, Oregon, 1973, p.54, Cat. No. 29c.
5. The inscription is in the arch of the eastern front with *bismillah* and *kalimah* in the same *nasta'liq* characters, and reads *"Mehr Banu qadimi-i Jahangir Shah"*. It has been translated inexactly by Carr Stephen (The Archaeology and Monumental Remains of Delhi, 1876; rpt. Delhi, Ashish Publishing House, n.d., p.199), as "[His] kind [Miharban] and old patron [is] Jahangir Shah". The gate bears no date but was probably erected at the same time as the bridge of Mehr Banu Agha, called Barahpulah about 1.5 km to its south east, dated by the *tarikh* of its inscription according to *abjad* reckoning to 1021/1612. The inscription is lost but preserved as a drawing published by Sayyid Ahmad Khan, Athar al-Sanadid, (Urdu text), ed. Khalid Nasir Hashmi, (Delhi: Central Book Dept, Jami' Masjid, 1965), p.426. The chronogram there gives 1021 but the date is indicated erroneously as 1030.
6. K.A. Thomas, Christian Paintings on a Mughal Monument, in: The Illustrated Weekly of India, May 10, 1981, p 30.
7. The Lahore Fort was founded by Akbar in about 1565 and altered during Mughal rule by Jahangir and Shah Jahan (1628-58). For the history of the Fort see especially Nur Bakhsh, Historical Notes on the Lahore Fort and its Buildings, in: Archaeological Survey of India, Annual Report, 1902-03, pp.218-24; Md 'Abdullah Chaghtai, A Brief Survey of the Lahore Fort, Lahore, 1973, (in Urdu); Muhammad Wali Ullah Khan, Lahore and its Important Monuments, 3rd.ed., 1961, Karachi, 1973, pp. 7-39.
8. The work was carried out in 1974/75 as projected by Md Ishtiaq Khan, in: Master Plan for Preservation and Restoration of Lahore Fort, Department of Archaeology Government of Pakistan, 1973, pp. 46, 58. I thank Dr. Syed Mohammad Ashfaque, Superin-

tendent of Archaeology, for the permission to study and photograph the so far unpublished wall paintings.

9. A complete plan of the Lahore Fort is given for instance by Nur Bakhsh, *op.cit.*, Pl.XXXIII, or Md Wali Ullah Khan. *op. cit.*, p.7. All plans so far published show only the outline of the Kala Burj, not its interior organisation, and are based on the plan published by Major H.H. Cole in: Preservation of National Monuments. India. Buildings in the Punjab, 1884, Plate No.1. Cole's plan is derived "from a drawing furnished by Syad Fakir Kamr-ud-Din, Honorary Magistrate Lahore" that shows the Fort buildings in the time of Ranjit Singh. It is kept today in the Department of Archaeology. Western Pakistan Circle, Lahore.
10. J.Ph. Vogel, Tile-Mosaics of the Lahore Fort, 1920; rpt. Karachi: Pakistan Publications, n.d.
11. See for example the central vault of Humayun's tomb in Delhi, about 1565-69, where the transition zone is formed by 16 arches. Reproduced by Andreas Volwahsen in: Islamisches Indien, Munich, 1969, p. 70.
12. Because of the height of the vault I could not examine the paintings from close but they were apparently executed *al fresco* on the damp plaster which is an even more cogent evidence for the contemporaneousness of the vault structure and the murals. The frescoe technique presumably employed is described by Ahmad Nabi Khan in: Maryam Zamani Mosque, Lahore. History and Architecture, Karachi, 1972, rpt. from Pakistan Archaeology, No. 7, 1972-73, pp. 10-12.
13. *Ibid*, Pl. LI a. The vault covers a room that is with 6.30 m by 6.30 m slightly bigger than the room of the Kala Burj.
14. The date 37 is found together with the name of the calligrapher Abd al-Nabi al-Qarshi on the inscription band of the south west corner *burj*. The date 1036 appears on the inscription band of the north wall in the upper chamber. A. Führer in: The Monumental Antiquities and Inscriptions in the North-Western Provinces and Oudh, 1891; rpt. Varanasi, 1969, p.55, records an inscription in the central ground floor chamber dated 1027/1617 the existence of which is doubtful. He does not mention the two other inscriptions read by Dr Yunus Jaffery from Dr Zakir Husain College (formerly Delhi College). The central ground floor chamber is with 5.65 x 5.65 m slightly smaller than the room of the Kala Burj, the vault is with 4.8 m height much lower. For a drawing of the vault see Volwahsen, Islamisches Indien, p. 129.
15. See for example the vault of the *hammam* in the Red Fort of Delhi (1638-1648), reproduced by J. Burton Page, The Red Fort, in: Splendours of the East, ed. Sir Mortimer Wheeler, 1965; Spring Books, 1970, p. 136.
16. Tuzuk-i Jahangiri, (Pers. Text), ed. Sayyid Ahmad Khan, Aligarh, 1864, p. 107.
17. The Tuzuk-i Jahangiri, transl. A. Rogers, ed. Henry Beveridge, 2nd ed., 1909-1914; rpt. 2 vols in one, Delhi, 1968, I, p. 219.
18. "*Tarh*" is used by the Mughal writers for "design" in regard to painting as well as architecture. See Abu'l Fazl's well known statement in the A'in -i Akbari, Pers. Text, II, Lucknow: Newal Kishore Press, 1869, p.157, about the five hundred buildings erected by order of Akbar in the Agra Fort in "the fine designs *(tarha)* of Bangala, Gujarat" and others.
19. The Tuzuk -i Jahangiri, transl., I, pp. 225, 376; II, p. 114.
20. Tuzuk, Pers. text, see above, p. 318. A. Rogers and H. Beveridge transl. II, p. 183, calculate the Christian equivalent of 5th Muharram 1030 as 20 November 1620. They follow in the transl. apparently the unreformed or Julian Calendar that was given up in England only in 1752 while the rest of Europe except Russia and Sweden had adopted the Calendar reformed by Pope Gregory XIII in 1582. My conversion of the Muslim dates is based on G.S.P. Freeman Grenville, The Muslim and Christian Calendars, 2nd

ed. London, 1977.
21. Nur Bakhsh, Historical Notes on Lahore Fort, p. 219.
22. Finch in Samuel Purchas, Hakluytus Posthumus or Purchas His Pilgrimes, Vol. IV, pp. 53-56.
23. The alternations done afterwards by Jahangir himself, Shah Jahan and in later times have changed the architecture of the Lahore Fort considerably. See A. Chaghtai, Brief Survey of Lahore Fort; Md Wali Ullah Khan, Lahore and it's Important Monuments.
24. Finch, p. 54.
25. Therefore the frescoes are more or less contemporary with Jahangir's wall paintings in the Agra Fort. These are not preserved but recorded in a letter of Jerome Xavier of September 24, 1608, the main substance of which is reproduced by Fernão Guerreiro, Relaçam .....V, 1607-08, Lisbon: Pedro Crasbeeck, 1611, pp. 13b-14b. Maclagan, Jesuits and the Great Mogul, pp. 238-40 translates apparently from the original letter, see his note 76, p. 261, because his translation differs slightly from Guerreiro's text. The following abstract is based on Maclagan's transl. The subjects of the representations were similar to the ones in the Lahore Fort described by Finch, but contained more Christian themes. The ceiling of an inner verandah behind the outer verandah where Jahangir used to show himself seems to have been painted with a Christian version of the ceiling of the Kala Burj, namely a picture of Christ in glory surrounded by angels. Jerome Xavier gives also an interesting description of the *procedere* of the painting. The models of the paintings were chosen by Jahangir from his collection of prints, he decided also where they were to be placed. Then his painters made large-size sketches on paper that were transferred to the wall. The Jesuit fathers were consulted in regard to the colours.
26. Examples can be seen among the wall paintings of Fatehpur Sikri, see Smith, Vol I, Pls. XV b; CIX, Fig. 2; CXX.
27. Erwin Panofsky, Renaissance and Renascenses in Western Art, 1965; London, 1970, pp. 147-50.
28. For the influence of Jesuit prints on Mughal painting see especially Maclagan, The Jesuit Missions and Mogul Painting, in: The Jesuits and the Great Mogul, pp. 222-67; Aśok Kumar Das, The Impact of Europe, in: Mughal Painting During Jahangir's Time, Calcutta, 1978, pp. 22-56; Beach, The Grand Mogul, pp. 155-57, with further literature, and the latest, my The Influence of the Jesuit Missions on Symbolic Representations of the Mughal Emperors, in: Islam in India: Studies and Commentaries, ed. C.W. Troll, Vol. I, Delhi, 1982, pp. 14-29.
29. Karl-August Wirth, Engel, in: Reallexikon zur Deutschen Kunstgeschichte, Vol. V, cols. 462-64.
30. *Ibid.*, cols. 353 ff.
31. For a further example see the engraving of the birth of the virgin by Cornelis Cort, dated 1581, and it's Mughal copy of ca. 1610 in: Beach, The Grand Mogul, Nos. 54 and 54A.
32. An example of Jahangir's time is discussed in note 49.
33. The political allegories of Jahangir painted by Abu'l Hasan and Bichitr are discussed by Richard Ettinghausen, Paintings of the Sultans and Emperors of India, New Delhi, 1961, pls. 11, 12, 13, 14 *id.*, The Emperors Choice, in: De Artibus Opuscula XL, Essays in Honor of Erwin Panofsky, ed. Millàrd Meiss, New York, 1961, I, pp. 98-120, and Aśok Kumar Das, Abu'l Hasan, Bichitr and the Iconographical [sic] Drawings in: Mughal Painting, pp. 213-28.
34. See my The Influence of the Jesuit Missions . . .pp. 19-21, where I analyse in particular the depiction of Jahangir standing on a globe and shooting at the head of his enemy Malik 'Ambar, of about 1620, by Abu'l Ḥasan, in the Chester Beatty Library.

35. The whole painting is reproduced by Robert Skelton, Two Mughal Lion Hunts, in: Victoria and Albert Museum Yearbook, No. 1, 1969, p. 44, pl. 12. This painting comprehends a whole compendium of European angel representations, i.e. puttos, angel heads and adolescent angel figures.
36. For the work of *ustad* Mansur see *inter alia* Beach, The Grand Mogul, pp. 137-43 and Asok Kumar Das, Mughal Painting, pp. 195-99, pls. 56, 57, 58, 61.
37. I thank Professor Annemarie Schimmel and Dr Desai for their help.
38. The Polyglot Bible had been edited by Dr Benito Arias Montanus, King Philip II's personal chaplain and was printed by Christophe Plantin in Antwerp from 1568 to 1572. For the genesis of the Bible see especially Max Rooses, Christophe Plantin Imprimeur Anversois, 2nd ed., Antwerp, 1896, pp. 111-48. The complete second frontispiece is reproduced in my The Influence .... pl. 2 where I discuss some of the so far underrated influence of this Bible on Mughal painting.
39. I thank Dr Ellen Smart for the indentification of this object. For an illus. of Humayun wearing this head-dress see for instance the representation of Timur handing his imperial crown to Babur, by Govardhan, c. 1630, Victoria and Albert Museum, The Indian Heritage, Court Life & Arts under Mughal Rule, ed. R. Skelton, London, 1982, Cat. no. 52.
40. "Persian miniatures from the fourteenth century onward always represent the Indian as blackish in color .... " Annemarie Schimmel, Turk and Hindu: A Poetical Image and Its Application to Historical Fact, in: Islam and Cultural Change in the Middle Ages, Fourth Giorgio Levi Della Vida Biennial Conference, Wiesbaden, 1975, p. 111.
41. Toby Falk, Rothschild Collection of Mughal Miniatures, in: Colnaghi, P. & D. & Co. Ltd. Persian and Mughal Art, London, 1976, p. 186, pl. 103 (colour). A short analysis of Govardhan's style relevant to our context is given by Stuart Cary Welch, Imperial Mughal Painting, London, 1978, pp. 87 and 95.
42. By Abu'l Ḥasan, circa 1618, Freer Gallery of Art, Washington. Often reproduced, latest by Milo Cleveland Beach, The Imperial Image. Paintings for the Mughal Court, Washington, D. C., 1981, Cat. no. 17b.
43. Robert Skelton, Indian Painting of the Mughal Period, in Islamic Painting and the Arts of the Book, ed. B.W. Robinson, London, 1976, pp. 259-60, pls. 37 (colour), 127.
44. A contemporary example from Jahangir's time is the *simurgh* attacking a lion, on the margin of a page of a manuscript of the Farhang-i Jahangiri, dating from c.1605 that was used as mounting for an Akbar Namah page. Toby Falk, Rothschild Mughal Miniatures, No. 86 ii.
45. ed. Syed Moinul Haq, Karachi: Pakistan Historical Society, 1961, Vol. I, p. 87. The passage is reproduced by Shah Nawaz Khan, The Ma'athir-ul-Umara, transl. H. Beveridge, rev. Baini Prashad, Vol. II, Calcutta, 1952, p. 818. 'Abd al-Samad, the Safawid court painter became one the co-founders of the Mughal school after he had been brought to India by Humayun in 1550. The house of the Khan -i A'zam or Mirza 'Aziz Koka (died in 1033/1624) in the Red Fort of Agra is not preserved.
46. British Library, Or. 7573, f. 218b. Aśok Kumar Das, in: Mughal Painting, attributes the miniature tentatively to Abu'l Hasan (p.87). The same manuscript contains another illustration with European putto-angels in clouds above dancing dervishes (f. 66 v.). The palette shows colours similar to the ones dominating the vault of the Kala Burj: light greens, purple, black, light sky blues, cloud, and body colours. Reproduced in colour in Douglas Barrett and Basil Gray, Indische Malerei, Lausanne, 1963, p. 101.
47. The scene is the visual embodiment of the verses above: "Heaven is drawing the horse of the support of religion [*Nusrat al-din,* allusion to Jahangir's *laqab Nur al-Din*], come and see: its angel has put his hand in his stirrup!" Cf. Diwan-i Hafiz, ed. Md Qazwini and Dr Qasim Ghani, Teheran, n.d., p. 292.

48. Hardly any Mughal writer or poet omitted the traditional allusions to one or the other aspect of paradise or heaven while describing a Mughal palace. For Jahangir's time see his *malik al-shu 'ara'* (poet laureate) Talib-i Amuli, Kulliyat, ed.T. Shihab, Tehran, 1346 sh./1967, p. 128, *qit'ah* in praise of an unidentified palace (line 2): "What a wonderful high roof, its ceiling is [of the height] of the throne of God [*'arsh*], it's arch is like [the arch of] the sky. It is always manifesting itself on the eyes of Jahangir"; alternative transl.: "It is always manifesting itself on the world capturing eyes." I thank Dr Yunus Jaffery for his assistance in the study of the Kulliyat.
49. Ingeborg Luschey–Schmeisser, in: The Pictorial Tile Cycle of Hašt Behešt in Isfahan and its Iconographic Tradition, Rome: Ismeo, 1978, mentions only one Indian example, significantly of Jahangir's time (p. 209, figs. 216, 217). It is the right half of the title page of the Jahangir Namah, Academy of Sciences, Leningrad, representing the inner front of a gate of the Agra palace with the festive crowd celebrating the accession of Jahangir. The painting was done in 1618 by Abu'l Hasan. The gate cannot be identified with certainty but shows resemblance to the inner fronts of the later gates of the Diwan-i 'Amm of Shah Jahan, ca. 1628-37. It is decorated with eight panels arranged vertically in four pairs. They show from top to bottom angels of the European adolescent type, *simurgh-s* fighting dragons, Laila and Majnun among the animals, and lions fighting bulls and represent therefore an instance where European angels take the place of their Iranian-Mughal counterparts in a traditional programme of Islamic palace decoration. I am not sure whether the depiction is a true portrait of a particular building as truthful topographic representations are rare in Mughal painting. More often architectural representations just show the general prevailing taste in architecture with features typical for the respective period.
50. Luschey Schmeisser, 1978, pp. 47-55.
51. *Id.*, 1976, see note 4, pp. 306, 308.
52. In poetry, too, where e.g. in *ruba'i* 84 of Talib-i Amuli, Jahangir illuminates the assembly of the angels by his presence. Kulliyat, p. 908.
53. Vogel in: Tile-Mosaics, p. 64, interprets "Banian Dews" as "Hindu Deities".
54. "Solomon" in T.P. Hughes, Dictionary of Islam, 1885; rpt. New Delhi, 1976, pp. 601-04; and "Sulaiman b. Dawud" in: Shorter Encyclopaedia of Islam, ed. H.A.R. Gibb and J.H. Kramers, Leiden, 1961, pp. 549-51, with further references.
55. Surah XXXIV, 11-13; XXXVIII, 36-38; Hughes, *op. cit.*, p. 603. Cf. Georg Salzberger, Solomons Herrschaft Über die Geisterwelt, in: Die Salomo-Sage in der Semitischen Literatur, Berlin, Nikolassee, 1907, pp. 92 ff.
56. Salzberger, pp. 74 ff.
57. For two Mughal examples (of about 1600) see Stuart C. Welch and Milo Cleveland Beach in: Gods, Thrones and Peacocks, Asia House Gallery Publication, 1965, No. 6, of ca. 1600, and Beach, The Grand Mogul, No. 1, fol. 157 recto of a Diwan-i Amir Hasan Dihlawi, dated 1602-3, executed by Salim's (the later Jahangir) studio in Allahabad.
58. Freer Gallery of Art, 50.1.; formerly Maria Sarre-Humann, Berlin. Cf. Laurence Binyon, J.V.S. Wilkinson and Basil Gray, Persian Miniature Painting, 1933; rpt. New York: Dover, 1977, Pl. XCIII-A. 157 and p. 136.
59. I suggest therefore distinguishing angels according to the object they are carrying. Birds and animals seem to be exclusive for Solomonic angels, e.g. the angels carrying antelopes on the spandrels of the arch of the gate of the Agra Fort during construction, illus. of the Akbar Namah, ca. 1590, 2-1896 (I.S.)-46/117, Victoria and Albert Museum. Plates with eatables like fruits, musical instruments and other objects pertaining to a princely life can also be carried by other angels, for example the ones who receive the Prophet on his ascent to heaven, i.e. representations of the *mi 'raj,* an

iconographic tradition related to the one of Solomon on his flying throne. See for instance Binyon, Wilkinson and Gray, Persian Miniature Painting, Pl. XCII-A. 152 (a).

60. Oleg Grabar, The Alhambra, (London, 1978, p. 150.
61. Kulliyat-i Talib-i Amuli, p. 44-45, *Qasidah* in praise of Nur Jahān, line 24; cf p. 960, *ruba 'i* No. 548 in praise of Jahangir. The same comparison will be used later for Shah Jahan and Mumtaz Mahal: "When the lady of the world *(banu-i jahan)* and Bilqis of the age *(Bilqis-i dauran)* went from the assembly of Solomon (*Shah Jahan*) to paradise . . ." Abu Talib Kalim, in: Diwan, ed. P. Baiza'i Tehran, 1336 sh./1957, p. 350 (*mathnawi* on Akbarabad and the Bagh-i Jahanara).
62. Vogel, Tile-Mosaics of the Lahore Fort, whith two elevations and 116 illus. The date of the tile-mosaics has been the subject of some controversy. 'Abd al-Hamid Lahauri in his Badshah Namah (Pers. text) ed. Kabir al-Din Ahmad and 'Abd al-Rahim, Calcutta, 1867-8, I, 1, pp. 223 ff.; trans. Nur Bakhsh, Historical Notes on Lahore Fort, pp. 222 f. says that the western substructures under the complex of the Shah Burj were begun by Jahangir in 1624 and completed by Shah Jahan during the first years of his reign. Muhammad Tahir "Ashna" or 'Inayat Khan (Mulakhkhas or Shah Jahan Namah, Pers. ms. British Library, Or. 175, f. 30 verso) gives an abridged version of Lahauri's passage. Muhammad Amin or Amina-i Qazwini in his Badshah Namah (Pers. ms. British Library, Or. 173, f. 307 verso, Pers. numbering) however mentions that the (whole?) base was done by Jahangir and the buildings on it by Shah Jahan. Muhammad Salih Kambo in: 'Amal-i Salih or Shah Jahan Namah (Pers. text), II, improved re-edition by Wahid Quraishi of the Calcutta ed., 1927 by Gh. Yazdani, Lahore: Majlis-i Taraqqi-i Adab, 1967, p.7, makes a similar statement. There is no stylistic difference in the tile mosaics facing the northern and the western front of the substructure of the Fort. Supposing Shah Jahan completed the western front he kept to the style and the programme of the tile work belonging to Jahangir's time. We can assume that all the work was executed by the same group of artists.
63. I refer here to a chronogram quoted by Jahangir in the Tuzuk (Pers. Text), p. 308, regarding the completion of his adaption of a ruinous pavilion of his father in the garden of the Fort of Srinagar on the Hari Parbat. The building (not preserved) which he calls picture gallery (*khanah-i taswiri*) was completed in 1029/1620 and painted with the likenesses of Humayun, Akbar and other relatives and *mansabdars* of Jahangir. There was also a picture of Shah 'Abbas. The complete *misra'* of the chronogram reads: *majlis-i shahan Sulayman hasham* (assembly of rulers with the retenue of Solomon). The Rogers-Beveridge transl. gives the verse as: "Pictures of kings of Solomon-like glory" (II, pp. 150-151, 161-162).
64. Vogel, Pls XIX No. 15; XXX No. 31; XXXVII No. 40; XXXVIII No. 42; L No. 55, LII, No. 58; LVIII No. 80; LIX No. 85.
65. *ibid*, Pl. XXVI Nos. 24 and 25.
66. Compare *ibid*, Pls. XXXVII No. 40; XXXVIII No. 42, with our Fig. 15.
67. *ibid*, Pls XIX No. 15; XXII Nos. 19, 20; LV No. 64; LXV No. 86; LXVII No. 89.
68. *ibid*, Pl. LXVII No. 89.
69. Cf. Luschey-Schmeisser in Hašt Behešt, pp. 52 and 54, Fig. 74, 115.
70. Mentioned as such in the Tuzuk (p. 114, trans. I, P. 234) in 1613.
71. Jahangir in his Tuzuk (trans. I, p. 7) says that the first order he gave after his accession was to set up the chain of justice. He describes it as a golden chain with sixty bells that was fixed to the Shah Burj of the Agra Fort so that those seeking justice could appeal directly to the emperor by shaking it. The chain of justice features also in his allegorical paintings as Jahangir shooting at the head of Malik 'Ambar (see note 34), or Jahangir as the Just Ruler triumphing over Poverty, probably Abu'l Hasan, c. 1625, Los

Angeles County Museum of Art, latest reproduced with a short analysis of its symbolism by R. Skelton in: The Indian Heritage, Cat. no. 48.

72. For the tradition of bird fights as symbol of the ruler see Luschey-Schmeisser, p. 70-73. Two *simurgh*-s fighting each other seem to be unusual, more common is the motif of a bird of prey descending on its victim. Two *simurgh*-s facing each other in a hostile way can be seen on an awning under which sits Shah Isma'il II Safawi (?), right half of the frontispiece of Isma'il II's Copy of the Shahnamah 1576/77. Rothschild collection, B.W. Robinson, Rothschild and Binney Collections: Persian and Mughal Arts of the Book, in: Colnaghi, Persian and Mughal Art, No. 19ii. The concept of the two hostile *simurgh*-s might go back to the heroic tradition of Iran where a good and a bad *simurgh* appear in the Shahnamah. See V.F. Büchner, Simurgh in *EI*[1], IV, pp. 426-428.

73. It is one of the often quoted passages of the A'in-i Akbarī on the painters of Europe: "The form leads to the one owning it [*khodawand* lit. master= body] and he leads to the inner meaning just as the written shape guides to letter and word and from there the content is found out. Although in general a picture represents a material form and [here in particular] the painters of *firang* quite often express, by using rare forms, our mental states and [thus] they lead the ones who consider only the outside of things to the place of inner meaning; whereas the written letter provides us with the experiences of the ancients and thus becomes a means to intellectual progress." in: Abu'l Fazl 'Allami, The A'in-i Akbari, (Pers. text), Vol. I, ed. II, Blochmann, Bibl. Ind., Calcutta, 1872, p.11. I have retranslated this passage with the help of Dr Christian W. Troll, because the translation of Blochmann (The A'in-i Akbari, second ed., rev. and ed. Lieut. Col. D.C. Phillott, Vol. I.1927: New Delhi, 1977 pp. 102f. misses an important point, namely the argument of Abu'l Fazl considering the potential of paintings as means to recognize a higher truth. It has apparently been formulated under the influence of the Tridentine argument for the use of images in the church. I have shown in my The Influence of the Jesuit Missions ..., pp. 21 ff. that the Jesuits had recourse to the treatise literature or the Counter-Reformation in the discussions at the Mughal court about the lawfulness of pictures. Not having access, then, to the Persian original, I quoted from the translation of Blochmann.

74. Tuzuk, trans., II. P. 199. For a discussion of these paintings see my forthcoming Notes on the painted and sculptured decoration of Nur Jahan's pavilions in the Ram Bagh (Bagh-i Nur Afshan) at Agra, in: Facets of Indian Art, ed. R. Skelton and A. Topsfield. The structure of the vaults in the two pavilions is developed from stars arranged in concentric circles but broken up in smaller facets than the group of vaults discussed in connection with the vault of the Kala Burj. The whole concept is closer to the structure of *muqarnas* vaults. Similar vaults are found among Mughal vaults from Eastern India, especially the vaults of the tombs in the Khusrau Bagh in Allahabad, constructed between 1603/04 and 1625 for Khusrau, Jahangir's ill-fated son, his mother and sister. The squinches of the half vaults of the porch of Khusrau's tomb dated 1031/1621-22 contain unskilled paintings representing a winged angel head and an angel in a long dress, a reflex of Jahangir's angels who here even invade the decoration of tomb architecture (Fig. 22).

75. The preserved angels represent a Mughal version of the Persian type with the long garment. In the central area of the vault of the southern pavilion and the verandah of the northern building, however, Jahangir's favourite winged angel heads can still be made out (Fig. 20).

76. The wall paintings have been dated by Hermann Goetz [The Early Rajput Murals of Bairat (ca. A.D. 1587), rpt. from : Ars Orientalis, I, 1954 in: Hermann Goetz, Rajput Art and Architecture, ed. Jyotindra Jain and Jutta Jain-Neubauer, Wiesbaden, 1978, pp. 123] on very weak grounds, namely the supposed resemblance of the figures

depicted in the vaults of the south western and north western roof *chhattri*-s with Akbar and Raja Man Singh. Goetz had not seen the paintings in the corner rooms of the half floors. The paintings in the net work of the transition zone of the north western corner room show angels, birds and *djinn*-s. The paintings are badly preserved and not of a high artistic standard. The architectural evidence provides us with a better base for a date. The building is an exact replica of the palace of Shah Quli Khan in Narnaul (dated by inscription to 1591-1593), but with a more elaborate central vault. Its central area with a medallion is embedded in a network developed from concentric circles of stars, a vault form — as we have seen — characteristic for the time of Jahangir.

77. The palace in the Lahore Fort; the palace in the Agra Fort, see note 25; the *khanah -i taswiri* in the Nur-Afza garden in the fort of the Hari Parbat, see note 63; the pavilions of Nur Jahan in the Ram Bagh, see note 74; and the palace Chashma-i Nur at Hafiz Jamal near Ajmer, completed 1615; described by Sir Thomas Roe, The Embassy of Sir Thomas Roe to India 1616-19, ed. William Foster, London, 1926, p.211.
78. Shah Jahan's writers underline that the buildings of his father were "not liked by the critical disposition of the world maintaining and art spreading Emperor." Abd al-Hamid Lahauri, Badshah Namah (Pers. text), Calcutta, 1867, I, 2, p.239, *et passim*. transl. Nur Bakhsh, The Agra Fort and its Buildings in Archaeological Survey of India, Annual Report, 1903-04, p.180.
79. For a short discussion of the origin of the flowers characteristic of the dado of Shah Jahan's buildings see Robert Skelton, A decorative Motif in Mughal Art in: Aspects of Indian Art, ed. Pratapaditya Pal, Leiden, 1972, p. 148. For the vegetabilization programme of the palaces of Shah Jahan see also my The baluster column—a European motif in Mughal architecture and its meaning in: J. of the Warburg and Courtauld Institutes. 45. 1982, p. 258.
80. Tarikh -i Firuz Shahi, quoted after H.M. Elliot and John Dowson, History of India as Told by its Own Historians, London, 1867 ff, Vol. III, p. 363. For the Pers. text see Tarikh-i-Firuz Shahi of Shams Siraj 'Afif, ed. Maulawi Wilayat Husayn, Bibl. Ind., Calcutta, 1891, p. 374 'Afif's statement is corroberated by the Futuhat-i-Firuz Shahi: "By divine guidance and heavenly favour, we directed that they should remove all figures and paintings from all articles and make those things which are not forbidden but sanctioned and approved by the religious Law; we commanded that they should obliterate all carved and engraved figures chiselled out on the houses, walls and palaces." N.B. Roy, The Victories of Sultan Firuz Shah of Tughluq Dynasty, English trans of Futuhat-i-Firuz Shahi, Islamic Culture, XV, 1941, p. 458.
81. Shah Jahan in Durbar ca. 1628, Bodleian Library, Oxford, reproduced by Percy Brown, Indian Painting under the Mughals A.D. 1550-A.D. 1750, 1924; rpt. New York, 1975, Pl. XXIV; or Shah Jahan Namah, Royal Library, Windsor Castle, f. 216 v. Later in his reign Shah Jahan had an important "relapse" regarding the decoration of real architecture: the Florentine *pietra dura* birds and the image of Orpheus set in the back-wall of the *jharoka* of the Diwan-i Amm in the Red Fort of Delhi (1638-48). Gordon Sanderson, Shah Jahan's Fort, Delhi in: Archaeological Survey of India, Annual Report, 1911-12, pp. 20-21, Pl. XI, fig 16, with further references.
82. Abu Talib Kalim, Diwan, ed. P. Baiza'i Tehran, 1336sh/1957, p. 373, *mathnawi*. Like the *simurgh* the *huma* is a mythical Iranian bird.
83. The pavilions are arranged on the stepped terraces of the dam of the Raj Samand in Kankroli. "The ceilings rupresent the apogee of the revivalist sculpture . . .certain details. e.g., the winged devatas, go back to Mughal, and finally to Christian prototypes." Hermann Goetz, The first Golden Age of Udaipur: Rajput Art in Mewar

during the period of Mughal Supremacy, rpt. from Ars Orientalis, II, 1957, in: Jain, Jain-Neubauer, Rajput Art and Architecture, p 102. pl. XXXI, 8/16 and 8/17. The angles, birds and the *simurgh* are found on the ceiling of the central pavilion.

The Image of India in European Antiquity and the Middle Ages

HEIMO RAU
Stuttgart

When, on his march to India, Alexander the Great arrived in the territory beyond the Hindu Kush mountains in the year 327 B.C., he granted his army a ten-day halt in Nysa. Not only were the local citizens treated mercifully, but the Greek soldiers also felt at home and were cordially received in the hospitable mountain city located in the Kabul Valley. For the inhabitants of Nysa claimed to be related to the Greeks through Dionysos-Bakchos, who, according to ancient traditional had been born at this very spot. The soldiers discovered ivy and vine—both plants sacred to Bakchos—growing there on the mountainside, and they were convinced that the dances and music which the citizenry performed for them were indeed Bacchanalian cults of the Dionysian mysteries. And they even thought to discern in the safron-yellow robes of the local people the sacred garment which Dionysos had brought with him to the West. Thus, these Greeks believed that in the city of Nysa they had met with one of their gods. In Aoronos, shortly thereafter, they felt they could perceive traces of one of their god-like heroes, Herakles, whom Alexander looked upon as one of his ancestors.

It is claimed in Greek tradition that after Herakles had finished performing his twelve tasks he proceeded to traverse the civilized world from West to East. But even his superhuman strength proved to be unequal to the rock-fortress of Aoronos, and he was forced to retreat without victory. What a moment this was then to become for Alexander, who entered the Indus Valley and was faced with the task of conquering the invincible fortress. On the south stood the mountain to which he had to lay siege, and which Sir Aurel Stein has indentified with Pir-Sar, its base washed by the waters of the Indus. On all other sides the fortress was protected by vertical rock walls, and was accessible only by means of a single path. On high there were cultivable fields providing food, and water was also available in abundance. Thus it was that the fortress was well-prepared to withstand even the longest of sieges. But Alexander's astuteness and tenacity as a commander were more than equal to the most invincible of hurdles. He proceeded to fill in a ravine with the trunks of trees, having felled the first ones with his own hand, and then went on to attack from a neighbouring hill of the same height. Finally, he mounted the rock and scaled it at a point least expected, and took the impregnable fortress by storm. Thus, Alexander succeeded in accomplishing a feat that had been denied to his demi-god ancestor Herakles.

These tales with which I have decided to introduce this brief survey dealing with the image of India in Europe during Antiquity and the Middle Ages were reported by Ptolemy and Aristoboulos, historiographers who both accompanied Alexander on his march through West Asia to India. They are later quoted by Arrian in his Anabasis, by Plutarch in his Moralia, in Polybios' History and in the Geographica written by Strabo.[1] It is curious to note, however, that there appears to be no mention anywhere within the corpus of Sanskrit literature of Alexander the Great.

These most ancient sources are mythological in nature. The tradition hints at the dark and mysterious secret cults and rites connected with the *pūja* of Dionysos. It was indeed India where, dressed in his ochre robes, he celebrated his most exuberant Bacchanalian triumphs, accompanied by Silen and surrounded by satyrs and nymphs. And when the assumption is made that the ancient image of India in the West may be bound up with this god and his cult, we may note that this is an image clothed in something deeply mysterious, a night-world opposed to the clear and rational daylight associated with the god Apollo. Here a deeper stratum is touched upon, more difficult to delineate, ancient in origin and rooted in that realm of darkness which preceeded Apollo's bright day.

This contrast is underscored by the religious belief among the ancient Greeks that Apollo dances with the Muses on Mt. Parnassos during the day, and Dionysos dances with them at night. Thus it is not surprising to discover that Alexandrian scholars called Nṛteśvara Śiva an Indian Dionysos. The myth of Herakles and its Indian connections may be interpreted in a similar light.

Quite different and distinct from these mythological-mystical traditions about India is the image which originated from the direct encounter with Indian travellers who journeyed to the West and from reports by Greeks who travelled to the East.

First of all, mention should be made of the *sādhus*. Some of them made their way to Persia and from there up to the Mediterranean at a rather early date. It is reported by Eusebios,[2] for example, that an Indian appeared one day in the famous marketplace of Athens, the *agora,* where he proceeded to contact the great sage Socrates. The *agora* was not only a place where fish and produce were sold, but also where teachers, the so-called *sophistai* or sophists, assembled, along with their students, and where news coming in from the four corners of the known world was communicated. The Indian *sādhu* is said to have asked Socrates about the final goal of his quest as a philosopher. The Greek then answered that his philosophy was centered on the human being. On hearing this response, he only laughed and wondered how one could study humanity without embracing the totality of the divine hierarchies.

Sādhus of different types and varying in appearance perturbed the soldiers of Alexander. These *sādhus* were found sitting along the roadside undisturbed by noise and military undertakings, their eyes closed in meditation. Some were devoted to different sorts of *tapas,* and the Greeks failed to comprehend how human beings could proceed to torture or mutilate themselves willingly by means of ascetic practices. One of these *sādhus* accompanied Alexander on his march, but finally burnt himself to death in ritual manner on a pyre set out in front of the entire army.[3] Since these *sādhus* were normally naked, they reminded the Greeks of Diogenes, the philosopher who had renounced all worldly comforts and lived in an empty barrel in the marketplace of Corinth. For this reason, they gave them the name *gymnosophistai,* the "naked sages". Aristotle himself even mentioned the Indian gymnosophists in his catalogue of names for sages among non-Greek peoples, as has been quoted by Diogenes Laertius.[4] Megasthenes made a distinction between Brahmans and ascetic "forest dwellers"; according to his description, the latter lived on leaves and wild fruits and wore little more than a loin-cloth made from bark. Megasthenes does not, however, mention the term "*gymnosophistai*".[5]

Mention has thus been made here in our remarks of one of the most important observers of ancient Indian life, Megasthenes,[6] Greek envoy of Seleukos, successor of Alexander in Seleukia, to the court of Chandragupta Maurya in Pāṭaliputra. Through his reports, Megasthenes contributed a great deal to the emerging image of India in the Hellenistic world and in the Roman Empire. Unfortunately, only a portion of these invaluable diplomatic source materials has survived in the form of quotations by Greek and Roman authors. Like Seleukos, Ptolemaios, the other successor of Alexander and residing in Egypt, also sent an envoy to Pāṭaliputra. His name was Dionysios and his reports were well known throughout the Greek and Roman world, as substantiated by a reference of Plinius.[7] Plinius lived in the first century A.D. and was to become famous through his tragic death during the eruption of the volcano Vesuvius in 79 A.D., when he was commander-in-chief of the imperial navy stationed at Misenum. The image which these envoys transmitted centres on the well-organized rule of the Maurya empire, and there is praise for the special concern with which foreigners were treated there. It is likely that there was a quite substantial colony of such foreigners at the Maurya capital. In addition, the splendour and wealth of the court are described, the love for gold and jewelry, precious textiles and colourful garments. All this suggests that the image of India which crystallized in the ancient Western world had two salient dimensions: on the one hand, India was regarded as a land of wise sages and ascetics; on the other hand, it was depicted as a country of boundless treasures, a land replete with gold, silver and precious stones.

Before adding a third dimension to this composite image, let us look at two more personalities who played a key role in the dialogue between East and West in this ancient period. One is Heliodoros, who served as ambassador of King Antialkidas of Taxila at the court of King Bhagabhadra in Vidiśa, which was the capital of an important kingdom at that time. The Greek Heliodoros had become a worshipper of Viṣṇu in the form of Vāsudeva, and erected a Garuḍa pillar, a monolith with a bell-shaped capital and a Brahmī inscription, in the year 90 B.C. at Besnagar, a village on the banks of the Bes riverlet near its influx into the Vetravatī where Vidiśa is located.[8] He left a stone monument to commemorate his conversion. Milinda,[9] the Greek-Bactrain King Menander, has left us a famous Buddhist didactic poem written in Pālī. The questions of King Milinda constitute a conversation between the scholarly king and the sage Nāgasena—the resultant form is indeed reminiscent of a dialogue by Socrates. It also approximates the question-answer form of Buddhist literature. But these monuments, one a piece of sculpture and the other a literary document, apparently did not have any discernible influence on the image of India in ancient Greece and Rome. They are, however, nonetheless quite remarkable as early examples of an Indo-Hellenistic dialogue.

Permit me to add one more example from the sphere of diplomacy. Like their fathers Candragupta Maurya and Seleukos, the kings' sons, Bindusāra and Antiochos, were friendly neighbours. Letters which they exchanged bear testimony to this fact. In one of the letters the Indian monarch requests Antiochos to send him figs and raisin wine, and also to buy for him a sophist as a teacher of Greek philosophy. Antiochos answered that he would be happy to send the figs and the wine, but that the unfortunately would be unable to supply a professor on hire, since it would be an offense against the laws of his country.[10]

The third dimension of the image of India in ancient Greece and Rome has already been alluded to in connection with these letters. It concerns the field of trade amd commerce, import-export and the general exchange of goods. In this respect, India was not only regarded as a treasurehouse of gold, silver and precious stones, but as a veritable cornucopia of spices, silks and valuable goods which added a touch of luxury to comparatively simple habits of dress and eating. These sources could only be properly exploited after a regular sea trade commenced starting from Alexandria in Egypt. The precondition for this was good knowledge of the patterns of the monsoon winds and their direction. It was Imperial Rome at the very height of its power, opulence and love of luxury which consumed goods from the East to supplement those available around the Mediterranean. Her merchants paid in pure gold, i.e., in the hardest of currencies, and since imports increased to fantastic sums, the economy of ancient Rome occasionally faced serious difficulties as a result of a currency crisis. There were important urban centres in western India, and Arikamedu in Tamilnadu was one of the trading posts for commerce with Rome; this Roman network extended as far as Indochina and the Sunda islands.[11] Of course, we must bear in mind that not only were Roman or Alexandrian merchants heading East; there were Indian merchants who came to Rome to do business, as well as diplomatic missions from the Kuṣāṇa and Śatavāhana kingdoms. Thus it was that the image of India acquired the dimension of a land full of the refinement and elegance of luxurious living. Indeed, ascetism and opulence came to be ranked side-by-side in the ancient Western image of Indian reality.

One should not forget the fact that India was known in the West as the land of ivory. The most beautiful example of exported ivory which reached Italy from India and has been preserved is the statuette of a Śālabañjikā found in the ashes of Pompeii,[12] which was buried by the eruption of Vesuvius in 79 A.D. This small gem of art looks exactly like a work carved by the *dantakāras* from Vidiśa who completed the last pillar of the southern *toraṇa* of the main *stūpa* at Sāñcī.

In conclusion, we can state that the image of India prevalent in Greek and Roman Antiquity has three salient dimensions: it is seen as the home of sages and the *gymnosophistai,* as a *mahārāja's* palace glittering with gold, silver, ivory and precious stones, and as a source for the West of the refined enjoyment of material pleasures.

The image of India during the Middle Ages in the West was shaped by the same dimensions as the ancient Greek and Roman world which preceeded it. India as a country of wisdom and a land of opulence, these two faces would seem to be opposed to each other at first glance, but upon closer examination prove to be complementary. It was Hrabanus Maurus (776-856, a contemporary of Charlemagne),[13] an abbot in Fulda (822-42) and later Bishop of Mainz (847-56) who presented the first written description of the South Asian subcontinent in his treatise De Universo. According to him, India — *vocata ab Indo flumine* — covered the immense area from the Caucusus to the rising sun. There were long rivers like the Gaṅgā, and, of course, the Indus and Hyphasis (Beas), from where Alexander had been forced by his soldiers to return. There were islands such as Taprobane, Chrysa and Argyris. There were high mountains covered with gold — *montes aurei, quos adire propter dracones et gryphes et immensorum hominum monstra impossibile est* — impossible to approach, since these mountains are guarded by dragons, griffins and immense human monsters. The inhabitants of India, however, possess the gold of wisdom, the silver of eloquence and gems of all virtues. The comparison of human talents and virtues with the glittering shimmer of jewels seems to be typical. The popular image of India combined the dream of fabulous treasures with the tradition of wisdom and priesthood, worldly treasures along with spiritual treasures.

It is, of course, an integral part of the image of India in medieval Christendom that Thomas, one of the twelve apostles of Christ, reached India on his mission to the East. In the New Testament[14] he is called the faithless Thomas, since he remained doubtful about the reality of Christ's physical resurrection until he was permitted to touch the wounds of the crucified Savior. Later the legendary tradition — and this is regarded by many scholars as highly probable — narrates that St Thomas preached in South India, suffered martyrdom on a hill near Madras and was buried at Mylapur. Though some contradictions remain to be clarified, most historians believe that this legend is based on reality. It is also reported in the legend that Thomas met the king Gundapher, who can be identified with Gondophares of Gāndhāra. The Acta Thomae,[15] which narrate his missionary activities and report on his subsequent martyrdom, were originally written in Syriac in the 4th century A.D., and were later translated into Greek and Latin. The framework of the narration is historical, but the speeches appear to be later additions — *propaganda fidei* — in this case Manichaean. Therefore the Acta were banned by Augustine as heretical. Their ascetic trend is obvious, and they are against marriage. They contain eucharistic prayers, but the priest offers only bread and water. Judas Thomas — this is his full name — is regarded as the twin brother of Jesus. Here, as in many other cases, Manichaeism also served as a mediator between India and Europe in the Middle Ages. Of course, pilgrims from the West who visited the place of Thomas' martyrdom and his tomb are very rare, though one has become famous, namely the German Minnesinger Heinrich von Morungen.[16] He accompanied the margrave of Meissen to the Holy Land in 1197 A.D., and proceeded on from there to seek out the site where Thomas died and was buried in 68 A.D. in India.

The tradition connected with Alexander and his miraculous deeds, culminating in his adventures in India — his *iter ad paradisum,*[17] as it was termed in the 12th century — took on considerable narrative colour over the centuries. As early as 200 B.C., an Alexander romance was written in Greek by an Egyptian. Its original has not survived, but it was translated into more than 30 languages. Its contribution to the image of India were two motifs: that Alexander met the Amazons there, and that he had conversations with the wise brahmins.[18] In this connection, it is useful to recall that there existed a group of tractates in Latin about brahmins which were widely read during the European Middle Ages. One of these — De Moribus Brachmanorum -- had been translated by St Ambrose[19] the bishop of Milan. In addition, there were letters in existence from an exchange between Alexander and the Brahmin Dindimus. Thus, the medieval image of India, as in classical Antiquity, remains closely associated with the figure of Alexander. The Alexander romance was followed by an even more fantastic folk epic, the so-called Pseudo-Callisthenes, and by the Res Gestae Alexandri Macedonis, composed by Julius Valerius at the beginning of the 14th century A.D.. In the 10th century, Leo of Naples wrote his Nativitas et Victoria Alexandri Magni. The popularity of the Alexander romance is reflected in the large number of laguages into which it was translated at the time. Versions can be found in English, Irish, French, Spanish, Italian, Dutch, Swedish, Slavonic, Czech, Polish, as well as in Syriac, Arabic and Malay, and even in the works of Firdausi and Nizami in Persia.[20] In Middle High German, the Annolied,[21] written in 1105 A.D., deals with Alexander's fabulous exploits. The Alexanderlied of one Pfaffe Lamprecht,[22] based on the epic poem by Alberich of Besancon, is another Middle High German work focusing on the Alexander theme, as is the Alexanderlied composed by the well known poet Rudolf von Ems (*c.* 1230-1255).[23] This poet, however, was to achieve special fame as the author of the epic poem Barlaam and Josaphat.

First let me briefly summarize its plot. Once upon a time there lived a king in India by the name of Abenner, who persecuted the Christians. A son was born to him and named Josaphat. The astrologers prophesied his greatness as a king, and only one of them denied the prospect of worldly fame and disclosed that he would come to accept the Christian religion. His father therefore had him guarded in a beautiful palace, so that he should know nothing of the ills of worldly life. However, the prince was troubled by his loneliness, and was finally allowed to venture out into the world outside. In spite of his father's precautions, he saw a blind man, an old man and a corpse lying by the roadside, and so learned that life meant suffering. Up to this point, the story will seem familiar due to its close similarity to the legend of Buddha's youth. It indeed would appear to be a kind of Christianization of the Buddha legend. The prince is then visited by a disguised monk, Barlaam, who instructs him in the Christian doctrine and finally baptizes him. His father tries to reconvert him by holding a public dispute between Hindus and Christians, but without success. Josaphat finally goes off into the jungle to meet Barlaam there. Neither of them ever returns.

The form of the name Josaphat — in Greek Joasaph — is correctly presumed to have been derived from the term *bodhisattva,* and the Barlaam from *bhagavān.* The story was transmitted to Europe from India through many channels, and has been used by a large number of different writers. Siegfried Schulz presented a lecture in Delhi recently entitled "Two Christian Saints?",[24] and stressed the fact that both Barlaam and Josaphat were canonized by the Roman Catholic Church. This theme fits quite well into the image of India prevalent during the European Middle Ages, when it was regarded as a home of brahmins, sages and ascetics who had renounced worldly life. The name of Buddha, however, does not appear anywhere in these texts.

We have as yet made no mention of the constant stream of stories which flowed from India to Europe, and of which Barlaam and Josaphat remains a prominent example. These tales underwent considerable change and modification on their journey West through many peoples and languages; their Indian origin was subsequently hardly recognizable and was, in the end, ultimately forgotten, The most famous source of such tales was the Pañcatantra.[25] Some time after the 4th century A.D., it was translated into Pehlevi, and from there into Arabic. It was later transmitted across North Africa into Spain, and translated there from Arabic into Hebrew by Rabbi Joel in the 13th century, and soon afterwards into Spanish in 1251 A.D. Directorium Humanae Vitae was the title of the Latin translation made by Johannes of Capua based on the Hebrew version (1263-1278 A.D.). It was translated and printed in Germany in Urach in 1480 or 1481, following the initiative of Graf Eberhard im Barte, the Count of Wuerttemberg, and soon became so popular that it was reprinted in 1483 in Ulm under the new title Das Buch der Weisheit (The Book of Wisdom). This valuable early book, illustrated with numerous excellent woodcuts, is still available in a fascimile edition done by Rudolf von Bayer-Thurn and published by the Wiener Bibliophilen-Geselleschaft in Vienna in 1925. In all, there are approx. 200 adaptations of the Pañcatantra which can be traced, and a total of some 54 languages into which it was translated. Similar statements could be made regarding two other collections of tales, the Hitopadeśa[26] and the Kathāsaritsāgara.[27]

The image of India in the High and the Late Middle Ages was intimately connected with the tradition of the priest-king Johannes. The earliest reference appears in the chronicle of Otto von Freising, written about 1145 A.D.: *Johannes quidam, qui ultra Persidem et Armeniam in extremo oriente habitans, rex et sacerdos, cum gente sua Christianos est*[28] (a certain John, who lives in the Far East beyond Persia and Armenia, king and priest, is a Christian along with his people).

The very important role which this priest-king John played in the European mind during this period becomes clear when viewed in connection with the theme of the Holy Grail. The poet Wolfram von Eschenbach mentions in his great epic Parzival that the priest-king is the son of Feirefiz and Repanse de Schoye, who earlier appears in the epic poem as the virgin carrying the Holy Grail.[29] Thus, the Indian ruler in the Far East is the nephew of Parzival, the king of the Grail; this, then, forges a thematic link between the highest embodiment of spirituality in the European Middle ages, the Holy Grail, and the land of India. Hermann Goetz has pointed out many other Indian features to be found in Parzival and other epic poems of the 13th century.[30]

We find another thematic link in the legend narrated by Oswald the Scribe. According to this legend, the priest-king John sent Emperor Frederick II of Hohenstaufen three gifts: a fireproof robe made of salamander skins, the water of eternal youth, and a ring containing three precious stones which enable the wearer to survive under water, to be invulnerable and to render himself invisible. In the so-called Rhymed Chronicle, the inhabitants of Salzburg express the wish that their abbot Henry of Admont might be with Priest John and Saint Thomas in India as a kind of patriarch. In this connection, we see how the medieval Christian world viewed India as some sort of paradise reigned over by rulers who indeed combined the virtues of regency and priesthood; Thomas and John became the symbolic figures for this type of idealized leadership. The Council of Constance (1414-1418) was an event of the greatest political and cultural importance at the close of the Middle Ages. It is of some interest in connection with the image of India in Europe as well, especially in respect to the theme of the priestly monarch. The Saxonian World Chronicle (Sächsische Weltchronik)[31] mentions that four monks appeared from distant India, and these monks had crosses burnt into their foreheads. The Emperor Sigismund[32] presented a document to the Council entitled the "Reformation of Sigismund" in which he outlined the union of worldly and ecclesiastical power in one hand. To quote: "Item, an emperor should be learned ... Were he a priest as well, he would be the worthier and all worldly law would be in his hand ... Melchisedek was priest and was annointed king in Jerusalem. A priest is emperor in India, where none can become emperor unless he is a priest."

The monks who journeyed from distant India to attend this Council reflect the fact that a new period had already dawned, one in which travellers from and through Asia brought authentic news and on-the-spot observations to the attention of Europe. We all know that Marco Polo (1254-1324) was the forerunner of this development. Though his contemporaries read his work Mirabilia Mundi (Miracles of the World) with great pleasure, they did not believe in his credulity and nicknamed him Messer Milione.[33] His sojourn in Asia (1271-1292) brought him over the ancient silk route to Kambuluk (Peking), and only on his return did he visit Sumatra and India. His book was subsequently also read by one Cristoforo Colombo, and influenced the latter's plans for the circumnavigation of the globe.

There were, however, other travellers who made the troublesome journey to the court of the Khan of Karakorum across Mongolia. The friars Rubruk[34] and Carpini[35] were sent on diplomatic missions, and their reports in Latin give detailed descriptions of their experiences and observations; William of Rubruk (1210-1270) travelled East during 1253-1255. After the breakdown of the Roman Empire and the failure of the crusades (1250 A.D.), those in power who felt responsible for the Christian West, namely Pope Innocent IV (1243-1254) and the French king Louis IX (1226-1270), looked for aid to the East, since they had noted the fact that the Mongols had crushed the Muslim kingdoms, and thus regarded these Mongols as potential allies. The ancient legend of the priest-king John was recalled, John who might come as a savior or redeemer for a Christendom in distress. As their envoys, the friars were delighted to meet Christians at the Mongolian court, Nestorians as well as Manichaeans and Buddhists. Of course, the priest-king John was nowhere to be seen, for he did not belong to the world of harsh political realities. The friars had travelled in the wrong direction, and not only in terms of geography.

With this observation, I would like to close our survey which has taken us through a colourful and varied historical panorama. Quite a number of additional details could be added to the picture already sketched. Three different dimensions have been underscored, and can be summarized once again: a) India as a holy land is not only inhabited by brahmins and *gymnosophistai,* but also by Christian priests and saints, and even governed by priest-kings, since these are the only individuals there who could truly aspire to rulership; b) India as a treasurehouse covered with gold and guarded by griffins becomes a motif in folktales; c) India beckons as a source of material goods which attracted trade and commerce. These different dimensions may be intertwined with each other in the human mind, but one motif binds them all together: the image of India is alluring from afar, full of features which one aspires to possess, whether the ideals of wisdom and holiness or the beauty of gold and precious stones or the stimulants of spices and refined luxury. It is always a country to be sought out and searched for. As reads a sentence formulated by the German philosopher Hegel[36]: "India has created a special momentum in world history as a country to be searched for."

NOTES

1. Flavius Arrianus, Anabasis, ed. Abich, Leipzig, 1876. Polybios, ed. Th.Büttner-Wobst, 1889-1905, 1922-24, tr. Haakh and Kraz, 1858-75, 1922. Plutarch, Moralia, ed. Daniel Wyttenbach, Oxford, 1795-1830, Leipzig, 1796-1834, tr. 1926-27. Strabo, Geographica, 17 vols, ed. Kramer, Berlin, 1844-52, ed. and tr. into Latin, C. Mueller and F. Duebner, Paris, 1853-57.
2. Vide Rawlinson in: Indian Art and Letters, London, X, 58.
3. His name was Kalanos.
4. Diogenes Laërtius, living at Laerte in the first half of the 3rd century A.D. His opus on life, views and sayings of famous philosophers was translated into German by O. Apelt in 1921.
5. Quoted by Strabo in his Geographica 703, 711-15.
6. Collected by Schwanbeck in Megasthenis Indica, Bonn, 1846, and C. Mueller in Fragmenta historicorum graecorum, Vol. 2, Paris, 1853.
7. M. Gaius Plinius Secundus (Maior.) (23/24-79 A.D.) Naturalis Historia, ed. C. Mayhoff, 1892-1933, tr. Wittstein, 1880-82.
8. Archaeological Survey of India, Annual Reports, 1908/09, 1913/14.
9. Milindapanho. The Questions of King Milinda, Oxford 1890-94, tr. Rhys Davids in: Sacred Books of the East XXXV, XXXVI.
10. Heimo Rau, Following Alexander's Tracks on the Indus, in: Reflections on Indian Art, Bombay 1976, 26.
11. W.H. Schoff, Periplus of the Erythrean Sea, tr. London, 1912. J.W. McCrindle, Ancient India as described by Ptolemy, Calcutta, 1827. E.H. Warmington, Commerce between the Roman Empire and India, Cambridge, 1928. W.W. Tarn, Hellenistic Civilisation, London, 1930. P.C. Bagchi, India and China, Calcutta, 1944. R.E.M. Wheeler, Report on the Excavation at Arikamedu, Ancient India II, 1946.
12. Now in the National Museum, Naples.
13. Patrologiae cursus completus accurante J.P. Migne tomus CXI: B. Hrabani Mauri tomus quintus, Paris 1852.
14. St. John 20, 24–29.
15. Acta Thomae, ed. Thilo, Leipzig, 1823. Acta apostolorum apocrypha, ed. Tischendorf, Leipzig, 1851. Apocryphical Acts of the Apostles, Syriac-English, 2 vols., by Wright, London, 1871. Supplementum codicis apocryphi, Greek, ed. Bonnet, Leipzig, 1883. A.E. Medlycott, India and the Apostle Thomas, London, 1905.
16. Michel, Heinrich von Morungen und die Troubadours, Strassburg, 1880. Rössner, Untersuchungen zu Heinrich von Morungen, Berlin, 1898.
17. Alexander's expedition to India was changed into March to Paradise imputing to the hero a religious motivation.
18. Vide the so-called Pseudo-Callisthenes, the Greek original ed. Meusel, Leipzig, 1871, Latin translation ed. B. Kübler, Leipzig, 1888.
19. Ambrosius *c.* 340-397 A.D. Opera ed. in Corpus scriptorum ecclesiasticorum latinorum, 1-4, Wien/Prag, 1897-1902. F.H. Dudden, The Life and Times of St. Ambrose, Oxford, 1935.
20. Spiegel, Die Alexandersage bei den Orientalen, Leipzig, 1851.
21. Anno II, Archbishop of Cologne (*c.* 1010-75) is lauded in the Annolied, ed. M. Opitz

Danzig 1639, ed. Rödiger in Monumenta Germaniae historica, Hannover, 1895.

22. Lamprecht composed his Alexanderlied, between 1120 and 1130 ed. Kinzel, Halle 1884.
23. Barlaam und Josaphat ed. Pfeiffer, Leipzig, 1843. Zingerle, Die Quellen zum-Alexander des Rudolf von Ems, Breslau, 1885.
24. Published in the India International Centre Quarterly, New Delhi, 1981.
25. Pañcatantra, fünf Bücher indischer Fabeln, Märchen und Erzählungen. Aus dem Sanskrit von Theodor Benfey, Leipzig, 1859. Johannes Hertel, Tantrākhyāyikā, die älteste Fassung des Pañcatantra. Mit Einleitung und Anmerkungen, Leipzig, Berlin, 1909. Pañcatantra, fünf Bücher altindischer Staatsweisheit und Lebenkunst in Fabeln und Sprüchen, ed. and tr. by Ludwig Alsdorf, Bergen (Obb.) 1952. Friedmar Geissler, Beispiele der alten Weisen des Johann von Capua. Übersetzung, der hebräischen Bearbeitung des indischen Pañcatantra ins Lateinische, ed. and tr. Berlin, 1960.
26. Hitopadeśa i.e. Introduction into the Useful.
27. Ocean of Stories.
28. Scriptores rerum Germanicarum in usum scholarum ex Monumentis Germanie Historicis separatim editi Ottonis Episcopi Frisingensis Chronica sive Historia de duabus civitatibus, Hannover-Leipzig, 1892, 364-65.
29. Ed. Karl Lachmann, 1833, 1965, 822, 23-27.
30. Hermann Goetz, Der Orient der Kreuzzüge in Wolframs Parzival, in: Archiv für Kulturgeschichte 49, 1, Köln-Graz, 1967.
31. Verses 16, 17 in: Deutsche Chroniken, Monumenta Germaniae Historica II, 1, Hannover, 1877, 363.
32. Monumenta Germaniae Historica VI, Stuttgart, 1964.
33. Marco Polo (1254-1324), Mirabilia mundi, many editions and translations: Marco Polo Veneziano delle Maraviglie de Mondo da lui vedute, Genua, 1298.
34. Wilhelm of Ruysbroek (*c.* 1210-*c.* 1270) travelled to Mongolia 1253-1255 by order of the French king Louis IX. H. Herbst, Der Bericht des Franziskaners Wilhelm von Rubruk über seine Reise . . . Leipzig, 1925.
35. Giovanni Piano Carpini (*c.* 1200-*c.* 1250) travelled to Mongolia 1245-1247 by order of Pope Innocent IV. His reports were Liber Tartarorum and Historia Mongolorum quos nos Tartaros appellamus, ed. d'Avezac in: Recueil de voyages et de mémoires, Vol. IV, Paris, 1839
36. Georg Wilhelm Friedrich Hegel (1770-1831), Philosophie der Weltgeschichte, Leipzig, 1917/18, ed. Georg Lasson, 344.

Revelation and Argumentation

Some References to the Relation of *śruti* and *tarka* in Śaṃkara's Bṛhadāraṇyakopaniṣadbhāṣya.[1]

HEIDRUN BRÜCKNER
Mainz

Considering the title of the present seminar, namely "India and the West", I have chosen to deal with some problems relating to the work of Śaṃkara since his teachings have been discussed extensively in India as well as in the West and his expositions have, moreover, been claimed by many different people for various purposes.[2] I wish to refrain, however, from entering into these controversies in a general way and shall concentrate here on trying to understand and interpret some passages from Saṃkara's Bhāṣya on the BĀU.[3] Such an analysis may then, in a second step, also permit conclusions relevant for these discussions.

In his BĀUBh, Ś. on the one hand himself applies reasoning on the basis of the different means of cognition (*pramāṇa*). He even quotes a Nyāya-sūtra twice and makes use of the logical method to which it refers. On the other hand, and in the same text, he strongly abuses the logicians (*tārkika*) as bulls without tails and horns, as chatter-boxes, etc.[4] How are we to understand these two different attitudes? What is Ś.'s own way of argumentation? In which context or under which presuppositions does he accept reasoning and in which respect does he condemn it? And what is the place of argument in relation to the revelation of the Sacred Texts?

A hint towards the understanding of this problem is—in my opinion—given by Ś. himself, when he speaks of the joint operation of *śruti* and *tarka*, of *āgama* and *upapatti*. He says that a matter which has been established by the Sacred Tradition as well as by reasoning is worthy of our trust because [then] there is complete agreement [between the cognition and the thing as it really is].[5] So, revelation and argumentation are not necessarily mutually exclusive; they can combine in such a way that argumentation serves to teach and reinforce the truths established through the Sacred Texts. It need not challenge the latter, it can complement them. Moreover, according to Ś.'s analysis these texts themselves occasionally apply "*tarka*" or "*upapatti*" to explain their message; they teach by mere statement as well as through similes and reasons.[6]

Thus, one way of "reconciling" *śruti* and *tarka* is to find reasoning applied by the *śruti* itself. Another is to assign different fields of operation to the *śruti* and to reasoning based on the worldly means of cognition. This second method will also provide a solution to the problem of the seeming contradiction in Ś.'s statements about *tarka* referred to above.

We shall now consider three passages where Ś. discusses the construction of the Upaniṣad. In doing so, he sometimes repeats his own explanation with slight variations. This gives us a chance to examine his terminology and clarify the specific meaning of certain terms.

... *upakramopasaṃhārābhyāṃ ca; sarvāsu hy upaniṣatsu pūrvam ekatvaṃ pratijñāya dṛṣṭāntair hetubhiś ca paramātmano vikārāṃśāditvaṃ jagataḥ pratipādya punar ekatvam upasaṃharati.* BĀUBh II. 1. 20 [296, 23-26].

["Another reason we can adduce for our conviction that BĀU II. 1. 20 teaches openness only] lies in the opening and the conclusion [of the passage in question]: because in all the Upaniṣads [the *śruti*] having first stated the oneness [and] having [then] explained by means of similes and reasons that the world is a part of the Highest Atman which represents a product of change, etc., again concludes oneness."

This passage is particularly interesting because of its terminology. "*Upakrama*" and "*upasaṃhāra*", in the first place, are technical terms of text exegesis as developed most probably by the Mīmāṃsā and adopted by other schools, too.[7] "*Upakrama*" refers to what is stated at the commencement of the discourse. If this does not help to discover the purport one should next look to the end of the passage, "*upasaṃhāra*." The four steps mentioned in the next sentence of the quotation, namely "*pratijñāya*", "*dṛṣṭāntaiḥ*", "*hetubhiḥ*" and "*upasaṃharati*", recall the Sāṃkhya-syllogism with its members "*pratijñā*", "*hetu*", "*dṛṣṭānta*", "*upasaṃhāra*", and *nigamana*, with the difference that in our passage, due probably to the actual development of the commented text, the *dṛṣṭāntas* are mentioned before the *hetus* and there is no fifth step like "*nigamana*".

In the above-quoted sentence, "*upakrama*" is taken up by the expression "*pūrvam ekatvaṃ pratijñāya*". Thus, the exegetic term "*upakrama*" seems to correspond to "*pratijñā*" when the categories and terms of logic are applied. Next, the initial statement is elaborated and proved by similes and reasons[9] and finally it is re-stated as the conclusion. Since, in this way, the text opens and ends with the statement of oneness the teaching of oneness is to be taken as the purport of the passage. At the same time, the structure of the passage can be looked at as an argumentative progression and thereby also fulfils the methodological requirements as postulated by the Nyāya-school. Being naturally concerned — in an Upaniṣad-*bhāṣya*—with both interpretation of scriptural passages and argumentation, Ś. uses methods and terms from both traditions. The term "*upasaṃhāra*" can figure in both contexts, in an exegetical one as well as in a syllogistic one. It can also be used in a non-technical sense.

There are two more passages relevant for the present analysis in which Ś. speaks of the *śruti* itself as applying "*tarka*". The first one is his introduction to BĀU II. 5 [363, 19-23], where he discusses the phase of *ātman*-realization as indicated in BĀU II. 4. 5 and in the parallel passage IV. 5. 6. This discussion is more elaborate than his respective *bhāṣyas* on II. 4. 5 and IV. 5. 6 themselves. Commenting on the expression "*śrotavya*", "*mantavya*", "*nididhyāsitavya*" in the Up-text, he paraphrases "*manana*" by "*tarka*" and in this connexion also refers to the structure of the Up. He says that the Maitreyī-section could be taken to give an initial statement and reasons. The ppp of the verb *prati-jñā* is used here to denote the first step, the following reasons are termed "*hetu*". For those who consider these reasons insufficient the next section can be understood to remove these doubts:

tatrāyaṃ hetur asiddha ity āśaṅkyata ātmaikasāmānyodbhavapralayākhyas tadāśaṅkānivṛttyartham etad brāhmaṇam ārabhyate. (BĀUBh II.5, intr. [363, 25-27]).

"[If] it is doubted that in respect to [the thing to be proved] this reason is unfounded, [viz. the reason which consists in the assertion] that [everything] is of one kind with the *ātman*, originates only from it and dissolves into it, [then] to remove this doubt the present chapter (section) is undertaken (i.e. taught)."

Ś. then summarises the underlying logic of the next *brāhmaṇa* as an answer to a possible objection, and proceeds to offer an alternative interpretation of the shape of the same Up. passage. In this context, he

refers to the Nyāya-scheme of syllogism, and quotes the definition of "*nigamana*" as given in NS 1.1.39. This second interpretation differs from the first one in taking the following section of the Up. to be the "*nigamana*" (conclusion) of the two preceding ones, instead of taking it as an additional explanation. Here, Ś. uses the terms "*pratijñāta*", "*hetu*" and "*nigamana*" and quotes NS 1.1.39 as a reference for the application of this pattern. He explicitly names the Naiyāyikas:
athavātmaivedaṃ sarvam iti pratijñātasyātmotpattiṣthitilayatvaṃ hetum uktvā punar āgamapradhānena madhubrāhmaṇena pratijñātasyārthasya nigamanaṃ kriyate. tathā hi naiyāyikair uktaṃ hetvapadeśāt pratijñāyaḥ punarvacanaṃ nigamanam iti. (BĀUBh II. 5, intr. [364, 14-17]).
"Or, after naming as the reason for the initially stated [sentence] 'All this is only the *ātman*' the fact that [everything] originates from the *ātman,* subsists in it [and] vanishes into it, again, the final statement of the initially stated matter is made by the *madhu*-section in which the Sacred Tradition (i.e. mere intimation of Sacred Truths) predominates. For it has been said by the Naiyāyikas: 'The final statement (conclusion) is the repetition of the initial statement (proposition) after the pointing out of reasons.' "

Thirdly, Ś. mentions the opinion of "others"(*anye*) about the passage in question who postulate three different *prakaraṇas* for the Upaniṣadic scheme of "*śrotavya*", "*mantavya*" and "*nididhyāsitavya*". While stating their interpretation he explains "*mantavya*" by using the term "*upapatti*" (reasoning) and subsequently concludes the topic by saying:
sarvathāpi tu yathāgamenāvadhāritaṃ tarkatas tathaiva mantavyam. yathā tarkato matasya tarkāgamābhyāṃ niścitasya tathaiva nididhyāsanam kriyata iti [364, 19-21].
"In any case, however, one should reflect through argumentation only in that manner in which it has been ascertained by the *āgama*. Meditation is practised only in that manner in which it has been thought correct by arguments [and] has been determined by Sacred Tradition and reasoning."[10]

He considers a separate injunction for meditation useless: one should not postulate different *prakaraṇas* of the Up. for *śravaṇa, manana* and *nididhyāsana*, as was done by the "others" quoted above.[11] He concludes further that in any case in this [*madhu-*] *brāhmaṇa* the meaning of the two preceding chapters is summarised:
sarvathāpi tu adhyāyadvayasyārtho 'smin brāhmaṇa upasaṃhriyate. [364, 23/24.

These first two chapters constitute the *"madhukāṇḍa"* the last section of which is the "*madhubrāhmaṇa*" (followed only by the list of teachers). BĀU II.4 is the "Maitreyībrāhmaṇa" which is repeated later on as BĀU IV.5. Chapters III. and IV. form the Yājñavalkya-*kāṇḍa* and thus the Maitreyibrāhmaṇa occurs in both the *kāṇḍas*. The following *khilakāṇḍa* is taken to be a kind of appendix.[12]

Before entering into a further discussion of the above quotations I want to refer to another very relevant passage. For in the introductory *bhāṣya* to BĀU IV.5. Ś. once again resumes the topic of the structure of the Up., and again, the terms *"tarka"* and *"upapatti"* are used. Whereas in the introduction to section II.5 of the BĀU the progression within the *madhukāṇḍa* was discussed, Ś. now analyses the shape of the entire Up.-text. In our aforesaid quotations, he had traced the argumentative structure in the different sections of the *madhukāṇḍa* dealing mainly with the Maitreyī- and the *madhu-brāhmaṇa*. Now, the *madhukāṇḍa* as a whole is treated and is described as merely communicating the Sacred Truths of the *brahmatattva*. The Yājñavalkya-*kāṇḍa*, on the other hand, expounds this truth by different types of reasoning and argumentation. In the fourth section of the fourth chapter (counted by Ś. as the sixth) the topic of the *brahmatattva* has been summarized (IV. 4. 25 [704, 13/14] . . .*tattvopasaṃhāra kṛtaḥ. tad upasaṃhṛtam* . . .). Applying NS 1.1.39, the following Maitreyī-*brāhmaṇa* can be considered the *"nigamana"*. It constitutes the last section of the Up. which, according to Ś., consists of four *prapāṭhakas* and ends with IV.5.15. IV.5.15 contains the *"upasaṃhāra"* of the whole text.[13]

BĀUBh IV.5, intr. [705, 6–10] runs:
āgamapradhānena madhukāṇḍena brahmatattvaṃ nirdhāritam. punas tasyaivopapattipradhānena yājñavalkīyena kāṇḍena pakṣapratipakṣaparigrahaṃ kṛtvā vigṛhyavādena vicāritam. śiṣyācāryasaṃbandhena ca ṣaṣṭhe praśnaprativacananyāyena savistaram vicāryopasaṃhṛtam. athedānīṃ nigamanasthānīyaṃ maitreyībrāhmaṇam ārabhyate.
"By means of the *madhukāṇḍa* in which Scriptural statement predominates the true nature of *brahman* is determined. Again, by means of the Yājñavalkya-section in which argumentation predominates — once it has been comprehended by means of [assuming] views and counter-views the same [*brahmatattva*] is deliberated on through debate. And in the sixth [section] it is summarised once it has been discussed at length by means of questions and answers between masters and students. And now the

Maitreyī-section is begun which takes the place of a conclusion (final statement)."

At this point, Ś. again quotes NS 1.1.39 but this time introduces it in the following way:
ayaṃ ca nyāyo vākyakovidaiḥ parigṛhītaḥ. (BĀUBh IV.5, intr. [705, 10])
In the passage quoted above (BĀUBh II.5, intr. [364, 16/17]) he had expressly attributed this *sūtra* to the Naiyāyikas (*naiyāyikair uktam*). If the Naiyāyikas are meant here, too, we must take "*vākya*" to mean "syllogism" or "logic" in the present context, and translate the sentence "this rule is followed by the experts of syllogism". I tend to adopt this translation instead of interpreting the expression to refer to the Mimāṃsakas with whom the term "*vākya*" is also very commonly associated.[14] The meaning "syllogism" or "logic" for "*vākya*" is attested for example in texts like the Yuktidīpikā.[15].

Ś. seems to refer to the Naiyāyikas to stress that the *śruti* progresses in a way which is methodologically correct and in accord with the rules developed by the worldly experts of dialectics and argumentation. The quotation of a NS by Ś. does by no means indicate his association with the Nyāya-school or his acceptance of their scheme of syllogism as an independant means of valid cognition. If there were such an association, he could have referred to NS 1.1.32. in which the five *avayavas* or parts of proof are enumerated, whereas in the definition of "*nigamana*" (NS 1.1.39) only three parts are mentioned. It is more probable that the technique and terminology developed by the Naiyāyikas for systematic reasoning had found favour with other schools of thought which then adopted whatever they thought convenient for their own purposes. The terms occurring in NS 1.1.39 apparently did not clash with Ś.'s own terminology, and could even be well-accommodated in it. In the above-quoted context they were easily applicable to the actual progression of the Up.

After quoting NS 1.1.39 (*hetvapadeśāt pratijñāyāḥ punarvacanaṃ nigamanam* [705, 11/12], transl. see above) to describe the structure of the Up.-sections under consideration, Ś. gives a second interpretation[16] which does not basically differ from the first one but adopts a slightly different perspective:
athavāgamapradhānena madhukāṇḍena yad amṛtatvasādhanaṃ sasaṃnyāsam ātmajñānam abhihitaṃ tad eva tarkeṇāpy amṛtatvasādhanaṃ sasaṃnyāsam ātmajñānam adhigamyate. tarkapradhānaṃ hi yājñavalkīyaṃ kāṇḍam. (BĀUBh IV.5, intr. [705 11-14]).

"Or, the *ātman*-knowledge accompanied by renunciation which has been declared by the *madhukāṇḍa,* in which Scriptural statements predominate to be the means to immortality, this very *ātman*-knowledge accompanied by renunciation is also realized through reasoning to be the means to immortality. For in the Yājñavalkya-section reasoning (argumentation) predominates."

Here, the *madhukāṇḍa* in which Scriptural statements predominate (*āgamapradhāna*) would correspond to the *"pratijñā"* in the terminology of the syllogism. Ś. uses the expression *"ātmajñānam abhihitam"*. After the *"ātmajñāna"* has been declared or stated by revelation it is also attained by reasoning *(tarkeṇāpy adhigamyate)*. Hence it is established on the basis of *āgama* and *tarka* that the *ātman*-knowledge combined with renunciation is the means to immortality:
tasmāc chāstratarkābhyāṃ niścitam etad yad etad ātmajñānaṃ sasaṃnyāsam amṛtatvasādhanam iti. tasmāc chāstraśraddhāvadbhir amṛtatva-pratipitsubhir etat pratipattavyam iti. āgamopapattibhyāṃ hi niścito 'rthaḥ śraddheyo bhavaty avyabhicārād iti. (BĀUBh IV.5, intr. [705, 14–18]).
"Therefore it is ascertained by the *śāstra* and by argumentation that this *ātman*-knowledge combined with renunciation is the means to immortality. Therefore this [means] should be obtained by those who have faith in the *śāstra* [and] strive for immortality. For a matter which has been ascertained by the Sacred Tradition and by reasoning is worthy of trust because [then] there is complete agreement [between the cognition and the thing as it really is]."
In the above quotation the compound *"śāstratarka"* is taken up again by the expression *"āgamopapatti"*. Earlier the word *"tarkāgama"* had also been employed (cf. note 10 above). It is essential that a matter is particularly worthy of credence when it has been established by both Scriptural statement and an argumentation which does not clash with the former. *"avyabhicāra"* is a non-diversion or, expressed positively, a complete agreement between the cognition obtained with the help of revelation and argumentation and the thing as it really is.

While here a twofold scheme is given, Ś. in the *bhāṣya* to BĀU IV.5.1. which immediately follows my last quotation has again recourse to the terminology of syllogistic reasoning and applies the threefold division of *"pratijñā"* (here: *pratijñāta)*, *"hetu"* and *"nigamana"* (here: *nigamyate)* to the text by splitting up the Yājñavalkya-*kāṇḍa* into an argumentative and a concluding portion. The *madhukāṇḍa* is — as before — considered to be the *"pratijñā"*:

hetupradhānāni hi vākyāny atītāni tadanantaram āgamapradhānena pratijñāto 'rtho nigamyate maitreyībrāhmaṇena. (BĀUBh IV. 5.1. [706, 13/14]).
"For the former statements were such that reasons predominated [in them]; immediately after those [statements in which reasons predominate] the matter which had been initially stated [by the *madhubrāhmaṇa* in which mere] Scriptural statement predominates is finally concluded by the Maitreyī-*brāhmaṇa.* "

In the compounds "*āgamapradhāna*" and "*āgamopapatti*" as well as "*tarkāgama*" "*āgama*" is used in a restricted sense, referring to the non-argumentative sections of the Sacred Text and merely giving authoritative factual statements. In a general sense, it can refer to the Upaniṣadic literature as a whole. The term "*sruti*" is mostly applied by Ś. for individual sentences or statements from the Sacred Texts, as for example the "*mahāvākyas*". He says on many occasions that a particular point he is making can be proved by "hundreds of *śrutis*" (BĀUBh II.I.20 ... *ityādiśrutiśatebhyaḥ)* and often uses the word in the plural for series of quotations, mainly from the Up.s, which could be continued further (*ityādiśrutayaḥ,* cf. also BSBh for this usage).

To sum up: While commenting on the BĀU Ś. makes use of different methods of understanding and interpretation of the text in order to penetrate the Scriptural teachings as deeply as possible. In the passages just quoted he offers several alternatives to analyse the progression or structure of the Up. This analysis is, to a certain extent, a formal one but has also implications with respect to the meaning conveyed by the text.

In BĀU II.5, intr., the pairs *āgama/tarka* and *pratijñā/hetu* are applied to the sections of the first *kāṇḍa* as well as a threefold scheme consisting of "*pratijñā*", "*hetu*" and "*nigamana*" and being referred to NS 1.1.39. It seems to be left to the choice of the reader/hearer whether he wants to take the *madhubrāhmaṇa* the latter is said to summarize or conclude in any case the meaning of the former (*upasṃhriyate*).[17]

Similarly, in BĀU IV,5, intr., several schemes are applied to analyse the structure of the entire text. The *madhukāṇḍa* is referred to as *āgama,* the first sections of the Yājñavalkya-*kāṇḍa* as *upapatti* which is concluded or summarized (*upasaṃhṛtam*) in the sixth section; the Maitreyī-*brāhmaṇa* takes the position of a *nigamana* (*nigamana-sthānīya*). For this scheme, NS 1.1.39 is quoted again. Subsequently, the twofold pattern expressed by the pairs *āgama/tarka, śāstra/tarka, āgama/upapatti* is mentioned one more time. This division is also elaborated in Ś.s introduction to the Yājñavalkya-*kāṇḍa* III.I) in which the *madhukāṇḍa* is designated as *āgama* and the Yājñavālkya-*kāṇḍa* as *upapatti.*[18] In

BĀUBh IV.5.1. finally, the threefold scheme is applied once again in terms (*pratijñāta, hetu, nigamyate*) recalling NS 1.1.39.

I have tried in the foregoing discussion to show that Ś. traces the application of "*tarka*" to the *śruti* itself, and in this way does not incur a confrontation between revelation and reasoning. Another way to achieve the same object is to assign different fields of operation or areas of application to the *śruti* and to reasoning based on the other means of cognition. The *śruti* governs the realm of transcendental subjects whereas the other means of cognition are valid in the empirical realm, or as additional support for the *śruti*. In their own area of application they should not be contradicted, even by the *śruti*. Ś. clearly says that not even hundreds of *dṛṣṭāntas* (similes) put forward by the *śruti* will convince us that fire is cold or that the sun does not burn, because there can be no contradiction between different means of cognition. The different *pramāṇas* have their specific spheres and enlighten us only about them. The same matter cannot be an object of different means of cognition.[19] Finally, this splitting of competences is a device of Ś.'s to arrive at the conclusion that only the *śruti* can speak about the highest *ātman*, and that there is no justification for reasoning about it on the basis of other, i.e. non-Vedic, sources of cognition/knowledge.[20]

It is at this point that we can understand why Ś., who freely makes use of the methods of argumentation and reasoning and relies on the worldly means of cognition will—on other occassions—condemn "*tarka*" and those who apply it. *Tarka, upapatti, anumāna,* etc. are not rejected as such but only when they are applied as independent *pramāṇas* in respect to non-empirical or transcendental matters. Much on the line of the Mīmāṃsā, they should—in Ś.'s opinion—mainly have a supporting function and confirm the teachings of the *śruti* (see above the quotation from BAUBh II.5, intr. *"yathāgamenāvadhāritaṃ tarkatas tathaiva mantavyam")*. Thus, the crucial point for Ś. is, whether the *pramāṇas* other than the *śruti* are applied in a field in which the *śruti* has priority. If this is done, Ś. finds the reasoning unacceptable and severely attacks those who rely only on their own thinking:

tatra paṇḍitaṃmanyāḥ kecit svacittavaśāt sarvaṃ pramāṇam itaretaraviruddhaṃ manyante tathā pratyakṣādivirodham api codayanti brahmaikatve. (BĀUBh II.1.20 [308, 10–12]).

"With respect to this some people who consider themselves to be learned believe on the basis of their own thinking that all means of cognition are mutually contradictory and they put forward with regard to the oneness of *brahman* a contradiction to sense-perception etc."[21]

Throughout the subsequent passage, Ś. makes use of arguments to point out absurd consequences in the *pūrvapakṣa*-arguments which are based on perception and inference. It is, therefore, not the application of these *pramāṇas* as such that is criticized, but their independent use with regard to metaphysical truths like the oneness of *brahman* which according to Ś. can be revealed only by the *śruti*. This is why he calls their reasoning "bad reasoning" *(kutarka)*.

So, for Ś., the contradiction is not between revelation and reasoning as such, but between the ends to which reasoning is directed. His polemic remarks in this passage culminate in the statement that the *pūrvapakṣin* does not enjoy the grace of the *śāstra* and of a *guru*, and hence is excluded from the fort where there is no fear *(abhayaṃ durgam)* . . . fear, probably, of the reasoning of others whose arguments may be still stronger.[22] Only those whose unquestionable basis is the *āgama* are, according to Ś., safe from refutation.

In short, I would like to stress that for Ś. himself there does not seem to be any conflict between *śruti* and *tarka*. Even the *śruti* itself makes use of reasoning. Both *śruti* and *tarka* collaborate in preparing the final step of *ātman*-realization. Reasoning is unacceptable for Ś. only when it is applied to question this goal.

NOTES

1. The present paper develops an aspect of the subject of the author's doctoral thesis "Zum Beweisverfahren Śaṃkaras. Eine Untersuchung der Form und Funktion von *dṛṣṭāntas* im BĀUBh und im ChUBh des Ś. Bhagavatpāda" (Berlin, 1979) in which the attention was focused exclusively on the mode of Ś. 's application of *dṛṣṭāntas*. Cf. also the author's paper: "On Ś. 's application of the *rajjusarpa-dṛṣṭānta*", in *Tattvāloka*, IV, 3, 1981, pp.17–31.
   The following abbr. will be used: BĀUBh = Bṛhadāraṇyakopaniṣadbhāṣya; Ś. = Śaṃkara; NS = Nyāyasūtra; BSBh = Brahmasūtrabhāṣya; ChUBh = Chāndogyopanisadbhāṣya.
2. For a detailed discussion of the problems involved in the application of western terms and categories like "mystic", "rationalist", "theologian", etc. to Ś. and other Indian thinkers, cf. W. Halbfass' excellent study "Indian und Europa. Perspektiven ihrer geistigen Begegnung", Basel/Stuttgart, 1981.
3. The limitation to the most interesting passages of only this one text is rather arbitrary and caused primarily by the limited space and the wish for lucidity. As far as I can see at the moment, my results are confirmed by the other work of Ś., too. Moreover, W. Halbfass in a forthcoming publication, a chapter of which he kindly made accessible to me after the completion of the present article, arrives, though on a broader textual basis, at results similar to those which will be outlined on the following pages. His monograph also contains a discussion of the extant secondary literature on the subject.
4. "*aho anumānakauśalaṃ darśitam apucchaśṛṅgais tārkikabalīvardaiḥ*"; "*tārkikacāṭabhaṭarājā*" BĀUBh II. 1.20 [310,6/7 and 311.29/301]. These and the fol-

lowing quotations refer to page and line of the (5th) Ānandāśrama-ed., 1953.

5. BĀUBh IV. 5, intr. [705, 16/17] *"āgamopapattibhyāṃ hi niścito 'rthaḥ śraddheyo bhavaty avyabhicārād iti."*
6. BĀUBh II. 1.20 [296, 25] *"...dṛṣṭāntair hetubhiś ca ..."* Cf. also ChUBh VI. 15,3 [386,9/10].
7. Prof. K.T. Pandurangi, Bangalore, pointed out a verse to me quoted by Madhva in his *bhāsya* on BS 1.1.4., in which exegetic devices are given to determine the purport of a scriptural passage. There, "*upakrama*" and "*upasaṃhāra*" figure as the first two of seven technical terms designating rules of text-interpretation.
8. I shall deal with the term *"nigamana"* below. With respect to the content of the statement, *upasaṃharati*" corresponds to a "*nigamana*" here. "*Pratijñā*" and *"hetu"* occur in the syllogistic reasoning of all the schools of Indian Philosophy who apply the latter.
9. Similes and reasons as means of instruction applied by the *śruti* are also mentioned in S.' s *bhāṣya* on ChU VI, 16,1 [386,9/10] where Śvetaketu is enlightened by his father by means of similes and reasons (see note.6).
10. In the compound *"tarkāgamābhyām" tarka* is mentioned first for grammatical reasons only. The order does not indicate any priority of *"tarka"*. That is why I have changed the order in my translation. Cf. synonymous expressions used by Ś. like *"āgamopapatti"* and *"śāstratarka"* (see quotation [705, 14–18] below).
11. *pṛthaṅ nididhyāsanavidhir anarthaka eva. tasmāt pṛthakprakaraṇavibhāgo 'narthaka ity asmadabhiprāyaḥ śravaṇamanananididhyāsanānām iti* [364, 22/23].
"A separate injunction for meditation is plainly useless. Therefore a splitting-up into different sections is useless; this is our opinion about hearing, reflecting [and] meditating."
12. Cf. also the intr. to Swāmī Mādhavānanda's Engl. transl. ot the Bhāṣya, Calcutta, 1965.
13. IV.5.15 [713, 18] . . . *etat pradarśanānta upasaṃhāraḥ 'sa eṣa neti netyādiḥ.*
14. For example in current expressions like "*padavākyapramāṇajña*" where *"pada"* refers to Vyākarana, *"vākya"* to Mīmāṃsā and *"pramāṇa'* to Nyāya. Hence there is also a possibility of taking "*vākya*" to Mīmāṃsakas, and the sentence to mean "this rule is accepted (or followed) by the Mīmāṃsakas", since Ś. refers to it in the context of Veda-exegesis.
15. I owe this reference to Prof. A. Wezler, Hamburg, whom I wish to thank here for stimulating discussions in connection with the present paper.
16. This again recalls his argumentation in BĀUBh II.5, intr. (see above). There also, an alternative analysis of the Up.'s progression was given and introduced by the word "*athavā*" as in the following quotation from BĀUBh IV.5. Here, the second statement, is occasioned, in addition, by a different understanding of the teaching intended by the Up. Above it was said that the *brahmatattva* is taught, now the *"amṛtatvasādhana"* is supposed to be conveyed.
17. For "*upasaṃhriyate*" cf. . . .also the quotation from BĀUBh II. 1.20 [296, 23–26] above.
18. *"Janako ha vaideha" ityādi yājñavalkīyaṃ kāṇḍam ārabhyate. upapattipradhānatvād atikrāntena madhukāṇḍena samārthatve'pi sati na punaruktatā. madhukāṇḍaṃ hy āgamapradhānam. āgamopapattī hy ātmaikatvapradarśanāya pravṛtte śaknutaḥ karatalagatabilvam iva darśayitum. śrotavyo mantavya iti hy uktam. tasmād āgamārthasyaiva parīkṣāpūrvakaṃ nirdhāraṇāya yājñavalkīyaṃ kāṇḍam upapattipradhānam ārabhyate.* (BĀUBh III. 1,intr. [389, 1–6]).
"Janaka of Videha..."etc., thus starts the *kāṇḍa* relating to Yājñavalkya. Although it has the same purport as the previous *(madhu-) kāṇḍa* it is not a repetition because

reasoning (argumentation) predominates [in it]. For in the *madhukāṇḍa* Scriptural statements predominated; [and] Scriptural statements plus reasoning [both] having been undertaken to show the oneness of the *ātman* can [indeed] show [it as clearly] as a *bilva* [–fruit] placed on the open hand. For it has been said [by the Up.] It is to be heard of, to be thought about. . . Therefore, to ascertain the meaning of the *āgama* only after prior investigation the *kāṇḍa* relating to Yājñavalkya is undertaken in which reasoning (argumentation) is discussed.

19. This is a paraphrase of BĀUBh II. 1.20 [295, 13–296, in particular of the following sentences:
na hy agniḥ śīta ādityo na tapatīti vā dṛṣṭāntaśatenāpi pratipādayituṃ śakyam. pramāṇantareṇānyathādhigatatvād vastunaḥ. na ca pramāṇaṃ pramāṇāntareṇa virudhyate. pramāṇāntarāviṣayam eva hi pramāṇāntaraṃ jñāpayati na ca laukikapada-padārthāśrayaṇavyatirekeṇāgamena śakyam ajñātaṃ vastvantaram avagamayitum.

20. *tasmāt prasiddhanyāyam anusaratā na śakyā paramātmanaḥ sāvayavāṃśitvakalpanā paramārthataḥ pratipādayitum.* BĀUBh II. 1.20 [296, 9-11].

21. Cf. also BĀUBh II.5.15 [375, 24/25] *tārkikāḥ kecit paṇḍitammanyāś cāgamavidaḥ*

22. Cf. Vākyapadīya I. 34, ed. Rau.

Indian and German Idealism

N.S.S. RAMAN
Varanasi

No historical study of philosophy can afford to ignore idealism, which may be said to constitute what is generally called *philosophia perennis,* though during the last one hundred years, much has been spoken and written against idealism. As in Indian tradition, so also in German intellectual tradition, the undercurrent of idealism is very strong. Transcendental Idealism in Germany is the counterpart of Empiricism in Great Britain and the Vedānta in India. It is very hard to say if idealism represents the true spirit of German philosophy. It would perhaps be more correct to regard it as a philosophy of the Prussian State, judging by the militant way in which Hegel expressed his philosophy of right and of the state. As students of German intellectual history have no doubt heard, Hegel's philosophy was characterized somewhat laconically as the "court philosophy" of Frederick Wilhelm IV of Prussia. Judged from the perspective that Germany has also played a leading role in the development of other philosophies like Dialectical Materialism, *Existenzphilosophie* and even logical analysis, it would hardly be correct to regard Transcendental Idealism as the only philosophy true to the Germanic tradition. I think the same could be said also of the Indian intellectual tradition; contrary to the claims of certain Indian idealists like Radhakrishnan, Raju, Mahadevan and others, the Vedānta cannot be given the status of the "official" philosophy of India. However, in the 19th century, many German students of Indology were quick to grasp the Vedānta and realized the significance and depth of this philosophy, perhaps because they were already acquainted with the main tenets of Transcendental Idealism in Germany, with which Vedānta clearly has an intellectual affinity. On the other hand, Indians were also quickly impressed by Transcendental Idealism of Kant and Hegel, with which they had become acquainted, though at second-hand from English sources. It is the purpose of this essay to discuss the historical and the conceptual affinities between idealism in Germany and Indian idealism.

It is very hard to define what "idealism" is, or to show what its main doctrines are. And the problem of definition becomes even more difficult when we consider the various so-called "refutations" of idealism, ever since Kant in his Critique of Pure Reason gave his famous refutation, *"Widerlegung"* as he called it, of idealism. Although Kant refers both to Descartes and Berkeley in this connection, he is more critical of what he calls the Dogmatic Idealism ("der dogmatische Idealismus") of Berkeley (B274-B279). Neither Descartes nor Berkeley seem to have had any great influence on German thinkers, at least not till Edmund Husserl wrote and published his well-known Cartesian Meditations sometime during the early years of this century. In spite of his refutation of idealism, Kant is rightly associated with the development of critical or transcendental idealist philosophy in Germany. Whatever its various forms may be, idealism is characterized by the central position it accords to mind, self or the spirit in its scheme of reality. These terms are sometimes freely interchanged by the idealists, and they are not agreed as to the exact definition of the status of the self in reality. Plato for instance talks very little about the self or mind in the structure of reality he conceives, and if the oft-quoted remark of A.N. Whitehead (who is sometimes referred to as an idealist), that the whole of Western philosophy constitutes a footnote to Plato's teachings is taken seriously, then "mind", "spirit","self", "consciousness", etc. would have no place in the history of European philosophy. This certainly is not the case because philosophers in Europe since the time of Kant, have been exploring into the structure of consciousness, lapsing only rarely into what Edmund Husserl has criticized as "psychologism". Husserl himself is not classed among idealists, but has devoted considerable attention to a descriptive and systematic study of consciousness in his philosophy.

There are such wide but acceptable definitions of idealism as that given by the well-known British Kantian scholar, Norman Kemp Smith: "All those philosophies which agree in maintaining that spiritual values have a determining voice in the ordering of the universe";[1] and such precise ones as that of Bernard Bosanquet, one of the leading British "Hegelians"; "The driving-force of idealism, as I understand it, is not furnished by the question, how mind and reality can meet in consciousness, but by the theory of *logical stability* which makes it plain that nothing can fulfil the conditions of self-existence, except by possessing that unity that belongs only to mind".[2] In ancient India, although there were very sharp philosophical controversies, which divided philosophical thought into various schools, these did not relate to "isms". In recent treatises in Hindi and other Indian languages on philosophy, one can find idealism being referred to by such varied terms as *"ādarśavāda"*, *"pratyayavāda"*, *"adhyātmavāda"*, etc., but these are recently coined terms, not at all applicable to the schools of the Vedānta.

The central place which the idealists assign to what they call the "mind" (or *Geist*) has however been the butt of criticism since the beginning of this century. (It may be seen in this connection that the German word *"Geist"* is very difficult to translate into English, just as the English word "mind" cannot exactly be translated into German, though these two words have a great deal in common.) The danger to the idealist position has come not so much from the philosophical criticisms of that doctrine by Kierkegaard, Nietzsche, Karl Marx, Willian James, Gilbert Ryle, Karl Jaspers and many others, each of whom attacked the idealist position from his own standpoint, but from its own terminological confusions. The idealist emphasis on "mind", "self", "ego", "consciousness", and a host of other terms bearing what Ludwig Wittgenstein has called "family resemblances" may be regarded as a clue to their point of view. The various corresponding Sanskrit terms are: *"ātman"*, *"jīva"*, *"buddhi"*, *"ahaṃkāra"*, *"manas"*, etc. We find a host of these terms in Sāṃkhya philosophy, which has also sharply distinguished between them. These terms have given rise to a great deal of misunderstanding and controversy amongst the supporters as well as critics of idealism both in the East as well as in the West.

All these difficulties amply show that it is by no means a simple philosophical theory. Idealism is expounded with a great deal of depth, sometimes bordering on the poetic, which is very often misunderstood and misinterpreted because of the barriers of intelligibility and communication. This is one of the reasons why a serious student of philosophy tries to read philosophical texts with the aid of commentaries. This tradition, which is very helpful, is common both to India and the West. This has also led unfortunately to some confusion in understanding the thought of the great masters. For instance, as a British interpreter of the philosophy of G.W.F. Hegel has observed, the interpreters of Hegelian philosophy have contradicted each other almost as variously as the several commentators on the Bible.[3] Hegel is claimed as their fountain-head by widely different schools of thought, all of which appeal to him as the original source of their main line of argument. At the beginning of this century, Hegelians all over the world were represented by a brilliant galaxy of thinkers. There was British Hegelianism represented by T.H. Green, F.H. Bradley, Bernard Bosanquet, Edward Caird, J.E. McTaggart and others; French Hegelianism associated with Emile Boutroux; Italian Hegelianism represented by Benedetto Croce and

Giovanni Gentile; and also American Hegelianism with Josiah Royce and George Howison representing it. What a treasure house of philosophical wisdom, depth and vision! All this coincided with a period of Indian intellectual renaissance, a period of revival of the ancient philosophy of the Vedānta. There was no need for any Indian to be a Hegelian; the Vedānta philosophy already had in it a rich fund of philosophical knowledge, and there was no need for any import from the West. However, curiously enough, it was an Indian philosopher, Hiralal Haldar, who wrote a comprehensive history of Neo-Hegelianism more than sixty years ago. Hiralal Haldar's Neo-Hegelianism was widely read at that time at least in India. The Indian student of philosophy was acquainted with German idealism only through English writings on the subject, because of the obvious barrier of language. Indians read avidly all about Hegel in the various histories of philosophy, (here again, I must state that German historians of philosophy e.g. Weber, Falckenburg, Erdmann have been quite popular with Indian students of European thought) and also through the writings of various British Hegelians. F.H. Bradley occupied an important place in British philosophical thought during the last few decades of the last century and the early years of this century. He was generally classed as a Hegelian, though his works have a British flavour about them. In some Indian universities, Bradley's Appearance and Reality and Ethical Studies are still read as textbooks, though he is hardly taken much notice of in the land of his birth. Unlike the British, Germans still treasure their tradition, which is evidenced by the activities of Kant-Gesellschaft and the Vereinigung der Hegelschen Philosophie, which bring out Kant-Studien and Hegel-Studien, the two outstanding periodicals from Germany.

Indeed Hegel occupies a position in European Philosophy comparable to those occupied by Śaṃkara and Nāgārjuna in the Indian tradition. About two hundred years ago, Madame de Staël (who was French) paid a rich tribute to the German mind, which is as much true today as it was in her time: "The Germans are the pioneers of the human mind. They blaze new trails, and venture experiments with unprobed means. Can one help being curious to hear what they have to report after returning from their journey into the infinite?"[4] Kant's transcendental method, his thing-in-itself and his Categorical Imperative, Fichte's Ego, Hegel's Absolute are all examples of such pioneering spirit as described by Madame de Staël. Most Indians unfortunately read German philosophical texts through the English language, and hence through the British perspective. What is interesting to note is that there has been some communication gap as far as Indians are concerned, which prevents them from knowing the German intellect at first hand; but as far as the German scholars are concerned, there does not seem to have been such a gap, judged by the pioneering work of some German scholars in the field of Indology in general, and of Indian philosophy in particular. This point has to be stressed now, because even Indians have stopped reading the classics, which are a part and parcel of their own heritage, Sanskrit being given stepmotherly treatment at the hands of our educational administrators now. In recent years, Indian thinkers have again been influenced by the philosophical trends in Anglo-Saxon countries (I mean in particular by logical and linguistic analysis), but this is not because of any affinities of temperament or of tradition, but simply because English language is more accessible to the Indians than any other language, except perhaps their own mother-tongue. There is perhaps more intellectual kinship between German idealism and the Vedānta, than between any two other trends of thought in the entire intellectual history of mankind. Thus in spite of the early enthusiasm in England for Hegelian philosophy, it was quite clear that it was foreign to the British mind. Thus the very first work to be written in Great Britain on Hegel, by Hutcheson Stirling and titled somewhat cryptically as The Secret of Hegel did not evoke a sympathetic response. It was humourously pointed out that nobody could understand the secret except the author himself. D.M. Datta, who was one of the most respected interpreters of contemporary European philosophy in India has paid a rich tribute to Hutcheson Stirling as follows: "Though it may be true as he says, I have not sought, and do not seek, to be considered a disciple, there is a consensus of Hegelian opinion as to the fact that Stirling secured for Hegel a large number of disciples who dominated British thought for more than a quarter of a century."[5] But the publication of the book marked a beginning in the study of idealist classics of great German philosophers both in England and India, though many Indians had to be content to read the great classics of German idealism (particularly Kant's Critique of Pure Reason) from second-hand sources through translations. It may be of interest to note in this connection that one of the well-known translations of Kant's first Critique was made by no less a person than the great F. Max Mueller.

There is, in our opinion, a greater scope for dialogue between German and Indian philosophies than between British and German philosophies, or even between Indian and British philosophies. It is wrong to bundle together many divergent systems of thought—divergent both in tradition and content — under the general heading "Western thought". It is astonishing to find on close examination that German idealism is indeed very close, at least in conceptual terms, to Indian idealism, in spite of the lack of communication between the two cultures till the end of last century. It may be recalled that Schopenhauer had spoken very highly about Indian philosophy; his noble words about the Upaniṣads are remembered by every keen student of Indian culture. But Schopenhauer's acquaintance with the Upaniṣads was through second-hand sources, to be precise, through the Latin translation of Dara Shukoh's Persian version of the famous texts, through Sirr-i-Akbar. But scholars who came after Schopenhauer became more interested in the study of the classics of Indian philosophy in original Sanskrit. Paul Deussen and F. Max Mueller were particularly attracted by Indian idealism. Max Mueller went as far to say that the Vedānta philosophy represented "a system in which human speculation seems to have reached its very acme" and further: "I make no secret that all my life I have been very fond of the Vedanta".[6] Unlike Schopenhauer, Nietzsche and Hegel, Deussen, Max Mueller and A.W. von Schlegel were acquainted with the classics of Indian philosophy in original. Many of these scholars had pioneered a study of ancient Indian thought in Europe, which brought a rich cultural heritage of the East nearer and nearer the German mind. It is our view that they also helped Indians themselves to acquire an abiding interest in their own heritage, and thus unwittingly, German Indology contributed a great deal towards Indian renaissance in the last century. The interest in the study of Indian philosophy, culture and literature was in fact keener amongst the German Indologists than among Indian intellectuals themselves, the Indian mind having become almost blank since the deaths of Appayya Dīkṣita and Prakāśānanda (16th Century A.D.). Nineteenth century India was still in the process of waking up from its long intellectual slumber. Barring Raja Ram Mohan Roy, who was more of a religious reformer than a philosopher, one can, during 17th and 18th centuries, hardly find any Indian intellectual of note. Hence it is not possible to underestimate the great role played by German Indology during this period.[7] The publication of the series, Sacred Books of the East, edited by Max Mueller contributed significantly towards bringing the Eastern philosophical and religious traditions closer to the European mind; the name of Georg Thibaut is associated with the series as the translator of Śaṃkara's and Rāmānuja's great commentaries on the Vedānta Sutras, one of the main sources for the development of the Vedānta.

Indians themselves started reading the Western philosophical classics a little later than they read the Bible. A close understanding of the German idealist tradition did not come about till Sarvepalli Radhakrishnan initiated a study of comparative philosophy, though he was handicapped by relying a little too much on the English sources for an understanding of the German philosophical tradition. Most Indians even today have to depend on bad or inadequate translations of German philosophical texts. The first comprehensive treatise showing the relevance of German idealism to the Vedānta was P.T. Raju's Thought and Reality - Hegelianism and Advaita. But by the time Raju's book was published in the thirties of this century, idealism had practically died out in the West, including

Germany, barring a few adherents here and there, but this was the period which saw the process of the revival of the Vedānta at its highest. Radhakrishnan, Raju, T.M.P. Mahadevan, Sri Aurobindo, K.C. Bhattacharya and many others had all started expositions of Advaita philosophy, each in his own way, while during the Nazi era in Germany, the adherents of the Marburg school of Neo-Kantians and the Heidelberg School had either died or were hounded out of Germany. Logical positivism on the one side and *Existenzphilosophie* had taken hold of European philosophy by storm, and each in its own way had tried to discredit idealism and had partly succeeded. Its present position both in the West and in India (perhaps more in the West than in India), is somewhat shaky.

We should now turn our attention to a more significant task; we have so far discussed the contacts between German and Indian idealism in their historical context. We have now to see in what conceptual aspects, German idealism comes close to Indian idealism. This would make a discussion of some of the basic ideas of both the traditions unavoidable. First, we shall deal with the differences in the two approaches, and then attempt to understand the conceptual affinities between them.

In many respects, the Vedānta shows a great deal of similarity with the Scholastic philosophy in medieval Europe. The Scholastics were interested primarily not in substituting religious knowledge by a secular philosophical outlook. They were only seeking a philosophical confirmation of Christian religious beliefs and in this task they freely adopted the so-called "pagan" ways of thinking of the ancient Greeks. The Vedānta in a similar way was also seeking confirmation of knowledge revealed by the *śruti* by philosophical knowledge. In Europe, by the time of the Age of Enlightenment, beliefs had become largely secularized. The publication by Kant of his major work in the field of philosophy of religion, Die Religion innerhalb der blossen Vernunft (1793), marks a shift in emphasis from revelation to reason. In contrast to the Christian philosophy of the medieval Scholastics, philosophy after the renaissance had indeed become more oriented by science and secular ideals than by a religious outlook. The Vedānta in sharp contrast is even now influenced by religious outlook, the *śruti* or the scriptural authority being regarded as supreme by it. In fact, many Vedāntins have spent a lifetime and all their intellectual energy in reconciling (what appears to me as an impossible task) contradictory passages in the sacred texts. The philosophical *Weltanschauung* (we have to thank the Germans for this happy word) of the Vedānta is also a religious one. Although many European philosophers (including Kant) had got into difficulties with religious authorities and were very cautions about what they said till recently, lest it should annoy the church, their philosophy cannot in any sense be called religious. Some persons in the religious sphere of influence even went so far as to adapt idealism to their own Christian beliefs. One might recall in this context the famous attack of Kierkegaard on Bishop Martensen, who had interpreted protestant theology in the light of Hegel's Absolute Idealism. Hegel himself had tried to reconcile his own ideas with those of orthodox Christianity, but even if he had not attempted such a task, still his philosophy would have been self-consistent in its own right.

Secondly, the history of German idealism shows a gradual historical development and fruition of ideas from Kant to Schopenhauer. The Vedānta on the other hand, consists of many subsidiary schools, each attempting to radically refute the other. For instance, Śaṃkara and Rāmānuja are radically opposed to each other. There are polemical texts like Śatadūṣaṇi and Śatabhūṣaṇi directed against each other. The followers of Madhva (e.g. Nārāyaṇa-Bhaṭṭa in his Maṇimañjarī) have even been abusive of Śaṃkara. The relationship between the German idealists on the other hand, is that of one being complementary to another; the entire movement represents a gradual blossoming of idealism, phase by phase. Hence, an interpretation of Hegelianism or Kantianism in the light of the Vedānta *as a whole* is not possible, and if attempted might lead to absurd conclusions. One can however take up for this purpose, a conceptual study of one school of Vedānta or one aspect of Vedānta. For instance, one might legitimately take up the logic or the dialectic of Advaita and compare it with that of Hegelianism (as P.T. Raju has admirably done). Paul Deussen has interpreted Advaita in terms of Kant, Raju in terms of Hegel. T.R.V. Murti has tried to draw a parallel between Nāgārjuna (the founder of the Mādhyamika School of Buddhism) and Kant in his well-known Central Philosophy of Buddhism. Scores of doctoral dissertations and books have appeared on such comparative studies, and have been useful for exchange of ideas between two cultures.

The well-known Scottish interpreter of Hegel, Edward Caird has remarked: "There is a sense in which every idealist must admit that the only object of mind is mind. Everyone who holds that the real is relative to mind and therefore that the difference between the mind and the object cannot be an absolute difference, must acknowledge that whatever is real (and just so far as it is real) has the nature of mind manifested in it. Reality cannot be alien to the subject that knows it, nor can the intelligence comprehend any object except as it finds itself in it."[8] But one should not infer from this that every object, which is in any sense real, is a thinking subject. Even as on the other hand no object should be seen in isolation from the selves for which it is an object. It is not the empirical self (which the Advaitins call the *jīva)*, which is real, but the transcendental Self, which is given the status of the Absolute (or becomes *brahman*, as the Advaitins would say). In other words, the thinking subjects, the selves so to say, are regarded by the Hegelians as integral elements of an Absolute Self, only when they are seen as having self-identical selves of their own. Thus the Absolute in Hegel is a plurality as well as a unity, an identity bracing all differences, a community of selves and regarded as a systematic whole not unlike *ātman* or *brahman* in Advaita philosophy. The transcending of lower forms of experience by going beyond them and yet including them in a process which Hegel has called *Aufhebung,* can be found also in the Advaitic analysis of experience. As in Advaita, so also in the whole of critical philosophy in Germany, a fundamental place is given to self-consciousness in all experience, and in this respect, there is a continuity of tradition from Kant to Schopenhauer. Indeed there is nothing in knowledge so certain as the consciousness of one's own being. There is a certainty which since the time of Descartes, thinkers have recognized to belong to the consciousness of the 'I'. It is this that is the starting point of all modern European philosophy, as it is indeed of the Vedānta. All the *mahāvākyas* indeed recognize the supreme character of self-consciousness.

We have therefore ultimately to fall back on the certainty of consciousness when we attempt to understand the foundation of all knowledge. Thus philosophy (which has been, not without reason, called *'darśana'* in India), while examining such foundations of knowledge, strikes upon the inner unity in the structure of consciousness, a detailed analysis of which is attempted for the first time in European philosophy by Kant, in the section on what he calls the "Transcendental Dialectic" in the Critique of Pure Reason.

As all students of philosophy know, there he comes to the conclusion that the unity of consciousness is presupposed in our experience of the unity of the external world. One might recall in this context the famous statement of David Hume: "I never can catch myself at any time without a perception, and can never observe anything but the perception".[9] Kant (who wrote using a more technical jargon) puts the same idea more critically: "The unity which the object makes necessary can be nothing else than the formal unity of consciousness in the synthesis of the manifold of representations".[10] Of course later writers[11] have objected to Kant's phrase "formal unity of consciousness" in describing the self, pointing out that the unity is actual. Coming in the wake of a scepticism, which denies all unity to the self and reduces it to a "bundle" of sensations, Kant's own view can be regarded as a re-affirmation of the unity of the subject, even if its unifying character cannot be expressed or even empirically discovered. This is somewhat similar to the Advaitic affirmation of the unity of philosophical experience in the transcendental *ātman,* which is categorically affirmed as the reality, in the wake of the sceptical position of the Buddhists (in particular of Nāgārjuna, though from the very beginning all Buddhist philosophy is anti-metaphysical, denying the reality of the soul and the world), which leads them to the denial of any reality of the self. This is the reason why Indian students of Advaita are reminded of Kant or rather, why a study of Kant reminds them of Advaita Vedānta of Śaṃkara. Indeed Kant's distinction between the empirical and the transcendental does bear a close resemblance to the Advaita distinction between the *vyavahārika* and the *pāramārthika* standpoints. (Nāgārjuna had similarly distinguished between *saṃvṛti* and the *paramārtha sattas.)* So also, Kant's distinction between appearance *(phainomenon)* and reality *(noumenon)* reminds us of the Advaita distinction between *mithyā* and *satyam.* Kant declares the world revealed by the intellect *(Verstand)* and sense experience *(Sinnlickkeit)* to be phenomenal. Of course Kant's distinction between reason *(Vernunft)* and intellect *(Verstand)* is based on the traditional scholastic distinction between *ratio* and *intellectus*, and therefore we do not find any such distinction in Śaṃkara. But Śaṃkara's idea of an integral experience (*anubhava*) cannot adequately be expressed by Kant's concept or concepts of intuition. Śaṃkara also characterized it as an *Erscheinung.* But the noumenal reality beyond is unknowable in Kant, whereas in Advaita philosophy it can be known by *anubhava,* by integral experience.

The scepticism of Hume in the European philosophical tradition and the scepticism of Mādhyamika Buddhism in the Indian tradition had an opposite effect. The latter's thought amounts to a rejection'of all metaphysics—of "consigning it to flames" as Hume wanted us to do though in a slightly different context. To some extent, Kant's agnostic position also dissuades us from any metaphysical pursuits. But the failure of scepticism in the history of human thought is demonstrated by the affirmation of a metaphysical reality most emphatically by the successors of sceptics and agnostics.

It has been pointed out that modern European philosophy since the time of the *Aufklärung* has evolved as a result of a reaction to the Copernican-Newtonian World-view (Kant refers to the mutual dependence of these two great scientists in his Critique of Pure Reason, BXXIIn). The reaction of Kant to this world-view is exemplified by his attitude to causality. He discovers two kinds of causality operative within the realm of human experience—mechanical causality as characterizing human knowledge and "free" causality as characterizing man's moral experience. Mechanical causality in the "scientific" or the empirical context had already been overthrown by David Hume as inconsistent; Kant only gives it a final push to throw it overboard. The empirical self is indeed governed by laws of mechanical causality (which is phenomenal, or *vyavahārika,* to put it in Advaita terminology), and is an object like any other object. The first step towards self-transcendence is taken in German idealism, when it is recognized that this self is indeed the conscious self, without which the experience of other selves and other objects is not possible. The student of Indian philosophy is immediately reminded of the principle of *sahopalam-baniyama* in Yogācāra idealism, by which any thing is identified with the consciousness of that thing. Consciousness therefore, is the link between two poles of experience, the subjective and the objective, which are mutually correlative. Kant's upgrading of the status of self-consciousness is indeed a Copernican revolution, but it is so only with reference to the European tradition. Such a "revolution" can be found in the transition from the Vedas to the Vedānta, from the discovery of an objective reality to a discovery of the self within.

The negative approach to reality by Nāgārjuna has been compared to Kant's.[12] This approach however does not deter the Advaitins (in the Indian context) and the successors of Kant (in the context of German idealism) to forge ahead. But the study of consciousness by these successors does land them into conundrums of transcendental logic—or to put it in the words Bradley, which the Italian idealist Benedetto Croce[13] quotes with approval in his critique of Hegelianism, a wearisome "ballet of bloodless categories finding a final rest in one supreme ultimate category" is the panlogism of pure rationalism, which weakens the subsequent development of post-Kantian German idealism. These extravagances of ultra-rationalism are perhaps avoided by the Advaitin, who rejects reason altogether as leading to categorical ways of thinking (*dharmabhūtajñāna*), and replaces it by *anubhava* or intuitive apprehension as leading to a direct and intimate knowledge of reality (*svarūpajñāna*).

It is a pity that the philosophy of Fichte is not studied any more in detail outside Germany. Even in Germany he is perhaps ignored. He is casually mentioned in the courses on the history of philosophy. For students of Advaita Vedānta his philosophy has a special relevance. In his emphasis on the self or the ego as the unifying principle, out of which a multiplicity of experience may be deduced, he comes nearest to Advaita Vedānta. Fichte had found that Kant had created many kinds of irresoluble dualisms—sense and understanding, knowledge and faith, *Vernunft* and *Verstand*, pure and practical reason, etc. These create gulfs which cannot be bridged easily, unless a single, all-embracing principle is postulated and Fichte puts forth the ego as such a principle. In Indian philosophy too, we find such "rainbow bridges of concepts" (to borrow a phrase from Nietzsche) as to be found in German idealism, in the metaphysics of the Sāṃkhya-Yoga and even the Vedānta, to explain the subjective and objective spheres of experience: *citta, buddhi, manas, ahaṃkāra, mahat,* etc. The search for a single, all-embracing principle mentioned in the Mahāvākya, *'Ekaṃ eva advitīyaṃ'* terminates in the discovery by Śaṃkara of the *ātman* which is identical with the *brahman.* Fichte says that no philosophy that is not idealistic can succeed, and treating the self as just one object among many other objects will not do. Like Śaṃkara, Fichte also talks of a universal ego as the ultimate reality, as different from the individual finite self, the *jīva.* Fichte has a word for it in German, *"Ich-heit",* to express the self-consciousness that constitutes this all-embracing ego.[14] Rejecting Kant's doctrine of the thing-in-itself, and subsuming all categories, space and time and objects under an all-inclusive self-consciousness, Fichte lays the foundation for later idealist philosophy. Bhagavan Das, the philosopher from Banaras was perhaps one of the few Indian philosophers in recent years to come close to Fichte in his interpretation of Vedānta philosophy.

The primary step in discovering the fundamental principle of experience lies in what we regard as a merely formal expression of self-consciousness in thought, as in Descartes. The first principle of all knowledge, therefore, is the affirmation by the self of itself, and this act of self-affirmation is the first act of experience. It constitutes an affirmation of the unity of self-consciousness, because without this unity, knowledge itself would not be possible. Thus it is an essential precondition of all other actions of the self, moral actions included. But the second principle of self-consciousness is that it is not possible to affirm the self-identity of consciousness without positing its negation, the not-self. This close relationship between identity on the one hand and its opposite, the difference, is the starting point of the dialectic, for which Hegelianism has become famous. In post-Śaṃkara dialectic also (especially in works like Śrī Harṣa's Khaṇḍana-khaṇḍakhadya), the logic of identity-in-difference plays a significant role.

It is not possible in this short essay to give a detailed account of the points of coincidence between idealist systems belonging to two different traditions. Throughout the great stream of post-Kantian German philosophy, there are ideas affirming a fundamental spiritual reality. Perhaps Marxism and logical positivism are the only exceptions and deviations from the main-stream of this *Geistesgeschichte.* It is in this sense too that German idealism comes close to the Vedānta, which is itself a kind of *Geistesgeschichte.* Kant had asserted the reality of a unity of consciousness, Fichte that of a transcendental ego, Schelling that of an objective Absolute, and Hegel that of an absolute reason, and in all these one finds shades of a perennial philosophy, which indeed is the highest point that speculative reason can attain. At this point is reached something which could only be described in terms of what Schelling has called the "neo-Platonic ecstasy of immediate intuition" or *"die geheime*

Mitwissenschaft mit der Schöpfung" (which is untranslatable but understood by all students of Schelling).[15] This is somewhat similar to the *ānanda,* the bliss (metaphorically so described) one experiences at the last stage in the realization of absolute self-consciousness identical with *ātman* or *brahman.* In Kashmir school of Advaita, writers like Abhinavagupta and Ānandavardhana identify this ecstasy with a kind of aesthetic enjoyment. Utpaladeva (who belongs also to Kashmir school of Advaita),[16] analyses this intuitive experience, which is akin to aesthetic oneness with the object of creativity or of enjoyment; the emotions start from our empirical consciousness and lift it "upwards" making the finite at one with the infinite. This state is described variously but symbolically and inadequately as *ānanda, śañti, anubhava, nirvāṇa,* etc. Such insights are perhaps the natural outcome of the gradual progress of thought. But a common outlook, a common temperament between the two strands of thought can lead to common insights, the similarity of which could only be amazing, when we consider that the spiritual communication between the two cultures was marked by a wide geographical, historical and linguistic gap.

In the above few pages, I have tried to focus attention on some points, where German idealism meets the idealism of the Vedānta. Many Indian writers (the names of some of whom have been mentioned in the above pages) have already made detailed comparative studies between Indian and German philosophy. The formula with which they approach the problem is not (to put it naively) West = East, but West+East, to borrow these expressions from F.S.C. Northrop.

One does not approach the problem with a view to finding out an exact one-to-one conformity between two sets of thought, but attempts to find out as far as possible, the common sources of inspiration and the common levels of insight, in so far as they become translatable in each other's modes of thinking. To attempt a cultural synthesis between the two in order to evolve a global philosophy may not be possible, because each kind of enquiry takes its birth within a specific cultural context, and it is impossible to ignore differences of tradition. This is one of the reasons that I have stated elsewhere[17] that comparative philosophy is not possible. Northrop gives a balanced view.[18] There are similarities of thought in East and West, there are also differences which are insurmountable and there is a danger that one is carried away by prejudices against the other. The East and the West must sympathetically understand each other, in order that each may supplement its insights by those of others. But it may be said that of all two systems of thought in different cultures, Indian and German idealistic systems are conceptually and temperamentally closest. It is not therefore surprising that the enquiry into the common intellectual heritage of India and Germany is still continuing in both countries. Uniformity of thought can never be our goal in the changing cultural patterns of the world. All the different ways of thinking, all the various conceptual formulations of thought, all the different values in various parts of the world must ultimately converge at some point, the gaps mentioned above notwithstanding. This should be our basic assumption in our study of the various cultures. I am glad that the Germans have a special name for this comparative study: *Vergleichende Kulturwissenschaft.* Incidentally, attainment of this ultimate universal goal within and in spite of all the differences is one of the cardinal aims both of German and Indian idealism. I hope the spirit of Hermann Goetz, in whose memory this international seminar is being organized and in which this humble essay is offered, is very much with us as the spirit of one who devoted all his life for realizing this inter-cultural understanding.

Romain Rolland, the French humanist has aptly remarked: "The truth is the same for all nations under the sun, but each people labours under its own delusion, which it calls its idealism. There can be nothing worse than being a slave of one's own way of thought and sacrificing everything at its altar". German Idealism and the Vedānta have been long superseded by other systems of thought, and therefore one cannot be dogmatic about the one or the other. They are nevertheless immortal in the history of mankind as great achievements.

NOTES

1. Prolegomena to an Idealist Theory of Knowledge, p. 1.
2. Meeting of Extremes in Contemporary Philosophy, p. 3.
3. W. Wallace, Introduction to his translation of Hegel's Logic.
4. Quoted by H. Ziock: Men Will One Day Reach the Point, p. 30.
5. Chief Currents of Contemporary Philosophy, p. 9.
6. Max Müller, Introduction to his Vedānta Philosophy.
7. We have to be indebted to the recently published account of German Indologists by the late Dr Valentina Stache-Rosen for a detailed account of work done by all German Indologists since the 17th century till the present day.
8. Edward Caird, Evolution of Theology in the Greek Philosophers, Vol. I, p. 193.
9. Hume, Treatise on Human Nature, Selby-Bigge, Part IV, Bk. 1.
10. The Critique of Pure Reason, A 105.
11. I refer in this connection particularly to the views of Sartre. Please see my article, "Kant's Doctrine of the Self and its Releavance to *Existenzphilosophie* in Immanuel Kant," Proc of a Seminar in Calcutta and Madras, 1974, ed. H. Herring.
12. I refer in this connection to the work of T.R.V. Murti in his Central Philosophy of Buddhism.
13. Croce, My Philosophy, Ch. 1.
14. The word has no equivalent expression in any language, but Dr Joachim Deppert assures me that its equivalent can be found in Kashmir Advaita.

15. The phrase can be inadequately translated as 'secret knowledge by communion with creation'. The sense of the phrase can be better expressed by the sense of a sudden revelation of ultimate being.
16. I am indebted to Prof. Raju for introducing me to the work of Utpaladeva: Īśvarapratyabhijñā.
17. Ref. to my essay, Is Comparative Philosophy Possible? in the volume, Indian Philosophy Today, N.K. Devaraja.
18. Meeting of the East and the West, Ch. XII.

The Mallāri/Khaṇḍobā Myth as Reflected in Folk Art and Ritual

GÜNTHER D. SONTHEIMER
Heidelberg

Hermann Goetz was one of the pioneers in showing how out-of-the way and seemingly insignificant monuments and works of regional art can afford evidence for the reconstruction of history and art history. He knew that the classical, e.g., Sanskrit texts, cannot alone unravel Indian culture and he ceaselessly recorded the testimony of antiquities which might have been lost by now if he had not done so. He also knew that only a combination of various sources would counter a one-sided picture of India and that only a balanced interpretation of apparently contradictory sources would reflect the true picture.

The following study utilizes a variety of sources which are brought together in order to portray, in an integrated way, the nature of a cult which is of considerable importance with respect to its spatial spread and historical antiquity.

The cult is that of Mallāri, popularly called Khaṇḍobā in Maharashtra, mainly Mailār (Mairāḷ) in Karnataka, and Mallaṇṇa in Andhra. Another name is Mārtaṇḍa Bhairava, especially used with reference to the form Śiva took when he fought the demon. For the sake of simplicity I shall use generally the name Khaṇḍobā. The emphasis here is on the reflection of the cult and the myth in folk art though I use other sources like oral literature, observed ritual performance and festivals (*jatrās*), and texts as well. Many published and unpublished manuscripts in Marathi of the Mallāri/Khaṇḍobā myth have been composed in the 18th and 17th century, some of which I have used here.[1] I have emphasized other aspects of the cult in previous publications.[2]

The myth of Mallāri, that is Śiva as the enemy of the *rākṣasa* Malla or of the two *rākṣasas* Maṇi and Malla, is extremely old though at a rather late stage it was somewhat loosely attached to the *Brahmāṇḍapurāṇa* as the *Mallārī Māhātmya.* Some elements of the myth may be found in the battle of Indra against Vṛtra, the demon who is described as a giant serpent, who arrogantly raises his head over a mountain and is in the possession of supernatural magic power (*māyā*). Vṛtra bars the waters enclosed in the mountain, robs and swallows the celestial rivers, until Indra kills him whence the waters are freed and run roaring like cows towards the sea.[4] In other myths Indra is also the liberator of the cows after a fight with the demon Vala who holds them captive in a mountain cave. In the postvedic literature Vṛtra and Vala are considered to be brothers as in our case the two brothers Maṇi and Malla.[5]

The association of demons with mountains prior to their defeat by gods is ubiquitous whether we think of the Veda or other (e.g., the old Tamil) literature.[6] The mountains, like the demons who either live on them or are sometimes homologous with them, are beyond the human habitat and are the embodiment of everything which is outlandish and dangerous. The demon Malla seems historically to be connected with the Mallas who were Kṣatriya Vrātyas according to the *Manusmṛti* (10.22) and they are mentioned as early as the *Jaiminīya Brāhmaṇa.* In this text actually an old relationship is found between Indra and the Mallas. Indra's charioteer Kutsa is chased away by Indra with the words "be a *malla*" or "be Malla" because he was sexually misbehaving with Indra's wife, just as the *daityas* Malla and Maṇi carried away the women of the Brahmins while raiding their hermitage.[8] Previously, when Kutsa had misbehaved with Indra's wife, he became the first to wear an *uṣṇīṣa.* This is a turban also worn by Rudra/Śiva and by the outlandish Vrātyas[9] whose association with Rudra was very close.

The Mallas were an ancient tribe and a kind of guild of pugilists and wrestlers. The *Harivaṃśa* mentions the wrestlers Cāṇura and Muṣṭika whom Kṛṣṇa and Baladeva defeated. Kṛṣṇa thereby acquired the name Mallāri: the enemy of Malla (or the Mallas). In this connection it is interesting that Malla and Śiva as Mārtaṇḍa Bhairava/Khaṇḍerāyā wrestle for nine days and nights according to the *M. V.* (18. 162 ff., 180).[10] Moreover wrestling bouts take place during the *jatrā* on the full-moon day of the Pauṣ month (December/January) at Jejuri.If I am not mistaken the encounter between Kṛṣṇa and Cāṇura and Muṣṭika is depicted in an old relief on one of the light-pillars (*dīpmāḷ*) in front of the temple of Khaṇḍobā at Jejuri. It may also be the fight between Mallāri (Khaṇḍobā) and the demons, Maṇi and Malla. It is well-known that many kings in the Deccan, in Rajasthan and Nepal had *malla* as their *biruda* in their name, e.g. the Kalacuri king Sovideva was called Bhujabalamalla, "the strong wrestler".[11]

Malla and Maṇi, though *rākṣasas,* are nevertheless great kings according to the *Mallārī Māhātmya.*[12] The *M. V.* says that Malla was the king of the *daityas* (11.26: *daityanāth*). *mallaṉ* in Tamil does not only mean "wrestler", but also "a great, important personage".[13] Maṇi and Malla are reputed to have destroyed the *mūrtis* of other gods and to have compelled people to worship their own *mūrtis* according to the *M. V.* 7.27. The *mūrti* of Malla in Jejuri, who became a devotee of Khaṇḍobā, is impressive and still ardently worshipped. The crown shows Malla's royal background. But the (popular ?) etymology of *malla* may also be Ta. *malai* = "hill, mountain", and we have the reference by Plinius to the Malli, who live in the territory of the mountain Mallus. [14]

The homology of the demons with the mountain is well-expressed in the *M. V.* 20. 49: the five sons of Malla become mountains after their defeat. In another passage it is said that on the Mountain Maṇicūl the *daityas* built their city and ruled over the three worlds *M.V.* 8.14; 9.57: near the mountain Maṇicūl) in consequence of a boon given by Brahmā. In the *M. M. Vi.* (16.26) we hear that Malla created mountains as his weapons against Śiva. The god who defeats the demon associated with the mountain is called Mallaṇṇa in Telugu, Mallayya in Ka. and Malaikiḻavōṉ in Ta. (the name of Murukaṉ), i.e. "the Lord of the Mountain", similarly as Śiva is *girīśa.*[15] After their "defeat" the mountain, or the demon identified with the mountain, becomes the seat of the god like Kailās is the throne of Śiva. In the *M. V.* Malla becomes the throne of Mārtaṇḍa Bhairava (*M. V.* 20.56). In short, the semantic connotations of Malla imply "pugilist", "wrestler", "king", "mountain dweller", "mountain", and "an outlandish hill demon".[16]

The mountain is occupied by the demon before the victory of the god. In the case of Indra's fight the demoniac enemy was the huge monstrous serpent Vṛtra. Similarly the anthill — a homologous representation of the mountain — is the seat of serpents (*nāg*) (see e.g., Sontheimer, 1976, pp. 182 ff., 204 f.). Thus the two demons may not only be identified with the mountain, but also with the serpents living in it. There is no reference to Maṇi and Malla connecting them with serpents in our texts. However, in the Khaṇḍobā temple of Mailarpur (Prempur/Pember, near Bidar), we find a stone image of a serpent in the place where one expects a *mūrti* of the *daitya* facing the god. The god may here be more properly Maṇi (Maṇimalla may also mean "Maṇi, the Malla"). Maṇi is perhaps still a reflection of Maṇibhadra, or Māṇibhadra, the *yakṣa,* who was the guardian deity of caravans.[17] If this is so, it fits well that Mailarpur was on an old north-south trade route and was notoriously unsafe because of waylaying robbers (Sontheimer, 1976, p. 151 f.).

When Śiva/Khaṇḍobā kills Malla, the demon is freed from his illusion and arrogance and before he dies he turns into a *bhakta* of Śiva/Khaṇḍobā. Śiva grants him a boon and Malla wishes to be absorbed in Śiva's name. Hence the name Mallāri or Mallakṛtānta.

Both features are clearly represented in the silver plaques (Ma. *ṭāk*) which show the demons under the feet of the god. This indicates the liberation from illusion and the achievement of union with Śiva (*śivasāyujya pavlā. M. V.* 20.98). Or the two heads of the demons, sometimes three,[18] are shown to support the seat of Śiva. Malla is actually *ahaṃkāra* personified (*M. V. 19.11*). Śiva/Khaṇḍobā shows mercy and removes the blindness and *avidyā* from the demon indicating the virtual consubstantiality of Śiva and the demon or any human soul.[19] The demons suddenly turn into followers of Khaṇḍobā, become members of his army or his doorkeepers as the *rākṣasas* in the famous Tripura myth.[20] Thus we come across in popular representations not only the heads of the two demons supporting the throne of Khaṇḍobā, but also two warriors preceding Khaṇḍobā and his entourage. The *M. M. Ś.* says that Maṇi and Malla seated on horseback became *dvārapālas* of Śiva forever (2. 115.) (Figs 1, 2, 3, and 4).

The *bhakti* for Śiva and Khaṇḍobā has occasionally taken such severe forms that religious suicide seems to have occurred in order to transpose oneself into the state of nearness or union with Śiva. Thus we find a number of *pādukas* of Khaṇḍobā surrounded by heads of rams, but also by rams *and* human heads.[21] From Kannada inscriptions we know that such memorial monuments indicate ritual suicide. Incidentally, it is curious that a somewhat similar arrangement occurs in the early prescription for the building of the fire-alter (*agnicayana*) which aims at the restoration of the primeval unity of Prajāpati. In the first layers of the fire-altar, in its centre, five skulls must be placed: a human skull in the middle, west, east, south, and north of it skulls respectively of a horse, a bull, a ram and a he-goat.[22] If we take into account that *pādukas* have replaced the human skull as the homologous representation of Prajāpati/Brahmā, and that Śiva in many respects has eventually replaced Prajāpati/Brahmā, ay be on the track of an old survival. However that may be, we find that all the above-mentioned animals survive in the Khaṇḍobā cult.[23]

Śiva/Khaṇḍobā is no doubt a perpetuation of the ancient Paśupati cult and Śiva is repeatedly referred to as Paśupati in the *M. V.* and *M. M. Ś.* Paśupati is the Lord of the *paśus,* that is, the Lord of the animals *and* the human beings, or the Lord of the souls. Thus the rams as the sacrificial animals may reach a higher state when they are sacrificed. The human being becomes free from his temporal limitations and merges into Śiva whether it is by sacrificial suicide — now no longer practised and forgotten — or by sheer devotion.

Malla also assumes the form of an elephant during his battle with Khaṇḍobā (*M. M. Vi.* 16.16; cp. 13.24). This reminds us of Śiva killing

Gajāsura and dressing himself in an elephant hide. Only if we know this incident of the battle described in the *M. M.* (Maṇi as *kunjara: M. M. 13.32;* Malla as *gaja:* 16.17), may we realize that the little elephant rider in front of Khaṇḍobā representations on plaques depicts Malla. This also explains the stone elephant which is placed in front and a little to the side, of Malla's *mūrti* in Jejuri. Like Malla, the elephant faces Khaṇḍobā. But the elephant rider can also be explained as another representation of Khaṇḍobā who turns the demon in the form of an elephant into one of his *vāhanas.* Śiva as Khaṇḍobā also means that he has assumed royal functions and rides in state on an elephant, similar to Indra. Thus at the marriage of Khaṇḍobā with Mhāḷsā, celebrated annually at Pali in the Satara Dt., the god rides on an elephant borrowed for the occasion from the ex-princely state of Aundh. Actually Khaṇḍobā is tied to the waist of the Pāṭīl (headman) of Pali in the form of a metal face mask of the god (Ma. *mukhavṭā*). Stone elephants as votive donations can also be seen on the way up to the temple in Jejuri, mostly placed to the side of *nandīs.*

Śiva in classical style invariably rides a *nandī* and arrives on his *nandī* according to the *M. M.* before he mounts a horse to fight the demon. Most of the texts tell us that the *nandī* turns into the horse (*turaṅga, haya*) though there are indications that the demons Maṇi and Malla owned the horse before Khaṇḍobā.[24] The connection of Malla, the hill demon, with the horse echoes the mythical, demoniac winged horses which dominated the mountains before the human beings.[25] It was Indra according to the *Ṛgveda* who cut off the wings of the mountains (= horses?) and thus rendered them immobile.[26] In many tribal myths of Middle India the creation of the first human beings by the god was endangered by a demon, mostly a horse, or more rarely, two horses. As a punishment the wings of the horses were cut off and they were reduced to the state of riding and pack animals.[27] The horse and the bull (bullocks) are conspicuous in the annual *jatrās* at Nimgav-Davdi in the Khed Taluka of the Pune Dt. Twice a year, on the fullmoon days of the month of Magh (January/February) and of the month of Caitra (March/April) carts decorated with five bunches of peacock feathers are driven up the hill towards the temple at breath-taking speed. The carts (*gāḍā*) have small solid wheels, are drawn by one or two pairs of bullocks, and are preceded by a rider on horseback. (Fig. 10)

The *M. M.* (13.16) and the *M. M. Vi.* (3.56) say that Maṇi (Maṇikā sura) was allowed to stay with his horse near Mallāri. This may account for bronze *mūrtis* which show a "groom" leading the horse with the god seated on the horse. Such a "groom" may also be a minor, but widespread god like the shepherds' god Bīrappa/Birobā (Murty/Sontheimer 1980, p. 173).

The representations of Śiva/Khaṇḍobā and of numerous similar gods with the horse as their *vāhana* are extremely widespread. They occur on silver plaques and as metal *mūrtis* and may be found in temples as well as in house shrines, especially in Maharashtra. Sometimes small plaques are used as charms tied around the neck. The myth of the battle of the god on the horse against the demons is also often depicted in murals on temples and in an old glass painting in the Municipal Museum of Nasik (Figs 3, 8, 9).

The omnipresent horse in the folk cults and rituals of the Deccan and Western India is so pervasive and historically so old that I wonder whether we should not emphasize this phenomenon much more. It is found as early as in the megalithic burials of the 7th cent. B.C. in the Deccan[28] and is part of an ancient complex which is essentially outside the brahmanical ritual and culture. Asko Parpola has suggested that Rudra, the Vrātyas and the Aiyaṉār are related to the megalithic burials.[29] The horse is connected with the hero-cult prevalent in Western India and the Deccan up to Tamilnadu at least from the time of the Caṅkam literature onwards. Thus Maṇi and Malla are repeatedly described as mighty *vīras* (*M.V.* 8. 14; 17; 9. 52; 11. 130; 12. 15 ff. Cf. 16. 27). Śiva, the *yogī* turned warrior, is also the Lord of the *bāvan vīr,* the 52 vīras who include several demoniac, mythological heroes, godlings or deified spirits, e.g. Bhairav, Jaypāl, Vīr Vikramājīt, Hanumān, Ismāl Jogī, etc.[30] The Rajputs and the Muslims have only added to the lore of the cult of the hero and to the reverence of the horse, symbol of the *kṣatra.*

Incidentally, in Jejuri, the most famous cult centre of Khaṇḍobā, the horses of the god are traditionally kept by a Muslim family. In some places Khaṇḍobā's is called Mallu Khān or Ajmat Khan — the latter said to be the name given to Khaṇḍobā in Jejuri by Aurangzeb who was compelled to flee from Khaṇḍobā's power. Many late medieval stone sculptures are scattered on the side of the stairs leading to the temple of Khaṇḍobā in Jejuri. They show the heads of heroes who died in battle. The stones are derived from the older innumerable hero-stones or (Ka.) *vīragaḷas,* (Ta.) *virakkals* of the Deccan and Western India. On these older widely varying stones the hero is often shown to have died in a raid defending his cattle and women, just as Khaṇḍobā came to the rescue of the Brāhmaṇas and their women folk when Maṇi and Malla attacked them. On the *vīragaḷas* the *apsaras* are shown to carry the hero towards heaven. There he dwells in the company of Śiva. It is noteworthy that the *yogī* with his *tapas* and the warrior in his fury who dies on the battle-field are often equated with each other. Both are able to pierce the orbit of the sun.[31] Thus we find a wealth of traditions which show warriors and even dynasties (like e.g. the Hoḷkars of Indore, who have Khaṇḍobā as their family god) emerging from a tribal or pastoral-nomadic past and merging into a religious context in which Śaivite gods and cults dominated.

From very early times the horse plays a great role in the myths and rituals of many tribals, the dynasties emerging from a tribal background, and in the culture of the *kṣatriyas*. Horse figurines, e.g., play a great role in the death rituals of the Bhīls. With the ritual called *nukto* in which brass figurines of a rider on a horse feature prominently, the purified spirit can ascend to reach the clan of ancestors and to dwell with Bhagavān in the beyond.[32] Thus the depiction of horse and rider in the memorial stones of the Bhīls is not only an imitation of prestigious Rajput styles — in fact, in the Rajput memorials the horse is not shown — but also reflects an incident of the death ritual. Generally, the horse is also a symbol of death and fertility. The horse is used by the shaman for his shamanistic flights to the upper and nether worlds in order to retrieve souls from there. But in the case of Śiva the obstinacy of his *bhaktas* has made him dwell on the human earth in the form of Khaṇḍobā/Mallāri. He was first seen by young herdsmen as he descended on horseback on the high mountainous plateau where the old temple is situated at Jejuri.

In the tribal context, the clan god on the horse is often interpreted as some form of Bhairava, a god who protects. He is a warrior, a deified hero, or a saint, and in any case a god which eventually merges into many of those major deities riding a horse. All these deities on horseback point towards gods like Mārtaṇḍa-Bhairava (the Khaṇḍobā of Maharashtra) or the Aiyaṉār of Tamilnāḍu, gods who express in a most complex manner this motif. They are mounted on a horse and surrounded by horses.

Bhairava, Mārtaṇḍa-Bhairava/Khaṇḍobā is accompanied by dogs or a pack of dogs whether he is on a hunt or defeating *rākṣasas*. The dog or pack of dogs is associated in the art, rituals and mythology of the Mallāri/Khaṇḍobā cult from the earliest times. Ekanāth (b. 1533 at Paithan) seems to refer to a golden *mūrti* of Khaṇḍobā seated on a dog. He says that "Khaṇḍerāv" and the dog are "not different" or are "identical" (*abhinna*) on account of their linkedness by gold.[33] In the *M. M. Vi.* (3.8; cf. 8.71) we read that Khaṇḍobā is surrounded by dogs, seated n a horse and is fond of turmeric powder (Ma. *bhaṇḍār,* Skt. *haridra,* Ma. *haḷad*). Turmeric powder is — apart from its medical properties — the poor man's substitute for gold. It also represents the substance of the god and especially during festivals of Khaṇḍobā like the Somvati Amāvāsyā festival at Jejuri everything is immersed in it. Even all the other gods are said to throw it on Khaṇḍobā in his praise at the end of the battle (*M. M. Vi.* 8.71). Thus *bhaṇḍār* provides the ritual and substantial link between god, men, *daityas,* and animals which reflects a "communitas" (Victor Turner) of all who are present at the festival. The *daitya* also receives a constant offering of *bhaṇḍār.* Even the black temple dogs in Jejuri or any ordinary stray dog receives a generous coating on his forehead (Fig. 5).

One of the earliest references to the dog of the god is in the *śatarudriya* of the *Taittirīya Saṃhitā.* Rudra is in the text a dog, the lord of the dogs, and the lord of those keeping dogs. In fact, there exists an oral legend in Karnataka telling us that in a previous *yuga* a group of special devotees went as a pack of hounds for a hunt with Śiva or to help him fighting the demon. The *M.M.Ś.* coincides with this: King Mārtaṇḍa is accompanied by seven hundred dogs (1.84; *M. M. Vi.* 8.16: "wild because of anger and accompanied by many dogs"). In our age these dogs have become human beings keeping a vow which involves that on special occasions they behave like dogs, barking and eating from a begging bowl in a dog-like fashion. It is noteworthy that their behaviour, appearance and outfit very much reflect the style of the ancient Vrātyas and again the Mallas, and the Pāśupatas with their peculiar vow.[34] Some of their attire and behaviour can very well be compared with the Cynics in Ancient Greece.[35] These devotees begging in the name of Khaṇḍobā / Mallāri are called *vāghyās* in Marathi and *vāggayya* in Kannada. *vāghyā* is invariably derived from Skt. *vyāghra.* It is said the *vāghyās* were tigers formerly, but having the *darśan* of Mārtaṇḍa their body became human. They were told by Mārtaṇḍa/Bhairava to bark like dogs. This reminds us somewhat of the ancient Pāśupata vow which involved *avitadbhāṣaṇa* — uttering senseless or contradictory words. Ka. *uggu,* from which *vāggayya* may be derived, similarly means to "utter repeatedly meaningless 'sounds".

In any case the Vāggayyas still occasionally act like dogs during *jatrās* performing a round dance accompanied by drums and chants. In the middle of the circle devotees throw coins on a black woollen blanket and the Vāggayyas pick up the coins with their mouths, entertaining the devotees. The coins in this instance tend to replace the food which devotees offer to the bowls of the Vāggayyas. One is reminded of the famous scene of the dog dance rite in the *Chāndogya Up.* (1.12) performed with the *udgītha* chant in order to procure food. This is in remarkable accordance with the explanation in the *M. V.* of the origin of the dog in the Mārtaṇḍa Bhairava / Khaṇḍobā cult: the *Sāmaveda* — somewhat impure when compared with the *Ṛgveda* and *Yayurveda* because it is sacred to the ancestors *(Manusmṛti* IV, 119–120) and thus has something to do with death (Monier Williams, *Sanskrit-English Dictionary,* s.v.) — became the dog of Śiva and would forever stay at Śiva's gate (*M.V.* 334.50).

The dog is often a metaphor for sexuality and sexual licentiousness, a trait which was, as we have seen, also characteristic for Malla. This feature seems to have been lost in the rites of the Vāghyās. However, I noticed devotees of Bīrappa in Andhra ritually drinking milk like dogs, barking and biting each other, and imitating the copulation of dogs (see Murty/Sontheimer 1980, p. 174 ff.).

The mixing of "tiger" and "dog" is chronic in myth, ritual, and in art. Rudra/Śiva — as presumably shown on the famous Indus seal — is also in the company of a tiger.[36] He is seated on a tiger skin or clad in a tiger skin (e.g. *dvipicarmanivāsin, Mahābhārata, Droṇaparva* 173, 32 a, crit. ed.; eg., *M. M.Vi.* 6.16). Thus Bhairava's *vāhanas* are occasionally the dog *and* the tiger or two animals which are a mixture of both, as, e.g., in a painting from Orissa and a glass painting from Tanjore.[37] The Vāghyās, on the other hand, have to carry a pouch made preferably of tiger skin or otherwise of deer's *(haraṇ)* skin. In this pouch they keep the sacred *bhaṇḍār,* the turmeric powder, the substance embodying Khaṇḍobā.

Rudra/Śiva or Bhairava is not normally shown in the texts as accompanied by his wife when he goes to hunt or to defeat the demons. Accordingly he occurs in a small brass *mūrti* as riding a horse, carrying a lance or a *triśul* and holding the head of one of the demons whereas the other head has fallen on the floor (Fig.6). This is more in accordance with our texts. In the *M. V.* and *M. M.* it is not mentioned that Pārvatī or Umā accompanies him though there are instructions in the *M. V.* what kind of *mūrti* should be used for *pūjā.* Here the wife is specifically mentioned.[38] Popular art frequently shows him with Pārvatī who is identical with Mhāḷsā in the Khaṇḍobā cult. In some more "classical" representations she sits in the Umāpati fashion more or less awkwardly on Śiva's left thigh. Both are seated on a horse in this style (Fig. 3). But very often she sits either in front or behind him. Rarely we may also find popular brass *mūrtis* where both wives are seated peacefully on the horse before Khaṇḍobā (Fig. 7).

Khaṇḍobā's second wife is Bāṇāī who comes from the shepherd community of the Dhangars. Khaṇḍobā and his equivalents in the Deccan and in South India always have a second wife from a community with tribal background. Thus Murukaṉ's "second" wife comes from the Kurava tribe.[39] It is Bāṇāī whom Khaṇḍobā dearly loves and who — coming from the forest — is more erotic, beautiful and earthy. Mhāḷsā, on the other hand, is from the higher community, but somewhat of a jealous nature, even cantankerous and too domestic. She sits high up on the horse, her nose turned towards the sky whereas poor Bāṇāī is standing on the floor holding a sheep in her arm and reaching Khaṇḍobā some fruit or other food. She essentially reflects the fertility and eroticism of the early Tamil Vaḷḷi in the old Tamil *(akam)* love poetry (Figs 4 and 5).

In popular pictorials it is Mhāḷsā who kills the demon with the lance, whereas Khaṇḍobā just lifts his sword as if he were about to strike. It is the *śakti* of Khaṇḍobā who seems to bring liberation to the demons. According to our texts (e.g., *M. V.* 8.90) the lance is often an embodiment of the *devī* (Figs 8 and 9, cf. 9).

Since Vedic times if not earlier, Rudra / Śiva is the great hunter armed with a spear or a bow and arrows. In an inscription of the year 1369 A.D. from Avinavōlu near Warangal in Sanskrit and Telugu it is said that the god Śiva, in order to protect Arjuna, assumed the form of a hunter (*śabara*), fought the demon Malla and killed him, thereby acquiring the name Mallār or Mailār.[40] Mallāri has always been the god of the hunting tribes, such as the Niṣādas, Śabaras or others. The 13th century text *Krīḍābhirāmamu* from Warangal says that Mailār is the god of those "who are fond of hunting with spears". Even today shepherds bring their ceremonial spears (another embodiment of the god) for the Somvati Amāvāsyā festival at Jejuri and participate in the ceremonial hunt of the god. Many of the Vāghyās or Vāggayyas are recruited from the shepherds and also carry spears. The same spear is also shown in old illustrations as Khaṇḍobā's weapon. A group of Dhangars was actually called Barge Dhangars and were said to go for a hunt with bear spears (*bargā*=staff?). The spear appears prominently in the Murukaṉ cult and in early texts Murukaṅ is called *vēlaṉ* after his frenzied attendants who carry a spear (Ta. *vēl*).[41] Murukaṉ, Skanda/Kārttikeya as well as Khaṇḍobā can, e.g., also be mutually connected because of possessing a lance or a spear (Fig. 6).

Thus folk art, rituals, oral myths and legends besides the written versions in Sanskrit and Marathi link up the age-old Rudra/Śiva cult with the Khaṇḍobā/Mallāri myth and cult. Taken together, these features form a body of evidence which is internally cohesive and mutually informative, and which illuminates the record of peoples outside brahmanical circles, people whose history is extremely ancient. Because of its vigorous and exuberant expression in visual art, oral literature and festivities this culture, with its irresistible mixture of temporal joy and potential otherworldly spirituality, has remained an invaluable treasure in the devastating spiritual and cultural emptiness of modern times. Khaṇḍobā / Mallāri combines *bhakti* and *mukti* and is accessible to all, irrespective of caste or religion including Mlecchas, i.e. Muslims. This the *M. V.* stresses repeatedly[42].

ACKNOWLEDGEMENTS

I am grateful for the financial support from the German Research Association (Deutsche Forschungsgemeinschaft) in the year 1979. Professor S.G. Tulpule has been helpful in reading with me the texts and mss. mentioned in fn. 1. Asko Parpola and Willem Bollée have made helpful observations. Jim Laine has made some important editorial comments as regards the English of this paper. I should also mention Mr Ramdas Atkar and Rajaram Zagade who have, as usual, assisted me in my field research. I am also grateful to Mr Richard Werny who has taken the photographs of Figs. 4, 5, and 6. The photograph of Fig. 3 was taken with permission of Mrs M. Happe.

ABBREVIATIONS

Ka.	=	Kannaḍa
Kh. Ā.	=	*Khaṇḍerāyāyacī Ādī*
Ma.	=	Marāṭhi
M. M.	=	*Mallāri Māhātmya* by Siddhapāl Kesarī
M.M.Ś	=	*Mallāri Māhātmya* by Śrīdhar
M.V.	=	*Mārtaṇḍa Vijaya* by Gaṅgādhara
M.M.Vi.	=	*Mallāri Māhātmya* by Vināyaka
Ta.	=	Tamil
Te.	=	Telugu

NOTES

1. The *Nirṇayasindhu* by Kāmalākarabhaṭṭa of the year 1612 refers to the Campaṣaṣṭhī festival on the 6th of the light half of the month Mārgaśirṣa as famous in Mahārāṣṭra and cites the *Mallārī Māhātmya* in the *Brahmāṇḍa-purāṇa*. Nirṇayasindhu, Nirṇayasāgara, Mumbaī, 1949, p. 228. Cit. by R.C. Dhere, *Khaṇḍobā,* Puṇe. 1961, p. 8. The *Caturvargacintāmaṇi* (1260–1271) of Hemādri mentions the *vrata* of Kumāra (Skanda) on Campaṣaṣṭhī, but not Khaṇḍobā/Mallāri. Dhere, *op. cit.* The *M.M.* was probably composed after that and before Siddhapāl Kesarī according to Dhere.
   The texts which have been used are:
   Śrī Mallārimāhātmya by Siddhapāl Kesarī (composed in Marathi in 1585 according to Dhere), Mumbaī (several editions).
   Śrī Mārtaṇḍa Vijaya by Gaṅgādhara. ed. R. C. Dhere, Pune, 1975 (composed in Marathi 1923).
   Śrī Malhāri Māhātmya by Śrīdharasvāmī Nājhareka, ed. R. C. Dhere, Pune, 1975. (Śrīdhara lived between 1580 and 1651.)
   Śrī Mallārī Māhātmya by Vināyaka, Bombay?, 1872 (composed in 1871).
   Khaṇḍerāyācī Ādī by Jagjīvan, xerocopy of unpublished ms. from Dhule, 8th cent.
2. Sontheimer, Birobā, Mhaskobā und Khaṇḍobā, Wiesbaden, 1976.
   Sontheimer, Some incidents in the History of the God Khaṇḍobā in: Gaborieau, Marc et Thorner, Alice (eds.), Asie du Sud. Traditions et changements, VIth European Conference on Modern South Asian Studies 1978, Paris, 1979, pp. 111–17.

Murty, L. M. K. and Sontheimer, Günther-Dietz, Prehistoric Background to Pastoralism in the Southern Deccan in the Light of Oral Traditions and Cults of Some Pastoral Communities, Anthropos, 75, 1980, pp. 163–84.

Sontheimer, The Dasarā Festival at Devaraguḍḍa (Karnāṭaka): Ritual and Dramatic Performance in the Cult of Mailār in: Proceedings of the VII European Conference on Modern South Asian Studies, London, 1981 (in press).

3. See fn. 2.
4. See Gonda. Jan, Die Religionen Indiens. Vol. I, 2nd edn., Stuttgart, 1978, p.55. Cf. *Ṛgveda* 5. 30. 6; 6. 17, 8, 9. Indra frees the rivers of Vṛtra: 4.17. 1. Rivers and cows are metaphors for food and are often mutually exchangeable according to J. Deppert, Rudras Geburt, Wiesbaden, 1977, pp. 121, 199 f. For Indra as the adversary of the demon Vṛtra and the subsequent parallels of Prajāpati and Namuci and of Buddha and Māra, see Bollee, A Note on Evil and its Conquest from Indra to Buddha, in Berkeley Buddhist Studies Series, 1977, pp 317–81.
5. Gonda, *op. cit.,* p. 57. Indra frees the cows locked up in the cave by Vala. *Ṛgveda* 1. 174. 4; 3. 32. 16, etc.
6. Deppert, *op. cit.,* p. 128. See Zvelebil, Kamil V., The Beginnings of *bhakti* in South India, Temenos, 13, 1977, pp. 223 ff., p. 234. The malevolent forces of the hills and the anxieties and terrors in the soul of men were personified as Cūraṉ whom Murukaṉ overcomes in battle. *Patiṟṟupattu* 11.5. Cūr is Murukaṉ's enemy who seeks to possess people, especially women. It is a personalized demonic force. *Naṟṟiṇai* 329. 7 – 9; 373. 5. See also Clothey, Fred W., The Many Faces of Murukaṉ, The Hague, 1978, pp. 28, 30. Cūr in his battle against Murukaṉ takes various terrifying forms, such as a huge mountain, See Shulman, David, Murukaṉ, Mango and Ekāmbareśvara-Śiva., IIJ, 21 (1979), pp. 27 – 40, at p. 31. Malla consecrates mountains by *mantras* using them as weapons in his fight against Mallāri *(M.M. Vi.* 16.26).
7. III 199 f. Bollée, Willem, The Indo-European Sodalities in Ancient India, ZDMG, 131/1, 1981, pp. 172 ff, at p. 178.
8. *M. M.* 1.53 ff. Malla raids the *āśram* of the Brahmans while on a hunt: *M. V.* 1. 88 ff.
9. For the *vrātyas* in this context, see Sontheimer 1981, *op. cit.* in fn. 2. R. N. Dandekar, Vedic Mythological Tracts, Delhi, 1979, p. 207 ff. Bollée, *op. cit.* 173 ff.
10. cf. 18.66 ff. Though the *daitya* may be a highly accomplished wrestler (*parama catur malla*) he can achieve nothing against Śiva, just as the Kolhāṭīs — a caste of acrobats — can perform acrobatic feats of a high order, but how can they measure themselves with Hanumanta! For Cāṇura and Muṣṭika, the "Mallas", and Kṛṣṇa as Mallāri see Bollée, *op. cit.* p. 183. Harivaṃśa 2. 121. 119 in the Poona edn. of 1936.
11. Sontheimer, 1976, p. 193. The Kalacuri king Someśvara Sovideva (12th cent.) adopted the *biruda* "Bhujabalamalla". One of his successors (Śaṅkama) had the *biruda* Niḥśaṅkamalla: "The wrestler without fear". His brother was called Ākavamalla: "The wrestler who is a challenge". See Maharashtra State Gazetteer, History, pt. I, Ancient Period, Bombay, 1967, p. 351 f. For the dynasties of the Mallas in Nepal, see Bollée, *op. cit.,* p. 184. For the Malla dynasty of the ancient kingdom of Mallabhum in West Bengal, see Ákos Östor, The Play of the Gods, Chicago and London, 1980, pp. 24–26, pp. 203–04. On the Malla as an ancient people in Buddhist and Jaina works, see Law, Bimala Churn, Tribes in Ancient India, 2nd edn., Poona, 1973, Chapter 50.
12. See, e. g., *M. M. 9.* 33, 13. 49: he is the *rājā* of the *daityas.*
13. Dravidian Etymological Dictionary, *s.v.* Sontheimer, 1976, p. 189. Sindhi *malu* means not only "wrestler" but also "brave man". See Turner, A Comparative Dictionary of Indo-Aryan Languages, 1907. I owe the reference to Asko Parpola.
14. R. C. Majumdar, The Classical Accounts of India, Calcutta, 1960, p. 341.
15. *Tirumurrukāṟṟuppatai* 317, 77. Sontheimer 1976, p. 20. Zvelebil, *op. cit.,* p. 235 ff.

Zvelebil tends to derive Skanda/Kumāra/Kārttikeya and Murukaṉ from an "Ur-Murukaṉ" (p. 236 f.), but I would believe that the Vedic Rudra, Śiva, Murukaṉ, Kārttikeya, etc. are all versions of one god genetically and historically connected with a proto-Indian pre-Vedic god. Note that Rudra is the *youngest* son of the Creator and that *kumāra* is one of the names of Rudra (this has been suggested by Asko Parpola). Rudra is also *inter al.* derived from *rud* which means "lament, cry" (cf. Ka. *uggu* = "repeatedly to utter unmeaning sounds" [sic], Kittel's Kannaḍa-English Dictionary, rev. and enl. edn., Madras, 1968, s.v., see below in text. Moreover, any god in folk religion as well as in the Veda, may assume the form of a young god. For Rudra as *giriśa, giriśanta, giritra* see *Taittirīya Saṃhitā* XVI, 2 f. *giriśa, Mahābhārata,* XIII. 6348 (Cal. ed.).

16. A rich *māla (=malla)* is mentioned in the 13th cent. Marathi *Līḷācaritra* (ed. V.B. Kolte, Bombay, 1978), *līlā* 30. He lived at Warangal and had 500 *mālās* under him. Here *mālā* means "masseur" rather than "wrestler" though the two professions are closely linked; cf. *koḷī* ="fisherman", "hunter" and "ferryman". Cf. Bollée, *op. cit.,* p. 184 fn. 97, and as regards *niṣāda* = "hunter", "fishermen", "robbers" etc. "ferry-men", ibid., p. 181.
17. See Sircar, D. C., The Nāgas and Yakṣas, in: Studies in the Religious Life of Ancient and Medieval India, Delhi, etc., 1971, p. 133 ff, p. 136 and fn. 3., pp. 144 ff. Sircar connects Maṇibhadra with Maniṇāga whose *tīrtha* at the ancient city of Rājagṛha is mentioned in the Mahābhārata.
18. According to the *Kantapurāṇam, kāṇḍam* 2–4 by Kacciyappar, the demon Cūr, together with his brothers Cinkamukaṉ (Skt. *siṃhamukha)* and Tarakan, worshipped Śiva and in this world won control over the universe. See Shulman, David, Tamil Temple Myths, Princeton Univ. Press, Princeton, 1980, at p. 30 f. and fn. 49. This may explain the three heads of demons shown in the *mūrtis* and their pictorial representations of Mallaṇṇa in Andhra, e.g., at Iloni (Ainavōlu) near Warangal and at other places in the Karimnagar Dt. See also Fig. 3. The three demons of the Tripura myth were Tārākṣa, Kamalākṣa, and Vidyunmālin facing the necessary destruction and death to gain Śiva. See Wendy Doniger O'Flaherty, Hindu Myths, Penguin Books, 1975, p. 125 ff.
19. *M. V.* 20. 98. See also 19.78: The flame of life from Malla's mouth enters the mouth of Mārtaṇḍa Bhairava and becomes identified with Śiva. On the *ahaṃkār* of the demon, see also Shulman, *op. cit.,* ch. V, p. 317 ff., p. 321 f.
20. Māṇikkavācakar's Tiruvācakam 14.4; 15.9. Glenn E. Yocum, Mānikkavācakar's Image of Śiva, in History of Religions, 17, 1977, pp. 20. ff., 23.
21. Sontheimer, Günther-Dietz, The Hero- and Sati-Stones of Mahārāṣṭra, in Settar, S., and Sontheimer, G.-D., The Memorial Stones of India, Dharwad/Delhi, 1982, p. 272 f. Figs. 21–23.
22. J. C. Heesterman, The Case of the Severed Head, in WZKSOA 11, 1967, pp. 22 ff., at p. 30.
23. I was told that the head with horns in the *kīrtimukha*style at the base of the threshold of the temple door is that of "Dakṣa". Besides "pure" animals, like "man", horse, bull, ram, having a function in the cult, there are great fairs for horses and camels at Malegaon (near Bid) in the month of Pauṣ (December/January) and of donkeys during the *purṇimā* day in Pauṣ at Jejuri. Gifts of bullocks, horses, buffaloes or cows to Mārtaṇḍa are recommended in fulfilment of a promise in exchange for a request for increase in cattle, *M. V.* 33. 43 ff.
24. According to *M. M. S.* 1.80; also *Kh. Ā.* 83; *M. M. Vi.* 8.25. According to *M. V.* 34.51 ff., Maṇi already had a horse. Śaṅkar ordered the moon to become a horse and, seated on it, he cut off the head of the *daitya.* Ever since the horse as a *vāhana*became dear to

the god. *M. M. Vi.* 13.24 tells us that Maṇi became "horse-faced" *(hayamukha)* after his head was cut off by Mārtaṇḍa and he started neighing. Eventually, the upper half of him became an elephant. According to the *M. M.* 13.59 the horse, chariot, and elephants derive from the demon.

25. See Jettmar, Karl, Die Religionen des Hindukush, Stuttgart, 1975, p. 295, cf. p. 252: flying horses. On the horses of the Hephtalite peoples of the Pamir area the Chinese have preserved a myth on the origin of these horses. There was a mountain in which a divine horse lived. Mares were driven into the mountain. See Eberhard, Wolfram, China und seine westlichen Nachbarn. Beiträge zur mittelalterlichen und neueren Geschichte Zentralasiens, Darmstadt, 1978, p. 146. (I owe the reference to P. Snoy.) Amongst the Dhangars of Maharashtra we find the belief that the horse was hidden in a mountainous cave in the form of wind, before Khaṇḍobā fetched it to ride to his beloved Bāṇāī of the Dhangars. Sontheimer, 1976, p. 190.
26. See *Ṛgveda,* 4.19.4; 6.30.3.
27. Kapp, Dieter B., Ein Menschenschöpfungsmythos der Mundas und seine Parallelen, Abhandlungen für die Kunde des Morgenlandes, XLIII, 2, Wiesbaden, 1977, *passim.*
28. Excavations of megalithic burials conducted by S. B. Deo at Mahurjhari and Vaikunth in the Vidarbha region of Maharashtra have yielded horse skeletons with horsebits *in situ* as well as skeletons of dogs (on which see below). Lances of the length of 2m. and arrow tips in the bodies of enemies point to a nomadic warrior community dominating over agriculturists. The site excavated is near a present-day Goṇḍ village. The Goṇḍs may sacrifice and eat any animal except the horse (and presumably the dog) — personal communication by S. B. Deo. This explains the continued importance of the horse *and* the dogs in cults, especially that of Khaṇḍobā. Lance and bow are still existant in representations of Khaṇḍobā. I once saw a beautiful brass figurine of Khaṇḍobā with a bow and on horseback, his wife seated behind. The persistent estimation of the horse is also reflected in its worship amongst tribals like the Goṇḍs and the Bhīls and others. They may not own horses themselves, but at least their gods are made to ride horses.
29. Parpola, Asko, Arguments for an Aryan Origin of the South Indian Megaliths, Madras, 1973, *passim.*
30. *Mahārāṣtra Vākyasampradāya Kośa, s. v. bāvan vīr.*
31. See Sontheimer, 1981. The famous *śloka:*
    dvāv imau puruṣau loke sūryamaṇḍalabhedinau
    parivrāḍ yogayuktaś ca raṇe cābhimukho hataḥ
    is alluded to in *M. V.* 16.27
32. Kramrisch, Stella, Indian Varieties of Art Ritual, in: Kitawaga, J. and Long, Ch. L. (eds.), Myth and Symbols. Studies in Honor of Mircea Eliade. The University of Chicago Press, Chicago, 1969, p. 23 ff.
33. *śvānārūḍha Khaṇḍerāvo/suvarṇācā karavilā pahā ho/*
    tethem pāhatām śvāna āṇi devo/survaṇānvayem abhinna.//
    Ekanāthaḥ Catuḥślokī Bhāgavata 580 in N.V. Paṇasīkara (ed.), Ekanāthakṛta Āṭha Grantha, Poona, 1968.
34. See Sontheimer, 1981, on the Vaggayyas of Devaraguḍḍa in Karnāṭaka. On the Pāśupatas see Lorenzen, David N. The Kāpālikas and Kālāmukhas, New Delhi, 1972, esp. ch. VI, p. 185: e.g. *avitatkaraṇa* (acting as if devoid of judgment) and *avitadbhāṣaṇa* (uttering senseless or contradictory words). The *Śaṅkaravijaya* refers to the followers of Mallāro at Ujjain "who were endowed with the dress and language of a dog which is the form of the *vāhana* of Mallāri". They pleased Mallāri with their dance and song. They wore as a special mark a necklace of cowries—which is still typical for *vāghyās* and Gorappas. Cf. the *niṣka* of Rudra. The followers of Mallāri based their

faith in Mallāri on the authority of *śatarudriya* reference of the "dogs and the lord of dogs." See N. Veezhinathan (ed.), Śrīśaṅkaravijaya of Anantānandagiri, Univ. of Madras, Madras, 1976, ch. 29, p. 117 f.

35. The Cynics were followers of the principles of Diogenes who had received the nickname of *kýon* (dog) because they rejected all conventions, tried to live on nothing, and advocated shamelessness *(anaidia)*, The Oxford Classical Dictionary, Oxford, 1949 (repr. 1957). The return to a state of nature and to the life of animals, not external wealth, but the possession of the soul, freedom from all desires were some of their teachings. They were dressed in a rough coat (cf. the rough woollen coat of the *vrātyas* and Vāggayyas), they had a satchel for keeping the almsfood and a staff. The life of the first human beings and of animals presents an example to them. The similarity with gods is seen in their complete exigency which leads to begging. The humiliation experienced when they beg unsuccessfully for food leads to spiritual merit. Corporal and spiritual asceticism, self-mortification were necessary to gain spiritual freedom. Sexual licentiousness in public and opposition to settled social life and institutions and the attempt to salvage the freedom of the individual are other features of the school of the Cynics. See Helm in Paulys Real-Encyclopädie der Classischen Altertumswissenchaft, 12 Band, Stuttgart, 1925, Kynismus. See Ingalls, Daniel H.H., Cynics and Pāśupatas: The Seeking of Dishonor, in Harvard Theological Review, 55, 1962, pp. 281-98.
36. For another, more plausible interpretation of the "proto-Śiva" seal see Hiltebeitel, Alf, The Indus Valley 'Proto-Śiva'. Reexamined through Reflections on the Goddess, The Buffalo, and the Symbolism of *vāhanas,* in: Anthropos, 73, 1978, pp. 767-97.
37. Bussabarger, Robert F., and Robins, Betty Dashew, The Everyday Art of India, New York, 1968, p. 153. Madurai Vīran in Appasamy, Jaya, Indian Painting on Glass, Indian Council for Cultural Relations, New Delhi, 1980, plate 4. "...Below the group is a dog chased by a cheetah ...". Rāmdās on (1608-1681) speaks of "dogs as big as tigers" in one of his *abhaṅgs* on Khaṇḍobā Anantadās Rāmdāsī (ed.), *Śrīsamarthāṃcā Gāthā,* Pune, 1982, *abhaṅg* 1170.
38. The instructions in the *M.V.* (24.57-63) on how *mūrtis* are to be made are worth quoting: "Preferably one should make for worship an image (*pratimā*) of gold, alternatiely of silver, or copper. Otherwise it can be made of stone or clay. There are two types [of images] for meditation: seated on the horse with Mhāḷsā. In the hand shine sword (*khaḍga*) and drum (*ḍamaru*), two hands are [thus] adorned, with the heads of Maṇi-Malla near the feet (57). The second type is prescribed according to *tantra* (*tantrokta*). The *mūrti* is adorned with four arms (*caturbhuj*), it shines with Ganga and Mhāḷsā on either side of the god (58). With *triśul*, *ḍamaru*, and drinking vessel (*pānpātra*), and the sword shining in the right hand. The *mūrtis* should be made beautiful with all ornaments (59). The horse should be nearby. In the front should be set the Nandī as well as a metal dog. Near the feet should be the heads (60). [Or] one should bring clay consecrating it with prayers and moisten it with water consecrated by *mantras*, make a square pedestal (*śāḷuṅkā*) and provide a channel (61). The shape of a horse out of clay should be made [at the end of the channel]. On the top one should from two liṅgs with highest devotion (62). The Mārtaṇḍa liṅg should be big, that of his dear Mhāḷsā one-third in size. On the head of the Mārtaṇḍa-liṅg one should place a lump of clay taking it to represent Gaṅgā (63).
39. Zvelebil, *op. cit.*, pp. 233, 244 f.
40. Sircar, D.C. (ed.) Annual Report on Indian Epigraphy for 1957-58, Delhi, 1961, pp. 8-9, 21. Murty, L.M.K., and Sontheimer, 1980, p. 168.
41. Sontheimer, 1976, p. 20 f.
42. *M. V.* 29. 30; 5. 12: *neṇe varṇa-jātī-kuḷā.*

Towards Reconciling Traditional and Modern Values: The Indian Experiment

T.K. OOMMEN
Delhi

The past is both an asset and a liability. To a large extent the success of a modernizing nation depends on its ability to convert the assets in its tradition to current advantages and to reject the liabilities which are obstacles in its social transformation. Our position assumes that notwithstanding the interdependence of system components, the constituting elements have some degree of autonomy. In all social systems some aspects are relatively more autonomous while others have a greater amount of reciprocal involvement vis-à-vis other system components. This means that in changing a system we can pursue the path of selective retention and replacement of its traditional elements.

Why not destroy the past and create a New Social Order in tune with the aspirations of the people and the spirit of the contemporary era? Our preference for a selective retention approach is dictated by pragmatic considerations and historical experiences rather than ideological presuppositions or national chauvinism. All systems are responsive to stimuli, although the degree and intensity of this response would vary depending upon the character of their antecedent institutional framework and historicity. To this extent their past is gradually but surely to be replaced. But at the same time all systems tend to preserve aspects of their past and even in those societies where revolutions have taken place, persistence of aspects of their past structures continues. If this is the reality, why not accept it and evolve one's strategy of change accordingly? But there is a significant difference here. Instead of fatalistically accepting the "natural tendencies" in the system, we opt for conscious planning and intervention in changing the system and hence the plea for selective retention and replacement.

In evaluating the assets and liabilities of Indian tradition we face certain specific problems and the requisite clarifications are required. India's is an ancient civilization with a deep historicity. It is difficult to demarcate India's hoary past into clear-cut time boundaries. Besides the Indian diversity is so stupendous that to speak in the singular about this nation is extremely hazardous. This is true not only in terms of the difference in folk and elite conceptions of Man and Society, but also in terms of the variations in her Little (micro) and Great (macro) Traditions. Yet one can conceive of a certain unity amidst this multiplicity and, when we speak of India's past tradition, we refer to this Unity. While India is an Old Society, it is also a New Nation.

When could modernity have had its beginnings in India? Broadly speaking India's modernization started in the 18th century. Her contacts with the West, particularly with the British colonial rulers accelerated the process of modernization in certain dimensions. However, the Indian Nation as a political entity emerged only in 1947. The blueprint of society towards which India strives today is embodied in her Constitution. Therefore, when we refer to modern India our frame of reference is independent India.

Here we propose to analyse the basic features of India's tradition and modernity. In undertaking this exercise we shall differentiate between the ideological and empirical components of the system. This is necessary because in all societies at all times there exists a gap between "what ought to be" and "what is", between the theory and the practice. This gap is not always and necessarily indicative of human fads and foibles alone but also of the imperfections of the goal itself or the impossibility of adequately translating ideologies into actions. Thus we recognize not only a "praxis-lag" but also a "theory-gap" in our attempt at an objective evaluation of any situation.

I must conclude these introductory remarks with a terminological clarification about the notion of values. Values are preferred modes of orientation to specifiable categories of human experience. That is, values define social preferences, specify societal choices, provide a vision for future action. It may be noted that hierarchy, democracy, etc., can be simultaneously an institutional form and a value system. Here I am concerned with them as value systems.

Traditional Indian Values

The Traditional Society in India was organized on the principles of Hierarchy, Pluralism, Holism, Renunciation, Tolerance, etc., among others. The value-themes listed here are by no means exhaustive but only illustrative and we will deal with the first three of them as these appear to be the cardinal ones and encompass several others. Hierarchy implies the ordering of the units which constitute a system in relation to the whole in a superior-inferior gradation. Hierarchy manifested itself not only in the system of caste and sub-caste stratification based on the notions of ritual purity and pollution acquired by birth, but also in the Hindu concept of occupational life-cycles and age-grades (*āśramas*) and moral duties (*dharma*). Marrying within one's own caste (*jāti*) was superior both to hypergamy and hypogamy, that is the practice of a male seeking his spouse from a lower caste and that of a female marrying into a lower caste. Of the triple objectives of marriage, religious duty (*dharma*) had precedence over securing progeny (*prajā*) or sexual pleasure (*rati*). The one who renounced the world (*saṃnyāsin*) was morally superior to one who still remained mundane.

The Brahmin who emerged from the mouth of the creator occupied an admittedly exalted position as compared with the Śūdra, who emerged from the feet of God. Thus the notion of hierarchy was omnipresent and all-powerful in regulating human conduct in every minute aspect of life. While the ideology of hierarchy institutionalized inequality in every conceivable aspect of human life, it allocated a secure and definite place to each individual and caste group. The valuation of individuals and groups and the distribution of societal resources was based on status and the status was ascriptive, even though birth into a group was believed to be based on moral merit, gathered during the previous birth, as implied in the theory of Karma and Reincarnation.

Pluralism as a value implied tolerance of other styles of life while preserving one's own. Hinduism, the dominant religion of India, was essentially tolerant and instead of abruptly converting, it gradually assimilated other faiths. In fact conversion to Hinduism was almost impossible as the contingency of placing the convert in the hierarchical order could not be easily solved. Hindus believed in the existence of multiple paths leading to the same ultimate goal. Thus the faiths of the Muslim conquerors, Christian colonial rulers, Parsi merchants and traders, etc., not only survived but prospered for centuries in India. The differences at the level of doctrines and rituals notwithstanding, the followers of different religions lived in relative harmony in India. However, the "modern" democratic politics made it necessary for each group to compete and vie with one another to maximise the benefits made available through state patronage.

The caste system provided an institutional basis for reinforcing the pluralistic tradition of Hinduism. Each caste had its own occupation, customs, rituals, traditions, and government. While each caste was insulated on the one hand, it was interdependent on several others. Autonomy co-existed with dependence and this led to an appreciation and recognition of others' distinctiveness. Apart from this, given the linguistic diversities and cultural differences, castes operated essentially as regional entities. This resulted in a localistic orientation of castes; castes with the same name differed sometimes substantially in their customs and traditions between different localities. This means that pluralism had not only a vertical dimension but also a horizontal one. And, co-existence of culturally diverse groups became a norm. However, co-existence was not always peaceful, particularly in its political context. Some groups dominated over others and superior-inferior relation was implied in so far as the inferior groups accepted the domination of superior groups without overt protest, which they often did due to the unequal distribution of resources. Thus the hierarchical principle was implicit here too.

Holism assumed a relationship between individual and group in which the latter had primacy over the former; the individual was expected to perform his duties and claim his rights always keeping in mind the wider interests of the community. The individual subservience to collectivity was manifested in a multiplicity of contexts, be it familial communism, village democracy or caste council meetings. The families were often joint in that they consisted of a large number of kin, including dependents — the aged, widowed, physically handicapped, etc. Although each contributed according to his ability, one was expected to draw from the familial store of wealth only according to one's need. Similarly the destitutes and dependents of a village community were the responsibility of the rich: the latter often operated as trustees of community wealth rather than private profiteers. This called for self-restraint of one's wants in the interests of fellow beings, the community-at-large. However, in so far as the individual was subservient to the community it implied a hierarchical relationship. Thus, in the final analysis, the hierarchical principle was all-embracing; it encompassed the values of pluralism and holism.

Notwithstanding the ideological prescriptions, practical aberrations were not uncommon. Thus the hierarchy was clear and sharp only at the polar points of the caste system, the disputes over caste rank being almost always endemic in the middle region, often facilitating mobility in spite of the rigid institutional framework. Further the indeterminancy over rank arose contextually, the king assuming superiority over the priest in secular matters and the priest claiming over-arching importance of the sacred over secular, thereby affirming his over-all superior status. Additionally, the problem of allocating status to the groups — tribals, Muslims, Christians, etc. — either assimilated into the Hindu fold or obtaining outside of it was also problematic as each person or group had to be placed in relation to others in a caste society. Similarly, pluralism, while it implied tolerance, had not infrequently led to bigotry and domination, creating hostility between groups. Finally, holism, while it implied collectivistic orientation, did not always impart the requisite altruism to sustain it. Individuals often felt the weight of the heavy yoke to which they were tied by group control, inhibiting their initiative, often leading to considerable tension in interpersonal and individual–group relations. All this is indicative of the dissensus that existed between theory and practice, prescription and performance in the traditional system of India.

Modern Western Values : Indian Adaptation

The fundamental values that the Indian Nation pursues today are embodied in the Constitution. These values are embedded in the basic goals of Socialism, Secularism, and Democracy. Although this value-package is western in origin, it is applied with the requisite adaptations and reinterpretations to the Indian context.

It is wrong to assume that everybody holds these values equally dear. Some think that socialism should be the most important goal to be pursued with immediacy, for the realization of other goals is contingent upon the establishment of socialism. Similarly, there are others who bestow primacy on the values embodied in democracy and argue that the pursuit of other goals in a manner endangering democracy is worthless. That is to say, notwithstanding the over-all consensus about the basic values, disagreements exist over their importance or the mode and sequence of their realization. We ignore this dissensus while pursuing the present analysis. Yet another clarification ought to be made here. None of the goals are achieved as yet and may be they will not be achieved in the near future and performance in relation to each varies substantially.

Although the word socialism found its entry in the Indian Constitution only in 1976, the Directive Principles prescribed that "the ownership and control of the material resources of the community are so distributed as best to subserve the common good". Further, it requires that the "operation of the economic system does not result in the concentration of wealth and means of production to the common detriment".

Admittedly, Indian socialism is different in theory and practice as compared with socialism elsewhere. While recognizing the "evils" in concentration of economic resources, Indian socialism does not attempt collectivization of private property but only seeks to limit it; the legitimacy of private property as an institution is not yet fundamentally questioned, only its cautious restriction is aimed at. Viewed against the background of the prevailing radical ideologies in the contemporary world this perspective is certainly less than radical but it is certainly progressive when it is matched against the backdrop of the pre-existing system of property relations. The Indian social system, with its all-pervasive institutionalized inequality, allocated resources and distributed rewards on the basis of status which in turn was based on birth. The recognition of the need for providing an opportunity structure which faciliated men to acquire material resources and move up in the social ladder ignoring their past background was radical only if viewed in terms of the antecedent social structure of India. Thus Indian socialism is based on the principle of allocation of resources and roles, based on merit. In so far as the erstwhile social system was characterized by extreme inequalities and in so far as a sudden break from the past did not take place, considerable continuity is in evidence. In effect then, those who have "merit" today are also the one's who had "status" in the past. The net result has been the gradual development of a capitalistic system which favours the economically enterprising in the distribution of resource and allocation of roles as against socialism which insists on need as the basis of distributive justice. While the shift from a feudal hierarchical system based on status to a capitalistic system hinged on "betting for the strong" is not smooth, the birth pangs of socialism are constantly felt and the process seems to be a long-drawn and difficult one.

Secularism in the Indian context meant in practice tolerance of other communities — particularly religious communities. The import of secularism as a primary value in the Indian Constitution should be seen against the back-drop of the circumstances which led to the split of the Indian subcontinent. India is a multi-religious nation in terms of its ideology and existential realities, but its birth was co-terminus with that of a Muslim nation — Pakistan, occasioned by animosity between Hindus and Muslims. India remains even today one of the biggest Muslim nations in the world with a population of over 65 million Muslims. Such a situation called for the explicit recognition of the distinctiveness of other religious groups and hence the importance of secularism as a value. Secularism meant not only non-interference in the affairs of other communities but also developing a positive appreciation for their distinct style of life. The timidity in evolving a uniform civil code for the different religious communities points to this. After independence, the need for recognizing cultural autonomy in the regional–linguistic context became compelling. The official recognition of the cultural autonomy of regional-linguistic entities became explicit in the late fifties when the Indian states were re-organized on the basis of language (culture). This may be viewed as another aspect of Indian secularism, if tolerance of diversity were the basic value in secularism. Notwithstanding the fact that secularism is fundamental to Independent India its institutionalization is far from achieved; communal riots, linguistic squabbles and caste conflicts are not infrequent.

While Indian democracy shares its form with other democratic societies and emphasizes equality of opportunity, its substance is certainly different. Democracy assumes the existence of autonomous and independent individuals capable of participation in the decision-making process. In the traditional social system of India the individual as an autonomous entity making decisions for himself was non-existent. The Indian tradition did not in fact admit of the concept of individual and the Indian individual emerged only when he renounced the world by assuming the role of *saṃnyāsin* or family ascetic. This all-pervasive holism was not conducive to the operation of democracy which presupposed the existence of autonomous individuals. This is the reason why Indian democracy is anchored in primordial loyalty structures such as religion, caste, linguistic groups, etc., wherein ideological polarization is nebulous and often incomplete and frequently mediated by traditional values and rigid institutional structures. The democratic man in so far as he wants to combine the values of socialism and secularism should develop a collectivistic orientation. At the same time this collectivistic orientation should be qualitatively different from existing primordial linkages, it should be based on universalistic values and should have a trans-local orientation. One of the basic dilemmas in bringing the traditional and modern values closer lies precisely here.

Congruence and Conflict

Having discussed the fundamental value-themes of traditional and modern India, we now propose to examine the possibilities of their being fused or synthesized. For purposes of brevity and clarity the three fundamental value-pairs are stated in Table I. We will examine two aspects of the problem presently. First, the possibility of reconciling these value pairs and second, unfolding their internal consistency so as to understand the possibility of effecting a consensus not only between tradition and modernity but also within each of the value-packages.

Table I

Traditional Values	Modern Values	Pre-requisite for realisation
I. (a) Pluralism	(b) Secularism	Tolerance and respect for others' style of life
II. (a) Hierarchy	(b) Socialism	Status based allocation of roles and resources for II(a) and need based allocation for II(b)
III. (a) Holism	(b) Individualism	Renunciation of self-interest for III(a) and assertion of self-interests for III(b)

It is clear from Table I that there is no basic contradiction between the traditional value of pluralism and the modern value of secularism since tolerance of others' style of life is basic to both. However, pluralism of the past was associated with distinct and deep traditions for each of the groups which often provided legitimacy for special privileges and prerogatives. This is turn rendered those with a disproportionate share of privileges, a dominating elite. But secularism as it is understood today in India calls upon the advantaged groups to orientate consciously their behaviour in such a way so as not to handicap the less previleged groups.

As pointed out earlier hierarchy was the over-arching value of the Traditional Order. The significant point in this context is the principle of allocation of resources and distribution of rewards based on birth. This is in direct contravention to the principle of need-based distribution implied in socialism. Perhaps one can discover a linkage here; in the traditional system status defined the need and in the modern system status is sought to be defined on the basis of contribution made by individuals and groups for the maintenance of the system and its change in a desirable direction. If those who occupied higher status are also taken to be the ones who contributed most to the system, the contradiction between the two principles of allocation can be resolved. But this cannot be done. The basis of status in the traditional society was birth and the definition of status in modern society is based on an individual's potentials to contribute to the system and hence the irreconciliability of the principles of hierarchy and socialism.

The traditional principle of holism required that the individuals should renounce their self-interest at the altar of collective goals. To the extent that no autonomy was bestowed on the individual and he remained encompassed in the current of collective life, there was no basic problem. However, with the introduction of democracy which impels individuals to be autonomous entities asserting their independence from the group, the inevitable development of self-interests, often at the cost of collective orientation, is in evidence. This is complicated because of the extreme distributional imbalance in terms of wealth, power and prestige which is a legacy of the antecedent social system. Thus we find the principles of holism and individualism (democracy) are mutually inimical. The upshot of our analysis, then, is that the possibilities of bringing about a reconciliation between India's traditional and modern values is limited except in the case of pluralism and secularism.

The modern values enshrined in the Indian Constitution are not fully translated into practice. Even as we recognize this praxis-lag, we should take into account the transmutations in the transitional stage during which a synthesis of the traditional and modern values is being evolved. Perhaps a couple of illustrations will clarify the situation. Traditionally castes were status-bestowing entities and they emphasized the ritual dimension (purity-pollution) of status. In modern India the castes are increasingly getting secularised in that they perform instrumental functions for their members. Thus, caste associations open educational institutions, establish financial agencies — banks, cooperatives etc., — institute funds for housing, travel abroad and the like, field candidates in elections through political parties. And all these for the material welfare of their own members which helps improve their secular status. This secularization of castes in terms of functions, particularly in urban India, changes their substance while retaining the traditional forms. The traditional caste pluralism which jealously guarded ritual purity is no more universally functional but the modern caste "secularism" which insists on the material improvement of the caste members is ever expanding. The recruitment to caste associations is based on membership in primordial groups and hence ascriptive but the goals these associations pursue are instrumental and achievement oriented.

Although the induction of democratic political framework assumes individual autonomy and freedom, the actual operation of the democratic process in India is infused with a high amount of traditional collectivism. For instance, decisions in the political context are rarely arrived at by individuals as independent entities; the prevalence of "group voting" by kin-groups, castes or territorial groups (villages) is not uncommon. The insistence on "consensus" in decisional process, avoiding the animosities associated with intense competition is quite frequent in political parties. Finally, given the present state of Indian economy social welfare measures to assist the unemployed, the aged, the invalid, etc., are rarely instituted by the State and the burden of supporting the dispossessed and disadvantaged is often accepted by the kin, caste and religious groups. In fact, most Indians who occupy well-off positions as compared with other members of their village, caste or kin would consider it to be their moral obligation to help their less fortunate brethren through educating them or finding a job or raising capital for them. Thus, while the context in which the modern Indian operates has undergone a partial change, the fulfilment of traditional obligations which calls for a collectivistic orientation persists. In the final analysis, what we witness in India today is neither the continuation of all the traditional norms nor the complete institutionalization of the newly introduced values but an intermediate situation containing elements of both tradition and modernity. It seems to me that this complex empirical reality cannot be dismissed as a transitional aberration but should be recognized as an evolving reality with distinct properties. It is important to remind ourselves that this perspective rejects the misplaced polarity often attributed to Tradition and Modernity.

Let us now examine the theory-gap in the two value packages — traditional and modern — so as to understand whether they are internally consistent. In the context of tradition, pluralism which is based on tolerance and holism founded on collectivistic orientation are not mutually inconsistent, because tolerance implies a collectivity orientation. However, hierarchy which is based on the principle of status led to a segmentalization of society leading to multiple group formation each of which was imprisoned in its narrow grooves. Additionally, pluralism fostered local or group pride overlooking wider interests thereby reinforcing hierarchy. Under such a situation holism in effect meant the collectivity orientation of insulated communities. This was not conducive to the growth of modern nationalistic values. But since the over-arching value of hierarchy enveloped other values, and an all-pervasive and dominating elite acted as the custodian of societal values, the requisite unity was forged for waging the anti-colonial struggle.

The basic inconsistency that we witness in the value package of modern India is that between socialism, as we have defined it, and individualism. If the basic tenet of socialism is a pattern of need-based allocation of resources and distribution of roles based on appropriateness, this calls for a high amount of collectivistic orientation and altruism. One cannot insist on one's share, in such a system, based on one's status or merit. One should be willing to contribute to the system as much as one can, that is based on one's ability, but should be prepared to accept the principle of need-based allocation. The spirit of individualism implied in democracy rebels against this as it ceaselessly emphasizes the importance of individual merit and it bestows undue importance on the welfare of individuals. It may be argued that maximization of welfare of all individuals will automatically lead to collective welfare and therefore common interests will not be endangered. But there are two problems here. First, such a system inevitably fosters acute competition between individuals for achieving socially prescribed and legitimate goals. Secondly, no system by definition can facilitate the maximization of welfare by all individuals who come to compose it, at any rate viewed from the subjective perceptions of the system participants. And, subjective evaluations are relevant in the context of heightening or lessening psychological deprivations. The options here are two: voluntary restraint by individuals keeping in mind the community interests or imposition of controls by an agency external to the individual, usually the State. While the latter will inescapably degenerate into totalitarianism, the former will inevitably require individuals who have internalized a high degree of altruism. If one is utopian, the other is dehumanizing.

Conclusion

Our analysis reveals that both traditional and modern values of India have assets and liabilities embedded in them. And we should consciously opt for a judicious combination of assets both in the traditional and the modern values in a consistent vein to secure the most appropriate mix.

Once again, we are at a new set of problems. What is the most appropriate mix? I can only assert that there is no mix which is universally appropriate; appropriateness will have to be defined contextually. The context is provided by the historicity of a system, and its present existential conditions.

We have seen that while the traditional value of holism fostered primordial collectivism with the introduction of democracy, individualistic values are gaining ground leading to the emergence of civil or instrumental collectivism, often degenerating into economism. What we need to inject into the system is ideological collectivism wherein men are motivated to plunge into collective mobilization with an altruistic orientation for systemic welfare rather than narrow individual and group interests. While retaining the collectivistic orientation found in our tradition, the content of collectivism should be transformed. We must recognize that a democracy innate to India can admit individual autonomy only sparingly. Traditional principles of allocation of roles and distribution of resources was based on hierarchy (status). Today although it is based on merit the persistence of institutionalized inequality is evident. What we should aim at is a system of need-based allocation. Notwithstanding the traditional value of pluralism individuals and groups were insulated in their narrow socio-cultural grooves, incapable of developing wider perspectives and fostering hostilities towards "others". Secularism of modern India only fosters a conscious indifference to other communal collectivities. It is necessary to harness the pluralistic orientation of traditional India to utilize it in order to transform the erstwhile but continuing hostility and the contemporary indifference to other communities into a conscious sensitization and appreciation of them. But in pursuing these objectives the current existential realities cannot be ignored.

Indian economy is predominantly rural and is characterized by substantial disparities in income and wealth. Indian industrial capital is concentrated in a few hands. The Indian nation is vast and consists of hetrogeneous populations with considerable cultural diversity. Indian polity is manned by an elite drawn from a relatively narrow base. Given these realities, for authentic social transformation to take place, what we need in India is a co-operative economy in which the primary producers directly own means of production more or less equitably and not state capitalism; a decentralized and not a delegated polity, which gives maximum opportunity to the men at the grass-root to shape their destiny and a secular pluralistic society which permits the optimum elasticity to maintain the diversities in culture.